MERTON COLLEGE

OXFORD

XX : KLE / STE

Heinrich von Kleist

The Dramas and Stories

Anthony Stephens

BERG

Oxford/Providence, USA

English edition
First published in 1994 by
Berg Publishers
Editorial offices:
150 Cowley Road, Oxford, OX4 1JJ, UK
221 Waterman Street, Providence, RI 02906, USA

Library of Congress Cataloging-in-Publication Data
A catalogue record for this book is available from the British Library.

British Library Cataloguing in Publication Data
A catalogue record for this book is available from the British Library.

ISBN 0 85496 708 7

Printed in the United Kingdom by WBC Bookbinders, Bridgend,
Mid-Glamorgan.

Contents

Acknowledgements

I would like to express my sincere thanks to Lü Yixu, Postdoctoral Fellow in German, University of Adelaide, for her invaluable help in working on the whole manuscript with me. I also thank Penny Boumelha for her helpful criticisms of my drafts. Hilary Stephens and Judith Wilson kindly read over versions of the text and gave advice. I owe a great debt to Gerhard Neumann for many years of fruitful dialogue, since we first gave a joint seminar on Kleist in Freiburg im Breisgau in 1981. I thank the Alexander von Humboldt-Stiftung for helping me to overcome the tyranny of distance, and for enabling me to attend conferences and pursue research in Germany over many years, and to the Australian Research Council for providing research assistance in the form of a major grant. This book is dedicated to the memory of Richard Samuel, in gratitude for many long conversations about Kleist.

Anthony Stephens
Melbourne, 1994.

Introduction

In an early scene from Kleist's first drama, *Die Familie Schroffenstein*, the dialogue between the young lovers, Agnes and Ottokar, reaches an impasse when Ottokar demands that she prove her unreserved trust in him by telling him her name. But Agnes finds herself unable to speak.[1] Ottokar persists, attempting to reassure her, whereupon she says: 'Von Liebe, hör ich wohl, sprachst du mit mir,/ Doch sage mir, mit wem sprachst du vom Morde?' (SW I, 78). In choosing these words as a thread to lead into the labyrinth of Kleist's dramas and stories, I draw attention to the dissonance that the coincidence of affection and threatened violence in the lovers' dialogue creates in the idyllic, natural setting, previously a refuge from the hostility which prevails in both their families. It is also worth noting that Agnes questions Ottokar about the relation between two of his own utterances, so that her words are marked as language about language, spoken in an attempt to elicit further meaning. When Ottokar insists she disclose her identity, which he already knows, she responds by asking whether the expressions of love and hostility in his own language are both directed towards the same person. For it is he who has previously introduced murder into their dialogue in the exclamation: 'O/ Mein Gott, so brauch ich dich ja nicht zu morden!' (SW I, 77).

That Ottokar should be relieved that he is no longer bound to murder her points up the theme of the transgression of social norms and imperatives of a darker kind which is joined to those of love and violence throughout Kleist's work. For Ottokar's father has made him swear bloody vengeance against Agnes's father and his whole household, so that in *not* murdering the person he loves he transgresses a paternal command. Since Agnes and Ottokar are related, and both are ultimately killed by their own fathers, the theme of the family as a set of potentially destructive relationships, which pervades all of Kleist's work, is fully present in these few lines. For in this first drama the family has usurped the place of the state, and thus bears the onus of such abstract values as justice and order, which are carried elsewhere in

---

1 'Drum will ich, daß du nichts mehr vor mir birgst,/ Und fordre ernst dein unumschränkt Vertrauen./ AGNES. Ich kann nicht reden, Ottokar. -' SWI, 77f.

Introduction

Kleist's fictional worlds by a wide range of other institutions. That the family is, at the same time, the locus of violence is also to have many sequels in Kleist's explorations of differing social structures, since the dynamics of family, wider social milieu and state frequently mirror each other.

Agnes's question to Ottokar also raises the problem of her own identity. Its terms are here deceptively simple: is she for him *primarily* the anonymous girl he has encountered in the mountains, safely away from both their houses, and fallen in love with, or one of a group he speaks of killing? Can he speak the same language with the one as he speaks with the other? Behind this are the additional questions of whether either of them can achieve an individuality distinct from their entanglement in the feud between their families and whether what they feel for one another is a basis for a new beginning, a discourse of emancipation.

Finally, it is worth pointing out that the dialogue has a ritual quality about it, for as far as the plot is concerned there is no need at all for this interplay of question and answer about their own and each other's identities. Two scenes earlier, Ottokar had his suspicions as to who Agnes might be confirmed at length by his half-brother, and his own offer to tell Agnes who he is becomes superfluous when, immediately before these lines, she calls him by his name. Ritual enactments of the ascertaining of truth by language are a source of fascination to Kleist, and provide some of the most memorable scenes in his works. It is characteristic of these scenes that language should first register its own limits: 'Ich kann nicht reden, Ottokar.' – and then go on to probe too deeply for comfort. As this brief dialogue indicates, an interrogation may reveal most when its ostensible object is already known, for when language produces truth in Kleist it is rarely on demand and often a different one from that which is consciously sought. Ottokar, knowing Agnes's name already, begins this exchange in an almost playful mode – 'Nun will ich heiter, offen, wahr,/ Wie deine Seele mit dir reden. Komm!' (SW I, 77) – yet Agnes's question turns the game into an unveiling of the core of the tragedy: whoever she might be for Ottokar in their encounters in the mountains, she is still the Agnes Schroffenstein whom he and all his family have sworn to kill.

Thus ritualized language can unexpectedly take a revelatory or sharply forensic turn, as Kleist's characters seek an illumination that promises some hope, rather than merely a confirmation of their worst fears or suspicions. In the previous scene, Agnes's father, Sylvester, reacts to the false accusations in which he has become enmeshed by announcing his intention to confront his accusers in words that could stand as an epigraph to Kleist's whole work: 'Ich muß mir Licht verschaffen,/ Und sollt ichs mir auch aus der Hölle holen' (SW I, 74).

There are two ironies here: first, that attempts to induce clarity into confused situations often only worsen them; second, that there is no hell worse than the internecine violence in which Sylvester is already caught and which will result in his mistakenly killing his own daughter.

The constellations produced by the dual themes of aggression and love, in constant interaction with social codes, abstract values, and the deceptive nature of human language, which is their common medium, form the substance of the interpretations that follow. Rather than exercise yet again the philosophical conundrums surrounding the crisis Kleist underwent in early 1801, I offer a detailed account of *Die Familie Schroffenstein* as an introduction to all of Kleist's work. This is done out of a conviction that Kleist's attitude to philosophical concepts and positions changes significantly from 1802 onward, once he begins creating literature. I therefore think it is best to approach his oeuvre through a literary work, rather than through his early letters.

If his letters prior to his crisis of 1801 show him willing to invest belief in doctrines culled from the Enlightenment, his practice as a creative writer is invariably to *quote*, with varying degrees of scepticism or irony, convictions he had once uncritically espoused. This applies equally to the thought of Rousseau, whom he never explicitly disowned and who remained a presence in most of his works, and to the 'Kantian' philosophy, which he blamed for his disillusionment.

Whatever his philosophical readings may have set in motion, the crisis from which Kleist began to emerge as a writer at the age of 23 encompassed much more than the problems of knowledge he expounds in his letters. It meant also the collapse of a teleological view of the world, a loss of trust in language as a means of producing truth, and a scepticism about the efficacy of moral development in the genesis of the individual. Some months before the crisis, he presents a vision of his personal development in terms reminiscent both of the Enlightenment and of Goethe's *Wilhelm Meisters Lehrjahre* in a letter to his fiancée, Wilhelmine von Zenge, with what appears in hindsight to be a grimly forced optimism and simplicity: '*Liebe* und *Bildung* das ist alles, was ich begehre, und wie froh bin ich, daß die Erfüllung dieser beiden unerläßlichen Bedürfnisse . . . nicht von dem Himmel abhängt . . ., sondern *einzig und allein von dir*' (SW II, 574).

From the perspective of the world of *Die Familie Schroffenstein*, such certainty has the aura of a lost paradise, a fantasy of individual fulfilment that may be posited as a goal, but usually is obscured by a cloud of inimical circumstances and illegible signs. For this reason, Kleist's literary technique is fundamentally experimental, and his intellectual positions are reactive rather than affirmative. The same thematic elements recur in his work in innovative, combinations, but he is much more often concerned with undermining the conceptual bases of the various conventional positions he quotes than with asserting confidence in a set of values distinctively his own.

Hence this study of Kleist's major works emphatically puts the literature first and allows its intertextuality with the writings of his contemporaries and predecessors to emerge where an understanding of the text demands it. In my view, there are no overriding external authorities for Kleist's complex fictional worlds. In keeping with my reading of his works as a series of experiments that was arbitrarily broken off by his suicide in 1811, this study does not have any single thesis. Rather, I am concerned with exploring the labyrinth for its own sake. I regret that the scope of the study could not include his poems, anecdotes, and occasional writings, but constraints of length have limited it to his dramas and major narratives. The plays are dealt with in the accepted chronological order; since the chronology of the stories is imperfectly known, I have placed two in each chapter on the basis of structural or thematic affinities. A chapter on *Über das Marionettentheater* is included, since I consider this text to be primarily a fictional narrative, rather than a treatise on philosophy or aesthetics, and have interpreted it in these terms.

There is no getting away from the extremes of cruelty evidenced by most of Kleist's experiments. Whilst it is not marked by the simplicity of being an end in itself, as it is in de Sade's concept of *jouissance*, it seems to be an inevitable accompaniment of attempts to elicit truth through the medium of language and, as well, the grim Other of all modes of human affection. Whereas I think Kleist remained sufficiently attached to those values of the Enlightenment which had dominated his formative years never to abandon an underlying humanism, this attachment often appears in the works as a final, helpless gesture in the face of destructive powers he uncovers in the individual and in society. Cruel violence within his fictional worlds can thus at times appear gratuitous, and I think there is no point in trying to deny it by excursions into a philosophical Idealism that Kleist as a writer did not espouse.

To render the cruelty innocuous by integrating it into a dialectic of history or social change seems to me equally spurious. Had Kleist apprehended contemporary European history in terms of the dialectical progressions that came so readily to Novalis, Hegel, and Hölderlin, then the societies he depicts could scarcely be so dominated by a discourse of savagery unfolding to no intelligible end, and the psychology of his characters would not be marked by those divisions in the self and dislocations of consciousness that so rarely achieve even a semblance of resolution.

Just as his vision of the family, through all of his work, amounts to a set of emotional dynamics with more potential for destruction than blessing, so his apprehension of Napoleonic Europe remains essentially one of incoherence, of a hiatus in time between an old order, which had foundered, and a new one whose shape could barely be glimpsed. While Kleist several times quotes from the body of utopian and apocalyptic myth that was current in Germany at the beginning of the 19th century, even the productions of his most patriotic phase in 1808-9 betray a strange vacillation between commitment and subversion. He had no particular reason to trust the Prussia he offered his somewhat belated devotion to, and I think his most succinct and characteristic expression of the terms in which he saw contemporary history is the following extract from his letter to Rühle von Lilienstern of November 1805, about a year before Napoleon's victory at Jena:

> Die Zeit scheint eine neue Ordnung der Dinge herbeiführen zu wollen, und wir werden davon nichts, als bloß den Umsturz der alten erleben. Es wird sich aus dem ganzen kultivierten Teil von Europa ein einziges, großes System von Reichen bilden, und die Throne mit neuen, von Frankreich abhängigen, Fürstendynastien besetzt werden. . . . Kurz, in Zeit von einem Jahre, ist der Kurfürst von Bayern, König von Deutschland. – Warum sich nur nicht einer findet, der diesem bösen Geiste der Welt [Napoleon] die Kugel durch den Kopf jagt. . . . Für die Kunst, siehst Du wohl ein, war vielleicht der Zeitpunkt noch niemals günstig; man hat immer gesagt, daß sie betteln geht; aber jetzt läßt sie die Zeit verhungern. Wo soll die Unbefangenheit des Gemüts herkommen, die schlechthin zu ihrem Genuß nötig ist, in Augenblicken, wo das Elend jedem . . . in den Nacken schlägt. (SW II, 761)

This is as lucid an explanation of the underlying pessimism of Kleist's work as one may find. That an end to Napoleon's empire was nowhere evident when Kleist decided to end his life, and that he felt betrayed by Prussia, figures strongly in one of his letters of farewell: 'Die Allianz, die der König jetzt mit den Franzosen schließt, ist auch nicht eben gemacht, mich im Leben festzuhalten' (SW II, 884). His resentment at the refusal of events to produce 'eine neue Ordnung der Dinge,' in which he could have any confidence, means that utopian conclusions to his literary experiments are invariably marked as comedy or fantasy. There is also the interesting dualism in his letter that makes 'ein einziges, großes System von Reichen' the virtual opposite of a new order in any sense that he could affirm.

In similar terms, his works show again and again the discrepant relation between elaborate symmetries and patternings of aesthetic form and the chaos that, for a time, they may mask – a tension already present in his first drama, *Die Familie Schroffenstein*. Where a text takes up the option of reordering this chaos into a comic or utopian ending, it invariably reveals at what cost to the plausibility of the fictional world this is achieved.

A further generalization about Kleist's work borne out by this study is that the dual thematic function of metaphorical language in the plays, as both a tool of cognition and a distorting of perception, corresponds in the stories to ambivalences in the relation between reader, narrator, and text. While Kleist's characters often find language inadequate to their need to express themselves, there is always another, ironic sense in which language communicates far too well, to the extent of subjugating the fictional situation to its own ludic imperatives. This is already fully apparent in *Die Familie Schroffenstein*, and I have used it to link together all the interpretations that follow.

Reviewing the course of Kleist scholarship in 1976, John Ellis objected to studies that take one prominent motif or idea and pursue it single-mindedly: 'This is not simply mistaken criticism but is in a way a recoil from Kleist's characteristic demand on his readers; for Kleist demands that the reader remain flexible and move with the text's changes of direction ... .'[2] This is quite correct, and an impatience with monomanic readings is fully justified, but I think Ellis undervalues two factors: first, the intertextuality between Kleist's *own* works is often the most revealing, because of the experimental character of his literary technique which operates by varying the shape of thematic and structural constellations used in earlier contexts; second, the amount of ambivalence generated in one text is often such that critical discourse may need to resort to cutting swathes as a means of maintaining its own coherence.

In the German essays on Kleist I have published over the last decade, I have tended to take one focus over several works, and I maintain that this is more valid than taking one aspect of one work, linking it to some external authority, and claiming for the result a general validity for understanding all of Kleist. But the present study, which I have tried to make accessible to the non-specialist reader, reverses this practice by offering more self-contained readings of all the dramas and stories.

In line with this book's having no single thesis, I have taken a consciously pluralistic approach to Kleist scholarship – at the risk of making no one happy. Quite pragmatically, the longer I work on Kleist, the more deeply suspicious I become of formulaic 'keys to the work' and shortcuts to the 'quintessential Kleist' that install one external frame of reference as an authority, whether this be the thought of Fichte or Kant

2 John M. Ellis, *Heinrich von Kleist. Studies in the Meaning and Character of his Writings*, Chapel Hill, 1979, p. 144.

or Adam Müller, or else the reform of the Prussian army.[3] This is not to declare possible influences or sources irrelevant, as I have recently established in some detail the intertextuality between the theme of sacrifice in Kleist's writings and in religious controversies of the popular Enlightenment[4] – rather, it is a question of maintaining balance. I have also pursued elsewhere my interest in the thought of Jacques Lacan, tracing its affinities to structures and motifs in Kleist's work,[5] but my conclusion is that, as far as literary criticism is concerned, Lacan makes a fractious servant and an unruly master. Therefore, while I find Lacanian readings of Kleist interesting, I do not find them more authoritative than other kinds, and am wary of the reductionist tendencies their global application might have. Hence I have tried to keep the present study comprehensive by installing no single external authorities and including the approaches of other critics I have found helpful. Kleist's work survives by its elusive richness of meaning, as does that of Kafka. To apply a simple formula for decoding either is to impoverish them.

Over the last two decades, writing on Kleist has tended to become more pluralistic as a whole, with a growing recognition of the role of irony and parody in his work and a loosening up of the dogmatism that had characterized moral judgements on his fictional characters and applications of concepts derived from *Über das Marionettentheater*. At the beginning of the 1980s, Erika Swales described *Prinz Friedrich von Homburg* as 'a text whose impulses are both integrative and subversive.'[6] At about the same time, Gerhard Kurz termed the main thrust of *Über das Marionettentheater* 'Kleist's subversive Kritik des Sündenfallmythos,'[7] and there has been any amount of 'subversion' in writing on Kleist since then, a trend I continually find healthy. Kleist's penchant for quoting and, at the same time, ironizing literary conventions and ideological positions that are unquestioned in the works of his predecessors and contemporaries makes readings of his works as 'subversive' entirely apposite, and I have cast the present study in this tradition.

The amount of dialogue with other critics is necessarily limited in a book that treats each of the major works. On many points, writing on

---

3 Cf. Wolf Kittler, *Die Geburt des Partisanen aus dem Geist der Poesle,* Freiburg im Breisgau, 1987, pp. 245–9.

4 Anthony Stephens, 'Der Opfergedanke bei Heinrich von Kleist,' *Heinrich von Kleist. Kriegsfall – Rechtsfall – Sündenfall,* ed. Gerhard Neumann, Freiburg im Breisgau, 1994, pp. 179-232.

5 Anthony Stephens, 'Verzerrungen im Spiegel. Das Narziß-Motiv bei Heinrich von Kleist,' *Heinrich von Kleist,* ed. Gerhard Neumann, pp. 233-80.

6 Erika Swales, 'Configurations of Irony: Kleist's *Prinz Friedrich von Homburg,*' in *DVjs* 56, 1982, p. 419.

7 Gerhard Kurz, '"Gott befohlen." Kleists Dialog *Über das Marionettentheater* und der Mythos vom Sündenfall des Bewußtseins,' in *KJb* 1981/82, p. 273.

Kleist has reached a consensus over the last decades, and it would be otiose to fill the notes with listings of critics who substantially agree with one another. Without imposing any firm rule, I have tried to confine using the amount of space that can be devoted to secondary literature to positions I either endorse or disagree with, or to formulations that bring together a great deal of critical opinion in a representative way. The volume of writing on Kleist shows no sign of abatement, and it has simply not been possible to refer to every valid perspective. I have cited my own essays on Kleist because they usually contain more elaborate treatments of particular points than is possible in this general study.

While there is as yet no definitive biography of Kleist, and while certain episodes in his life remain poorly documented, the two volumes collated by Helmut Sembdner, *Heinrich von Kleists Lebensspuren* and *Heinrich von Kleists Nachruhm*, when read with his letters, are still the best biographical introduction. I have consistently quoted from Helmut Sembdner's edition of the works, but have also made frequent reference to the volumes in the Deutscher Klassiker Verlag that have appeared so far, as the notes to this edition assemble a great deal of useful information and commentary in one place.

–1–

Die Familie Schroffenstein

A Plurality of Discourse

Die Familie Schroffenstein is as extraordinary a first work as exists in modern European literature. The power of its language, the density of its themes, and the complexity of its relations to the literary and philosophical currents of the time all mark it as a work of genius. That a great deal of Kleist criticism has not recognized its quality can be attributed, in the main, to two causes: first, to the influence of Kleist's own disparaging remarks on the play and of an anecdote that reinforces them,[1] and second, to the undeniable fact that, from the end of the fourth act, after Ottokar survives unscathed a suicidal plunge of fifty feet onto a stone pavement, the play begins to destroy its own credibility.

Kleist seems quickly to have forgotten his first completed drama, which he had published anonymously, and there is no sign of the emotional tie between author and work that was to bind him to *Robert Guiskard* or *Penthesilea*. Nevertheless, *Die Familie Schroffenstein* shows Kleist mounting bold experiments with dramatic form and the language of metaphor. If the drama, as is generally agreed today, undermines its own coherence, then this is due mainly to antagonisms between the disparate elements of a complex text that Kleist holds in a precarious balance until, in the closing scenes, he allows it to lapse into pastiche.

Kleist composed the work in 1802 with an eye to current literary fashion.[2] Melodramas of chivalry, banditry, and fatal passion set in a romanticized past were in vogue, and he readily found a publisher. As in all his later works, both dramatic and narrative, whenever Kleist takes up the conventions of an established genre or style, he begins to change them into something else. *Die Familie Schroffenstein* gave all that the fashion demanded and more – indeed so much more that in the end the conventions of melodrama are confronted with their own absurdity. What then emerges from the wreckage is no single, new form, but a number of alternative forms, none of which is quite realized.

1 Cf. SW II, 731; also Hinrich C. Seeba, KW I, 581 and LS, 58.
2 Cf. KW II, 534-40.

I suggest the play might be read, in structural terms, as a palimpsest, where one incomplete drama is, as it were, written over another.[3] When Kleist embarked on a literary career after his abortive attempts in other fields, it was with an extreme ambition that his letters frankly admit.[4] He seems to have planned his literary début as an attack on two fronts: *Die Familie Schroffenstein* was aimed at the popular market and rapid success; at the same time, Kleist set out to storm the citadel of high tragedy, and was working on the theory he attempted to realize in *Robert Guiskard*, a work that meant much more to him than his first drama.[5] But one of the factors that subverts *Die Familie Schroffenstein* as a popular melodrama is that Kleist also cast most of it as a tragedy, in the full seriousness of the genre.

Another factor that gives the play the quality of a palimpsest is its abundance of literary borrowings. In various places the text quotes Shakespeare, Lessing, and Schiller, and its intertextuality is by no means limited to such clear allusions in the imagery.[6] Schiller's *Don Carlos,* for instance, prefigures the themes of conflict between father and son and of a world in which trust is both demanded and hard to sustain.[7] Shakespeare's influence is not confined to the plot's obvious affinities to *Romeo and Juliet*,[8] nor to more distant ones to *Macbeth* and *King Lear*. The vocabulary of malediction, with its wild beasts and reptiles, is strongly reminiscent of *Richard III*. Indeed, the following lines from Richmond's closing speech sum up a world very similar to that of *Die Familie Schroffenstein*:

> England hath long been mad, and scarr'd herself;
> The brother blindly shed the brother's blood,
> The father rashly slaughtered his own son,
> The son, compell'd, been butcher to the sire.[9]

3 I have borrowed this metaphor from Gérard Genette, 'Proust palimpseste,' *Figures I*, Paris, 1966, p. 51: 'Ce palimpseste du temps et de l'espace, ces vues discordantes sans cesse contrariées et sans cesse rapprochées par un inlassable mouvement de dissociation douloureuse et de synthèse impossible, c'est sans doute cela, la vision proustienne.'
4 Cf. SW II, 726.
5 For a summary of Kleist's probable phases of work on *Robert Guiskard* see Richard H. Samuel and Hilda M. Brown, *Kleist's Lost Year and the Quest for 'Robert Guiskard,'* Leamington Spa, 1981, pp. vi-ix and 28; also KW I, 659-75.
6 For details of such reminiscences see SW I, 920; LS, 86.
7 Cf. Gerhard Kluge, 'Der Wandel der dramatischen Konzeption von der *Familie Ghonorez* zur *Familie Schroffenstein*,' *Kleists Dramen. Neue Interpretationen*, ed. Walter Hinderer, Stuttgart, 1981, p. 61.
8 Last observed by Peter Michelsen, 'Die Betrogenen des Rechtgefühls. Zu Kleists *Die Familie Schroffenstein*', in *KJb* 1992, p. 65.
9 *King Richard III*, Act V, Scene 5; compare: '- Selbst das Band,/ Das heilige, der Blutsverwandtschaft riß,/ Und Vettern, Kinder eines Vaters, zielen,/ Mit Dolchen zielen sie auf ihre Brüste.' SW I, 52f.

Shakespeare's influence is also reflected in Kleist's penchant for mixing genres. Critics have often pointed to the pronounced symmetry in the plotting, but without recognizing that it owes more to the typical structures of Shakespearean comedy than of tragedy.[10] This is only one of several experiments with tragic form in *Die Familie Schroffenstein*, but it indicates something of Kleist's unique manner of assimilating and transforming literary influences: his allusions generally signal a critical attitude to his source, and are rarely simple reminiscences.

The metaphor of the palimpsest is to be understood in two senses. First, the published text of *Die Familie Schroffenstein* preserves successive stages in the concept of the drama that the earlier manuscript material allows us to identify. Originally, the play set out to illustrate the workings of a malign destiny: 'Das Schicksal ist ein Taschenspieler – Sturm der Leidenschaft, Raub des Irrtums, Himmel hat uns zum Narren' (SW I, 833). This is overlaid with the beginnings of a drama of social decadence in Rousseauistic terms, in which the hostilities set up within the House of Schroffenstein by a contract of inheritance produce a climate of suspicion that turns domestic order into chaos. Besides these, the final text reveals numerous other strands which Kleist was unable or unwilling to combine into a conventional aesthetic unity. Second, therefore, it may help to visualize this plurality of discourse in the text as different axes along which the one play may be read.[11]

Most obviously, the play exists as an imitation of fashionable melodrama which drifts toward self-parody. Next, it may be read along the axis of tragic form which, as George Steiner has pointed out, underwent a crisis in the period in which *Die Familie Schroffenstein* was written.[12] In this regard the play reveals itself not only as a dialogue with the conventions of classical and Shakespearean tragedy, but also with those of the 'middle-class tragedy,' the *bürgerliches Trauerspiel*, which was one of the main literary innovations of the Enlightenment in Germany. It is on this axis that Kleist poses for the first time a question that recurs in all his later work, namely: how can one reconcile the conflict between love and power within the sphere of the family?

We may also read the play along the axis of a religious drama. It opens in a chapel in which a bizarre rite is taking place. Graf Rupert compels his immediate family to swear bloody vengeance against Graf

10 Hinrich C. Seeba, 'Der Sündenfall des Verdachts. Identitätskrise und Sprachskepsis in Kleists *Familie Schroffenstein*,' in *DVjs* 44, 1970, p. 74.

11 The metaphor of axes is used in French literary theory as the concept of 'isotopies,' cf. A. J. Greimas, *Du Sens. Essais sémiotiques*, Paris, 1970, pp. 212f; F. Rastier, 'Systématique des isotopies,' *Essais de sémiotique poétique*, ed. A. J. Greimas, Paris, 1972, pp. 80-106.

12 George Steiner, *The Death of Tragedy*, London, 1961, pp. 127-36 and 216-28.

Sylvester's branch of the wider family, and the oath is taken upon the Eucharist. Kleist thus grafts Old Testament traditions of vengeance upon the Christian sacrament of reconciliation, and this creates a dimension of religious reference that is sustained – although never rendered quite coherent – throughout the play. It is characteristic of Kleist's later writing as a whole to introduce religious themes with a maximum of tension, thereby echoing, but also questioning, the dominant modes of thought of the European Enlightenment.

In general, commentators on religion within the European Enlightenment had regarded the Eucharist as a humane progression beyond the sacrificial rituals and narratives of the Old Testament. Lessing's *Die Erziehung des Menschengeschlechts* argues, as had Diderot before him, that Christian doctrines and sacraments are to be understood in a progressive sense.[13] By forcibly welding together what the Enlightenment had been content, in the main, to leave separate, Kleist establishes the axis of religious themes as one of conflict and experiment. It is then little wonder that the young lovers, Ottokar and Agnes, celebrate new sacraments of Ottokar's own devising and that the imagery of the play is permeated by religious motifs. Divine vengeance and divine providence are often invoked, but both the frequency and the lack of success of these appeals ultimately serve to debase the coinage of religious reference.

A further axis proceeds from Kleist's personal crisis of 1801 and offers an exposition of the fallibility of human perception. Walter Müller-Seidel has demonstrated the importance of this theme for Kleist's whole work.[14] Reading the play along this axis yields a similar critical dialogue with the epistemological assumptions of the popular Enlightenment in Germany to that which takes place on the axis of religious themes.

The play may also be read as a drama about language itself. The abundance of simile and metaphor in the dialogue has been often remarked, and the characters discuss more than once the problems that beset verbal communication. The nature of metaphor in the play has been analyzed at length, and there is little doubt that the imagery in general tends to become independent of its immediate dramatic function

---

13 For this line of argument see Lessing, 'Die Erziehung des Menschenge- schlechts,' *Lessings Werke. Mit einer Auswahl aus seinen Briefen und einer Skizze seines Lebens*, ed. Franz Muncker, vol. 12, Stuttgart 1890, §16, 27, 34, 64, 75, 86, 93; cf. also the article by Diderot, 'Sacrifices des Hébreux,' *Encyclopédie ou Dictionnaire raisonné des sciences, des arts et des métiers*, reprint, Stuttgart-Bad Cannstadt, 1967, vol. 14, p. 484.

14 Walter Müller-Seidel, *Versehen und Erkennen. Eine Studie über Heinrich von Kleist*, Cologne and Graz, 1961, pp. 89-109 and 172-78.

and to lead, as it were, a life of its own.[15] On this axis, the play is an extended debate about the strengths, limits, and pitfalls of metaphoric language conducted largely within the field of metaphor itself.

All these different dimensions of the play pose problems for which the text offers no solution. The play does not succeed in transforming itself entirely from a melodrama in the fashionable mode into a new model of tragic form; the religious themes foreshadow, in the love between Agnes and Ottokar, a rebirth of humanity, but the lovers are killed by their own fathers, indicating Kleist's unwillingness to present a new beginning as a tangible reality; the characters' insights into their own plight as victims of linguistic confusion do not yield any hints as to how language might be turned into a means of producing truth.

What imperils the dramatic coherence of *Die Familie Schroffenstein* is not only the number of different paths that Kleist pursues simultaneously, but also the fact that each axis along which the play may be read unfolds a conflict that the catastrophe can terminate but not resolve. The action ends in a scene of reconciliation whose helplessness is obvious. The two fathers stand over the corpses of the children they have murdered; Rupert proposes a reconciliation to Sylvester; Sylvester says nothing, but extends his hand to Rupert while averting his face. In neither version of the text does the stage direction indicate how Rupert responds to this gesture. The two mothers, Eustache and Gertrude, do embrace, but the whole scene is shifted into the grotesque by the ravings of Johann, Rupert's illegitimate son, who has lost his wits, in best Shakespearean style, and proclaims the whole grim spectacle to be a farce.

These dissonances signal that the play has taken on more issues than it can settle. The ending is well nigh unplayable as serious drama, for unlike many dissonant endings the final conflicts do not produce an aesthetic value of their own, but destroy such continuities as the text has already created. A recent production of *Die Familie Schroffenstein* by the Berliner Ensemble points up the incompatibility between the body of the work and its ending. By treating the chaotic ending as the essence of the play rather than as an embarrassing appendage, this production successfully turned the whole work into black comedy. Subordinating the whole text to its ending rendered farcical many scenes Kleist obviously meant to be taken seriously, and this further evidenced a drama at odds with itself.

15 Cf. Robert Labhardt, *Metapher und Geschichte. Kleists dramatische Metaphorik bis zur 'Penthesilea' als Widerspiegelung seiner geschichtlichen Position*, Kronberg/Ts. 1976, p. 113; for a commentary on Labhardt's view of Kleist's metaphors see my article: 'Zur Funktion der Metapher beim frühen Kleist,' in *Akten des VI. Internationalen Germanisten-Kongresses Basel 1980*, Bern, Frankfurt/M and New York, 1980, pp. 372f.

Readings that treat the text reverently for as long as possible will tend to locate the dramatic climax in the first scene of the final act, in which Ottokar and Agnes exchange clothing in a cave.[16] Ottokar devises this strategy to save Agnes from his own father, who is intent on murdering her, but the language of the scene goes far beyond this to imply at once a spiritual marriage and a blending of identities. But, significantly, these positive outcomes remain a projection into a future that will never come to pass.[17] What ensues is the negation of this vision by murder, and the helplessness of the reconciliation scene makes plain that there is no mediation between a glimpse of paradise and the fallen state of the present.

The plurality of discourse in *Die Familie Schroffenstein* illustrates a paradox which is fundamental to all of Kleist's works and which one might term the demiurgic principle of aesthetic creation. In Gnostic philosophy, the demiurge is the creator of this world, but is not identical with a benevolent supreme being – rather an antagonistic opposite. In shaping his first fictional world, Kleist seems to have discovered that a wealth of structural principles may underlie a creation that is emphatically not the well-ordered universe of the Enlightenment, but is instead self-destructive and ultimately chaotic. From this derives the constant tension in his works between highly integrated formal patterns, which evoke the appearance of a teleological world model, and the thematic negativity, verging on incoherence, that lies at their core.

The World of *Die Familie Schroffenstein*

The multiplicity of texts within the one text produces, for most of the work, a thematic density which anticipates that of Kleist's later writing. *Die Familie Schroffenstein* presents us with a world that seems adrift in space as well as in time. Both earlier versions, *Die Familie Thierrez* and *Die Familie Ghonorez*, supposedly take place in Spain, but there is so little to tie them to this locality that Kleist simply changed the names of the characters when he decided to situate the action 'in Swabia,' and none of the other textual alterations between versions seems directed toward making the change of setting more plausible.

The action takes place in a society that is feudal to the point of travesty – Rupert literally treats his servants like his dogs – but quite lacking

---

16 Cf. Ingeborg Harms, '"Wie fliegender Sommer." Eine Untersuchung der "Höhlenszene" in Heinrich von Kleists *Die Familie Schroffenstein*,' in *JbSchG* XXVIII, 1984, pp. 270-314.

17 Cf. Anthony Stephens, '"Was hilfts, daß ich jetzt schuldlos mich erzähle?" Zur Bedeutung der Erzählvorgänge in Kleists Dramen,' in *JbSchG* XXIX, 1985, pp. 309f.

in historical specificity. There is an impression of the late Middle Ages, but this can scarcely become more concrete, because the play literally knows no world outside the one divided family. The whole superstructure of feudal society is missing: there is no appeal to a higher authority, whose vassals Rupert and Sylvester might be, or to a state within which their hegemony might be contained. It is as if Kleist wanted to force the one family in upon itself with the same violence as marks Rupert's blending of the communion rite with the oath of vengeance in the first moments of the drama.

In a sense, the play is as much a critique of the values of middle-class society as it is of any feudal world. Themes such as the abuse of paternal authority, the attempt by children to emancipate themselves from the world of their fathers, and the lack of mediation between familial love and despotic authority are very much part of the *bürgerliches Trauerspiel*, while other aspects of the play clearly refer to the aristocratic society in which Kleist had grown up.[18] The relationships between Rupert and his wife and sons may have something of the claustrophobic quality of the middle-class family in Germany at the end of the 18th century, but in the first scene Rupert still compels Ottokar to swear vengeance not only upon Sylvester, but upon his whole clan – 'sein ganzes Haus' (SW I, 52) – a term that was current in Kleist's time for the extended, aristocratic family.[19] Thus the society of *Die Familie Schroffenstein* is a curious hybrid of the feudal and the middle-class. The late 18th century was a time when the nature of the European family was being re-thought,[20] and all of Kleist's works reflect this to a significant degree.

What differentiates this family from those in most of Kleist's other works is the absence of any authority above that of the father: the family has replaced the state. Appeals to God, as in all of Kleist's works, either go unheard or are answered so ambiguously that the divinity seems virtually reduced to a function of language. This points up the question as to how power of this kind might relate to such other values as the family stands for. Paternal authority is put on trial in *Die Familie Schroffenstein* and found guilty in terms that seem to go beyond the par-

18 Cf. Peter Horst Neumann, *Der Preis der Mündigkeit. Über Lessings Dramen. Anhang: Über Fanny Hill*, Stuttgart, 1977, pp. 9-28.

19 Cf. Otto Brunner, 'Das "Ganze Haus" und die alteuropäische "Ökonomik"'. *Neue Wege der Verfassungs- und Sozialgeschichte*, 2. vermehrte Auflage, Göttingen, 1968, pp. 103-27; Anthony Stephens, 'Kleists Familienmodelle,' in *KJb* 1988/89, pp. 225f.

20 Cf. Michael Mitterauer and Reinhard Sieder, *The European Family. Patriarchy to Partnership from the Middle Ages to the Present*, trans. Karla Oosterveen and Manfred Hörzinger, Oxford, 1982, pp. 129f; Günter Saße, *Die aufgeklärte Familie. Untersuchungen zur Genese, Funktion und Realitätsbezogenheit des familialen Systems im Drama der Aufklärung*, Tübingen, 1988, pp. 248-51 and 258-62.

ticulars of the plot, yet which reappear throughout the rest of Kleist's work. The theme of an equivocal paternal authority is no less dominant in Kleist's last drama, *Prinz Friedrich von Homburg*.

In the characterization of Rupert and Sylvester, Kleist shows great skill in his blending of symmetry and differentiation. Whilst Rupert's course from the oath of vengeance to the murder of his own son is only slightly troubled by reflection, Sylvester begins the play as Rupert's cautious and humane opposite. He then undergoes his own negative development until he espouses the cause of vengeance with all of Rupert's intransigence. By the time each father mistakenly kills his own child, they have become, as it were, mirror images of each other. There is an element of destructive narcissism in paternal authority that becomes more evident as the play nears its conclusion, and I shall later show how this process is paralleled in the imagery.

Only two areas in the play are not immediately discernible as extensions of the fathers' power. The first is the idyllic, natural setting in the mountains where Agnes encounters both Johann and Ottokar. The text very clearly segregates this region from the fathers' spheres of control and, as critics have long recognized, it has connotations of a Rousseauistic paradise regained. On the religious axis of the play, 'paradise' is to be taken almost literally, and when the fathers invade this region with murder in their hearts, then we may regard this as a process of profanation – the first of many in Kleist's works.

Nature appears, in the scenes between Agnes and Ottokar, to be not only a sanctuary from the violent world of the fathers, but also the embodiment of values which remain intact despite the mistrust and hostility that pervade the social sphere. But this is a simplification. Nature is also dominant in the discourse of the two fathers and ambivalent from the outset. In the first scene of the play, Rupert dismisses Nature as a fiction no longer relevant to a world turned upside down.[21] The experiences of Johann, Ottokar, and Agnes at first seem to offer an effective contradiction to this. Yet, when Sylvester stands by the corpse of Ottokar, which he believes to be that of his daughter Agnes, he invokes the power of Nature in terms that deprive it of any moral authority:

> Laß einen Augenblick mich ruhn. Es regt
> Sich sehr gewaltig die Natur im Menschen,
> Und will, daß man, gleich einem einzgen Gotte,
> Ihr einzig diene, wo sie uns erscheint.
> Mich hat ein großer Sturm gefaßt, er beugt

21 'Doch nichts mehr von Natur./ Ein hold ergötzend Märchen ists der Kindheit,/ Der Menschheit von den Dichtern, ihren Ammen,/ Erzählt. Vertrauen, Unschuld, Treue, Liebe,/ Religion, der Götter Furcht sind wie/ Die Tiere, welche reden' SW I, 52.

Mein wankend Leben tief zur Gruft. Wenn es
Nicht reißt, so steh ich schrecklich wieder auf,
Ist der gewaltsam erste Anfall nur
Vorüber. (SW I, 146)

This is one of many passages in which the motif of a descent into death and the hope of a resurrection determines the imagery. Kleist seems deliberately to conflate the Old Testament myth of the Fall with New Testament elements of a descent into death and resurrection.[22] He was to do something similar with the Adam of Genesis and Luther's 'old Adam' in *Der zerbrochne Krug*.[23]

As far as the place of natural forces in this complex is concerned, the ambivalence does not lie purely in the fact that Nature appears as a power outside morality. For the sanctuary has been invaded, Ottokar has been struck down mistakenly by his own father, and Sylvester is in the process of resolving an act no less bloody than Rupert's. But, beyond this, the text contains a strand of images of violent natural forces that correlates with the 'tempest' Sylvester here invokes. In this area of reference, Nature is not the sacred counterpart of the profane confusion of social relationships, but an alternative way of describing and justifying violence.

When the characters see their own actions, present or future, in the guise of natural forces, the act of perception itself renders these opaque to critical scrutiny. It is characteristic of the metaphors in the play as a whole that the image tends to become more powerful than whatever it might originally designate, and this is especially the case with those taken from nature. Here Sylvester renders his own past and future behavior immune to self-criticism by transposing his explanation of it into natural imagery.

In the perspective of Kleist's whole work, this is no process of mere embellishment or exaggeration. One of the challenges Kleist's imagery still presents to readers in the late 20th century is the difficulty of recognizing that it does not necessarily imply a substrate of 'reality' of which metaphors are mere disguises. Even Ottokar, whose love for Agnes becomes an attempt to emancipate both of them from the world of their fathers, renders the nature of paternal authority opaque to criticism in this way. When Agnes asks him if he cannot mollify Rupert's attitudes, he replies:

22 Cf. Timothy J. Mehigan, *Text as Contract. The Nature and Function of Narrative Discourse in the Erzählungen of Heinrich von Kleist*, Frankfurt/M, Bern, New York and Paris, 1988, pp. 63-76.

23 For a summary of Luther's variations on the phrase from Paul's Epistles see Georg Büchmann, *Geflügelte Worte. Der Zitatenschatz des deutschen Volkes*, 32. Auflage, Berlin, 1972, pp. 92f; cf. also KWI, 816 and SW I, 177.

Ich mildern? Meinen Vater? Gute Agnes,
Er trägt uns, wie die See das Schiff, wir müssen
Mit seiner Woge fort, sie ist nicht zu
Beschwören. (SW I, 103)

The play at first appears to establish a clear polarity between divine nature and unholy society, only to blur this distinction as the action progresses toward its end, and to offer nothing in its place. Kleist's subversion of Nature as an authority is analogous to the erosion of the ethical standing of natural paternity in the *bürgerliches Trauerspiel*, but without the saving alternative of adoptive paternity, which was also to be celebrated by the late Goethe.[24] In this we may see a certain bitter nostalgia on Kleist's part for the celebrations of natural goodness he knew so well from Rousseau, as he forces them to exist side by side with the bleaker view that Nature, like all seemingly absolute authorities, can reveal itself as nothing more august than a sad proof of the creative function of human language run riot. Far from representing a standard against which the aberrations of human conduct may ultimately be measured, its authority becomes weaker the more frequently it is invoked. Nothing can render it immune to the all-pervading relativism of metaphor.

The other area that seems free from the fathers' power is the peasants' hut where Barnabe and her mother, Ursula, prepare their magical brew. With the exception of Gerhard Neumann, interpreters of the play have been largely unsuccessful in integrating these scenes with the rest of the plot.[25] Before Act IV, Scene 3, there is no hint that the cottage and its inhabitants exist at all, and one might be tempted to regard Barnabe and her mother as survivors from an earlier draft of the work. In Kleist's first scenario, the dramatic roles of both Barnabe and her mother are assigned to a figure designated simply as 'a woman' (SW I, 721f). The magical incantation and the severing of the drowned child's finger to use as a protection against the devil are then introduced in *Die Familie Ghonorez*, and the relevant parts of the text are significantly modified in *Die Familie Schroffenstein*. Ursula's appearance with the severed finger in the last scene is as crass as anything in the play's final moments, but by contrast the speeches and dramatic function of her daughter are fine-

---

24 Peter Horst Neumann, *Der Preis der Mündigkeit*, p. 21; on adoptive paternity in Goethe's *Wilhelm Meister*, see Gerhard Neumann, '"Ich bin gebildet genug, um zu lieben und zu trauern." Die Erziehung zur Liebe in Goethes *Wilhelm Meister*,' *Liebesroman – Liebe im Roman*, *Erlanger Forschungen*, Series A, vol. 41, pp. 78-82; also his commentary in Johann Wolfgang Goethe, *Wilhelm Meisters Wanderjahre*, eds. Gerhard Neumann und Hans-Georg Drewitz, *Sämtliche Werke*, vol. 10., Frankfurt/M, 1989, pp. 937f.

25 Gerhard Neumann, 'Hexenküche und Abendmahl. Die Sprache der Liebe im Werk Heinrich von Kleists,' in *Freiburger Universitätsblätter*, No. 91, March 1986, pp. 9-31.

ly wrought, and this element of the play cannot simply be dismissed as part of the chaotic ending.

The cottage in the mountain wilderness is the only place in the play in which femaleness dominates. Barnabe's father is dead, and the first part of her incantation dwells on this, wishing him rest and a joyful resurrection – Kleist's witches are as Christian as any other characters in the play. In this sense, the world of Barnabe and Ursula stands in direct opposition not only to that of both castles, where the fathers' authority is absolute, but also to the idyll in the mountains in which Agnes remains subordinate to Ottokar. Barnabe's incantation, in its conclusion, evokes the powers of the body, in the forms of sexual intercourse and birth, with a directness that is evident at no other point in the play:

> Freuden vollauf: daß mich ein stattlicher Mann
> Ziehe mit Kraft kühn ins hochzeitliche Bett.
> Gnädiger Schmerz: daß sich . . . die liebliche Frucht
> Winde vom Schoß o nicht mit Ach! mir und Weh! (SW I, 127f)

Interestingly, the lines in *Die Familie Ghonorez* that correspond to the last two quoted here make no mention of birth, but conjure a general healthfulness: 'Blüte des Leibs: das mir kein giftiger Duft/ Sudle das Blut, Furchen mir ätz in die Haut' (SW I, 802). It is thus clear that the final version of the play intensifies the female aspect of the region into which Ottokar strays and where he learns the truth about his brother's death. In contrast to the oath of blood-vengeance on the Eucharist, all of Barnabe's wishes, as she stirs the cauldron, are benevolent.

There is a strong temptation to see in this one of the conventional mythicizations of the feminine at the beginning of the 19th century that endow it with an elemental purity, and thus set it apart from the imperfections of historical processes. Julia Kristeva has aptly pointed to European literature's tendency to stylize a specifically 'female' time.[26] Certainly history, to the extent that it exists within the world of the play, is the domain of the fathers and their initial preoccupation with the contract of inheritance. Historical continuity is both patriarchal and doomed. Moreover, the region Barnabe inhabits also contains the knowledge necessary to solve the puzzle of the death of Rupert's youngest son.

But one must not overlook the element of hyperbole Kleist uses to

---

26 Cf. Julia Kristeva, 'Women's Time,' *The Kristeva Reader*, ed. Toril Moi, Oxford, 1987, p. 191: 'As for time, female subjectivity would seem to provide a specific measure that essentially retains *repetition* and *eternity* from among the multiple modalities of time known through the history of civilisations.'

ironize Ottokar's receiving the news: 'Du hast gleich einer heilgen Offenbarung/ Das Unbegriffne mir erklärt' (SW I, 131). For when Ottokar acquires this knowledge from Barnabe, it is far too late to avert the catastrophe. Nothing she tells him has the force of divine revelation, and the things he does not understand about his own situation go far beyond the question of what has become of a dead child's finger. The text thus, once again, plays with the illusion of certainties, offering the simulacrum of a clear antithesis between a destructive male dominance and a more autonomous role for a 'female principle' than Agnes can ever assume. Against this, however, are the facts that the forest hut is tucked away on the fringes of this society, marginalized in a quite literal sense, and the source of an *ignis fatuus* of clarity, which Ottokar pursues to his own death.

If we now consider the role of female characters in general in the drama, then they are certainly less violent than their male counterparts, but quite unable to influence them. In chiastic symmetry with the initial contrast in character between Rupert and Sylvester, Rupert's wife, Eustache, consistently pleads for caution and restraint, whilst Sylvester's wife, Gertrude, consistently represents the voice of suspicion for as long as Sylvester is prepared to give Rupert and his clan the benefit of the doubt. But in the final scene of the play, the two wives actually embrace, whereas the reconciliation of the fathers, as we have seen, is rendered much more equivocal.

The role of Eustache seems to correlate best with the conclusions we may draw from the introduction of Ursula and Barnabe into the play as to the opposition between female and male. In the first scene, Rupert assigns his wife, and women in general, a passive and subordinate position in the scheme of things:

Ich weiß, Eustache, Männer sind die Rächer -
Ihr seid die Klageweiber der Natur.
Doch nichts mehr von Natur.
Ein hold ergötzend Märchen ists der Kindheit,
Der Menschheit von den Dichtern, ihren Ammen,
Erzählt. (SW I, 52)

Eustache takes the point, but does not necessarily accept it. She does not cease pleading with Rupert to reconsider his actions, and in the course of one such plea acknowledges her own subjugation, calling herself 'dein unterdrücktes Weib' (SW I, 116). It is she who recognizes the fatal symmetry of suspicion between the two houses and, in one of the most perceptive speeches in the whole play, attempts to convince her husband that a pattern of mistrust and violence may be completing its own design at the characters' expense.[27] This is a rare insight for any of Kleist's fictional characters into the nature of the reality they face and of which they are part. It is likewise Eustache who finds the words that indicate most accurately how the social world of the play is constituted. Pleading once more with Rupert, she proclaims that repentance is the innocence of the fallen: 'Denn Reue ist die Unschuld der Gefallnen' (SW I, 120). Here a perspective is briefly opened onto the composition of metaphorical reality. It is a fallen world, and in it the traditional human values and qualities no longer correspond to their names. The characters commit error after error because their own language has become opaque to them, but they continue to use it as if it were still transparent to an underlying reality. Eustache's words imply that what is needed is a set of new equivalences. Innocence cannot be regained, but repentance may function in its stead in a fallen world. The tragic irony in *Die Familie Schroffenstein* is that all such insights are ignored by those who need most to act upon them. Rupert is so taken with self-pity in the scene where Eustache speaks these words that he gives no sign of even hearing them.

Just as the witches' cottage can be seen as a repository of the key to the puzzle, but a key that can never be used in time, so all of Eustache's pleas and intuitions are clearly articulated, but cannot deflect Rupert from his course. There is nothing specifically medieval about the male and female roles in the play, as exemplified by Rupert and Eustache. If one reads Fichte's views on the subject in his *Deduktion der Ehe* – which is part of his *Grundriß des Familienrechts*, an appendix to his *Grundlage des Naturrechts*, published in 1798 – then Rupert's views on women may appear, by contrast, as almost enlightened.[28] Kleist certainly knew Fichte's work, as he virtually quotes from it in letters to his fiancée.[29]

---

27 'Warum nicht mein Gemahl? Denn es liegt alles/ Auf beiden Seiten gleich, bis selbst auf die/ Umstände noch der Tat' SW I, 121.

28 Johann Gottlieb Fichte, 'Deduktion der Ehe,' *Werke 1797-1798*, ed. Reinhard Lauth and Hans Gliwitzky, Stuttgart-Bad Cannstadt, 1970: p. 102: 'Ihre eigene Würde beruht darauf, daß sie ganz, so wie sie lebt, und ist, ihres Mannes sey, und sich ohne Vorbehalt an ihn und in ihm verloren habe. . . . Nur mit ihm vereinigt, nur unter seinen Augen, und in seinen Geschäften hat sie noch Leben und Thätigkeit. Sie hat aufgehört, das Leben eines Individuum zu führen; ihr Leben ist ein Theil seines Lebens geworden . . .'

29 'Da findet nun die Urteilskraft zuerst, daß der Mann nicht bloß der Mann seiner Frau, sondern auch noch ein Bürger des Staates, die Frau hingegen nichts als die Frau ihres Mannes ist; . . . daß folglich das Glück des Weibes zwar ein wichtiger und erlaßlicher, aber nicht der *einzige* Gegenstand des Mannes, das Glück des Mannes hingegen der *alleinige* Gegenstand der Frau ist; . . . daß zuletzt der Mann nicht immer glücklich ist, wenn es die Frau ist, die Frau hingegen immer glücklich ist, wenn der Mann glücklich ist, und daß also das Glück des Mannes eigentlich der Hauptgegenstand des Bestrebens beider Eheleute ist.' Letter to Wilhelmine, 30 May 1800, SW II, 506f.

These echoes of Fichte's views in *Die Familie Schroffenstein* empha-
sise two things: first, Kleist's proclivity for quoting in his poetic works
views he had espoused prior to 1801, but almost always in a context that
should alienate them from the audience or reader; second, the fact that
the world of his first drama is neither timeless nor meant as an image of
historical feudalism, but relates very concretely to the debates on the relevance of gender roles to the relation of individual and society in the latter phases of the German Enlightenment. Such a relation, however,
should not be confused with a crude partisanship for one or the other
position.

I have suggested elsewhere that the theme of rebirth which pervades
Kleist's works must be seen in contemporary terms: it is a cipher for the
problematic nature of the concept of individualism at a time when the
confident solutions of the mid-18th century were more and more failing
to convince.[30] I consider that this is the real sense of the play's religious
dimension. The antithesis between Old Testament vengeance and New
Testament reconciliation is ultimately a pretext for a religious debate
whose terms are much more secularized, and which is conducted around
the question of the self-realization of the individual at the beginning of
the 19th century.

Humanity reborn?

The theme of a new beginning recurs throughout Kleist's work. In *Das
Erdbeben in Chili*, the interlude in the valley after the earthquake presents itself as a regeneration of society; the Amazon State in *Penthesilea*
is founded in the cause of an emancipation from tyranny; the betrothal
between Gustav and Toni in *Die Verlobung in St. Domingo* is understood by her as an act of liberation from a past in which she has often
been an accomplice to murder. In Kleist's first drama, the onus of a new
beginning falls on the children, Agnes and Ottokar. The opening scene
of Act III shows that they are not immune to the misapprehensions that
beset other characters. Agnes believes for a good part of the scene that
Ottokar intends to poison her, and she is only convinced of the truth by
his willingness to drink the same water himself. Ottokar knows who
Agnes really is, yet he seems to resist this knowledge for as long as he
can, insisting that Agnes name herself to him. The elaborate ritual con-

---

30 Cf. Anthony Stephens, '"Wie bei dem Eintritt in Ein andres Leben."
Geburtsmetapher und Individualität bei Kleist,' *Das neuzeitliche Ich in der Literatur des
18. und 20. Jahrhunderts. Zur Dialektik der Moderne. Ein internationales Symposion*, eds.
Ulrich Fülleborn and Manfred Engel, Munich, 1988, pp. 195-214.

structed around the naming of Agnes links, in fact, the theme of distorted perception with that of the opacity of language.

At the beginning of Act III we encounter a piece of exposition that strains the credibility of the plot. Agnes asks why Ottokar calls her Maria, and Ottokar embarks on a long account of their first meeting, which Agnes can scarcely have forgotten. Ottokar has taken water from the stream and baptized her with the name Maria because she is 'an image of the mother of God.' In Act I, Scene 1, which stands later in time than these *narrated* events, Ottokar proposes to Johann that they should also 'baptize' her with the name Maria. When Ottokar addresses her as Maria in Act III, this surprises her to the extent that a long explanation appears necessary. After they have proven their trust in one another by their willingness to share the drink Agnes believes to be poisoned, Ottokar is, unusually, able to address her by her real name, and they discuss strategies for dissolving the suspicion that exists between their families.

To make sense of these implausibilities, it is necessary to begin with the fact that Agnes, in the first moments of her first encounter with Ottokar, denies she has a name at all. It is significant that she has just woken from sleep, a motif that, as I have shown elsewhere, functions consistently in Kleist's work as a metaphor of rebirth.[31] Agnes's reluctance to name herself suggests her intuition that by doing so she will only return herself to the world of family hostilities that she has momentarily escaped. The fact that Ottokar cannot share the freedom of anonymity with her, but is immediately impelled to 'baptize' her with a name that is full of extraneous connotations, seems poetic in the immediate context, but, from the perspective of the whole action, is ominous.

For the text of the play is saturated with images derived from Christian mythology, and to call Agnes 'Maria' is to tie her to the world of social discourse as securely as by giving her her real name. This seems to be the sense of the puzzling fact that her second 'baptism' as Maria in Act I, Scene 1, takes place – in her absence – in the chapel at Rossitz in the immediate aftermath of Rupert's ritual of vengeance, which, as we have seen, conflates the values of the Old and New Testaments.

Ottokar's action illustrates the irony that surrounds the use of language in the play. By naming her Maria he is trying to place her in a region above and beyond that where suspicion and vengeance dominate; but there is no language that is genuinely private and exclusive to intimacy, and a name such as Maria is compromised precisely because of its wealth of accumulated meanings. It is significant that both narrative

31 Ibid., pp. 208f.

sequences that include the 'baptism' of Agnes with the name Maria go on to confirm her social identity as Sylvester's daughter. Once more we may see these as anticipations of the end of the play, for Agnes, despite all attempts to make her someone else, reverts in death to being Agnes Schroffenstein.

Another aspect of her 'baptisms' that deserves notice is the extent to which she becomes the object of Ottokar's manipulations. In the episode that precedes the action of the play, and which Ottokar recounts at the beginning of Act III, Agnes has no choice in acquiring the name Maria, although her preference is clearly to remain nameless. In the dialogue between Ottokar and Johann, she is 'baptized' a second time in her absence, and Ottokar never tells her that his private name for her has been shared with Johann. The exchange of clothing in Act V, Scene 1, anticipates a marriage between them that will never take place, and the culmination of the scene is a fiction woven by Ottokar to conceal from Agnes the real danger of the situation. Whilst the vision conjured up by Ottokar's words is one of loving union, Agnes has virtually nothing to say as it unfolds and is, in effect, once more the passive object of Ottokar's discourse.

In concrete terms, Ottokar's strategy fails because it leaves Agnes deluded as to the real situation. Whereas Ottokar deliberately provokes his father into murdering him by declaring himself to be Agnes, her own incomplete knowledge of what is happening leaves her quite silent when confronted by Sylvester, so that he strikes her down without knowing that this is his own daughter. The only passage in which Agnes and Ottokar become equal partners in dialogue is in the latter half of Act III, Scene 1, after Ottokar drinks the water Agnes believes to be poisoned. While Ottokar knows very well that this is all make-believe, Agnes, thinking that she is already dying, is convinced that Ottokar wishes to join her in death. Drinking the supposedly poisoned water thus becomes for Agnes a rite of passage, for after it she is much more vocal and self-assertive than in any of her other scenes with Ottokar. This moment of emancipation in the shadow of death, however, does not change the course of the tragic action. A similar thematic pattern recurs with Toni and Gustav in *Die Verlobung in St. Domingo*.

If one reads the play along one axis as a debate about the constitution of a new kind of individuality in the wake of the discrediting of the Enlightenment's more facile convictions, then the course the love between Ottokar and Agnes takes surely implies that traditional gender roles must be transformed if a new beginning is to become possible. Ottokar's dominance in most of his dialogues with Agnes indicates that more than love in its conventional idealizations and an idyllic, natural setting are necessary to redress the balance of the sexes. The sudden liberation of Agnes's speech after the metaphorical transition through death and her subsequent return to passivity in Act V, Scene 1, suggest that emancipation will not become a lasting reality within the world of the play.

If we recall the programmatic subordination of women in Fichte's *Deduktion der Ehe*, then what Kleist implies about gender roles and individuality in *Die Familie Schroffenstein* seems revolutionary in terms of the understandings of these current at the time. The individual as the subject of an exemplary process of development is emphatically male. As Kleist's essay for his fiancée, *Über die Aufklärung des Weibes*, written in September 1800, proclaims, women have much more modest goals, namely to bear children and ensure their moral education (SW II, 318). But Kleist, in his first drama, seems intent on subjecting the beliefs and attitudes he had affirmed before the crisis of 1801 to critical scrutiny and, in this particular instance, complete reversal, so that it is entirely characteristic of his later work that his first pair of lovers poses – despite all the literary conventions with which their feelings are overlaid – the question of the equality of the sexes and of the possibility of an emancipatory discourse. One may, therefore, read the tragedy of the young lovers as a protest on Kleist's part against the dominance of conventional gender roles. Indeed, the whole play may be understood as a critique of the more repressive aspects of German family life at the time. For a successful example in Kleist's works of female emancipation within the framework of a male-dominated society, one has to wait for the essentially comic structure of *Die Marquise von O....*

Die Familie Schroffenstein thus raises the question of how meaningful social innovation can occur, and answers it with a pessimism that owes much to Kleist's disillusionment with the aftermath of the French Revolution and the onset of the Napoleonic era. Kleist's first disparaging remarks about Napoleon are from a letter written during the composition of *Die Familie Schroffenstein*, on 19 February 1802.[32] In the play, the theme of social innovation is clothed in the metaphorical garb of the sacraments Ottokar devises for himself and Agnes. These improvised sacraments are at once courageous attempts to create relationships that are genuinely new and, at the same time, proofs of the virtual impossibility of success – because the only available instrument is language, and all language is a repository of customary codes and meanings.

---

32 'So leicht indessen wird es dem Allerwelts-Konsul mit der Schweiz nicht gelingen. Zwar tut er sein Mögliches, dieses arme Land durch innere Unruhen immer schwach zu erhalten, und jetzt in diesem Augenblicke noch ist Zürich im Aufstande; indessen gewiß, wenn er sich deutlich erklärt, vereinigt sich alles gegen den allgemeinen Wolf.' SW II, 718.

The message implicit in the text is that new sacraments are necessary if the promise of rebirth is to be realized, but that the Christian sacraments familiar to all – and by extension their secular equivalents in post-Revolutionary European society – cannot be radically transformed. Religion has forfeited the emancipatory promise it held out in Lessing's *Die Erziehung des Menschengeschlechts*. Kleist's forecast of the stagnation of Christianity in the 19th century and beyond is thus an acute diagnosis. Rupert can make the Eucharist an emblem of vengeance, and Ottokar can make a variant of it into a sacrament of trust, but the derivative nature of these actions works for Rupert and against Ottokar and Agnes.

As *Die Familie Schroffenstein* clearly shows, Kleist is haunted by the discrepancy between events and their representations in language, and this applies to contemporary history as much as to the fictional events in his first play. The incongruities between language and the actions it supposedly reflects or produces lead Kleist to create, in *Die Familie Schroffenstein*, a world that is metaphorically over-determined, one in which every event has a plurality of linguistic guises, but where the characters lack a criterion for choosing among them.

But there is also the problem of making ideals, such as truth or a genuinely new concept of humanity, concrete in language. Kleist had already, two full years before the crisis of 1801, encountered this barrier with regard to the Enlightenment ideal of 'Tugend':

> Sie erscheint mir nur wie ein hohes, erhabenes, unnennbares Etwas, für das ich vergebens ein Wort suche, um es durch die Sprache, vergebens eine Gestalt, um es durch ein Bild auszudrücken. Und dennoch strebe ich diesem unbegriffenen Dinge mit der innigsten Innigkeit entgegen, als stünde es klar und deutlich vor meiner Seele. Alles, was ich davon weiß, ist, daß es die unvollkommenen Vorstellungen, deren ich jetzt nur fähig bin, gewiß auch enthalten wird; aber ich ahnde noch etwas Höheres, und das ist es wohl eigentlich, was ich nicht ausdrücken und formen kann. (SW II, 475)

Scepticism about the adequacy of language as a 'means of communication' (SW II, 626) is, like his scepticism concerning the direction of contemporary history, one of the very few elements of Kleist's thinking that survives the transition from his early letters to his beginnings as a writer of dramas and narratives without being rejected or reversed. Ironically, he seems more suspicious of language when working as a poet than when he was thinking in terms of becoming a philosopher or scientist. This scepticism becomes evident if we consider the frequent religious references in the play's imagery.

At first sight, the religious dimension of the play's language seems cluttered to the point of losing all coherence. The characters tend to perceive one another as angels or devils, rather than as mere human beings. Most revelatory is the moment in Act IV, Scene 5, when Rupert, on his way to do murder, sees his own reflection in a stream: 'Eines Teufels Antlitz sah/ Mich aus der Welle an' (SW I, 132). Besides this, there are various strands of natural imagery with religious connotations, ranging from the lightning bolt of God's vengeance in the Old Testament to reminiscences of pagan mythology. When Johann describes his first encounter with Agnes in Act I, Scene 1, he relates how his horse bolts in the mountain wilderness and plunges with him into a river. He loses consciousness and is rescued by a naked girl who is bathing there. He first perceives her as a goddess, and one is reminded of the myth of Diana and Actaeon, for Johann's glimpse of the naked Agnes bathing proves ultimately as fatal to him as Actaeon's sight of the naked Diana.[33] When Agnes clothes herself and comes to attend to Johann's wounds, she then reminds him of an angel (SW I, 61), and Ottokar, to whom the story is being told, proposes they together 'baptize' her Maria because of her resemblance to the Mother of God. A little later Johann reveals what Ottokar already suspects, namely Agnes's real name, and thus her place in the grim family constellation. In the one dialogue she has thus appeared, by turns, in the guise of the virgin goddess Diana, of an angel of mercy, of the Virgin Mary, and finally as the daughter of their supposed enemy, Sylvester.

While the new beginning is perforce presented in divine terms, the sheer amount of religious reference in the text that points back into the world of the fathers rather than forwards to an emancipation makes this metaphorical dimension, on the whole, a hindrance. A further hindrance is the structure of society itself.

The passage most often quoted in studies of the play as a key to understanding its central theme is from the first scene, in which the Kirchenvogt explains to Jeronimus the contract of inheritance, which supposedly accounts for the hostility between the two branches of the one family: if the one branch produces no successor, then the whole property reverts to the other. While the passage is within the conventions of dramatic exposition, there is still a fundamental implausibility about the need to explain the contract at all. Jeronimus is no newcomer to the action, for he belongs to a third branch of the Schroffenstein clan and has planned to marry Agnes for some time.

---

[33] This motif recurs in Meroe's narration of Achilles' death in *Penthesilea* (SW I, 412f).

Nevertheless, he challenges the relevance of the contract of inheritance to the present turmoil, which gives the Kirchenvogt the opportunity to say:

> Ei, Herr, der Erbvertrag gehört zur Sache.
> Denn das ist just als sagtest du, der Apfel
> Gehöre nicht zum Sündenfall. (SW I, 57)[34]

The usual interpretation of these lines is that the contract causes a degeneration of social relationships equivalent to that of humanity's first fall into sin in the garden of Eden. Kleist is commonly supposed to be reproducing certain ideas of Rousseau in a very simplified form.[35] But Kleist, in his poetic works, never simplifies anything, and the lines deserve closer inspection.

For the Kirchenvogt suggests that the contract 'belongs' to the present situation in the same way as the apple 'belongs' to the primal fall from grace. This is *not* to posit a causal relationship or say that the contract is the ultimate foundation of all discord in the society of the play. For it is Satan's playing on the weakness of human nature and not the apple itself that brings about the Fall. The fruit is an emblem of the mythical action, but it does not cause it, nor is it in any sense the myth's primal foundation. Similarly, we may say that in *Die Familie Schroffenstein* the contract is both the pretext and cipher for the lamentable state of human relationships, without its being the prime cause of catastrophe in crudely Rousseauistic terms.

Such a reading accords better with the way in which the world of the play is constituted, because it becomes increasingly evident that faulty deductions, suspicion of others, the inability to take notice of clear perceptions when they are articulated, and the opacity of speech to the speaker are so deeply entrenched in human conduct that one could almost remove the contract of inheritance from the action without making things any better. Significantly, the characters refer less and less to the contract as the play progresses, until all mention of it ceases, and Rupert becomes wholly obsessed with his thirst for vengeance as an end in itself.

The imagery of the play suggests again and again that aspects of the human predicament have their equivalents in supernatural or mythical terms, and that these aspects appear to be as real to the characters as the actions of others or, indeed, their own feelings. If the human may be so

---

34 Cf. Hinrich C. Seeba, KW I, 595f.
35 Cf. Oskar Ritter von Xylander, 'Heinrich von Kleist und J.-J. Rousseau,' *Germanische Studien,* vol. 193, Berlin, 1937, pp. 270f; Siegfried Streller, 'Heinrich von Kleist und Jean-Jacques Rousseau,' in *Weimarer Beiträge,* 8, 1962, pp. 545f.

readily transformed into the supernatural, then the play constantly challenges an audience or reader to identify the dominant reality: is it a drama of social conflict embellished with a wealth of religious themes and images, or a reenactment of a primal myth in the guise of a social tragedy?

Once again, the text as a whole is so constructed as to tempt us toward one answer or another, but refuses to confirm that either answer is correct. In this sense, Kleist's first work does almost to excess what all his subsequent works also do in one way or another, namely place the audience or reader in the same predicament as the fictional characters. Kleist's characters as a rule find the text of reality a challenge to decipher, and when it appears least ambiguous it is most likely to be misread.[36] Hence his figures become obsessed with finding the one right answer to the problems that confront them, and the history of Kleist criticism shows amply that this affliction overpowers scholarly readers as well, for the quest for right answers is pursued as passionately and ineffectively in writing about Kleist's fictions as it is within them.

If we ask why this is so, then the answer may lie outside his works and in the philosophical climate of the time. The Enlightenment had seen a progressive secularization of religious values to the point where distinctions between the religious and the social were very readily blurred. The French Revolution and its aftermath had given a powerful impetus toward viewing the historical present in mythical terms. Both these tendencies are amply documented in Kleist's letters both before and after he began composing literary works.

Kleist ultimately failed to discern any mythical pattern in contemporary history, although it was not for want of trying. But whereas Hölderlin, Hegel, and Novalis all managed to fix a coherent mythical vision of their age, Kleist's mythicizations of contemporary events are marked by a lack of lasting commitment. This seems, in turn, to drive him back into an incessant brooding on the myths of the Enlightenment, especially on their tendency to conflate social and religious issues. *Die Familie Schroffenstein* takes up an issue, such as the possibility of the emergence of a new order from the ruins of an old one, and explores it in terms that continually test the validity of the secularized religion of the late Enlightenment as an adequate description of the human condition – but without coming to a final conclusion. What distinguishes Kleist from his Romantic contemporaries is not any reluctance to experiment with myth, but his unwillingness to allow such experiments to produce coherent results.

---

36 Although he does not discuss Kleist, Hans Blumenberg has treated this general issue in *Die Lesbarkeit der Welt*, Frankfurt/M, 1981, pp. 199f.

I suggest that the theme of a new beginning in *Die Familie Schroffenstein* is best understood in these terms. The two fathers are not so much villains, as prisoners of the power they wield. This is exemplified by the following exchange between Eustache and Rupert, in which the question of how Rupert intends to use his power is posed in the most direct terms, but answered in a metaphor that effectively conceals the moral dimensions of his action from the protagonist:

EUSTACHE.   Das Mädchen? O
Mein Gott, du wirst das Mädchen doch nicht morden?
RUPERT.   Die Stämme sind zu nah gepflanzet, sie
Zerschlagen sich die Äste. (SW I, 122)[37]

The children, Agnes, Ottokar, and Johann, clearly fall prey to this captivation expressing itself in their fathers' violence. But they are also, to some extent, victims of their own modes of perceiving others and themselves. This is most extreme in Johann's case. Both he and Ottokar have fallen in love with Agnes in their separate first encounters with her, but Johann's perceptions of reality fluctuate wildly from the outset, and it is this distortion of perception as much as his unsuccessful rivalry with Ottokar that makes his descent into madness in the second act credible. In the first scene of the play he fantasizes about being a sacrificial victim at a point where no one is sufficiently concerned with him to offer him violence (SW I, 63). His perceptions of Agnes give her an aura of the supernatural, although Johann already knows who she really is. In Act II, Scene 3, where he kisses her and then tries to force her to stab him, he pronounces her, in rapid succession, to be both a corpse and a saint. For all their extravagance, there is clairvoyance in Johann's visions. Just as Agnes will end the play as a corpse, there is a sense in which the text itself – and not just Johann – also endows her with an aura of sanctity. Johann survives to the final scene, but apparently only so that he can force the audience to view the reconciliation of the parents as grotesque and farcical. But here again, his ravings offer as valid a perspective on the action as any other.

Johann is linked to Ottokar by more than the fact that they are half-brothers. He and Ottokar are the first of a long series of paired characters in Kleist's work who may be regarded as alter egos, doubles, or substitutes for one another. In their first long dialogue in Act I, Scene 1,

---

37 Cf. Lessing, *Nathan der Weise*, Act 2, Scene 5: 'Mit diesem Unterschied ist's nicht weit her./ Der große Mann braucht überall viel Boden;/ Und mehrere, zu nah' gepflanzt, zerschlagen/ Sich nur die Äste. . . .,' *Lessings Werke*, vol. 4, p. 71; on Kleist's relation to the works of Lessing, see Ruth K. Angress, 'Kleists Abkehr von der Aufklärung,' in *KJb* 1987, pp. 101f.

they seem almost to be complementary halves of the same identity. When it rapidly becomes apparent in Act II that Agnes welcomes Ottokar, but flees the sight of Johann, the latter's desire for Agnes immediately becomes self-destructive, and in Scene 3 he attempts to force Agnes to kill him. Jeronimus intervenes and wounds him, thinking he is trying to kill Agnes, but instead of dying Johann succumbs to madness.

There is much in Johann's fate that summarizes the course of the whole action. His plunge into the stream, loss of consciousness, awakening to the vision of the naked Agnes, and subsequent descent into madness are a condensation of the theme of the new beginning – and one that anticipates the future. The impossibility of finding any mediation between Agnes's role within the family feud and the new identity Ottokar tries to create for her outside it is ultimately the mainspring of the tragic plot. The self-destructiveness that surfaces so rapidly in Johann as soon as he is thwarted (SW I, 80f) is a salient feature of the whole world of the play. Finally, his fantasy, in the very first scene of the play, of being dragged as an unwilling sacrifice to an idol which is a 'bloody caricature' (SW I, 63) seems quite unmotivated at the time, but in fact anticipates the final slaughter. All three children end as pointless sacrifices to a paternal authority that has, in effect, become a 'bloody caricature' of what it initially represents itself to be. The fate of Johann and the reasons for it thus anticipate in a variety of condensed forms the unfolding of the main plot.

Kleist was to use this device again and again in later dramas and narratives, and it becomes one of the most distinctive features of his structuring of fictional plots. Its obvious function here, as often elsewhere, is to show the limits of insight within a world constructed around a core of the incomprehensible and the failure of fictional characters to decipher a text of which they themselves are part.

It is not difficult to translate the problem of social innovation in the text into terms that correspond to what we know about Kleist's attitudes to the course of contemporary history. The speeches of Rupert and Sylvester reveal a common obsession with the future security of their own bloodlines.[38] Ironically, they each kill the only child remaining to them that can continue their dynasties. The world of the fathers is the locus of violence, and, remarkably, of mob-violence. In Act II, Scene 2, it is reported to Sylvester that the herald sent by Rupert has been stoned to death by his retainers while he was unconscious.

In Act III, Scene 2, Rupert stands by while Jeronimus, who is still trying to mediate between the two houses, is bludgeoned to death in the

---

38 Cf. Anthony Stephens, 'Kleists Familienmodelle,' pp. 230f.

courtyard at Rossitz, and it later becomes clear that Rupert has ordered the killing. In both cases, the dialogue refers to the mob as 'das Volk,' whereas elsewhere in the text the households seem to be of modest size. That all violence in the play is within the sphere of the fathers, even the apparently spontaneous outbreak in Sylvester's castle, suggests that Kleist sees little difference between revolutionary violence and that sanctioned by the *ancien régime.*

Power productive of violence is, in a sense, always that of the fathers, and it will always seek its own expansion in space and time. Its most ready and obvious means of expansion is language, particularly the metaphorical language that is so abundant in the play. Gerhard Gönner, in his recent study of force and violence in Kleist's works, speaks of Rupert's 'alienation from language' ('Sprachfremdheit'), but surely the opposite is the case.[39] Rupert's consciousness is so strongly identified with the way language works in the play that its opacity to him is absolute. Thus he can even describe quite accurately the manner in which language functions as an extension of paternal power without gaining the slightest distance from it, or deriving from his own words the slightest control over his further actions:

> Das eben ist der Fluch der Macht, daß sich
> Dem Willen, dem leicht widerruflichen,
> Ein Arm gleich beut, der fest unwiderruflich
> Die Tat ankettet. Nicht ein Zehnteil würd
> Ein Herr des Bösen tun, müßt er es selbst
> Mit eignen Händen tun. Es heckt sein bloßer
> Gedanke Unheil aus, und seiner Knechte
> Geringster hat den Vorteil über ihn,
> Daß er das Böse wollen darf. (SW I, 117)

It is thus Rupert's closeness to the language of power, rather than any 'alienation' from it, that makes him so securely its victim. This also renders effortless the expansion of paternal authority into areas that may at first have seemed immune to it. A margin of alienation from language might indeed have produced in him some realization that his blood-thirsty quest becomes increasingly a self-reinforcing process and more and more distanced from whatever external causes may have set it going.

But what makes even Rupert a tragic figure is that his complete lack of distance from his own language blinds him. Rupert does not begin the

39 Gerhard Gönner, *Von 'zerspaltenen Herzen' und der 'gebrechlichen Einrichtung der Welt.' Versuch einer Phänomenologie der Gewalt bei Kleist*, Stuttgart, 1989, p. 68.

play without values. As the father of an apparently murdered child, he demands justice and sees the supposed murder as yet another symptom of a world out of control. That he ends the action proclaiming that he must become a murderer because others have branded him as one (SW I, 133), and then goes on to turn this curse into reality, shows what an unequal struggle takes place within him between morality and the words of others. It also introduces the major Kleistian theme – developed most fully in *Penthesilea* – of the determination of an individual by the language of which he or she is the object.

The analogy between Kleist's diagnosis of this relationship in *Die Familie Schroffenstein* and his perception of historical events is not far to seek, so long as we remember that the false relationships in which his fictional characters are entrapped are precisely those which the text as a whole sets out to unmask in all their falsity. The expansionist policies France had pursued since the outbreak of the Revolutionary Wars in 1792, whilst maintaining the fiction of bringing 'Liberty, Equality and Fraternity' to the rest of Europe, and the inescapable fact that Napoleon was building his own empire in the aftermath of the French Revolution and of the 18 Brumaire 1799 were sufficient examples, to anyone seeking confirmation, of the inability of the language of popular representation to reveal the nature of its own relationship to power.

My intention is not to reduce Kleist's works to allegories of the Napoleonic era, but to make visible what links his fictions to their social and historical context. That both Rupert and Sylvester end by negating the future of their own houses, thus destroying the very dynastic principle with which they are preoccupied, can, in this sense, be read as a sceptical comment on the violence of Kleist's own times, be it grounded in the French Revolution or in the old monarchies of Europe. Kleist's scenario for the renewal of humanity in his first drama is thus both abortive and strongly pacifist. This was not always to be his position, but it is the position from which he began as a creative writer, and to such beginnings he returned more than once.

The Deceptions of Language

In keeping with the play's character of a palimpsest, one level of explanation directs us to another beneath it. We have seen how the themes of a social contract and the fall of humanity are linked together by the Kirchenvogt in the first scene in a manner that purports to offer an explanatory model for the whole play. But the contract of inheritance by no means 'explains' all the false perceptions and confusions in the dialogue, and the inadequacy of this model refers us to the nature of perception in the work as something underlying both the religious and social dimensions of the action. Once more, there is no lack of explanatory models in the text itself. The most often quoted is Sylvester's diagnosis of mistrust as a 'sickness of the soul' in Act I, Scene 2:

> Das Mißtraun ist die schwarze Sucht der Seele,
> Und alles, auch das Schuldlos-Reine, zieht
> Fürs kranke Aug die Tracht der Hölle an. (SW I, 69)

To portray suspicion as an 'illness' of perception has a similar effect to clothing paternal authority in images of irrestible natural forces, namely to endow it with connotations of physical inevitability. If it is an illness, then it may be incurable or simply have to run its course. There is no suggestion in these lines that Reason, the panacea of the Enlightenment, can be applied to cure it. The inadequacy of the rational consciousness as an antidote is borne out by the text as a whole, for such discursive insights as some characters may have are consistently ignored by others or lost in the general confusion.

Most interestingly, Sylester's words set up a metaphorical equivalence – 'mistrust *is* the soul's dark addiction' – which goes unchallenged for the rest of the play. This is characteristic of metaphorical equations as a whole in Kleist's work, for once made they seem to resist being unmade with a tenacity that is stronger than rational discourse. The inadequacy of language is an integral part of Kleist's intellectual world before he sets out to become a poet, and the most striking formulation of this occurs in a letter to his half-sister, Ulrike, of 5 February 1801.[40] The unreliability of language as a 'means of communication' can be documented in virtually any scene of *Die Familie Schroffenstein*. But there is an irony attending this that is absent from the discursive statements in Kleist's letters before he begins writing dramas. For, within his fictions, language turns out to be an unreliable instrument not because of any inherent weakness, but because it is *stronger* than the characters who ostensibly control it.

Hence we may find in the nature of figurative discourse a further explanatory model for events within the play, which underlies the thematics of mistrust and distorted perception, just as these underlie the myths of the fall of humanity and the social contract. The remainder of the speech in which Sylvester speaks of mistrust as a disease presents an

---

40 'Und gern möchte ich Dir alles mitteilen, wenn es möglich wäre. Aber es ist nicht möglich, und wenn es auch kein weiteres Hindernis gäbe, als dieses, daß es uns an einem Mittel zur Mitteilung fehlt. Selbst das einzige, das wir besitzen, die Sprache taugt nicht dazu, sie kann die Seele nicht malen, und was sie uns gibt, sind nur zerrissene Bruchstücke' SW II, 626.

explanatory model of the nature of figurative language, but once more one that none of the characters can apply in a critical sense:

Das Nichtsbedeutende, Gemeine, ganz
Alltägliche, spitzfündig, wie zerstreute
Zwirnfäden, wirds zu einem Bild geknüpft,
Das uns mit gräßlichen Gestalten schreckt. (SW I, 69)

Trivial and innocuous things are woven into an 'image' that then appalls with horrid visions. If we ask who does the weaving and in what medium it occurs, the answer is surely that the characters themselves must create these 'images' in language, and are then deluded and terrified by their own creations. But Sylvester's use of an impersonal construction leaves it open to conclude that language itself does the deceiving. This correlates with what I term the ludic or demiurgic function of the 'whole text' in Kleist's practical aesthetics. Once an image is complete, its own creator no longer recognizes it as a mere assemblage of oddments, a linguistic *bricolage*, and it thus acquires the opacity of a reflecting surface. The figures in the drama cannot see through the image to its origins, but treat it as if it were a concrete reality. In this way the process of image-making is, as a rule, irreversible, even though later events might contradict what various images imply. Once Rupert has equated Sylvester and his clan with beasts, specifically reptiles, in the first moments of the play, there seems no way to escape from this mode of perception. When Rupert murders Ottokar, believing he is Agnes, in Act V, his henchman, Santing, demonstrates the undiminished power of this strand of imagery by remarking: 'Die Schlange hat ein zähes Leben' (SW I, 144).

Two further examples will serve to show the power that figurative language acquires over the speaker. When Jeronimus is killed by the mob in the courtyard of Rossitz in Act III, Scene 2, it is rapidly revealed that Rupert has given instructions that he be murdered. In the following scene, Rupert broods about the nature of power, pardons the servant who has first struck Jeronimus and, for a brief time, seems to repent of his action. His wife, Eustache, seizes on Rupert's mood as evidence of genuine regret and straightway magnifies it into an image:

O laß mich bleiben. – O dies menschlich schöne
Gefühl, das dich bewegt, löscht jeden Fleck,
Denn Reue ist die Unschuld der Gefallnen.
An ihrem Glanze weiden will ich mich,
Denn herrlicher bist du mir nie erschienen,
Als jetzt. (SW I, 120)

Eustache's perception of her husband takes the form of a metaphorical equation, but no sooner is the image formed than she declares her intention to bask in its 'radiance,' whereas Rupert simply reaffirms his wretchedness: 'Ein Elender bin ich' (SW I, 120). The 'splendour' of this moment has no existence outside her own excessively hopeful perception of her husband, and such 'radiance' as may be present is quite literally the reflection of her own humane and charitable feelings from the image she has made of Rupert. Despite all the signs that he is very far from attaining a lost innocence through repentance, she persists, throughout the rest of the long scene, in attributing her own perceptions and motives to him, and thus finally betrays the whereabouts of Ottokar and Agnes in the mountains. Rupert, who apparently absorbs nothing of her pleas and reasoning but this one piece of information, duly sets off at the end of the scene to find and kill Agnes.

The second example occurs in Act IV, Scene 5, while Rupert is still searching for Agnes. He pauses by a stream, sees his own reflection, and turns from it in disgust, saying 'a devil's visage' has looked back at him from the water (SW I, 132). Santing laughingly tells him that the face he has seen is his own, but so far is Rupert from being able to take advantage of such insights that he ignores the implications of his own vision entirely. Moreover, after his brief dialogue with Barnabe, he can admit his own predicament as a prisoner of language without drawing any conclusion from it except to reaffirm the power of words over reality. He now is what the language of others has made him:

So führ ein Gott,
So führ ein Teufel sie mir in die Schlingen,
Gleichviel! Sie haben mich zu einem Mörder
Gebrandmarkt boshaft, im voraus. – Wohlan,
So sollen sie denn recht gehabt auch haben.
– Weißt du den Ort, wo sie sich treffen? (SW I, 133)

Just as a destructive narcisssism determines the overall relations of the two branches of the family to one another, so the same principle here becomes apparent in the relationship of the speaker to language. What language reflects back upon the speakers has acquired such power that they cannot penetrate its surface. Once more, it is the excessive *power* of language, rather than any inherent defects in it, that diminishes its usefulness as an instrument for deciphering reality and communicating the result.

The text as a whole points to this phenomenon by the frequent use of the verbs 'erklären' and 'beschwören' as opposite ways of denoting the power of language.[41] To use language as a means of creating clarity in a given situation is often presented as an ideal, but never realized in time to do any good. The power of language to 'conjure up' visions is also remarked upon, but without diminishing its force in any way.

Significantly, the best known lines in the play expressive of a yearning for clarity clothe this in an image that is prophetic of still darker confusion. Confronted with Rupert's accusation that he is a murderer, Sylvester exclaims: 'Ich muß mir Licht verschaffen,/ Und sollt ichs mir auch aus der Hölle holen' (SW I, 74). In a very real sense, the only illumination available to the figures of the drama is a deceptive 'light from hell,' namely the distorting effect of imagery upon feelings and events. If we ask why the cognitive function of metaphor should amount to an infernal illumination, then the answer lies in the axiom, for Kleist's works, that metaphor is no mere play of language on the surface of things, but penetrates beyond factual discourse to the substrates of potential violence: the metaphorical Other of the loving father is, ultimately, the murderer.

By way of summarizing the pitfalls of imagery in the whole text, I shall single out three main aspects. First, metaphorical associations and equivalences seem to have largely supplanted causal argument in the language of the play. There is a strong tendency for characters to see themselves and others in a distorted fashion, not because of what has actually taken place, but because an image, once formed, resists rational deciphering. Moreover, such images can propagate themselves in the dialogue irrespective of which character uses them in a given context. The very first words of the play refer to Rupert's infant son Peter in the image of an 'angel' crushed by an 'impious foot': 'Sah ein Frühling/ Einen Engel./ Nieder trat ihn ein frecher Fuß' (SW I, 51). The image then recurs much later in Act V, Scene 1, when Sylvester contemplates the corpse of Agnes: 'Sie blühte wie die Ernte meines Lebens,/ Die nun ein frecher Fußtritt mir zertreten' (SW I, 147). It is as if the linking of the generation that carries the future with angels and with the image of being trodden to death, once implanted within the text, must sooner or later be repeated – irrespective of the identity of the speaker. For the imagery begins as part of Rupert's ritual of vengeance and ends in Sylvester's lament over the corpse of the daughter he has himself murdered.

---

41 Examples of this antithesis are: 'Wir haben viel einander zu erklären,/ Viel zu Vertraun. – Du weißt mein Bruder ist – / Von deinem Vater hingerichtet' SW I, 99; 'Ich mildern? meinen Vater? gute Agnes,/ Er trägt uns, wie die See das Schiff, wir müssen/ Mit seiner Woge fort, sie ist nicht zu/ Beschwören. . . .' SW I, 103. I have provided a commentary on the problems of 'explanation' in my essay '"Eine Träne auf den Brief." Zum Status der Ausdrucksformen in Kleists Erzählungen,' in *JbSchG* XXVIII, 1984, pp. 342f.

Second, the characters are impelled to go onward with the images they have themselves created. There seems no possibility of their retracing their steps, of undoing the metaphorical connections that lead them into further confusion. In the dialogue between the blind Sylvius and the mad Johann in the final scene of the drama, Johann makes a remark that also applies to the figurative dimension of the play's language. Sylvius demands that he be led back home, to which Johann replies: 'Ins Glück? Es geht nicht, Alter. 's ist inwendig/ Verriegelt. Komm. Wir müssen vorwärts' (SW I, 148).[42] The lines allude to a lost paradise, and are one of those statements in which Johann's madness possesses its own clairvoyance. They also aptly describe the way in which the characters of the play are driven forward from one misleading image to another, with no respite and no possibility of going back to undo the damage. The motif of nostalgia for a more happy state, real or imagined, and of the desire to 'return home,' has a strong presence throughout Kleist's works and may be summarized in the conceit that humanity has been expelled from a paradise, in which language enacts only the truth, into a world in which truth is lost among metaphorical distortions.

Third, the play sets up various ideals of communication, and, as we have seen, even points directly to the manner in which language can deform the perception of reality, yet without altering the course of events in the slightest. Appropriately, the ideal forms of communication and perception are sketched out in dialogues between Ottokar and Agnes. First, there is an ideal of perfect communication without any mundane speech at all. In Act III, Scene 1, Ottokar speaks of 'reading' Agnes's soul at their first encounter as if it were a book 'that explains the world in the language of the gods.'[43] Later in the scene, Ottokar imagines a confrontation between the two fathers in which they understand each other perfectly 'without speech.'[44]

There is also the ideal of a spontaneous dialogue. It is close to being realized in Act III, Scene 1, after Agnes and Ottokar survive their test of confidence in one another. Sylvester has already envisaged a frank conversation with Rupert as the only means of disentangling events, but it is fated to remain a vain hope (SW I, 86). For it is the dynamics of language itself that entrap the characters and lead them ever further away from any paradisal state of complete understanding. There is a tragic

---

42 Cf. Hinrich C. Seeba, KW I, 597f and 707.
43 'Deine Seele/ lag offen vor mir, wie ein schönes Buch,/ . . . doch immer kehrt er wieder/ Zu dem vertrauten Geist zurück, der in/ der Göttersprache ihm die Welt erklärt . . .' SW I, 95f; on the motif of 'reading souls' cf. Anthony Stephens, '"Eine Träne auf den Brief",' pp. 340f.
44 '- O Gott, welch eine Sonne geht mir auf!/ Wenns möglich wäre, wenn die Väter sich/ So gern, so leicht, wie wir, verstehen wollten!/ . . . – Und schuldlos, wie sie sind, müßt ohne Rede/ Sogleich ein Aug das andere verstehn' SW I, 102.

irony in the fact that the creative powers of language are shown by Kleist to be identical with those of delusion. For the fantasies that enable Johann to see Agnes as a goddess or an angel, or Ottokar to conjure up a credible vision of the marriage he and Agnes will never celebrate, depend as much on the ability of metaphor to detach itself from present reality as do the endless fatal mistakes and confusions. It is only because figurative language can successfully obscure reality that the play attains a kind of apotheosis in the scene in which Ottokar and Agnes exchange clothing in the cave; it is equally because of this quality of metaphor that Rupert, on the way to do murder, can perceive himself as a 'devil' and yet draw no redeeming conclusion from it.

Kleist experienced his own age as a time of many incomplete transitions. As well, his was an age in which the Aristotelian view of metaphor, as an ornament or rhetorical embellishment, was being replaced in poetic practice by an acknowledgement of metaphor as one of the prime resources of language.[45] Instead of being something added to rational discourse to make it more vivid or persuasive, metaphorical transformation was increasingly seen as the creative strength of language *par excellence*. This development was to reach its culmination in French Symbolism and its reflections in other European literatures.

Kleist's modernity is nowhere more in evidence than in his recognition of the power inherent in metaphor to supplant rational discourse. In *Die Familie Schroffenstein*, metaphorical language appears to run riot, but this is only the case if we approach the play with expectations derived from the Enlightenment or Weimar Classicism. The ultimate incoherence of the metaphorical dimension of the text is deliberate, and is a proof of the thesis that there is no criterion of objective reality by which all aberrations or distortions may ultimately be judged, but that such reality as there is, is no more than the mode in which rival subjectivities encounter one another and fail to agree.

The autonomy which the metaphorical dimension gains in the play is one of Kleist's great achievements, for all that it tends to throw the plot and characterization out of balance and disappoint conventional expectations. The best way of reflecting the many uncertainties that beset him in this regard was to abandon the Aristotelian principle of using metaphor as a series of projections from a stable, underlying reality and, instead, to allow it to unfold its full 'creative' powers at the expense both of his fictional characters and of the metaphysical or social authorities that are entrenched in language itself.

---

45 Cf. Wilhelm Köller, *Semiotik und Metapher. Untersuchungen zur grammatischen Struktur und kommunikativen Funktion von Metaphern*, Stuttgart, 1975, pp. 30-8.

The Recalcitrance of Tragic Form

Kleist was to struggle for the whole of his creative life with the problems of writing tragedy. None of the plays he wrote after the beginning of 1808 was designated as a tragedy, even when they contained many tragic elements. Thus a drama such as *Prinz Friedrich von Homburg* displays its full tragic potential before opting for a conclusion that reconciles some of the major thematic conflicts, while leaving others in suspension. If we can see beyond the conventional, melodramatic aspects of *Die Familie Schroffenstein*, then there is no lack of points of contact between the text and the mainstream of European tragedy. Much of what Lucien Goldmann says of the world of Racine's tragedies may be applied to that of Kleist's first drama. God, if he exists, is a silent spectator, Janus-faced, from whom the characters may appear to receive imperatives that conflict with one another in human action.[46] Through the bewildering play of perspectives he sets in motion, Kleist emphasizes the subjectivity of human experience of the divine to the point where it holds no firm contours. But if there is a god in his tragedies, then this god is hidden. Whilst various characters, including the vengeful Rupert, are convinced they are implementing the will of God, the ambiguous status of the divine in this world is best captured in Sylvester's words to Jeronimus: 'Ich bin dir wohl ein Rätsel?/ Nicht wahr? Nun, tröste dich, Gott ist es mir' (SW I, 93).

The phenomenon of 'tragic conversion' that Goldmann sees in Racine is also evident in *Die Familie Schroffenstein* as the caesura in an individual's experience, marking the beginning of a new kind of consciousness. This is certainly the way in which both Johann and Ottokar represent their first encounters with Agnes. Where Kleist departs from the Racinian pattern is in showing the 'conversion' to be less than complete. Ottokar vacillates between the world of old authorities and the new existence his love for Agnes allows him to glimpse. The beginning of his long fantasy about their wedding night in Act V, Scene 1, begins most incongruously with the words: 'Wenn erst das Wort gesprochen ist, das dein/ Gefühl, jetzt eine Sünde, heiligt – -' (SW I, 141). It is hard to understand this as other than a relapse into ways of thinking beyond which the lovers have already advanced. For they have previously been free of any awareness of 'sin' – indeed the text has represented their love as the only possible redemption of the two families. That Ottokar here invokes the authority of 'the word' in an orthodox Christian sense to sanctify a love that the rest of the play implies is sacred and in no

---

46 Cf. Lucien Goldmann, *The Hidden God. A study of tragic vision in the 'Pensées' of Pascal and the tragedies of Racine*, London, 1964, pp. 36f and 317f.

need of further sanctification betrays an uneasiness on Kleist's part about the efficacy of 'tragic conversion,' for all that other parts of the text may present it with no reservations.

Once more the example of Ottokar's alter ego, Johann, provides an additional perspective on the experience of the tragic hero. As we have seen, Johann's life is changed decisively by encountering Agnes in the mountains, and the terms in which he describes it mark a transformation in his existence, which he interprets as being led by 'a god' into 'eternal life' (SW I, 60). But powerful as the moment of conversion is, it heightens rather than diminishes the tension between Johann as a being reborn and Johann as the bastard son of Rupert. Johann's descent into madness in Act II, Scene 3, is a grotesque alternative to the fall of the tragic hero, and it is the grotesque that dominates the final scene of the play. We may thus see Kleist's tragedy as testing the idea of a decisive caesura in the life of a character, at first affirming it, but then finding reservations and suggesting alternatives that are virtually parodistic.

In his essay *Tragedy and its Validating Conditions,* R. J. Kaufmann suggests that tragedy only thrives when the existence of the gods is questioned, when such issues as teleology, providence, and the relation of human to divine action undergo a process of revaluation, in the course of which ultimate authorities may be varied or exchanged for new ones.[47] Once again, *Die Familie Schroffenstein* offers such abundant examples of the discrediting of authorities that the question is whether any at all remain at the end of the play. The divinity is invoked so often and to such ill-assorted ends that any authority it may carry is dissipated by the end of the action. Nature is declared by Rupert in the first scene to be an outdated fiction and remains, at best, equivocal. The scenes between Ottokar and Agnes suggest the contrary, but Kleist cannot content himself with the polarity he has thus established, and the play goes on to render nature as ambiguous in terms of human values as the distant, hidden god. The authority of the fathers seems, for most of the play, much more stable than the higher powers to whom they constantly appeal, but the text increasingly reveals the destructive narcissism inherent in it, and the murder of the children discredits it totally in moral terms.

The values we glimpse in the scenes between Ottokar and Agnes can be summed up as replacing the negatives of the fathers' world with positive opposites: trust instead of suspicion; love instead of revenge; a greater equality of gender roles instead of the fathers' subordination of their wives; the innocence of a new beginning instead of the compro-

47 R. J. Kaufmann, 'Tragedy and Its Validating Conditions,' in *Comparative Drama*, vol. I, 1967, pp. 12f.

mised values of a 'fallen' society. It is, however, a proof of Kleist's genius in his first dramatic work that the idealistic vision never quite emancipates itself from its discredited Other. Thus all the positive elements of the new beginning prove to be unstable in the subsequent course of the action. Even more importantly, they all derive from the world of family conflict, as reversals of qualities already present there, just as the sacramental actions Ottokar devises derive from the outworn models of Christian ritual. In this sense, the new beginning never really emerges from the shadow of the old authorities, even when these are more like a heap of ruins than a sacred edifice.

With the death of Ottokar and Agnes and the dubious reconciliation of the fathers, the audience or reader is left asking what future the world of the play could possibly have. The moral force of all authorities has been successfully challenged – perhaps so successfully that the cosmos itself ultimately appears to lose all coherence in the confusion of the ending. The Hegelian concept of tragedy is one in which both sides of the conflict are equally justified in themselves, whereas they perceive their own roles only as an 'infringement or transgression' of the other's authority.[48] It is not difficult, from an external point of view, to see Agnes's and Ottokar's attempts to emancipate themselves from the world of the fathers as fully justified; it is well-nigh impossible to find any justification on the side of paternal authority, as the play progressively subverts any moral basis it may have to the point where Sylvester and Rupert are each other's wholly negative mirror images. But the sphere of the fathers is where power resides. It is significant that the moment of disclosure, when Ursula throws the dead child's finger among the surviving family members, is clearly also one of alienation, for the harm the characters have inflicted upon themselves goes far beyond the initial cause of the confusion.

Kleist's handling of tragic form in *Die Familie Schroffenstein* thus takes up many aspects that are central to the European tradition and tests them in the experimental framework of a world reduced to a single, self-destructive family. In the process, the familiar elements of tragic form tend to be exaggerated to the point where they lose conviction or lapse into self-parody. Rupert's inability to gain any profit from Eustache's explanations of the real state of affairs and his own vision of himself in the stream as a fiend from hell amount to a parodistic exaggeration of

---

48 Cf. Peter Szondi, *Versuch über das Tragische*, Frankfurt/M, 1964, p. 25. Szondi quotes the following passage from Hegel's *Ästhetik*: 'Das ursprünglich Tragische besteht nun darin, daß innerhalb solcher Kollision beider Seiten des Gegensatzes für sich genommen *Berechtigung* haben, während sie andererseits dennoch den wahren positiven Gehalt ihres Zwecks und Charakters nur als Negation und *Verletzung* der anderen, gleichberechtigten Macht durchzudringen imstande sind und deshalb in ihrer Sittlichkeit und durch dieselbe ebensosehr in *Schuld* geraten.' (Jubiläums-Ausgabe, vol. 14, pp. 528f).

the tragic blindness of, for example, King Lear, and the same may be said of other conventionally tragic aspects of the drama.

Kleist seems bent on demonstrating that, while the familiar elements of tragic form may still have life on stage, they readily lose validity under the pressure of such a world as he creates in *Die Familie Schroffenstein*. The shambles in which the play ends surely indicates that a new concept of tragic form is called for, in a historical situation where the old order seems moribund and the 'new beginning' of the French Revolution has already discredited itself. Since *Die Familie Schroffenstein* can only give some indication of what this form might be and stops short of realizing it, the play appears to turn upon itself shortly before the end and do everything possible to subvert its own credibility. But Kleist had achieved too much in this first work for its ending to ruin it. His next attempt at tragedy, *Robert Guiskard*, was to be more ambitious still.

Robert Guiskard

Only the first ten scenes survive of the tragedy Kleist regarded as the masterpiece that was meant to establish his fame. His failure to complete the play in late 1803 was a personal catastrophe that prompted fantasies of self-destruction. We have no evidence as to when this fragment was composed in the form in which it was published in 1808, but he began the play in 1802.[1] Among the many legends which have grown up around Kleist and his works, and which Kleist himself had no small part in propagating during his lifetime, the composition of *Robert Guiskard* holds prime place. His 'discovery' of a new concept of tragedy, which the fall of an 11th century Norman warrior-prince was meant to realize, his struggle to complete the work, and his destruction of the manuscript in 1803, once he was convinced he had failed, are all portrayed in his letters in such a way as to make the creative process into a tragedy in its own right.[2] The pattern of intense ambition, hope, struggle, and finally violent despair at a lesser outcome was one Kleist was to repeat throughout his life. But the initial challenge was never to be so great, nor the disappointment so bitter, as with his first attempt to complete *Robert Guiskard*. In the following discussion, I can make only some tentative suggestions, based largely on a study of the imagery, as to what the play might have become, for the data we have are too inconclusive to say more.

While all crises in Kleist's life have histrionic elements, especially in the manner in which Kleist himself presents them to correspondents, there is Wieland's testimony as to the quality of the scenes of the play he heard the author recite when Kleist was staying in his house as a guest in early 1803. Wieland wrote in April 1804 to Dr Georg Wedekind, who played his own enigmatic role during Kleist's life in these years, that the young poet, a friend of his eldest son, had confessed to him that he had

---

1 Cf. SW I, 921f and KW I, pp. 663-75; Hans Joachim Kreutzer, *Die dichterische Entwicklung Heinrichs von Kleist*, Berlin, 1968, p. 154f and Richard Samuel, 'Heinrich von Kleists *Robert Guiskard* und seine Wiederbelebung 1807/1808', in *KJb* 1981, pp. 315-48.

2 See the letters to Ulrike von Kleist of 13/14 March 1803 (SW II, 730), 3 July 1803 (SW II, 733), 5 October 1803 (SW II, 735f.) and 26 October 1803 (SW II, 737).

such an exalted concept of his unfinished tragedy in his mind that it was impossible for him to realize it on paper.[3] Tragic drama was held in more esteem in German literary circles at the time than any other form of writing, and it is no accident that Kleist's text alludes to Sophocles' *King Oedipus*.[4]

That a young writer should aspire to a new kind of tragedy was the height of ambition or, indeed, presumption, but Wieland gained an immediate appreciation of Kleist's potential. One afternoon Kleist declaimed from memory several of the important scenes of his unfinished play to Wieland. He was, in fact, soon to take lessons in declamation as a more effective means of presenting his tragedy 'live,' since a letter to Ulrike of March 1803 shows that he had doubts as to how it would fare in one of the slapdash theatre productions that were the rule, rather than the exception, on German and Austrian stages at the time.[5] Wieland recalled his astonishment at the talent revealed to him, and went so far as to say that if the shades of Aeschylus, Sophocles, and Shakespeare had concerted their efforts to produce a tragedy, then it would be something like Kleist's 'Death of Guiscard the Norman,' if the whole of the work lived up to what Kleist had recited to him.[6]

Kleist was to promise a complete version of the work again in 1808, when he published the first scenes as a sample of more to come, but it is unclear whether this fragment was principally a reconstruction from memory or a reworking of material that had survived his burning of the manuscript in Paris in 1803. From the evidence of his own and others' letters, he certainly intended to complete the play between the winter of 1807 and mid-1808, and may have come close to doing so.[7]

In the letter of October 1803 to Ulrike, in which he claims he has burned the manuscript and that he rejoices in the thought of dying in the course of Napoleon's invasion of England, he announces that he is at last quit of the hopeless task of completing *Robert Guiskard*. But there is good evidence to support the conclusion that he remained obsessed with his failure to complete the work until April or May 1804.[8] The evidence of style and imagery shows that the published fragment has affinities to the tragedy *Penthesilea*, which Kleist completed in the autumn of 1807, so that, whatever may have been preserved or remembered of the

3 Cf. LS, 75.

4 For a summary of the influence of Sophocles' tragedy on *Robert Guiskard*, see Jochen Schmidt, *Heinrich von Kleist. Studien zu seiner poetischen Verfahrensweise*, Tübingen, 1974, pp. 230f.

5 'Ich lerne meine eigne Tragödie bei ihm deklamieren. Sie müßte, gut deklamiert, eine bessere Wirkung tun, als schlecht vorgestellt.' SW II, 730.

6 Cf. LS, 75f.

7 Cf. KW I, 673f.

8 Cf. Richard Samuel and Hilda Brown, *Kleist's Lost Year*, pp. 100f.

version Kleist rejected in 1803, the text was reworked for publication in 1808 and bears traces of Kleist's preoccupations in those years.[9]

Much speculation has surrounded what the work might have become and what prevented Kleist from finishing it to his own satisfaction. There is no doubt as to the magnitude of the task Kleist had set for himself. To have his hero, who is close to reaching his goal of conquering Constantinople, die on stage of the plague, without diminishing the force of the first act conflicts, was a formidable challenge. For these conflicts are of an essentially political nature and scarcely susceptible to resolution by having a charismatic leader of his people succumb to 'fate' in the form of mortal illness.

In sharp contrast to *Die Familie Schroffenstein*, where the vassals and common people are ultimately no more than extensions of the power of the two fathers, the 'people' in *Robert Guiskard* become a power in their own right. Indeed, Guiskard's subjects open the play, speaking as if they were a chorus in classical Greek tragedy. In this first, long, expository speech and later, through the outspoken old man who acts as the people's voice, feelings and attitudes are expressed that may at first seem to be subject to all the fluctuations of temper of a Shakespearean mob. But, in fact, the people put forward a forceful, articulate viewpoint on the dynastic quarrel that threatens Guiskard's authority and the survival of the reign he has established.

If Kleist's first completed tragedy, *Die Familie Schroffenstein*, sometimes comes close to being an allegory of a single identity divided against itself, *Robert Guiskard* is clearly the work of an author who had brooded on the role of the common people in the French Revolution and the consequences of this for the history of Europe. As Gerhard Schulz has recently observed, the play exemplifies the problematic relationship of language to power in the post-Revolutionary epoch.[10]

The play opens at dawn in the camp of the Normans, who are besieging Constantinople. The people have chosen a deputation of 12 proven and respected warriors to demand an audience with the Duke, as many of their number are dying each day of the pestilence, and they fear their existence is threatened both by Guiskard's ambition and his apparent indecisiveness. Parallels to events in Napoleon's Egyptian campaign are undeniable and doubtless intended by Kleist to be recognized by a reader or an audience, but the Normans in Kleist's play are more than just an army on an expedition of conquest in a foreign land. They are, above all, a whole community concerned with their survival in generations to

9 Cf. Iris, Denneler, 'Legitimation und Charisma. Zu *Robert Guiskard*', *Kleists Dramen*', ed. Walter Hinderer, pp. 75f.

10 Gerhard Schulz, *Die deutsche Literatur zwischen Französischer Revolution und Restauration. Zweiter Teil, 1806-1830*, Munich, 1989, p. 637.

come, and it is remarkable how much of the imagery is concerned with marriage and progeny. Hence a simple equation of Guiskard with Napoleon can only be reductionist. Our lack of knowledge as to how the plot would have developed in detail obliges us to examine the imagery of the fragment in search of clues. In the opening lines, there are other dimensions of reference than those that link Guiskard with Napoleon:

> DAS VOLK *in unruhiger Bewegung.*
> Mit heißem Segenswunsch, ihr würdgen Väter,
> Begleiten wir zum Zelte Guiskards euch!
> Euch führt ein Cherub an, von Gottes Rechten,
> Wenn ihr den Felsen zu erschüttern geht,
> Den angstempört die ganze Heereswog
> Umsonst umschäumt! (SW I, 155)

The angel, signifying the righteousness of their cause, is a familiar motif from other works of Kleist, but biblical imagery is not significantly developed in the text as we have it. Indeed, one of Kleist's uncertainties seems to have been precisely what higher powers the characters in this play can meaningfully invoke, for the next lines allude to Zeus' thunderbolt and, for the remainder of the fragment, the religious dimension fades from view as all interest is focused on the conflicts of purely human wills.

The identification of Guiskard with a cliff and the people with waves breaking against it is the beginning of a significant strand of imagery, for the ferment of a possible 'rebellion' or 'uprising' is repeatedly likened to the surge of an ocean. In grim counterpoint to this image of Guiskard stands the vision of the land where the Normans are at that moment encamped, towering over the sea like a 'grave-mound' over the single corpse of his whole people. Consonant with this is the warning by the chorus that Constantinople may become for Guiskard himself nothing but a 'splendid tombstone.'[11]

But by far the most vivid and sustained line of imagery in the chorus's opening speech is the evocation of the pestilence. At first it appears as a frightening caricature of the Angel of Death, striding through the camp. Then it becomes associated with 'schauerliches Raubgeflügel' and finally seems reminiscent of some of the descriptions of the Furies and their attendant Harpies in Greek and Roman litera-

---

11 Richard Samuel and Hilda Brown, *Kleist's Lost Year*, point out the parallel in Kleist's letter to Ulrike concerning his intention to die taking part in Napoleon's invasion of England: '. . . unser aller Verderben lauert über den Meeren, ich frohlocke bei der Aussicht auf das unendlich-prächtige Grab' (SW II, 737).

ture.[12] This establishes a link to the imagery of *Penthesilea*, which I shall comment on later. At the outset, the pestilence appears as a destructive and distinctly female presence in opposition to the 'bride,' the equally female emblem of fulfilment, which has no one referent, but a range of positive connotations, such as 'liberty' and 'fame.' Thus, in the chorus's first speech, the plague is seen as effecting by death a series of separations, among them 'die Braut vom Bräutgam' (SW I, 155).

In the second scene, an 'ancient' is made spokesman of the people. This alters considerably the impact the voice of Guiskard's subjects may have on the course of events, since the old man has had a long and close association with the ducal family and can address them with various modulations of respect, but with no trace of subservience. From this point on, the action hinges on the question of whether Guiskard himself has succumbed to the plague. His daughter addresses the crowd, but fails to convince their spokesman to disperse them. A report that the Duke's physician has attended him that night in disguise is kept from most of the Normans, though neither from the old man nor the audience, and then Guiskard's son and nephew, the rival claimants to the succession, openly compete with one another in commanding the allegiance of the people. Robert, the son, and Abälard, the nephew, belong, like Ottokar and Johann in *Die Familie Schroffenstein*, to the category of paired characters in Kleist's work.

Here the rivalry raises the issue of the legitimacy of power, one of obvious relevance to contemporary events in the Napoleonic era. Abälard, as the son of Guiskard's elder brother and predecessor as Duke, claims authority by the 'law of inheritance,' while Robert, the son of an acclaimed and successful usurper, demands that the new order take precedence over all else. The dispute is complicated by the fact that the people's spokesman clearly prefers Abälard and declares he has all those qualities that made the Normans idolize Guiskard himself when his elder brother died and he assumed power. Moreover, Robert is arrogant and unskilled in his attempts to exact obedience from the crowd, while Abälard plays to their affections, praising their love of freedom in terms that, once again, use the imagery of marriage, although with oddly destructive overtones: 'Und heilig wäre mir das Ehepaar,/ Das mir den Ruhm im Bette zeugt der Schlacht' (SW I, 162).

Kleist then introduces further subtleties into the contest. No sooner has Abälard appeared as the paragon of all the qualities the Normans prize than he adds an element of dangerous instability to the already pre-

---

12 'Und statt des Segens unsrer Kinder setzt/ Einst ihres Fluches Mißgestalt sich drauf,/ Und heul'nd aus ehrner Brust Verwünschungen/ Auf den Verderber ihrer Väter hin,/ Wühlt sie das silberne Gebein ihm frech/ Mit hörnern Klauen aus der Erd hervor!' (SW I, 156).

carious situation by accusing his rival of concealing the fact that Guiskard is ill. Disingenuously, he denies the Duke has the plague, but confirms in the same breath that he has all the familiar symptoms. He clearly intends to use the desperation his announcement unleashes to advance his cause in the people's hearts, but all he achieves is to provoke the appearance of Guiskard himself, who sets about restoring calm and rebukes his nephew. Challenged to deny he has the pestilence, and eager to end the confrontation and return to his tent, Guiskard prevaricates. A sudden weakness overcomes him and he carefully sits on a large drum that his daughter positions behind him at the right moment. The spokesman of the people analyzes the situation acutely: even if Guiskard is not infected, he argues, the Normans are so weakened by the plague that any plans of conquering Constantinople are futile. The fragment ends with his resounding appeal to Guiskard to lead his people back to Italy.

Doubt and apparent certainty alternate with one another in the audience's perspective on the action, which keeps them constantly off balance. No sooner does Abälard seem to justify the crowd's affection for him by giving them the truth, which the rest of the family is trying to conceal, than Guiskard shows himself and apparently discredits his nephew. The Duke's evasiveness as to his state of health and his sudden attack of weakness shift the perspective again, but not to Abälard's clear advantage. Has his forcing Guiskard to confront the crowd really improved the situation for anyone? If Guiskard has used his remaining strength to put on a show, who is now capable of controlling the course of events? By these frequent shifts of perspective, Kleist poses questions about the relationship of truth to political power and explores ways in which language may serve as a medium for both.

As I have shown elsewhere, similar questions are posed very clearly, but receive consistently negative answers, in *Die Hermannsschlacht*, a political drama completed in December 1808.[13] The fragment of *Robert Guiskard* leaves political questions genuinely open, chiefly by giving the spokesman of the people such an eloquent voice, as he constantly reminds the ruling family and the audience that there is more at stake than dynastic rivalries or military glory. For his speeches compel these issues to be seen in terms of their implications for the survival of a whole community threatened by extinction. In *Die Hermannsschlacht* the people are no more than an expendable resource in the service of Hermann's manipulations toward a flatly nihilistic end.

13 Cf. Anthony Stephens, "'Gegen die Tyrannei des Wahren." Die Sprache in Kleists *Die Hermannsschlacht*', '*Die im alten Haus der Sprache wohnen*'. *Beiträge zum Sprachgedanken in der Literaturgeschichte*, ed. Eckehard Czucka, Münster, 1991, pp. 175-95.

With the development of the theme of community, *Robert Guiskard* is obviously a long way from being a mere gloss on Kleist's fixation on Napoleon. Rather, there seems to be an undercurrent of criticism of the view that history is primarily the creation of exceptional individuals. The imagery repeatedly conjures the vision of an ideal family, which serves to show up the destructive impulses active in the ducal household and emphasizes the right to survival of all those families that make up the common people.

The community certainly accepts a firm leadership that is also in their best interests. But the final speeches of the old man draw a compelling analogy between the pointless destructiveness of bad leadership and the madness that overcomes victims of the plague in their final agony:

> Ja, in des Sinns entsetzlicher Verwirrung,
> Die ihn zuletzt befällt, sieht man ihn scheußlich
> Die Zähne gegen Gott und Menschen fletschen,
> Dem Freund, dem Bruder, Vater, Mutter, Kindern,
> Der Braut selbst, die ihm naht, entgegenwütend. (SW I, 172)

In his successful attempt to charm the crowd, Abälard proclaims 'liberty' to be the Norman's true bride, and in this context their child is fame and their marriage bed the battlefield. Later in the scene he openly accuses Guiskard's son of treating the army as if it were 'a pregnant woman' whose sensitivities must be spared, when he accuses his rival of concealing the truth about Guiskard's illness. But the imagery also mirrors the dual perceptions that the price of an individual's glory may be the destruction of future generations and that, in this sense, a leader who sacrifices his people to his own thirst for conquest is like a plague victim turning, in his last sufferings, against his own family in a homicidal frenzy.

It is the outbreak of pestilence that forces this issue, but it does not require a leap of imagination to equate the disease with the wider consequences of war for a civil population, since the imagery has persistently suggested this from the outset. This, in turn, raises the question of what was to become of Robert Guiskard in later scenes. If he, after thirty years of rule, is already stricken by the plague at the moment the drama commences, it is hard to see how the action might develop his characterization further. One may observe of Kleist's characterization in general that he is most reluctant to allow his characters to 'develop' in a conventional sense.

The struggle between his son and nephew and the decisive role the interests of the people, as represented by the old man, might play in deciding its outcome clearly have great potential for dramatic elaboration, but it is hard to make out a tragic conflict within Guiskard himself. His prevarication about his own health when confronting the crowd is oddly reminiscent of that of the guilty judge Adam in *Der zerbrochne Krug*, whose character undergoes no change whatsoever in the course of the action.[14] He is not interested in the moral dimension of his own guilt, and it is only a matter of time before his delaying strategies are exhausted and he is exposed. This affinity may point to one of the major problems Kleist experienced with the character of Guiskard. He is a successful usurper who does not appear worried by the legitimacy of his power. Nor do the people, for as long as he is capable of leading them without destroying their claim to a future.

In terms of the imagery, Guiskard has two potential 'brides': victory or the plague. If the die is already cast in these early scenes, what variations on the theme could sustain dramatic interest? I have suggested elsewhere that the theme of emancipation from a state in which the individual is compromised by his or her past may have been as important for the concept of tragedy in *Robert Guiskard* as it is in *Penthesilea*.[15] Part of Penthesilea's tragic conflict stems from the fact that, as Queen, she is meant to embody the ethos of the Amazon state, which is both inhumane and rigid, while, in loving Achilles she aspires toward a new and freer mode of human relationships, even if she cannot define it in clear terms and vacillates between familiar models. It is possible that Guiskard's tragedy might also have developed as an attempt to win free of the taint of the usurpation by which he came to power and which the discord within his own household embodies in the present. Within this hypothesis, the plague could appear as a metaphor of Guiskard's inner disunity, and his death from it could be read as his failure to overcome this disunity and achieve emancipation. If this seems to read too much of *Penthesilea* into the fragment, it is worth pointing out that one of Penthesilea's most perceptive summations of her own plight matches closely the beginning of the old man's final exhortation to Guiskard:

PENTHESILEA.
Wo sich die Hand, die lüsterne, nur regt,
Den Ruhm, wenn er bei mir vorüberfleucht,
Bei seinem goldnen Lockenhaar zu fassen,
Tritt eine Macht mir hämisch in den Weg –
– Und Trotz ist, Widerspruch, die Seele mir! (SW I, 344)

---

14 This point is made by Gerhard Schulz, *Die deutsche Literatur. Zweiter Teil*, p. 638.
15 Anthony Stephens, 'The Illusion of a Shaped World: Kleist and Tragedy,' in *AUMLA*, vol. 60, 1983, p. 201.

DER GREIS *gesammelt.*
Du weißts, o Herr – und wem ists so bekannt?
Und auf wem ruht des Schicksals Hand so schwer?
Auf deinem Fluge rasch, die Brust voll Flammen,
Ins Bett der Braut, der du die Arme schon
Entgegenstreckst zu dem Vermählungsfest,
Tritt, o du Bräutigam der Siegesgöttin,
Die Seuche grauenvoll dir in den Weg –!
Zwar du bist, wie du sagst, noch unberührt;
Jedoch dein Volk ist, deiner Lenden Mark,
Vergiftet, keiner Taten fähig mehr . . . (SW I, 172)

The lines from *Penthesilea* show clearly that the external 'power' that blocks her way to victory correlates with an inner conflict, and the similarity of metaphor makes it tempting to come to the same conclusion regarding *Robert Guiskard.*

The difficulty with this is essentially Guiskard's opacity to a reader or audience. While Penthesilea frequently gives us glimpses of her own attempts to comprehend what is taking place within her, Guiskard gives away as little as possible, and nothing vouches for the correctness of other characters' surmises. The more serious problem is whether Guiskard, within such moral terms as the fragment establishes, has incurred any guilt strong enough to make the plague credible as an objective correlative of his inner state. The conflicts that derive from his usurpation of power are already visible in the dissimulation and wrangling within his household, but it places strains on the credibility of an interpretation to maintain that his opportunism carries the same stigma and brings down the same curse upon the Normans as does Oedipus' unwitting incest upon Thebes. Abälard was a child when Guiskard had himself crowned Duke, rather than merely acting as regent for his nephew, and this reign has endured for 30 years. Certainly, there is a question as to the legitimacy of Guiskard's power, but it seems to me exaggerated to see the plague as a projection of this.[16]

For the rivalry between his two possible successors, which does derive from his long-ago usurpation of power, seems almost incidental to the devastating effects of the pestilence. The plague thus appears as a metaphor with no clear referent, and this may have contributed to Kleist's abandoning the project. To be more than mere chance, it should

---

16 I thus do not agree with Lawrence Ryan, 'Kleists "Entdeckung im Gebiete der Kunst." *Robert Guiskard* und die Folgen,' *Gestaltungsgeschichte und Gesellschaftsgeschichte*, ed. Helmut Kreuzer, Stuttgart, 1969, p. 245: 'Vorläufig soll uns das an die Person des Helden geknüpfte Schuldmoment beschäftigen, das im neuen Drama in der Pest zweifellos eine symbolische Gestalt gewinnt.'

correspond to some past or present conflict within the hero, after the pattern suggested both by *King Oedipus* and by the references to the Furies in *Penthesilea*. But the fragment leaves us with an unsatisfactory choice among a number of possible equivalents, none of which lends itself to being magnified into a cause, intelligible in moral terms, of the wholesale suffering of the people. There is a similar problem with the imagery of marriage, since Guiskard, after thirty years of successful rule and conquest and now a plague victim, seems ill-fitted for the role of 'bridegroom,' which is surely more appropriate to one of his younger possible successors. For neither his son nor his nephew has yet had a chance to 'wed' victory on their own initiative.

We should be careful, however, of applying too rationalist a scheme to this text. Kleist's fictional worlds often make a mockery of strict causal relationships. The references to the myth of the Fall that abound in his work are rarely linked to the breaking of a prohibition. *Die Familie Schroffenstein* presents, from the outset, a world in a fallen state that owes more to the characters' entrapment in their own language than it does to any guilt that may accrue to their actions or to those of their forebears in concluding a contract of inheritance. Similarly, the plague that dominates the imagery of *Robert Guiskard* may well be a doom out of all proportion to any guilt inherent in the political constellations and there simply to outweigh the fantasies of marriage and birth that are also prominent in the characters' evocations of their plight.

Even Abälard's betrayal to the crowd that Guiskard is ill is qualified by two unexpected images of vitality: a tiger crouched to spring and a strategist reborn:

> Doch das hindert nicht,
> Daß er nicht stets nach jener Kaiserzinne,
> Die dort erglänzt, wie ein gekrümmter Tiger,
> Aus seinem offnen Zelt hinüberschaut.
> Man sieht ihn still, die Karte in der Hand,
> Entschlüss' im Busen wälzen, ungeheure,
> Als ob er heut das Leben erst beträte. (SW I, 167)

Guiskard himself is an enigmatic text that the other characters struggle to decipher. It is in keeping with this that there should be indications that he himself might, paradoxically, be regenerated out of the disaster that has overtaken his world. The tragedy of his fight against the infection in himself and the dissensions in his family could, within the almost surrealistic imagery, take on the terrible irony of a dying man's struggle to be reborn of victory in defiance of the other female presence, the plague. Could it be Guiskard's own rebirth – a fantasy of autogenesis doomed to remain a tragic illusion – to which the imagery so insistently alludes?

Questions such as these cannot be answered from the fragment Kleist published. What we can say with certainty is that the scenes display the same awareness of the family as a destructive set of relationships as pervades *Die Familie Schroffenstein*, yet continually allude to an ideal community of family ties in terms that are much more powerful and concrete than, for example, the possibility of a marriage between Ottokar and Agnes in Kleist's first finished tragedy. If we take this together with the new independence of the voice of the common people, then we may see in the unresolved tensions between individual glory and communal well-being a final obstacle to the successful unfolding of a tragic plot.

It seems as though the emergence of Napoleon's rule from the aftermath of the French Revolution challenges Kleist to make of the power of the common people a dramatic protagonist in its own right, but that he is unsure of how this goal may be achieved within a dramatic tradition dominated by larger-than-life individuals. In *Penthesilea*, Kleist could find no other solution to this problem than to dissolve the Amazon State itself, and in *Die Hermannsschlacht* he reverts to the formula of *Die Familie Schroffenstein*, whereby the people from the outset are no more than another puppet for Hermann to manipulate.

Since *Robert Guiskard* seems to point to neither of these outcomes, the conclusion is open that Kleist had exhausted his possibilities of devising a credible resolution and thus abandoned the play.[17]

---

17 Further conjectures about his theory of tragedy based on an account by Christian Gottlieb Hölder are possible, but I shall not pursue them beyond what has already been published, as I incline to the view that Hölder likely garbled whatever it was he might have heard, cf. Hermann F. Weiss, *Funde und Studien zu Heinrich von Kleist*, Tübingen, 1984, especially pp. 47-57; Hilda Brown, 'Kleists Theorie der Tragödie - im Lichte neuer Funde,' *Heinrich von Kleist. Studien zu Werk und Wirkung*, ed. Dirk Grathoff, p. 116.

–3–

Der zerbrochne Krug

The third of Kleist's dramas to have its origin in his stay in Switzerland in 1802 is *Der zerbrochne Krug*. Kleist began writing the play in Dresden in the early summer of 1803 and finished it in August 1806.[1] It was published at the beginning of 1811 as a book, but had already earned some notoriety through Goethe's production of it at the Court Theatre in Weimar on 2 March 1808.[2] It is characteristic of the nemesis that seemed to hang over Kleist's literary productions that the play should have sufficiently appealed to Goethe for him to undertake the production himself, but then should effectively erect a barrier of embarrassment between these two great talents when the production failed.[3] Two days after reading the play for the second time, Goethe consigned it in a letter to Kleist's friend, Adam Müller, to 'the invisible theatre,'[4] at the same time declaring that it had undoubted merits. He would scarcely have exposed himself to ridicule by continuing with the production had he not expected it to work on stage. His strategy of dividing into three acts the text Kleist wrote as one continuous scene only served to exacerbate the play's main weakness, namely the absence of dramatic tension. We can only surmise that Goethe expected the acrobatics of the play's language to carry the day. While *Der zerbrochne Krug* did not receive its next performance until 1816, this performance in Munich was the first of many successes, showing that, with judicious pruning, the text could make effective theatre. The play has since become the most performed of Kleist's dramas and a staple of the German repertoire.

In a prologue Kleist omitted from the published version, but which is preserved in a manuscript, he identifies the play's main sources in an engraving illustrating the proverb from which the title is adapted and in Sophocles' *Oedipus Rex* (SW I, 176). The central character, the judge Adam, has attempted to seduce a village girl, Eve, on false pretenses,

---

1 Cf. KW I, 732-6.
2 Cf. KW I, 746f.
3 Cf. Katharina Mommsen, *Kleists Kampf mit Goethe*, Frankfurt/M, 1979, pp. 36-41.
4 'Der zerbrochene Krug hat außerordentliche Verdienste, und die ganze Darstellung dringt sich mit gewaltsamer Gegenwart auf. Nur schade, daß das Stück auch wieder dem unsichtbaren Theater angehört.' LS, 146.

and he is forced to preside at the trial that will establish his guilt. The relationship of Kleist's play to that of Sophocles is one of parodistic reversal, since Adam is aware of his own guilt from the beginning and devotes all of his energies to postponing its inevitable coming to light.[5] It is hardly to the play's advantage that the audience is also convinced of Adam's guilt from very early on, and often reminded of it in asides from Adam that the other characters supposedly do not hear.

The third main body of allusion in the text is to the myth of the Fall, and here again Kleist lays it on extremely thickly. Parodistic reversal is once more apparent since Adam is the tempter, not the tempted, and his fall is not from any state of grace, but merely from one in which he can use his wits, official status, and education to manipulate the rustics in his charge into exposure and removal from office. Even then, the figure of authority in the play, Walter, emphasizes that he will be spared harsh punishment.[6] The Fall is thus merely one from a barely sustainable concealment into disclosure – but a disclosure to which the reader or audience is party from the beginning.

Next to its length, the play's heavy-handedness accounts most for its hostile first reception, as contemporary verdicts indicate.[7] Indeed, Kleist's penchant for subverting the forms in which he was working seems to have led him toward turning the conventions of comedy into something else. His friend Fouqué suggested in 1811 and again in 1816 that the play might best survive if it were considered a 'comic idyll' rather than a comedy,[8] and Goethe's reservations about the play and his consequent choice of a mode of production that made it even harder for the play to succeed in familiar comic terms could indicate a similar recognition.[9]

From the perspective of Kleist's entire work and the time that has elapsed since it was written, it is apparent that one of the factors that sets *Der zerbrochne Krug* apart from conventional comedies of the early 19th century is the author's fascination with rituals. It is no coincidence that the first scene of *Die Familie Schroffenstein* takes place in a chapel where a ritual is being conducted that is a blasphemous variation of the Christian Eucharist, or that the text of *Penthesilea* assigns so much

5 Cf. John Milfull, 'Oedipus and Adam – Greek tragedy and Christian comedy in Kleist's *Der zerbrochne Krug*,' in *German Life and Letters*, N.S. 27, 1973/74, pp. 7-17.

6 'Von seinem Amt zwar ist er suspendiert,/ Und Euch bestell ich, bis auf weitere/ Verfügung, hier im Ort es zu verwalten;/ Doch sind die Kassen richtig, wie ich hoffe,/ Zur Desertion ihn zwingen will ich nicht./ Fort! Tut mir den Gefallen, holt ihn wieder!' SW I, 244.

7 Cf. LS, 390f.

8 See Fouqués Letter to Varnhagen of 2 May 1811, LS, 390; for the later version of this see KN, 192.

9 Cf. KW I, 759f.

importance to the rituals of the Amazon State. For Kleist, the workings of the law were very close to religious ritual, and he was later to combine them in the masterly courtroom drama of the first act of *Das Käthchen von Heilbronn*.[10] Ascertaining truth through language was for Kleist a process of endless fascination, which partakes in all his works of a ritual formality. But the essence of a ritual action as such is that the spectators already know its course before it begins, whereas a comedy dispenses with surprise elements at its own peril.

Audience hostility to the first production of *Der zerbrochne Krug* was focused on the end of the play, and a contemporary review singles out Eve's long narration of Adam's deception of her as the most painful part of the evening.[11] In the printed version, Eve's disclosure that Adam is the guilty party is completed in ten lines, whilst in the manuscript her account of what has occurred draws out the ending, after Adam has fled the court, for over 350 lines. Kleist's attachment to an ending that he had to acknowledge made poor theatre is attested by his including Eve's long narration as an appendix in the printed version, under the title of 'Variant.'

The question must still be asked: Do we gain anything by knowing all the ins and outs of Adam's deception? The answer may well be: only if we are prepared to experience the play in its ritual mode, in which most interest focuses on the *how* rather than the *what* of the dramatic process. Even in a production that omits the longer ending, Kleist's affection for the ritual mode poses serious problems for the actor playing Adam and for the audience's understanding of the psychology of the character. For Adam's position is lost so early in the action that the credibility of his role is strained before the play is half over. Before Adam's superior, Gerichtsrat Walter, appears on the scene and the hearing begins, the court's clerk, Licht, has already drawn out the essentials of Adam's crime in their opening dialogue, and Adam has confided to Licht the details of a dream he has just had that anticipates the conclusion of the action. A further anticipatory motif is contained in the news that the judge in a nearby village, Holla, has been found guilty by Walter of malfeasance and has attempted suicide. The hearing has scarcely begun before Adam confides his fear, in an aside to the audience, that he will end up as the accused (SW I, 195), and the play, in its shorter version, is not yet halfway through when Walter announces, in the hearing

10 'Wir, Richter des hohen, heimlichen Gerichts, die wir, die irdischen Schergen Gottes, Vorläufer der geflügelten Heere, die er in seinen Wolken mustert, den Frevel aufsuchen, da, wo er, in der Höhle der Brust, gleich einem Molche verkrochen, vom Arm weltlicher Gerechtigkeit nicht aufgefunden werden kann' SW I, 431.

11 'Demois. Elsermann, die eigentliche plagende Erzählerin, Jungfer Eve, hatte sich recht gut kostümiert.' LS, 205.

of all, that this is the last case Adam will ever conduct (SW I, 206). Not long afterward, Eve's mother, Frau Marthe, makes a protest at the length of proceedings that has probably struck a chord with many audiences:

> Hör du, mach mir hier kein Spektakel, sag ich.
> Hör, neunundvierzig bin ich alt geworden
> In Ehren: funfzig möcht ich gern erleben.
> Den dritten Februar ist mein Geburtstag;
> Heut ist der erste. Mach es kurz. Wer wars? (SW I, 216)

In terms of a conventional comedy, one is at a loss to know what Adam can hope to gain by dragging out the conclusion. The hearing has yet to commence, and Walter, the inquisitor, has barely appeared on stage when he spells out his own tolerance and leniency:

> Doch *mein* Geschäft auf dieser Reis ist noch
> Ein strenges nicht, sehn soll ich bloß, nicht strafen,
> Und find ich gleich nicht alles, wie es soll,
> Ich freue mich, wenn es erträglich ist. (SW I, 188)

What Adam has done is clearly beyond the bounds of tolerance, yet the paradox remains that the strategic intelligence which enables him to defer his exposure by spinning improbable inventions should also tell him there is no point in going on. Skillfully played, this could be turned into a comic paradox in the manner of the businessman who acts like a millionaire precisely because he is going bankrupt, but it requires a talent rarely seen on German stages.

Much the same applies to the characterization of Eve in the longer version. An innocent and naive village girl she may be, but her extended resistance to Walter's attempts to convince her that all will be well with her betrothed's military service in the 'Variant' cannot help but make her seem less intelligent than in earlier scenes. To restore credibility to the characters, it helps to see them as performing a ritual dance around a centre of truth, which is veiled and disclosed in turn by the play's language.

The quality of Kleist's dialogue also presents problems, for it is uneven. Adam is most enjoyable when he is most fluent, but his speeches are larded with a plethora of oaths, curses and ejaculations that rapidly become tedious. The same applies to the excess of Shakespearean punning that dominates the early scenes of the play, but, mercifully, does not pervade the whole dialogue in such quantity.

The clear elements of parodistic reversal in the play raise the question of how seriously we are to take the play's various fields of reference. The myth of the Fall is all-pervasive, but may tend to be trivialized by the absence of a credible lost paradise or state of grace. Eve is innocent, but part of her innocence is a chronic suspicion of anyone in authority. She expects Ruprecht to trust her absolutely, although this means his conniving at her false version of events. Her self-disclosure in the longer ending shows that she has little hesitation in accepting the arrangement Adam proposes to free Ruprecht from military service – what she balks at is the price he demands in sexual favors.

It is therefore doubtful whether the frequent biblical references endow the play with as oppressive a religious dimension as some critics maintain.[12] If one is partially sketched in, then it is to provide a framework for the tragic potential in the character of Eve. None of Kleist's works moves very far away from tragedy, and his two comedies develop a tragic subplot around the main female character. In the case of Eve a potentially tragic conflict develops around the themes of trust, truth, and language. Like Toni in *Die Verlobung in St. Domingo* and various other female characters in Kleist's works, Eve understands her betrothal as more than just a social contract. She feels it as an absolute commitment, and there is tragic potential both in the intensity of this bond and in the way it tends to blind her to other people's attitudes. With no particular evidence, she has assumed an equally total commitment on the part of her betrothed, Ruprecht, and his failure to live up to her expectation of him undermines her feeling of self in a way that Adam's sexual blackmail cannot. The speech in which she reproaches Ruprecht for not supporting her version of events is very finely crafted by Kleist to convey these complex feelings, without making her language too sophisticated for a village girl:

> Unedelmütger, du! Pfui, schäme dich,
> Daß du nicht sagst, gut, ich zerschlug den Krug!
> Pfui, Ruprecht, pfui, o schäme dich, daß du
> Mir nicht in meiner Tat vertrauen kannst.
> Gab ich die Hand dir nicht und sagte, ja,
> Als du mich fragtest, Eve, willst du mich?
> Meinst du, daß du den Flickschuster nicht wert bist?
> Und hättest du durchs Schlüsselloch mich mit
> Dem Lebrecht aus dem Kruge trinken sehen,
> Du hättest denken sollen: Ev ist brav,
> Es wird sich alles ihr zum Ruhme lösen,
> Und ists im Leben nicht, so ist es jenseits,
> Und wenn wir auferstehn ist auch ein Tag. (SW I, 216f)

12 Cf. Oskar Seidlin, 'Was die Stunde schlägt in Kleists *Der zerbrochne Krug*,' *Mythos und Mythologie in der Literatur des 19. Jahrhunderts*, ed. Helmut Koopmann, Frankfurt/M, 1979, p. 74; Hinrich C. Seeba, KW I, 795f.

Her reference to the resurrection of the dead for the Last Judgement signals the full seriousness of a conflict that is as incongruous within the comic convention of the time as it is in the character of a peasant girl on stage. The bumbling Ruprecht remains entirely in character by not understanding her. In the longer ending of the play, Kleist allows Eve's separateness from her social context to verge on caricature through her obstinate refusal to recognize the sincerity of Walter's intentions toward her and Ruprecht, although, like all the other characters, she has witnessed him behaving with complete probity throughout the whole hearing.

Eve is one of many characters in Kleist's works caught up in the uneasy relationship between truth and language. In one sense, her own position is compromised from the moment she agrees to Adam's spurious plan to save Ruprecht from being shipped off to the East Indies with the militia by means of a fake medical certificate. By conniving at what she later describes as 'List gegen List' (SW I, 844), she puts herself in possession of an unpleasant truth that she believes she cannot reveal to the hearing for fear that Adam will take revenge on Ruprecht.

Such a fear seems to ignore both the presence and authority of Walter and the fact that Adam is, from the first moments of the hearing, clearly under Walter's control and showing every sign of desperation. But the enigmas of her conduct tend to add depth to the characterization of Eve, rather than render it implausible. Like many of Kleist's heroines, her expectation that absolute trust will not be misplaced poorly equips her to deal with situations in which it is. This is blended very skillfully with the confusion of her attitudes toward authority. In his only perceptive remark in the whole play, Ruprecht tries to explain to Walter why Eve did not unmask Adam immediately: 'Es war ihr Richter doch, sie mußt ihn schonen' (SW I, 839). Adam was a friend of Eve's dead father, and, within the confines of village life, his position as judge is vested with paternal authority. Moreover, Georg Lukács was quite correct in seeing the play as having a significant dimension of social criticism, for part of Eve's confusion is the deep-seated mistrust of the peasantry toward the power of the state, which both Walter and Adam represent.[13]

This is revealed most clearly in the 'Variant' at the point where Walter is forced to confront the fact that Eve expects him to lie about what is in store for the militia as part of his duty: 'Gut, gut. Auf Eure Pflicht./ Und die ist, uns, was wahr ist, zu verbergen' (SW I, 844). In trying to seduce her in exchange for a forged medical certificate, Adam has not so much appalled Eva as fulfilled her pessimistic expectations of

13 Cf. George Lukács, 'Die Tragödie Heinrich von Kleists', *Deutsche Realisten des 19. Jahrunderts*, Bern, 1951, pp. 19-48, especially p. 42; Helmut Arntzen, *Die ernste Komödie: Das deutsche Lustspiel von Lessing bis Kleist*, Munich, 1968, pp. 198f.

all servants of the state. This explains some of her unwillingness to believe, despite all the evidence, that Walter is different.

Kleist enriches the theme of the elusiveness of truth by associating it with that of violence. The connection is first made when Adam invites Frau Marthe to respond to Ruprecht's entirely truthful account of what he witnessed the previous night:

> Was ich der Red entgegne?
> Daß sie, Herr Richter, wie der Marder einbricht,
> Und Wahrheit wie ein gakelnd Huhn erwürgt.
> Was Recht liebt, sollte zu den Keulen greifen,
> Um dieses Ungetüm der Nacht zu tilgen. (SW I, 212)

Kleist's manuscript shows that, before settling on the image of the relationship of language to truth as being like a small beast of prey killing a fowl, his impulse had been to use the much more incongruous and hyperbolical one of a boa constrictor – 'Königsschlange' – crushing a bleating lamb.[14]

The violence inherent in the disturbed relationship of language to truth is further brought out by two parental reactions to statements by children. When Eve admits that she had lied to her mother the night before in blaming Ruprecht for breaking the jug, Frau Marthe comes close to a physical attack on her daughter: 'Hör, dir zerschlag ich alle Knochen!' (SW I, 217). In a piece of ironic symmetry, Veit Tümpel threatens his son, Ruprecht, in almost identical words, after the latter has yet again made a true statement that is at odds with Frau Marthe's latest allegations: 'Hör, du verfluchter Schlingel, du, was machst du?/ Dir brech ich alle Knochen noch' (SW I, 222).

This should not be dismissed as purely conventional, or the casual violence of peasant life as viewed by Kleist the aristocrat. For the text is careful to give some substance to Eve's fear that the sons of the peasantry might be called on to go to war against Spain or be shipped off to the East Indies to fight and die. Violence is therefore an integral part of this world. Walter does not deny that the second is possible; he merely states that this is not in store for Ruprecht, and that the government always tells troops in advance if they are to be sent abroad. Kleist is therefore careful to place the violence in the villagers' language in the wider perspective of a somewhat shadowy historical dimension, which in Frau Marthe's account of the history of the jug alludes to the turbulent

---

14 '[Was]/ [Ich dazu sage? Daß die Rede sich,]/ Herr Richter, wie [die Königsschlange aufbäumt,]/ Und Wahrheit, [mit geschmeid'gem Gliederbau,]/ [Geknäuelt, wie ein blöckend Lamm, erdrückt.]/ Was Recht liebt, sollte zu den Keulen greifen,/ [Das] Ungethüm[, zusamt dem Nest,] zu tilgen.' KW I, 840.

history of the Netherlands, the colonial war in Bantam of 1685, and the war of the Spanish Succession, which commenced in 1701.

Despite an appearance of chronological precision, Kleist does not trouble to make the historical dimension cohere. It is sufficient for the purposes of the play that Adam's playing on Eve's fears for Ruprecht's safety should be credible to all the other characters. It is therefore possible to interpret the violence in the villagers' language as a reflection of the threats posed to the life of this small community by the state-sanctioned violence of contemporary history, which is exacerbated by their helplessness before the intrusion of the recruiting commission on their wedding plans (SW I, 841) and by their lack of insight into the politics of nations.

Eve's mistrust of Walter's veracity must thus be seen in a social frame of reference in which truthfulness is uncompromisingly demanded from those one holds dear, but not expected to cross class barriers. Adam's position is very much on the border. He is the one inhabitant of Huisum with access to the workings of the state, and he can successfully use his status to deceive Eve. Still worse, one of his attempts to maintain pressure on her during the hearing emerges as a parody of a witness' obligation to be wholly truthful, and also introduces the motif of the Last Judgement, which Eve is later to take up in her reproach to Ruprecht:

> Sprich, Evchen, hörst du, sprich jetzt, Jungfer Evchen!
> Gib Gotte, hörst du, Herzchen, gib, mein Seel,
> Ihm und der Welt, gib ihm was von der Wahrheit.
> Denk, daß du hier vor Gottes Richtstuhl bist,
> Und daß du deinen Richter nicht mit Leugnen,
> Und Plappern, was zur Sache nicht gehört,
> Betrüben mußt. Ach, was! Du bist vernünftig.
> Ein Richter immer, weißt du, ist ein Richter,
> Und einer braucht ihn heut, und einer morgen. (SW I, 214)

Eve's unwillingness to believe Walter in the 'Variant' is thus well-motivated in the earlier text of the play, and the plot could certainly be swung toward a tragic outcome were Ruprecht's fate made to depend on her inability to believe that authority is incompatible with truth. Since the play is a comedy and requires its happy ending, Walter must ultimately convince her, which he does. But Kleist points to the lasting discrepancy between truth and language by making the act of conviction entirely implausible in terms of rational discourse.

It is credible that Eve's conviction as to the contents of a letter she cannot read, and for which she has no other guarantee than the words of

Adam, should exert its own force on her mind. It strains credibility only when, after Adam has fled the scene, she refuses to connect Walter's behavior throughout the hearing with his assertion that Ruprecht is not bound for service in Batavia, demanding, in effect, that Walter prove what he has already proven:

WALTER   Steh auf, mein Kind.
EVE   Nicht eher, Herr, als bis ihr Eure Züge,
Die menschlichen, die Euch vom Antlitz strahlen,
Wahr macht durch eine Tat der Menschlichkeit. (SW I, 840)

Eve's disbelief persists through many additional speeches, and it begins to crumble only when Walter produces a purse of guilders and offers it to her. The money would enable her to buy Ruprecht's freedom. Walter raises the stakes by declaring that the money is hers if he is shown to be misleading her about Ruprecht's service, and that he will have it back from her with interest if he is proven truthful.[15] But what finally convinces Eve is a dialogue between them that makes no sense at all:

WALTER   Das Geld? Warum das?
Vollwichtig, neugeprägte Gulden sinds,
Sieh her, das Antlitz hier des Spanierkönigs:
Meinst du, daß dich der König wird betrügen?

EVE   O lieber, guter, edler Herr, verzeiht mir.
– O der verwünschte Richter!

WALTER   So glaubst du jetzt, daß ich dir Wahrheit gab?

EVE.   Ob Ihr mir Wahrheit gabt? O scharfgeprägte,
Und Gottes leuchtend Antlitz drauf. O Jesus!
Daß ich nicht solche Münze mehr erkenne! (SW I, 853f)

It would be understandable if, after her ordeal with Adam, truth could not reside in mere words for Eve but must be as tangible as coins. But the problems of this dialogue about truth go far beyond such a simple explanation. Eve's only previous mention of the Spanish has been of a tyrannical enemy threatening the Netherlands, and Walter has confirmed this as a real danger (SW I, 841). Why the head of the King of Spain on a coin should then persuade her of *anything*, let alone be greeted as 'Gottes leuchtend Antlitz,' is a question most commentators prefer

15 Cf. Ruth K. Angress, 'Kleists Abkehr von der Aufklärung,' p. 105.

to pass over, since it is answerable neither from the text nor from Kleist's historical sources.[16]

The Netherlands became independent of Spain in 1648. Walter is thus unlikely, in a scene that appears to take place at some time between 1685 and 1701, to have in his pocket a purse of newly minted Spanish coins. This incongruity aside, the hyperbole of the words 'Gottes leuchtend Antlitz' suggests that Eve is speaking in delirium, yet her next words show her planning in most practical terms to visit Ruprecht during his military service:

> Und ich geh einen Sonntag um den andern,
> und such ihn auf den Wällen auf, und bring ihm
> Im kühlen Topf von frischgekernter Butter:
> Bis ich ihn einst mit mir zurückenehme. (SW I, 854)

One can only conclude that the text here subverts its own credibility as violently as it does in *Die Familie Schroffenstein* at the end of Act IV. Kleist had every opportunity to moderate the anachronistic effect of this passage, much as he changed the incongruous image of language crushing truth as a boa constrictor crushing a lamb. But his insistence on printing in 1811 the 'Variant' as an appendix to the shorter version of the text implies he was determined to retain this incomprehensible moment.

I suggest that such a genuinely opaque piece of dialogue, which revolves around the theme of truth and leads directly to the happy ending, can only signal to a reader or audience that truth, in the sense the text has implicitly defined it, is not to be found in the artifice of a stock comic ending. Rather, it maintains its own inaccessibility and, indeed, absurdity in the face of such fictional contrivance. In the real world, Kleist seems to imply, Walter would long since have lost patience with Eve's obstinacy and Ruprecht would have to take his chances with the draft. Perhaps, in the real world, Walter would not even have appeared to take charge of the hearing, and there would have been nothing to mitigate Eve's tragedy. That this tragedy is averted may be as implausible as Walter's and Eve's exchange over the coins.

Certainly, violence is done to the characterization of Eve in the 'Variant'. In the shorter version, the painful discrepancy between her

---

16 Of the commentators who do take up the question, Dirk Grathoff provides a courageous, but in my view over-elaborate, explanation in his essay 'Der Fall des *Krug*. Zum geschichtlichen Gehalt von Kleists Lustspiel,' in *KJb* 1981/82, pp. 303-10; less probable explanations are offered by Ruth Angress, 'Kleists Abkehr von der Aufklärung,' pp. 105f and Wolf Kittler, *Die Geburt des Partisanen aus dem Geist der Poesie: Heinrich von Kleist und die Strategie der Befreiungskriege*, Freiburg i. Br., 1987, pp. 97f.

expectations of Ruprecht's trust in her and his stereotyped and rather simple-minded reaction to her imagined infidelity give her role a depth that the other characters lack, making her one of the most memorable creations among Kleist's female figures. Agnes in *Die Familie Schroffenstein* is in a potentially tragic conflict, but right up to the moment of her death she remains a puppet of the male characters, especially Ottokar. Eve is alone in *Der zerbrochne Krug* in her struggle to come to terms with a need for absolute trust that is not reciprocated, and her suffering is intensified by the fact that she is the bearer of a truth, disclosure of which can halt her ordeal at any time, but which she still fears will have fatal consequences for Ruprecht once Walter has departed. One of the most successful aspects of Kleist's dramatic technique in *Der zerbrochne Krug*, as it is usually performed, is that these aspects of Eve's plight come through the garrulous interchanges of the other characters quite forcefully. Her characterization scarcely gains from her occupying the center of attention for most of the 'Variant,' for no new conflicts are revealed, the play's chief tension has been lost with Adam's flight, and her obstinate refusal to believe Walter's reassurances makes for a poor substitute. The main interest of the 'Variant' lies in the further exploration of the more abstract issue of the antagonism between truth and language – one which, as we have seen, cannot be resolved without disrupting discourse itself. The dislocation of rational dialogue by the exchange concerning the golden coins at the end of the 'Variant' is like the hole in the broken jug in which the founding of the Netherlands, the fictitious historical context of the play, has to be imagined to occur.[17]

If Eve, in the shorter version of the play, can communicate so much while saying relatively little, we are bound to ask why the dominant character, Adam, can say so much without engaging the feelings of the audience. The obvious answer is that everything is disclosed about Adam so early in the play that only his virtuosity in wriggling can sustain audience interest, whereas the moral earnestness and depth of Eve's distress can well come as a surprise to an audience expecting her to be as stereotyped as the other villagers.

Another possible explanation is that Adam is, at best, only a partial character, and for this reason not susceptible to any development. Already in *Die Familie Schroffenstein*, Kleist had experimented with paired characters, such as Ottokar and Johann or Rupert and Sylvester, as one expression of the theme of the divided self. He was to continue to do so in his later works. To force one character to contain all the major conflicts in a work, as is the case in *Penthesilea*, creates a ten-

17 Cf. Hinrich C. Seeba, KW I, 801f.

sion that may threaten the figure with disintegration. The alternative, which sacrifices tension to a more elaborate dramatic exposition, is to assign different aspects of the one complex to different roles, as happens with Rupert and Sylvester in *Die Familie Schroffenstein*. Rupert can be single-mindedly vengeful and ruthless because all of the moral scruples he might be expected to feel have been transferred to Sylvester during the early acts of the play. By the conclusion, the two fathers have become virtually indistinguishable from one another through the erosion of Sylvester's morality by the fatal coincidences of the plot.

Similarly, Adam may be seen as being paired with both Walter and Licht. Walter functions as Adam's moral self, as the upright judge Adam knows he ought himself to be. As the progress of the hearing increasingly makes Adam the real accused, so Walter exchanges the role of observer for that of judge. Adam's dream has prefigured just such a division of the self:

– Mir träumt,' es hätt ein Kläger mich ergriffen,
Und schleppte vor den Richtstuhl mich; und ich
Ich säße gleichwohl auf dem Richtstuhl dort,
Und schält' und hunzt' und schlingelte mich herunter,
Und judiziert den Hals ins Eisen mir.

LICHT   Wie? Ihr Euch selbst?

ADAM   So wahr ich ehrlich bin.
Drauf wurden beide wir zu eins, und flohn,
Und mußten in den Fichten übernachten. (SW I, 187)

Since Adam, from a judicial point of view, knows from the outset what the implications of his attempted blackmail and seduction of Eve are, he has no discoveries to make about himself, and his frank, if indulgent, characterization of the judge in Holla is effectively a self-portrait:

Ei, Henker, seht! – Ein liederlicher Hund wars –
Sonst eine ehrliche Haut, so wahr ich lebe,
Ein Kerl, mit dem sichs gut zusammen war;
Doch grausam liederlich, das muß ich sagen. (SW I, 181)

Licht, unlike Walter, has no moral presence, but represents, as Adam's relative, those survival skills that have maintained Adam as judge in Huisum until he concocts his plot to seduce Eve. Licht lets Adam's implication of him in financial irregularities pass unchallenged, and, while he clearly lacks Adam's vitality and eloquence, an audience has no grounds for thinking that things will be different in Huisum from what they have been, if he becomes Adam's successor.

As proof of the affinities between them and the judge as criminal, both Walter and Licht understand Adam extremely well. In the opening scene, Licht immediately connects the wounds Adam bears on his face and head with some sexual misdemeanor, establishing Adam as a 'sinner' in the eyes of the audience well before Frau Marthe has appeared with her broken jug. Walter fulfills, in his dialogues with Eve, the role of the 'good father,' which Adam, the friend of Eve's real father, has totally disgraced. But Walter is no puritan or moral fanatic. He declares at the outset that there is a considerable degree of tolerance in his application of ethical criteria, and this is borne out by his promise of leniency and some measure of rehabilitation for the unmasked culprit. For Adam has not produced a single extenuating circumstance for his crime, and his total lack of feeling for the pain of his victim cannot help but diminish him. Indeed, as the hearing wears on, his credibility as a character is reduced as his stratagems lose any rational point. By the time Walter commands him to conclude the hearing, Adam has become a mere embodiment of rhetorical panache.

When interpreting *Die Familie Schroffenstein*, I used the metaphor of the palimpsest to characterize the various fields of reference that are overlaid in the text. The text of *Der zerbrochne Krug* is similar. Attention is repeatedly directed to the myth of the Fall; there are numerous other direct allusions to the Bible in the dialogue; both Adam and Eve evoke the Last Judgement, if for totally different reasons. The history of the Netherlands offers another field of reference that is present throughout the text, and much the same could be said of the tensions between a small peasant community and the state in which it is located.

From a survey of critical writing on the play, it is clear that each of these fields of reference represents a strong temptation to conduct schematic readings of the text. The problem is that none of these fields of reference is wholly unified, and this forces critics to go outside the work to make their readings cohere. Thus, it is not unusual to link the mythic or religious dimension of the text with quotations from Kleist's essay *Über das Marionettentheater*, especially those that associate self-awareness with the Fall and other motifs from the Book of Genesis.[18] Similarly, interpretations along the historical axis of the text may appear capricious in the singling out of details as being of prime importance for understanding the play.

The fundamental enigma remains: Why should Kleist, whose works as a whole display a very fine attention to detail, leave inconsistencies in

---

18 Cf. Oskar Seidlin, 'Was die Stunde schlägt,' pp. 77f.

a text that was almost nine years in the making, from the genesis of the concept in 1802 to the first publication of 1811? For the inconsistencies extend from a very concrete level to the furtherst reaches of mythical allusion. For example, at the beginning of her long account of the jug, Frau Marthe presents it as being 'entzwei geschlagen,' with a convenient hole in the middle of the historical tableau painted on the side. When she comes, at the end of her story, to the events of the night before, the jug has suddenly become a heap of fragments: 'Den Krug find ich zerscherbt im Zimmer liegen,/ In jedem Winkel liegt ein Stück' (SW I, 203).

Oskar Seidlin has shown that the characters are especially concerned with fixing the time of the events of the previous night, but that their accounts do not agree, or rather can cohere only if Ruprecht spends an entire hour walking through the small village to Frau Marthe's house.[19] Similarly, for all the wealth of historical detail, we cannot fix the year in which the action is supposed to occur to within a decade. For all the references to the 16th and 17th centuries, there is much in the awareness of class tensions displayed in the dialogue to suggest the social ambience of post-Revolutionary Europe.

The difficulty with the field of mythical or religious reference is to demarcate what is significant from what is trivial. When Adam cautions Eve: 'Denk, daß du hier vor Gottes Richtstuhl bist' (SW I, 214), his intention to intimidate her makes a travesty of the religious allusion. The tone is quite different when Eve takes up the same motif in the lines: 'Und ists im Leben nicht, so ist es jenseits,/ Und wenn wir auferstehn ist auch ein Tag' (SW I, 217). Finding herself burdened with a truth that she cannot articulate for fear of ruining Ruprecht and their future together, she projects a resolution of the conflict, which she experiences in this moment as completely intractable, into a future when all mundane conflicts will perforce be resolved.

The problem is that the text offers no internal criterion for borderline cases. The drama abounds in references to falls of one sort or another, and it seems equally possible to read them as trivializing the myth of the Fall by equating it to Adam's abrupt descent from Eve's window, or else to give it the more portentous and sophisticated reading of a fall into divided consciousness in the terms of *Über das Marionettentheater*. Licht's teasing reference to 'der erste Adamsfall,/ Den Ihr aus einem Bett hinaus getan' (SW I, 179) clearly points to the former mode of reading; Adam's dream has been interpreted to support the latter.[20]

---

19 Ibid., pp. 61f.
20 Cf. Hinrich C. Seeba, KW I, 803f.

It should not surprise us if a text in which the discrepancy between truth and language is a prominent theme also exemplifies this gap when it refers to bodies of knowledge outside itself, such as myth and history. The essence of fiction is that it might flirt with its audience or reader in a way that modern historical or scholarly writing is supposed to eschew, and this can very well apply to areas of shared knowledge. The strong tendency in *Die Familie Schroffenstein* for the metaphorical level of dialogue to become independent of what the text itself posits as 'fact' has already been stressed. If *Der zerbrochne Krug* plays on its own ostensible historicity in a manner that leaves this field of reference as a congeries of semi-autonomous metaphors, then this may be a salutary reminder that the whole play is not mimetic of any one set of real or even probable circumstances. After all, Kleist's original foreword signals that the plot is predetermined both by a contemporary etching and the shape of a well-known Greek tragedy. The first scenes open the further possibility that what follows is less determined by external circumstance than by the dream in which Adam, as his own judge, pronounces sentence on himself. If the play then appears to dovetail with external fields of reference, we have no good reason for expecting that this need be more than appearance, just as dreams may scoop up much of their content from daily life but distort it according to more powerful determinants from within the unconscious.

The most famous of the various narratives in the play, Frau Marthe's recitation of the jug's pedigree, offers the model of a playful interchange between poesis and fact. Her account moves from what she can credibly know in great detail, namely the scene painted on the side and visible in its entirety until the previous day, to a series of vignettes from the jug's history. She purports to unfold a continuous history from the sacking of the town of Briel by the 'Wassergeusen' in 1572 up to the present. Her narrative is richly circumstantial, but the following lines introduce an element of self-parody into the oral tradition:

Drauf fiel der Krug
An den Zachäus, Schneider in Tirlemont,
Der meinem sel'gen Mann, was ich euch jetzt
Berichten will, mit eignem Mund erzählt.
Der warf, als die Franzosen plünderten,
Den Krug, samt allem Hausrat, aus dem Fenster,
Sprang selbst, und brach den Hals, der Ungeschickte,
Und dieser irdne Krug, der Krug von Ton,
Aufs Bein kam er zu stehen, und blieb ganz. (SW I, 201)

If the tailor broke his neck, it is unlikely, to say the least, that he survived to tell the tale to Marthe's husband, but the point is surely that it does not matter what really happened to any of the jug's previous owners. The important things about Marthe's narration are that it is comic and that it gets the jug unscathed through a century and a half of happenstance to the moment of its being broken the night before. Eve's father might have invented the pedigree; Frau Marthe might have forgotten some episodes, including one in which someone else saw the tailor break his neck and recounted it to her husband – the audience cannot know.

Just as Adam is stigmatized by his clubfoot and the wounds on his face and head, so Eve's betrothal to Ruprecht is stigmatized by the hole in the jug which, quite literally, breaks the painted figures in two. Besides its comic effect, the sense of Frau Marthe's narrative is to lend force and apparent meaning to the non-verbal sign. The whole circumstantiality of her account has the implicit purpose of bolstering the credibility of her description of Ruprecht standing helplessly in Eve's room while the jug lies in pieces on the floor. But as the jug she has just displayed does not bear out her graphic evocation of its fragments lying in every corner of the room, so the detail of her narrative is not guaranteed by anything within or outside the text.

If we seek a common denominator for this wide range of inconsistencies, then it is surely that they all work against the convergence that is so firmly programmed into the text. The forensic ritual of eliciting truth is a most convergent form of dramatic dialogue, and the presence of Walter ensures that none of Adam's attempts to break out of its narrowing perspective can be successful. Moreover, Adam's opening scene with Licht, the account of his dream, and his asides to the audience reinforce the convergence to the point where the play easily becomes ineffective as theatre. If we read the longer version of the play, then it contains three long narratives that all converge on the breaking of the jug, plus a fourth that traces Adam from the scene of the crime to the scene of the play.

To balance this, the text permits itself inconsistencies, most blatantly in the moment when Eve is finally convinced by Walter's money. These vagaries represent the only margin of freedom in an otherwise over-determined world of language. Without exception, they enlarge the scope of the text. The potentially tragic conflict within Eve takes the play beyond the purely comic convention; both the mythical and historical fields of reference open the village setting out so that it offers wider perspectives; but the fact that nothing quite adds up prevents it from regressing into the convergence of allegory.

Der zerbrochne Krug

In one sense, the character of Adam may suggest an analogy to the Romantic crisis of self-awareness; in another, he is just a middle-aged lecher who has fallen off a trellis after being beaten about the head with a door-latch. The essential point is that neither perspective comes to dominate. The play insists on the tension between the forensic ritual of the courtroom that can arrive at truth, in terms of a simple, almost banal facticity, and the multiple refractions of more elusive truths in the opening of perspectives onto other, more diffuse and portentous frames of reference.

–4–

Amphitryon

Kleist's second comedy appears to have been finished by the end of 1806, and was published with a foreword by his friend Adam Müller in May 1807.[1] It is not clear when Kleist began work on it, and there is no sign that the idea of adapting Molière's comedy of the same name goes back as far as 1802, when *Der zerbrochne Krug* was begun. But as *Amphitryon* has many phrases in common with this work, it is likely they share a period of composition in Königsberg (1803-1805) and Dresden (1805-1806). *Amphitryon* was not to receive its first performance until 1899, although the play did not lack admirers when it was first published, and today it is often staged successfully.

While Goethe disapproved of the play, he did not relegate it to the 'invisible theatre,' as he did with *Der zerbrochne Krug* even before he tried producing it. It also posed no problem for political censorship, as had Molière's *Amphitryon* in the Paris of Louis XIV. The main inhibitions against producing it in the 19th century were probably religious. For, while the play is not aggressively blasphemous, it does hold up a mirror to the confusions of Christian theology in a manner that 19th century directors and audiences could well have found uncomfortable.

Adam Müller, who published the play as a way of raising money for Kleist while he was a prisoner of the French in Fort Joux, was a Catholic convert, whose fervor many found irritating. His foreword to the first edition may have been the initial reason for Goethe's unfavorable reaction, which described the play as 'mystisch' in a strongly derogatory sense.[2] The foreword also claims that in this work Kleist has continued a task, begun by Goethe, of blending the ancient with the modern, thus borrowing Goethe's seal of approval for the type of Romantic literature

---

1 Cf. KW I, 861f.
2 Cf. KW I, 877f; LS, 145; Joachim Maas, *Kleist. Die Geschichte seines Lebens*, Bern and Munich, 1977, pp. 164-69; Hans Dieter Zimmermann, *Kleist. Die Liebe und der Tod*, Frankfurt/M, 1989, pp. 270-84.

Müller favored and Goethe emphatically did not.[3] In terms of contemporary German literary politics, Müller's prologue began a provocation that must have been intensified in Goethe's eyes by the undeniable fact that a drama set in the realm of Classical mythology, like Goethe's own *Iphigenie auf Tauris*, contains in its dialogue an obtrusive strand of Christian reference.

It is the crassness of the allusions, rather than the simple mingling of Christian and pagan elements, that must have displeased Goethe. For his *Iphigenie auf Tauris* adds more than a tincture of Christian humanism to Euripides' plot and characters, of which Goethe was well aware. In a letter from Rome while he was finishing the play, Goethe went so far as to compare his Iphigenie with the 'wholesome virginity' of Raphael's St Agatha, and promised he would give his own Ancient Greek priestess nothing to say that would be incongruous in the mouth of Raphael's figure.[4] But this admission is contained in a private communication, and the text of Goethe's play presents its Christian dimension most discreetly. The Christian allusions in Kleist's *Amphitryon*, by contrast, are blatant to the point of disrupting the Classical fiction. The text deals freely in terms of sin, devils and hell, alludes to verses in the Gospels of Matthew and Luke on the conception and birth of Jesus, and even goes so far as to have Jupiter address Alkmene as follows:

Mein angebetet Weib, was sprichst du da?
Was könntest du, du Heilige, verbrechen?
Und wär ein Teufel gestern dir erschienen,
Und hätt er Schlamm der Sünd, durchgeiferten,
Aus Höllentiefen über dich geworfen,
Den Glanz von meines Weibes Busen nicht
Mit einem Makel fleckt er! Welch ein Wahn! (SW I, 286)

Such passages are quite incongruous in the mouth of a god who is notorious for including the rapes of mortal women among his pastimes,

---

3 'Mir scheint dieser Amphitryon weder in antiker noch moderner Manier gearbeitet. Der Autor verlangt auch keine mechanische Verbindung von beiden, sondern strebt nach einer gewissen *poetischen Gegenwart*, in der sich das Antike und Moderne – wie sehr sie auch ihr untergeordnet sein möchten, dereinst wenn getan sein wird, was Goethe entworfen hat – dennoch wohl gefallen werden . . .,' LS, 134; cf. Katharina Mommsen, *Kleists Kampf mit Goethe*, pp. 24-35.

4 See the extract from Goethe's diary for Charlotte von Stein, Bologna, 19 October 1786, HA V, p. 404: 'Im Palast Ranuzzi hab' ich eine St. Agatha von Raphael gefunden, die, wenn gleich nicht ganz wohl erhalten, ein kostbares Bild ist. Er hat ihr eine gesunde sichre Jungfräulichkeit gegeben ohne Reiz, doch ohne Kälte und Rohheit. Ich habe mir sie wohl gemerkt und werde diesem Ideal meine "Iphigenie" vorlesen und meine Heldin nichts sagen lassen, was diese Heilige nicht sagen könnte.'

and they can only produce discord in proximity to the abundance of material in the text from Classical mythology. Goethe might be forgiven for understanding their presence as a kind of Romantic ineptitude on Kleist's part. Religious syncretism was in vogue among the Romantics in Germany, and Goethe probably thought that here was an especially heavy-handed instance of it. Having read no other work of Kleist's in July 1807, he was scarcely to know that contrived dissonances were essential to his artistic technique.

Another glaring anachronism in the work, namely Sosias' craving for a very German 'Bratwurst' and cabbage, might well have given Goethe pause, had he not been so affronted by his first encounter. For surely an author who could get so many of his Classical allusions right could have provided Sosias, had he wanted to, with an acceptable Ancient Greek dinner, just as he has Jupiter and Alkmene dining on ortolans. For Sosias' 'Bratwurst' is as deliberate a dissonance as Jupiter's Christian allusions, and we must ask why the play risks its own credibility in these ways.

Certainly, those contemporary readers who approved of the play took the Christian references at face value, and saw them as adding to the profundity of the work.[5] So have the bulk of critics writing on it in this century – to the point where its profundity has swamped its comic character. Although designated 'Lustspiel nach Molière,' the play's content has been treated with such utter seriousness in the secondary literature that the writing often resembles scriptural exegesis. In particular, the speeches of Jupiter and Alkmene's reactions to them have attracted such ingenious attempts at decipherment that this scholastic mode of interpretation leaves the reality of a comic drama on stage far behind. An unfortunate side-effect of this is to isolate *Amphitryon* from the rest of Kleist's works as the only text in which he was, allegedly, prepared to articulate a concept of godhead and to clarify his views concerning the proper relations between the human and the supernatural. It is advisable to ask why this should be, and what is wrong with it, before going into the intricacies of the text itself.

Kleist did nothing to weaken the social satire that had Molière's *Amphitryon* taken off the stage after its premiere in 1668 and forbidden in France for many years thereafter. Sosias, Amphitryon's servant and the most clear-sighted of all the characters, makes the cynical point early in the play that acts and words have a different quality in the eyes of society when they are attributed to the great of this world:

5 Cf. KW I, 872f.

So ists. Weil es aus meinem Munde kommt,
Ists albern Zeug, nicht wert, daß man es höre.
Doch hätte sich ein Großer selbst zerwalkt,
So würde man Mirakel schrein. (SW I, 270)

Grafting the makings of a religious drama onto this satire of social hierarchies must make for puzzlement, because the very authority that the former convention posits as absolute is repeatedly challenged in the latter. As with *Die Familie Schroffenstein*, the concept of Kleist's text as a palimpsest may be helpful here. Just as the melodramatic convention of Kleist's first drama is overlaid, first, with Rousseauistic themes that center on the contract of inheritance, and these in turn with a dimension of religious imagery full of angels, devils, and modified sacraments, so Kleist has superimposed a theological debate in *Amphitryon* on the conflicts arising in Alkmene from her sexual encounter with the god Jupiter. It is part of the nature of the palimpsest in *Die Familie Schroffenstein* that these overlays are not legible as unified discourses throughout the text; the characters seem to lose interest in who inherits what halfway through the play, and the religious drama remains fragmented.

Der zerbrochne Krug also has its comic plot overlaid with a religious dimension that opens a perspective onto the myth of the Fall. Indeed, it plays so often on the names Adam and Eve that a reader or audience can only be left wondering: From what paradise could this unlikely pair have been expelled, or what transgression could possibly unite them? One will ask in vain, for this dimension of *Der zerbrochne Krug* remains as inchoate as it is made obtrusive.

In both these dramas, the fragmentary nature of the religious dimension is less of a problem than in *Amphitryon*, for it enhances the scope of the action without ursurping the center of interest. The main problem in interpreting *Amphitryon* is that Jupiter's long and grueling interrogation of Alkmene in Act II, Scene 5, places religious questions squarely in the play's central focus, with the consequent danger that a reading which finds their presentation ultimately incoherent runs the risk of seeming to condemn the whole play.

So anxious have most critics been to avoid this danger that they have consistently taken refuge in theological special pleading, rather than address directly the consequences of Kleist's making Jupiter's representations of himself a potpourri of the ideas of the divinity fashionable in Germany at the turn of the 19th century. In this way, writing on the play usually loses sight of it as a comedy directed against an unquestioning acceptance of authority. The absurd effect of forcibly endowing Jupiter's speeches with coherence is to turn Alkmene's suffering into a harsh training in metaphysics, thus shifting the play toward a theological didacticism that never links up with its comic dimension.

Alkmene's situation presents a genuine difficulty, for it is a tragedy encapsulated within a comic context. The easiest way of getting around this obstacle is to adapt the context to it by inventing a potential tragedy for Jupiter as well, during which what he says about himself is claimed to be both serious and coherent. This is quite contrary to what Merkur gives the audience to understand about the god's intentions at the start of the action. Explaining his need to get rid of Sosias' presence, he says:

> Wenn ich den ungerufnen Schlingel dort
> Beizeiten nicht von diesem Haus entferne,
> So steht, beim Styx, das Glück mir auf dem Spiel,
> Das in Alkmenens Armen zu genießen,
> Heut in der Truggestalt Amphitryons
> Zeus der Olympische, zur Erde stieg. (SW I, 249f)

While there can be no doubt that, in Kleist's version, Jupiter's adventure takes an unusual turn, I can find no grounds in the text for arguing that it moves away from purely selfish enjoyment in one or other sense. This remains the reason for the play's satirizing the Olympian, regardless of how much compassion it invites us to feel for Alkmene.

All versions of the myth concede that there is potential for suffering in Alkmene's situation, and no critic contests that her interrogation by Jupiter in Kleist's play intensifies her suffering to the point of creating a tragic conflict between knowledge and feelings, or between imperatives she cannot reconcile. But there is a great emotional reluctance in the literature on the play to understand Jupiter's rhetorical strategies, which clearly intensify her suffering, as anything other than quite consistent and morally edifying. Wolfgang Wittkowski, who does see through the ideology of the divine, has documented the voices for and against a questioning of Jupiter's authority, and thus there is no need to restate the debate once more here.[6]

It is worth remembering that, to convince a reader or audience, the origins of a tragedy need not make sense. The tragedy of King Lear and Cordelia has its origin in an act of crass foolishness on the father's part, when he confuses his youngest daughter's unwillingness to proclaim her love for him in the manner of her sisters with a lack of love, but the events that ensue are not the less tragic for it. Likewise, we may perceive the various ploys in Jupiter's interrogation of Alkmene as strategies in a cruel game that the god, in an aside, can dismiss as 'madness' –

---

6 Cf. Wolfgang Wittkowski, *Heinrich von Kleists 'Amphitryon'. Materialien zur Rezeption und Interpretation*, Berlin and New York, 1978, pp. 1-17 and 157-64.

'Verflucht der Wahn, der mich hieher gelockt!' (SW I, 292) – without diminishing in the slightest the compassion we must feel for her.

There are two main factors responsible for the emotional resistance to seeing Jupiter critically, and both bear on different kinds of authority. There is, first, the authority of the convention of mythical fiction in which gods are good until they prove themselves otherwise. Second, Jupiter benefits from the authority of the successful rhetorician, even though his victories turn out to be mainly bluff, for *Amphitryon* is as much a play about the workings of language as *Die Familie Schroffenstein* or *Der zerbrochne Krug*.

The admixture of Christian allusions in Jupiter's speeches and their ready acceptance by Alkmene enhance rather than weaken the plausibility of Jupiter's divine authority within the mythical convention because readers are so used to registering, but immediately discounting, the irrational and despotic aspects of the Christian god. If Jupiter shows himself to be jealous of Alkmene's love of her mortal husband, then the Christian tradition has a niche into which a sexually jealous god can readily fit. The infidelities of Israel, so execrated by Old Testament prophets, even prevent a reader from blinking twice at what Jupiter is jealous *about* – as long as one forgets or ignores the whole critique of anthropomorphic divinities in such Enlightenment works as Voltaire's *Dictionnaire philosophique*.[7] It is unlikely that Kleist ever forgot the central doctrines of the Enlightenment for very long, even if, after 1801, he treated them as sceptically as many Enlightenment writers in France had treated dogmatic Christianity.

I suggest that Jupiter's discourse mimics the incoherence of Christian theology in the expectation that a reader or audience will initially *accept* it at face value, rather than find it preposterous or outrageous. The reception of the text as a whole may thus be as trusting as Alkmene under Jupiter's interrogation. Theology is full of inconsistencies, and these may, on closer inspection, expose themselves and set us wondering how a pantheistic divinity can suddenly find himself demanding something of his creation that it refuses to give. But Jupiter's inconsistencies are likely to pass, on first acquaintance, because they follow well-trodden paths of doctrinal incoherence and because an audience can have no idea of what ploy he is going to use next.

If one compares Jupiter with Adam in *Der zerbrochne Krug* and Alkmene with Eve, this may lead to a better understanding of *Amphitryon*. Both Jupiter and Adam are brilliant rhetoricians, but Adam's hand is fully disclosed in the opening scenes, before the hearing commences, and the purpose of all his strategies and evasions is clear to

---

7 See, for example, in the Old Testament, the Book of Hosea, Chapters II-IV.

the audience before he formulates them. Moreover, the high moral ground in the play is fully occupied by Gerichtsrat Walter, so that Adam's scope for action is severely circumscribed. Jupiter clearly wishes to enhance his enjoyment of Alkmene by having her admit she prefers him to Amphitryon, and to this end he deploys a wealth of inquisitorial skills with a virtuosity that contrasts favorably with Amphitryon's semi-articulate rages. But a reader or audience has no way of knowing how far Jupiter will pursue his game, and there are no predetermined limits on his deployment of moral arguments, as there are in the case of Adam, whose hypocrisy is under Walter's constant surveillance. His underlying intentions have therefore to be deduced in retrospect, or from Alkmene's reactions, and these are made harder to assess by the uncertainty into which she is plunged.

Jupiter is no more concerned by Alkmene's protest that he is tormenting her than is Adam by Eve's evident distress:

> Wenn sich Amphitryon mir – ach, du quälst mich.
> Wie kann sich Amphitryon mir zeigen,
> Da ich Amphitryon in Armen halte?
>
> JUPITER.
> Und dennoch könntst du leicht den Gott in Armen halten,
> Im Wahn, es sei Amphitryon.
> Warum soll dein Gefühl dich überraschen?
> Wenn ich, der Gott, dich hier umschlungen hielte,
> Und jetzo dein Amphitryon sich zeigte,
> Wie würd dein Herz sich wohl erklären? (SW I, 294)

Eve and Alkmene undergo a prolonged verbal inquisition that is ostensibly directed at uncovering a truth that both fear will destroy what they hold most dear in life. Just as one may well ask why Walter takes so long to intervene to end the hearing, so one may also wonder why Jupiter so prolongs his interrogation when he must know in advance the answers to all his own questions. One of his grandiloquent self-descriptions – 'Ihn, der der Menschen Herzen kennt' (SW I, 281) – is verified by his being able to tell Alkmene details of her thoughts and feelings that no one else can know. In these terms, he must know what Alkmene reveals to her servant, Charis, in Act II, Scene 4, and confirms by her choosing Jupiter as the real Amphitryon at the end of the play, namely that the divine version of her husband exerts more power over her. In both cases, the protracted verbal ordeal moves the play away from anything identifiable as comedy.

The contrast between the two plays lies not in what the female characters are made to suffer, but in what the male characters can get away with. Adam is as much a victim of the forensic process as Eve, whereas Jupiter has the ultimate refuge of his own omnipotence. Whatever an audience may feel about the game Adam plays with Eve's feelings, his intentions are perfectly transparent, whereas Jupiter's are so enigmatic as to transform, in many interpretations, the Olympian libertine of the play's beginning into a divine pedagogue with a taste for making his charges suffer. One may well argue that compassion with the fates of Eve and Alkmene prevents either play from reunifying itself as a comedy. Adam's simply giving up and running away and Jupiter's recourse to the trappings of a deus ex machina are both notoriously hard to stage as effective comedy in the light of the direction the two plays have taken toward their end. If one wishes to prove the contention that the religious dimension of *Amphitryon* is no more coherent than that of *Der zerbrochne Krug*, then it is rewarding to pursue similarities in the thematics of language between both works.

Amphitryon begins with Sosias rehearsing the account he will give to Alkmene of the battle he has not witnessed. While the battle was on, his cowardice made him hide in a tent, where he enjoyed some food and drink, yet his verbal enactment for his general's wife, although a fiction, will fulfill the function of a true account. The play thus begins with an emphasis on verbal disclosure similar to the way Adam's dream at the beginning of *Der zerbrochne Krug*, which sees him as judge pronouncing sentence on himself as a criminal, anticipates in metaphorical condensation the course that the hearing will take. Sosias imagines Alkmene commanding him to narrate:

> – Sie weichen, tot ist Labdakus, ihr Führer,
> Erstürmt Pharissa, und wo Berge sind,
> Da hallen sie von unserm Siegsgeschrei. –
> 'O teuerster Sosias! Sieh, das mußt du
> Umständlich mir, auf jeden Zug, erzählen.'
> – Ich bin zu Euern Diensten, gnädge Frau.
> Denn in der Tat kann ich von diesem Siege
> Vollständge Auskunft, schmeichl' ich mir, erteilen.
>
> (SW I, 249)

Sosias' spurious eyewitness account soon gets into trouble when he misplaces the main body of the army – 'Mit dem Hauptkorps ists nicht richtig' (SW I, 249) – and his interruption by Merkur means that his account remains incomplete for the rest of the play. Its completion has, in fact, already been anticipated by Jupiter's no less spurious firsthand account of Amphitryon's victory at Pharissa, as she reveals when her husband orders her to rehearse the events of the previous night – 'Nein;

doch du wirst den Hergang mir erzählen' (SW I, 275) – with the obvious difference that Jupiter, being omniscient, does not have the main army in the wrong place:

> Wir setzten uns – und jetzt erzähltest du
> Mit kriegerischer Rede mir, was bei
> Pharissa jüngst geschehn, mir von dem Labdakus,
> Und wie er in die ewge Nacht gesunken
> – Und jeden blutgen Auftritt des Gefechts. (SW I, 276)

These lines are the narration of a narration, produced on demand to someone who must know their content anyway. The pressure on Alkmene to make verbal disclosures that will satisfy both Jupiter and Amphitryon, and the impossibility of her doing so without convicting herself of adultery, come to dominate the action of the play in a way quite similar to the forensic process in *Der zerbrochne Krug*. If Sosias' unfinished narration signals anything to a reader or audience, then it is surely that the language of disclosure may take on a life of its own, and that there is no necessary correspondence between a report and its factual basis. There is an ironic reversal of this model in Alkmene's plight, for much of her suffering proceeds from the fact that, no matter how hard she tries to match her disclosures to the truth as she has experienced it, she cannot really satisfy either of her interrogators.

A further irony is that Jupiter ostensibly does not need to know her answers, any more than Adam needs Eve in *Der zerbrochne Krug* to tell the truth, since he can fish them out of her mind just as readily as he can the fact that when she prays to him she gives the deity the appearance of her husband. But perhaps the pleasure he undoubtedly derives from forcing her disclosures is not enough to explain the tortuous length of his interrogation and the difference that winning or losing seems to make to him.

The emphasis Jupiter lays on an explicit confirmation of what he wants to hear is only fully intelligible if we recognize that the expression of feelings may, in turn, modify the feelings that are expressed, a proposition that would surprise no attentive reader of *Die Familie Schroffenstein*, but one which remains to be tested in the world of *Amphitryon*. In this sense, we may reread the lines quoted above, placing the emphasis on 'sich . . . erklären,' the act of verbal disclosure:

> Wenn ich, der Gott, dich hier umschlungen hielte,
> Und jetzo dein Amphitryon sich zeigte,
> Wie würd dein Herz sich wohl erklären? (SW I, 294)

What Jupiter can possibly hope to gain from his inquisition is always puzzling, since he shows himself to be genuinely omniscient. His desire may well have as its goal that Alkmene might be brought, by a series of forced disclosures about hypothetical states of feeling, to a point where she must declare her exclusive devotion to Amphitryon to be a fiction. In the scene before Jupiter's long interrogation of her in Act II, Scene 5, she has already revealed to Charis what Jupiter wants her to declare to him, and what she will confirm by disowning the real Amphitryon before his generals and the people of Thebes at the end of the play:

> Er stand, ich weiß nicht, vor mir, wie im Traum,
> Und ein unsägliches Gefühl ergriff
> Mich meines Glücks, wie ich es nie empfunden,
> Als er mir strahlend, wie in Glorie, gestern
> Der hohe Sieger von Pharissa nahte. (SW I, 283)

Thus, Jupiter's interrogation of her has a distinct affinity to Walter's prompting Eve to spell out all details of her story in the longer version of *Der zerbrochne Krug*, although nothing that she reveals can make any significant difference to the factual outcome. In both plays, ritual disclosure is thus assigned a value of its own which seems to be at odds with effective comedy. For all his scepticism about the relationship between language and truth, Kleist could never resist the temptation to devise inquisition scenes for his plays and stories, perhaps because he wrote them so brilliantly. But since the ritual extraction of truth through language always demands a heavy emotional cost from the fictional characters, there is a strong tendency for such scenes to veer toward a tragic outcome for the object of interrogation. When a female character becomes such an object for a male interrogator in Kleist's dramas, the mingling of love, in whatever sense, with violent aggression may produce such justified accusations of cruelty as occur here and in Act I of *Das Käthchen von Heilbronn*.

The irony that all Jupiter's rhetorical skills cannot manipulate Alkmene into making a declaration in the precise terms he wants does not justify her excessive suffering throughout his inquisition. What it achieves is to hold up a mirror to the religious clichés of the age and to demonstrate a supposedly supreme moral authority discrediting itself. But an audience is just as likely to miss the point, as has the majority of Kleist scholars in their sincere, if misguided, attempts to make Jupiter as respectable as Kant or Fichte.

If the quite esoteric value the text places on verbal disclosure is to make sense within the dramatic fiction, it must be plausibly integrated into the psychology of the characters. Disclosure has always been one of the mainsprings of comic action on stage, and the dramas of both Plautus and Molière on the Amphitryon theme make much of the disclosure to the characters of what the audience already knows, namely the identity of the adulterous god.[8] Kleist's most significant development of this motif emerges as the characters' excessive dependence on what others say to them about themselves.

Once more, the opening scenes present a model that is varied throughout the rest of the play. Finding that Merkur has usurped his role and is more than willing to enforce his usurpation with physical violence, Sosias capitulates to superior force and asks to be told who he now is:

Ich sehe, alter Freund, nunmehr, daß du
Die ganze Portion Sosias bist,
Die man auf dieser Erde brauchen kann.
Ein mehreres scheint überflüssig mir.
Fern sei mir, den Zudringlichen zu spielen,
Und gern tret ich vor dir zurück. Nur habe die
Gefälligkeit für mich, und sage mir,
Da ich Sosias nicht bin, wer ich bin?
Denn etwas, gibst du zu, muß ich doch sein. (SW I, 258)

Amphitryon, too, is placed in the position of having his own sense of who he is depend on what Alkmene tells him about his own supposed actions the previous night:

Du hörst, ich zweifle nicht.
Man kann dem Diadem nicht widersprechen.
Gewisse Gründe lassen bloß mich wünschen,
Daß du umständlich die Geschichte mir
Von meinem Aufenthalt im Schloß erzählst. (SW I, 275)

Lacking Sosias' flexibility and being used to autocratic privilege, he reacts to Alkmene's narrative with rage and threats of further violence, but is no less a victim of what she has told him about 'himself' for all that:

Treulose! Undankbare! –
Fahr hin jetzt Mäßigung, und du, die mir
Bisher der Ehre Fordrung lähmtest, Liebe,
Erinnrung fahrt, und Glück und Hoffnung hin,
Fortan in Wut und Rache will ich schwelgen. (SW I, 277)

8 Cf. Wolfgang Wittkowski, *Heinrich von Kleists 'Amphitryon,'* pp. 27-42.

There is a clear and ironic symmetry between Amphitryon's dependence on what Alkmene says here and her own declaration to Jupiter,
whom she believes to be Amphitryon, at the beginning of Act II, Scene
5, that what he says will decide between life and death:

> Mein Herr und mein Gemahl! Vergönne mir,
> Daß ich dir knieend dieses Kleinod reiche.
> Ich lege treu mein Leben dir zu Füßen,
> Hast du mir diesen Stein, betracht ihn wohl,
> Mit eines fremden Namens Zug gegeben,
> So küss ich ihn vor Lust und wein auf ihn;
> Gabst du ihn nicht, und leugnest du ihn mir,
> Verleugnest ihn, so sei der Tod mein Los
> Und ewge Nacht begrabe meine Schmach. (SW I, 284)

The intensifying repetition 'leugnest . . ./ Verleugnest' underlines
Alkmene's decision to make her life depend on what her husband says,
rather than on what she herself believes to be the case, or any objective
truth that might lie beyond the language of the situation. The outbursts
of the real Amphitryon and the puzzling sophistries of Jupiter mas-
querading as her husband have scarcely encouraged her to have faith in
what others say, and yet here she places her fate in the words of another, just as Amphitryon is later to make his own fate depend on the verdict of the crowd of officers and citizens of Thebes. For the whole play,
the locus of conviction has shifted away from inner certainty and
toward objectification through language. There is an implicit assumption that, if the enigmas that torment Alkmene and Amphitryon are to
be solved, then it will be through the declarations of others. There is a
comic irony in the fact that Jupiter, in pursuing his game with the mortal characters, takes full advantage of the capacity of language to misrepresent.

The human dilemma is put most succinctly by Alkmene to Charis in
Act II, Scene 4, before her long interrogation by Jupiter: 'Wie soll ich
Worte finden, meine Charis,/ Das Unerklärliche dir zu erklären?' (SW I,
281). The irony here is that, even if she could find the appropriate
words, it is unlikely that they would help her, for it is her faith in words
that is misplaced. This is not the position from which Alkmene begins,
but one that she is forced to adopt. In her first confrontation with the real
Amphitryon, she maintains with a confidence later events can only
undermine that her inner conviction is proof against the vagaries of language. If her husband denies what she knows to be true, she will be
wounded by his cruelty, but not shaken in herself:

Sehr ruhig siehst du um den Ausgang mich.
Kannst du im Ernst ins Angesicht mir leugnen,
Daß du im Schlosse gestern dich gezeigt,
Falls nicht die Götter fürchterlich dich straften,
Gilt jeder andre schnöde Grund mir gleich.
Den innern Frieden kannst du mir nicht stören,
Und auch die Meinung, hoff ich, nicht der Welt:
Den Riß bloß werd ich in der Brust empfinden,
Daß mich der Liebste grausam kränken will   (SW I, 273f)

The ironies surrounding these words are manifold. Far from punishing mortals for lying, it is the gods themselves who are masters of deceit. Far from preserving her inner peace intact, Alkmene, by relying on what others say, is to become a victim of one uncertainty after another for the remainder of the drama. The cruelty toward her, which she here attributes to Amphitryon, has already been begun by Jupiter's insistence that she distinguish between her husband and himself in terms that must create a hiatus in her existence:

Versprich mir denn, daß dieses heitre Fest,
Das wir jetzt frohem Wiedersehn gefeiert,
Dir nicht aus dem Gedächtnis weichen soll;
Daß du den Göttertag, den wir durchlebt,
Geliebteste, mit deiner weitern Ehe
Gemeinen Tag'lauf nicht verwechseln willst.
Versprich, sag ich, daß du an mich willst denken,
Wenn einst Amphitryon zurückekehrt –?   (SW I, 262)

Acceptance of such a hiatus can only mean a declaration of guilt for Alkmene, and she defends herself against making such a concession for as long as circumstances permit. In the terms of the play, declaring herself to be guilty means admitting something alien into her self-awareness, and it is illuminating to pursue the career of the word 'fremd' through Kleist's text.

A further irony attends the fact that it is Alkmene herself who introduces it into the dialogue in her first speech to Jupiter:

Was brauchen wir, als nur uns selbst? Warum
Wird so viel Fremdes noch dir aufgedrungen,
Dir eine Krone und der Feldherrnstab?   (SW I, 260)

As Peter Szondi points out, this marks a significant departure by Kleist from Molière's text, where Alkmene proclaims: 'Je prends,

Amphitryon, grand part à ta gloire.'[9] Alkmene's wish to exclude everything but their purely personal happiness from her relationship with Amphitryon seems innocent enough, but the word 'fremd' is to return to haunt her in Scenes 4 and 5 of Act II, when she is confronted with 'ein fremdes Zeichen' in the form of the initial J on the diadem. This signifies the intrusion of something much more alien into her existence than Amphitryon's role as Theban general, and Jupiter has effected the change of initial from A to J for no other reason than to create an insoluble problem for his mortal victims. By then, she has come to trust external evidence more than her own feelings, and she consciously revokes her own previous assurance that nothing external can disturb her inner peace:

Mein zuversichtlich Wort hat dich beleidigt,
Ich fühlte damals schuldlos mich und stark.
Doch seit ich diesen fremden Zug erblickt,
Will ich dem innersten Gefühl mißtrauen:
Ich glaubs – daß mir – ein anderer – erschienen,
Wenn es dein Mund mir noch versichern kann. (SW I, 285)

The final line once more brings out Alkmene's extreme vulnerability to what others say to her. Her tragedy lies not only in her love for her husband being compromised by Jupiter's intrusion, as the change of initials on the diadem testifies, but also in her reliance on the words of others to reestablish the truth of a situation she has been forced to conclude is false. This leads to the tragic irony of her not realizing she has come victoriously through her interrogation by Jupiter in Act II, Scene 5 by adhering to her love of Amphitryon above all else. While her final utterances in the text are too brief to be interpreted conclusively, it seems that at the end of the play she remains a passive victim and an unwilling vessel for the birth of Hercules.

I agree with Wolfgang Wittkowski that Alkmene's main preoccupation is not with any real or imagined loss of identity, but, much more concretely, with the question of whether she is guilty or not.[10] Of all her attempts to formulate her own conflict in words, the one to which she adheres most consistently seems to be expressed in the following

9 Cf. Peter Szondi, 'Amphitryon. Kleists "Lustspiel nach Molière",' *Schriften II*, Frankfurt/M, 1978, pp. 161f.

10 Wolfgang Wittkowski, *Heinrich von Kleists 'Amphitryon,'* p. 135: 'Als sie endlich diese Behauptung aufgeben muß, geht ihr darüber das Gefühl der eigenen Identität jedoch keineswegs verloren. Sie wird, so müßte man stattdessen sagen, für sich selbst identisch sein als diejenige, die sich irrte und schuldig wurde. Es geht nicht um das Problem der Identität oder der Wahrheitserkenntnis, sondern um das der Schulderkenntnis . . . .'

words to Jupiter: 'leben will ich nicht,/ Wenn nicht mein Busen mehr unsträflich ist' (SW I, 286). Nothing in her words at the end of the play indicates that she is any closer to being reconciled to an alien intrusion into her relationship with Amphitryon than she was when confronted with the evidence of the J on the diadem. In this sense, she poses the question to Jupiter in the same scene: 'Kann man auch Unwillkürliches verschulden?' (SW I, 291), with the implication that, if the answer is yes, she would rather die than remain in a world in which she is guilty of adultery, whether she has consciously incurred the guilt or not. This is consistent with her frequent references to death and the netherworld, perhaps most poignantly in her reversal of the myth of Orpheus: 'So würd ich folgen dir, wohin du gehst,/ Und wärs auch, wie Euridike, zum Orkus' (SW I, 293). In the myth, Eurydice follows no one into Hades, but such is the strain of Alkmene's interrogation by Jupiter that she quite understandably transposes its terms to make Orpheus' devotion beyond death into an image of her own exclusive love for Amphitryon.

The question arises as to whether Alkmene, through all her ordeals, becomes alienated from herself to the extent of losing her identity. Once more, I tend to agree with Wittkowski that she does not, and to accept the parallel he draws between her and Sosias. Once Sosias becomes aware that Merkur will enforce his claim to their joint identity by physical violence, he declares himself willing to renounce it, but in reality does nothing of the kind. He simply reverts to being himself whenever Merkur is not about. Similarly, Alkmene, through all her ordeals, clings to her own identity as defined by her exclusive love for Amphitryon, even if this means consigning herself to death. The text certainly insists on the theme of alienation from oneself as relentlessly as does *Der zerbrochne Krug* on the myth of the Fall, but Kleist's ironic conclusion seems to be that Alkmene may indeed go through all the emotional confusion that the situation and the other characters can inflict on her without undergoing any fundamental change. The tragic irony that no divine intervention can dispel is that remaining herself and coming to a full awareness of what has happened to her together deprive her of the desire to continue living.

When Jupiter curses, in an aside to the audience toward the end of Act II, Scene 5, the 'madness' that has embroiled him with Alkmene, his words may be taken at face value, since it is one of the very few points in the scene where he is not keeping up the pretense of being her mortal husband, or where his words are not primarily directed toward manipulating her into rejecting Amphitryon in favor of himself. It is his only aside in the course of this very long scene, although at a few other points he appears to lose his grip on the role of Amphitryon and speaks to

Alkmene directly as the god, which confuses her further. We are thus bound to ask what lies behind Jupiter's 'madness.'

Kleist found a version of the story in Molière in which Alcmène calls Jupiter a monster, and he, in a fit of remorse, falls to his knees before her, threatening to stab himself if she does not forgive him and cease to hate him. The whole of Act II, Scene 5, has no basis in Molière and is Kleist's own invention. Since Kleist returns to Molière for the details of Act III, one's initital assumption is that Jupiter remains a god of comedy, and certainly this is what his aside suggests. His other speeches in Act II, Scene 5, are, however, taken so seriously by writers on the play that, if Jupiter thinks what he is doing is madness, many critics firmly believe, on the contrary, that he is giving a straight-faced demonstration of German Idealism in action.[11] Since Jupiter continues in this scene a dialogue he began with Alkmene earlier in the play, we must go back to Act I, Scene 4, to find the origin of what he calls his madness.

Immediately we are faced with a choice as to how Jupiter's whole behavior is to be read. The most intransigent Idealist view, which takes his omniscience and omnipotence entirely seriously, will ignore Merkur's explanation that Jupiter has visited Alkmene to take his pleasure and will see his sexual enjoyment of her as part of a pedagogic programme, a kind of softening-up to prepare her for her introduction to metaphysics. But it is also possible to argue that in his first speech he is intending to take his leave, having enjoyed her, and that something in her words sets him along the course he is later to describe as madness. If this is so, the most likely stimulus is Alkmene's complaint 'Warum/ Wird so viel Fremdes noch dir aufgedrungen . . .?' (SW I, 260), for it expresses a desire, absent in Molière, to distinguish between Amphitryon as he is to her in their sphere of intimacy and his public persona as a general in the service of Thebes. Moreover, it is the night he describes as 'stolen' from the war so as to be with her that has made her aware of what his duties prevent her from enjoying:

Ach was das Vaterland mir alles raubt,
Das fühl ich, mein Amphitryon, erst seit heute,
Da ich zwei kurze Stunden dich besaß. (SW I, 260)

As Niklas Luhmann has shown, the theme of the value of intimacy was topical in Kleist's Germany, and there is nothing unusual in

---

11 The most extreme example of this is the essay by Lawrence Ryan, '*Amphitryon*: doch ein Lustspielstoff!' *Kleist und Frankreich*, ed. Walter Müller-Seidel, Berlin, 1969, pp. 83-121, especially pp. 94f.

Alkmene's complaint.[12] It is Alkmene's misfortune that Jupiter takes up the implications of the word 'fremd' in a way she could scarcely anticipate and identifies the alien element as the law binding her in marriage to Amphitryon: 'Sieh dies Gesetz, es stört mein schönstes Glück' (SW I, 261). Alkmene's wish to separate, for herself, the intimate and public areas of her husband's life is turned by Jupiter into the Kantian dichotomy between inclination and duty.[13] He tries to persuade her here – and will persist in his attempt throughout Act II, Scene 5 – to distinguish between him as the object of her inclination and Amphitryon as the man to whom duty binds her: 'Entwöhne,/ Geliebte, von dem Gatten dich,/ Und unterscheide zwischen mir und ihm' (SW I, 261).

The distinction is foreign to Alkmene's way of thinking, although later in the play her statements will make clear that the presence of the god in the guise of her husband arouses more intense feelings in her than Amphitryon alone. Jupiter's determination to get her to say so to him may seem a very slender basis for a verbal ordeal that will see him invoke, by turns, the divine presence in the whole of creation; the creator's separation from his creation; the divine privilege of jealousy at the conduct of his creation; the creator's need to be loved by his creation; indeed, to love himself in the love of his creation; and the divine right to tell his creation to be silent when it says something he does not like. Viewed this way, Jupiter seems very much a god of shreds and patches, not very distant from Molière's ludicrous spectacle of a Jupiter on his knees, threatening to stab himself. What inhibits the comedy in Kleist's version is the intensity of Alkmene's suffering and Jupiter's command of eloquence, which never slips into the bathos of Molière's text. Having chosen language as the arena for his contest and set the rules himself, Jupiter seems to become absorbed in winning as an added spice to the sexual pleasure of the night before.

Jupiter's game, which is as cruel as any other in Kleist's work, becomes clearer through a further comparison with the situation in *Der zerbrochne Krug*. Whilst there the roles of moral authority and sexual delinquent are split between Walter and Adam, Jupiter combines them in himself, and he has, like Walter, the power to break matters off and produce the dénouement at any time. This makes any subversion of his authority problematic. In *Der zerbrochne Krug*, Walter comes into the situation from outside and is guilty of nothing, so that there is no need for anyone to test the basis of his control. In *Amphitryon*, Jupiter will

12 Niklas Luhmann, *Liebe als Passion. Zur Codierung von Intimität*, Frankfurt/M, 1982, p. 150f.

13 Theodore Ziolkowski, in a recent article, 'Kleists Werk im Lichte der zeitgenössischen Rechtskontroverse,' in *KJb* 1987, p. 43, has referred the issue of the 'Gesetz der Ehe' to the realm of the Prussian 'Allgemeines Landrecht.'

eventually unmask himself as an adulterer, but use divine privilege to
abolish the moral issues, saying to Alkmene's husband:

> Zeus hat in deinem Hause sich gefallen,
> Amphitryon, und seiner göttlichen
> Zufriedenheit soll dir ein Zeichen werden. (SW I, 319)

Since Kleist's Jupiter does not imitate Molière's to the extent of
making himself ludicrous, any subversion of his authority must come
from the human characters. Amphitryon has no verbal subtlety. Right
up to the final scene he reacts to the puzzle confronting him with
threats of violence and bluster, and never more so than when confronted with Jupiter in his own image: 'Tod! Teufel! Wut und keine
Rache!/ Vernichtung!' (SW I, 315). His rages are no match for
Jupiter's suavity. Sosias is much more quick-witted and pragmatic,
and he ends the play by saying that, if this is a divine visitation, then
he wants nothing of it. But all his confrontations are with Merkur,
who treats his role as a chore he must perform for Jupiter and remains
quite uninvolved. We may, of course, extend what Sosias says about
Merkur to a critique of Jupiter, but it is not very likely that an audience will put together what the play keeps apart. If Jupiter's authority
is to be questioned, then the role falls to Alkmene as the only character to sustain long dialogues with him. She is handicapped by the fact
that she continues to believe he is her husband, and she does not
understand what is happening in those moments when he drops his
role and speaks as the god, if only because he keeps reverting to mas-
querading as Amphitryon, until the transformation in the last scene of
the play.

Moreover, to give Jupiter his satisfaction, she has to declare that
adultery has occurred and that she prefers the adulterer to Amphitryon, a
disclosure she resists since it has also become clear to her that if she
bears the guilt of adultery – whether she intended to incur it or not – she
does not want to live. Her repeated exclamations of 'Entsetzlich!' or
'Entsetzlicher!' register her protest at the choices with which Jupiter
confronts her and her helplessness before them. For her, not declaring
that Jupiter-as-Amphitryon produced in her a more intense experience
than her memories of Amphitryon becomes a matter of survival. Hence,
she is simply not in a position to comment satirically on Jupiter's abuse
of divine authority, although she has no hesitation in branding Jupiter's
disclosure of what has really happened the previous night as a criminal
act. Jupiter promptly reprimands her for blasphemy, since gods, by definition, cannot be criminals:

Jupiter sagt ich,
Und wiederhols. Kein anderer, als er,
Ist in verfloßner Nacht erschienen dir.

ALKMENE.
Du zeihst, du wagst es, die Olympischen
Des Frevels, Gottvergeßner, der verübt ward?

JUPITER.
Ich zeihe Frevels die Olympischen?
Laß solch ein Wort nicht, Unbesonnene,
Aus deinem Mund mich wieder hören. (SW I, 287)

This exchange is as comic as the dialogue between Adam and Eve in *Der zerbrochne Krug*, where he enjoins respect for himself as her judge as a means of preventing her from coming out with the truth. Jupiter has here received an answer from the unwitting Alkmene that strips him as god of any moral pretentions, so that he has to resort to bullying to save face, as, indeed, he must also do to win their next exchange:

Ob du der Gnade wert, ob nicht, kömmt nicht
Zu prüfen *dir* zu. Du wirst über dich,
Wie er dich würdiget, ergehen lassen.
Du unternimmst, Kurzsichtige, ihn zu meistern,
Ihn, der der Menschen Herzen kennt. (SW I, 288)

Metaphysics was clearly not meant to be fun. The problems, as far as the play as comedy is concerned, are that this exchange takes place early in the scene and that Jupiter, observing that Alkmene has not noticed anything peculiar about what she believes to be Amphitryon's intimidating words, and still persisting with the debate, thereafter limits his tactics to endearments and flattery. Intimidation then occurs by means of a whole arsenal of theological arguments, whose inconsistency does not yield much in the way of comic effects, because Christian theology is incoherent anyway, while the intensity of Alkmene's suffering is as great as ever and eloquent in its simplicity.

Indeed, Jupiter's description of himself as 'Ihn, der der Menschen Herzen kennt' seems to mark a threshold beyond which the dialogue enters a realm of ritualized absurdity. For Jupiter is to give proof that he does indeed know the secrets of Alkmene's heart, in particular the extent to which the human and divine are conflated in her image of Amphitryon. He therefore has nothing to gain, beyond a sadistic pleasure, from manipulating her into separating what she continues to experience as a unity, when he must also know that, forced into a corner, she will choose the Amphitryon who is immediately present to her, be he man or god.

Kleist seems, at this point, to forsake the comic vein in favor of a satire of conceptions of the divine that were current in the literature and philosophy of the time, but the satiric point can only be glimpsed in retrospect, since a reader or audience has no way of anticipating where and when Jupiter will end the game. There is scarcely any limit to the stratagems he may employ, and when he apparently tires of the game, the ending has a certain arbitrariness about it.

Having pronounced himself the connoisseur of human hearts, Jupiter seems surprised that Alkmene is only saddened by the suggestion that a god has visited her – 'doch meine Seele kehrt/ Zu ihrem Schmerzgedanken wiederum zurück' (SW I, 288) – and directs her attention to the miraculous change of initials on the diadem. When Alkmene then asks if she is to think of 'der Götter ewger, und der Menschen, Vater' in these terms, namely as an amoral miracle-worker, he asks who else could deceive a sensibility such as hers and announces that if 'die Allmächtgen,' 'die Allwissenden,' 'die Allgegenwärtigen' wish to be intimate with her, then they must do so in the guise of Amphitryon (SW I, 289). Still believing the god to be her husband, Alkmene kisses him out of relief that he is not alleging she has had to do with anyone but Amphitryon, in whatever guise. It is not possible to say how much of his argument she has understood, since she persists in her belief that her husband is testing her in ways that make little sense.

Jupiter then goes on the offensive and asks whether she perceives the god in his pantheistic identity with his creation, or whether she does not commit idolatry by worshipping an inner vision of Amphitryon. Alkmene tries to defend herself by proclaiming her piety and recalling her acts of worship, but the god knows better and refutes her. At this point, Alkmene pronounces the words that bring her significantly closer to a confession of guilt:

Ach, ich Unsel'ge, wie verwirrst du mich.
Kann man auch Unwillkürliches verschulden?
Soll ich zur weißen Wand des Marmors beten?
Ich brauche Züge nun, um ihn zu denken. (SW I, 291)

Jupiter seeks to capitalize on the first point he has won in the course of his interrogation by proclaiming his divine right to punish her for this idolatry:

Gewiß! Er kam, *wenn* er dir niederstieg,
Dir nur, um dich zu *zwingen* ihn zu denken,
Um sich an dir, Vergessenen, zu *rächen*.

ALKMENE. Entsetzlich! (SW I, 291)

Well may she protest, since Jupiter has left behind any pretense of a fiction of Classical Antiquity, in which gods were notoriously anthropomorphic and commonly amoral, and has shifted the debate into the sphere of the Old Testament, where the divinity is equally anthropomorphic, but an irascible and punitive moralist. The shift itself is not contrary to the conventions of comedy, since it is not unusual in comic drama for figures of power to change the rules as they go along.

The difficulty is that neither the audience nor Alkmene knows where the dialogue is going. For as long as Alkmene remains the ironic victim, the audience may laugh at her, cruel as it may be. But, by this point, any audience will have lost the superiority that derives from anticipating blunders on the part of the characters on stage. It is more likely to be simply bemused by Jupiter's sudden switch from the pantheistic concept of the gods as 'die Allgegenwärtigen' – for whom it can scarcely matter in what appearance they are worshipped – to the familiar Old Testament concept of a sexually proprietorial god venting his displeasure on a disobedient humanity.[14]

Jupiter then exacts a promise from Alkmene that she will not confuse this version of divinity with her husband any longer, under threat that the god may visit her again. Alkmene agrees, but immediately spoils the god's victory – purely in verbal terms – by stating:

Gut, gut, du sollst mit mir zufrieden sein.
Es soll in jeder ersten Morgenstunde
Auch kein Gedanke fürder an dich denken:
Jedoch nachher vergeß ich Jupiter. (SW I, 292)

Jupiter treats this apparent defeat – apparent because he has already revealed his complete understanding of what Alkmene feels but has not said – as an opportunity to introduce yet another concept of divinity, and shifts to an invocation of the *numen tremendum* of the Book of Job, with

14 Cf. Arthur Henkel, 'Erwägung zur Szene II, 5 in Kleists *Amphitryon*,' *Festschrift für Friedich Beißner*, eds. Ulrich Gaier and Werner Volke, Bebenhausen, 1974, p. 163: 'Hochtheologisch? . . . Jupiters gewissermaßen wechselnde Masken von Theologumena. . . : der allem Moralischen überlegene Gott, der allmächtige Gott des Kosmos, der eifrige, der rächende, der Gott des Hen kai Pan, der Pascalsche, – und als metaphorische Basis solchen göttlichen Gestaltwandels dient die erotische Sprache der Mystik, von der Gottesminne, dem Einwohnen Gottes in der Seele.'

pagan reminiscences of Semele's being consumed by Zeus' manifesting himself directly to her. Once more, the contradiction to the idea of a god present in the whole of creation – and thus also in Alkmene herself – is crass, and it could be exploited for a comic exchange – were Alkmene not unused to theological argument and still preoccupied by the question of her own guilt.

So it is that when Jupiter states that if the god were now to reveal himself to her – 'Ja, wenn er deine Seele jetzt berührte. . . .' – she would weep when he departed to Olympus, she contests this and insists that she would prefer it if the previous night had never happened. Her point is that whatever pleasure she may have derived from a divine visitation, it is as nothing if, as a consequence, she has to bear a guilt she cannot come to terms with. At this point, Jupiter makes his one aside to the audience and curses his own madness.

Alkmene, not hearing this, registers his displeasure and asks if she has offended him. Jupiter then announces himself to be a *deus abscondi-tus* – misunderstood by his human creation, miserable in his separation from it; 'auch der Olymp ist öde ohne Liebe' – and in need of a narcissistic fulfillment that only Alkmene's soul can afford him:

> In ewge Schleier eingehüllt,
> Möcht er sich selbst in einer Seele spiegeln,
> Sich aus der Träne des Entzückens widerstrahlen. (SW I, 293)

Yet again, the scene could become comic if Alkmene were to realize she was arguing with a god and had the presence of mind to point out that Jupiter has already declared gods to be omniscient and omnipresent. Since she persists in understanding Jupiter's statement as a hypothetical question asked by Amphitryon, she replies hypothetically and with an acceptance of absolute authority: 'Ward ich so heilgem Amte auserkoren./ Er, der mich schuf, er walte über mich' (SW I, 293).

The scene might end at this point were she not to spoil her gesture of submission with the afterthought:

> Läßt man die Wahl mir –
> JUPITER.
> Läßt man dir –?
> ALKMENE.
> Die Wahl, so bliebe meine Ehrfurcht ihm,
> Und meine Liebe dir, Amphitryon. (SW I, 293)

Jupiter is provoked into a further hypothetical question: 'Wenn ich nun dieser Gott dir wär –?' – which plunges Alkmene into confusion

again. Two additional hypothetical questions follow, one of which
brings the protest: 'ach, du quälst mich' (SW I, 294). An audience
will be inclined to take Alkmene at her word, since Jupiter's persis-
tence has possibly become as tedious to them as it is distressing to
her. Her final answer is to the effect that her love is for the
Amphitryon who is present and holding her in his arms, which still
fails to make the distinction Jupiter has been angling for since Act I,
Scene 4:

> Wenn du, der Gott, mich hier umschlungen hieltest
> Und jetzo sich Amphitryon mir zeigte,
> Ja – dann so traurig würd ich sein, und wünschen,
> Daß er der Gott mir wäre, und daß du
> Amphitryon mir bliebst, wie du es bist.   (SW I, 294)

The two most probable ways of interpreting Jupiter's reaction are
that, having decided to end the game as futile, he is compelled to an
admiration of Alkmene's staying power, or else that, since earlier in the
scene he found bullying ineffective, he has consistently pretended that
all his defeats are really wins, and now does so again.

Of the various divine attributes he has given himself during the interrogation, he chooses to affirm himself for the time being as a narcissistic creator who is not coextensive with his creation, although he is to
revert to a pantheistic self-description in the last scene of Act III:

> Mein süßes, angebetetes Geschöpf!
> In dem so selig ich mich, selig preise!
> So urgemäß, dem göttlichen Gedanken,
> In Form und Maß, und Sait und Klang,
> Wie's meiner Hand Äonen nicht entschlüpfte!   (SW I, 294)

Alkmene, of course, responds by calling him 'Amphitryon,' since the
divine import of his words once more escapes her.

So must that of his last words in this scene, since the final moments
of Act III reveal her still to be confused, heaping violent reproaches on
the real Amphitryon for presuming to address her as 'Geliebte!' (SW I,
316). Kleist has returned to following Molière, and how much of the
comic effect is preserved in an actual production will depend on how
much of Act II, Scene 5 is cut. Interpretations dominated by subservience to German Idealism tend to have Alkmene understand Jupiter
by the end of Act II, Scene 5, and thus have no real explanation of why
she is still confused about his identity in Act III, for here she understands only that she is resigned to her own death.

Finally, we must return to the question of what kind of comedy Kleist has created with this text, and what he meant to achieve by its many dissonances. The degree of cruelty in Jupiter's treatment of Alkmene does not entirely rule out a comic ending. The text's treatment of both Malvolio at the end of Shakespeare's *Twelfth Night* and Alceste in Molière's *Le Misanthrope* is cruel, without altogether destroying the comic convention. Jupiter's proclaiming that Alkmene will become the mother of Hercules, in words reminiscent of the birth of Christ, is yet another dissonance to bring home to a reader or audience, who will scarcely need reminding, that the play's version of Classical – or indeed Christian – Mythology is deliberately ragtag and bobtail. But I think it unlikely that the text's prime comic intent is meant to reside in this alone. Indisputably, Christian theology takes a beating through the inconsistencies of Jupiter's self-representation, but, when Kleist wrote the play, the times were long past when a critique of dogmatic Christianity could create anything like the effect Lessing produced when he published parts of Reimarus' clandestine attack on the contradictions of religion.[15]

I suggest that the play never loses sight of the subversion of authority as the prime goal of its comic and satirical dimension, and that the authority here contested is, in the first instance, the intellectual one of the popular Enlightenment, which was a much stronger force in Germany at the time than, for example, Weimar Classicism or dogmatic Christianity. In *Penthesilea,* Kleist was to create his own counter to Goethe's *Iphigenie auf Tauris*, but here he seems to be satirizing the widespread tendency of the German Enlightenment in the early 19th century toward complacency regarding its own ability to assimilate virtually any view of the deity, no matter how disparate. The self-representations of Kleist's Jupiter read like a haberdasher's catalogue of the concepts of the divine then in fashion, with the tacit implication that it little matters which one you buy.

There is perhaps a comic hybris in Jupiter's claim to embody them all, and still remain a credible fictional character. His intellectual sovereignty is surely reminiscent of the omnivorous mind of the Enlightenment, which was always ready to assimilate yet another aspect of the divine into a serendipitous, if muddled, Deism.

This view is lent credence if we consider that Kleist has endowed his Jupiter with omniscience and omnipotence, but still has him losing a game in which he can and does change the rules as he goes along. Jupiter's dominance is a dominance of language, and yet he is defeated

15 Cf. *Hermann Samuel Reimarus. Handschriftenverzeichnis und Bibliographie*, ed. Wilhelm Schmidt-Biggemann, Göttingen, 1979, p. 13.

in the area of discourse, the very vehicle of his power. We may recognise in this a satire of the Enlightenment's deification of Reason – 'Vernunft' – a position the young Kleist enthusiastically espoused.[16] Kleist's tendency in his literary creations to subvert views he had uncritically affirmed before 1801 is so marked as to need no argument. In *Amphitryon*, he turns a jaundiced eye on the 'Herrschaft der Vernunft' (SW II, 484) he had once affirmed, demonstrating, through the inconsistencies of his Jupiter, the wealth of irrationality the sovereign discourse of the Enlightenment might absorb without betraying the least anxiety. Because this, in turn, exposes the naivety of a deified Reason in its approach to the, for Kleist, problematic relationship of language to truth, we see Jupiter, the master rhetorician, deploy his full powers in vain against Alkmene and expose the full irrationality of that Deism favored by the priests of Reason in the process. That this satire should sometimes take on the appearance of a serious exercise in that religious syncretism so dear to the German Romantics was a sign of changing times and certainly an aspect of the play that annoyed Goethe, but the prime target of Kleist's comedy of subversion was an intellectual arrogance whose great time was past, but which, in the Germany of 1806, was comfortably oblivious of the fact.

---

16 'Aber ich bezweifle diesen möglichen Schritt; weil ich die goldne Unabhängigkeit, oder, um nicht falsch verstanden zu werden, die goldne Abhängigkeit von der Herrschaft der Vernunft mich gewiß stets zu veräußern scheuen würde, wenn ich erst einmal so glücklich gewesen wäre, sie mir wieder erworben zu haben.' SW II, 484.

5

Penthesilea

Written between the summer of 1806 and the autumn of 1807, *Penthesilea*, which has a strong claim to being Kleist's masterpiece, was his last completed tragedy.[1] It was less understood by his contemporaries than any other work he published during his lifetime, mainly because it was so unlike the prevailing literary currents of the age that it was easy to dismiss it as an aberration.[2] The world of *Penthesilea* is as far from Kleist's beginnings in the popular thinking of the Enlightenment as can be imagined, and it also sets itself in strident opposition to the main tenets of Weimar Classicism. It does not merely present a violent fiction of Classical Antiquity as an alternative to the enforced harmony of the world of Goethe's *Iphigenie auf Tauris*, but the text clearly alludes to that of Goethe's drama in ways that reveal its provocative intent.[3] While the banishing of the Furies that torment Orestes is one of the chief victories won by the 'voice of truth and humanity' in *Iphigenie auf Tauris*, Kleist's heroine not only summons them near the play's climax, but she is also perceived by the other characters to be one of them.[4] Such reversals go far beyond a parodistic intent, and they serve as a starting point for a critique of the ideal of the individual as a *harmony* of antithetical forces that is as radical as anything European literature has produced.

When Kleist sent a published fragment of the play to Goethe, asking for his blessing in quasi-religious terms, it was almost a foregone conclusion that Goethe would reject the work, not because its savage and negative elements were wholly foreign to his own creations, but because he now felt that the triumph of art lay in their containment, whereas Kleist had given them free rein. Goethe liked to think that the violent and bloody aspects of Greek mythology were perceptible as a 'mon-

---

1 Cf. KW II, 676-85.
2 Cf. KW II, 693-708.
3 Cf. KW II, 749f, 769f and 830; Jochen Schmidt, *Heinrich von Kleist*, p. 233f.; Katharina Mommsen, *Kleists Kampf mit Goethe*, p. 160f; Anthony Stephens, '"Menschen/ Mit Tieren die Natur gewechselt." Zur Funktionsweise der Tierbilder bei Heinrich von Kleist,' in *JbSchG* XXXVI, 1992, pp. 135 and 139.
4 Cf. Anthony Stephens, ibid., p. 134f.

strous opposition' in the background of his *Iphigenie auf Tauris*,[5] whilst Kleist had allowed chaos to take center stage.

In his reply to Kleist, Goethe's comments address the play as if it was the heroine, and thus set in motion a set of ambivalences in the reception of the work that has lasted to the present.[6] The complex relationship between the text and its central character continues to bedevil readings of the play. In many ways, the external world of the action is reduced to reflections or refractions of what is taking place inside the central character in a manner that anticipates such diverse fictional creations as Wagner's Wotan, Nietzsche's Zarathustra, or Rilke's Malte Laurids Brigge. In other respects, the text asserts an autonomy through its withholding of the desired object from the center of desire. This is essential to Penthesilea's tragedy and, paradoxically, shatters a solipsistic cosmos without displaying any more encompassing order in its place than the formal unity of a world of metaphor that is totally relativistic, in the sense that no level of reference is allowed to dominate.

The resulting text is, in my view, the most complex Kleist composed. In terms of shifting perspectives and unresolved tensions, its obvious comparison is with Goethe's *Die Wahlverwandtschaften*, which was finished in 1809. While Goethe's novel was as easily misread by contemporaries as Kleist's drama, it was far less easy to dismiss because what is incommensurable in it has to be sought beneath a highly disciplined surface. By making the surface of his own text mimetic of the chaos that is one of its explicit themes, Kleist laid himself open to the charge of producing nothing but 'bombast.'[7] This was reinforced by stage directions that brought on elephants and packs of savage dogs, and also by the sheer horror of Penthesilea's going beyond the slaughter of Achilles to commit acts of necrophilic cannibalism on his corpse.

---

5 Goethe, HA V, 406: 'auch die Kühneren jenes Geschlechts, Tantalus, Ixion, Sisyphus, waren meine Heiligen. In die Gesellschaft der Götter aufgenommen, mochten sie sich nicht untergeordnet genug betragen, als übermüthige Gäste ihres wirthlichen Gönners Zorn verdient und sich eine traurige Verbannung zugezogen haben. Ich bemitleidete sie, ihr Zustand war von den Alten schon als wahrhaft tragisch anerkannt, und wenn ich sie als Glieder einer ungeheuren Opposition im Hintergrunde meiner *Iphigenie* zeigte, so bin ich Ihnen wohl einen Theil der Wirkung schuldig, welche dieses Stück hervorzubringen das Glück hätte.'

6 SW II, 806f: 'Mit der Penthesilea kann ich mich noch nicht befreunden. Sie ist aus einem so wunderbaren Geschlecht und bewegt sich in einer so fremden Region daß ich mir Zeit nehmen muß mich in beide zu finden. Aber erlauben Sie mir zu sagen (denn wenn man nicht aufrichtig sein sollte, so wäre es besser, man schwiege gar), daß es mich immer betrübt und bekümmert, wenn ich junge Männer von Geist und Talent sehe, die auf ein Theater warten, welches da kommen soll. Ein Jude der auf den Messias, ein Christ der aufs neue Jerusalem, und ein Portugiese der auf den Don Sebastian wartet, machen mir kein größeres Mißbehagen.'

7 Cf. KW II, 694f.

The temptation to reject the drama on the grounds of its obvious excesses was strengthened by an awareness of its ultimate negativity. In an era where there was little distinction between aesthetic categories and those of conventional morality, even those willing to admire the work were stricken with profound unease.[8] So uncompromising is Kleist's onslaught on the values of Enlightened individualism that it is hard for critics to accept that he has nothing to put in its place except a muted appeal to the tenets of that very humanism which the central thrust of the tragic action appears to deny. But this is the essential limitation of Kleist's talent, and may underlie Goethe's consistent rejection of his works.

The innovative strength of *Penthesilea* is that no previous work of German literature had confronted the problems of the poetic representation of chaos with anything like its directness. The only setting for the single, continuous action is a battlefield, and unremitting conflict is the only external possibility for what is taking place within Penthesilea. This poses a formidable challenge to staging the play. While most of its action must occur in lulls in the battle, an atmosphere of constant warfare must be established and remain credible throughout the more lucid and tranquil episodes. The text continually asserts the presence of chaos, perhaps most clearly in the following speeches from Scenes 3 and 7:

Staub ringsum,
Vom Glanz der Rüstungen durchzuckt und Waffen:
Das Aug erkennt nichts mehr, wie scharf es sieht.
Ein Knäuel, ein verworrener, von Jungfraun,
Durchwebt von Rossen bunt: das Chaos war,
Das erst,' aus dem die Welt sprang, deutlicher.   (SW I, 336)

Nichts, gar nichts sehen wir!
Es läßt kein Federbusch sich unterscheiden.
Ein Schatten überfleucht von Wetterwolken
Das weite Feld ringsher, das Drängen nur
Verwirrter Kriegerhaufen nimmt sich wahr,
Die im Gefild des Tods einander suchen.   (SW I, 355)

It is characteristic of the text that both evocations are spoken by minor characters – the first by a Greek soldier, the second by an Amazon girl – and that both function to make real for an audience what it cannot see on stage. The prevalence of actions reported from offstage is both a strength and weakness of the play's technique. On the one hand, Kleist uses it to create a new kind of narrative theatre that, from

8 Cf. LS, 236f; KW II, 703f.

today's perspective, seems to demand the resources of film; on the other, the epic tendencies of the text work toward the involvement rather than the detachment of the audience. There is nothing to guarantee that the spell, which passages such as the above seek to cast, will be at all effective. The play depends so much upon creating a successful chiaroscuro, in the sense of the emergence of moments of lucidity or illumination from the prevailing turmoil, that it is little wonder that it has survived chiefly as a drama for readers, or that it had to wait until 1876 for its first stage performance. For it is in the play's demand for a simultaneity of order and chaos in its audience's response, rather than in the cumulative effect of its breaches of dramatic convention, that its main challenge for any theatre resides.

In opting to weave his plot around a minor strand of the mythological tradition in which Penthesilea slays Achilles, and not vice versa, Kleist was once more showing his penchant for reversals. It is Euripides' *Bacchae*, rather than any other work of Classical Antiquity, that gives substance to the details he took from Hederich's *Mythologisches Lexikon*.[9] But beyond this, the choice to develop the figure of the Amazon queen over that of Achilles completes a development that becomes increasingly more visible in *Der zerbrochne Krug* and *Amphitryon*. In *Die Familie Schroffenstein* there is an implication that Agnes and Ottokar are ideal halves of one identity, although the male half is clearly dominant. With Eve in *Der zerbrochne Krug*, Kleist begins to sketch a female heroine who does not hesitate to project the resolution of her conflicts into a realm beyond the mundane: 'Und ists im Leben nicht, so ist es jenseits,/ Und wenn wir auferstehn ist auch ein Tag' (SW I, 217). Alkmene is then forced, in *Amphitryon*, to undergo the torment of being a tragic heroine enmeshed in a comic plot. Jupiter's failure to do other than exacerbate Alkmene's sufferings shows Kleist's view of the inadequacy of divinity to resolve extremes of human conflict. *Penthesilea* takes the theme of the inadequacy of the divine a stage further, since whatever the gods represent partakes of the essential chaos of human action. If Eve and, to a much greater extent, Alkmene are at odds with the comic fictions that provide them with dramatic context, and their development as characters is constrained accordingly, no such limit is set on Penthesilea as a tragic figure. Her character can expand to where it seems about to usurp the function of external events in the play, and it is her inner division projected upon the world that produces the catastrophe. The text makes no secret of this. Diagnoses of what is dangerous in the situation and in the characters' reactions to it are as common as in *Die*

---

9 Cf. KN, 498f; Johannes Niejahr, 'Heinrich von Kleists *Penthesilea*,' in *Vierteljahresschrift für Litteraturgeschichte* 6 (1893), pp. 506-33; Jochen Schmidt, *Heinrich von Kleist*, pp. 234-41; KW II, 685-90.

Familie Schroffenstein. As in that work, explanations are rarely offered in the presence of those who could benefit from them, and when this does happen, they are neither heard nor heeded. Thus, at the conclusion of Scene 7, well before the dialogue between Penthesilea and Achilles, the Oberpriesterin pronounces a verdict that substantially anticipates the end:

> O sie geht steil-bergab den Pfad zum Orkus!
> Und nicht dem Gegner, wenn sie auf ihn trifft,
> Dem Feind in ihrem Busen wird sie sinken.
> Uns alle reißt sie in den Abgrund hin. . . . (SW I, 358)

The quantity of action that is reported from offstage in *Penthesilea* introduces a different kind of dependency on the language of others from that which is dominant in *Amphitryon*. There, even the god makes his win or loss depend on the words Alkmene utters to him, although he knows what her feelings are before she speaks. That they might change through being spoken is presumably what keeps him interested. In *Penthesilea*, the two main characters are as much creations of what is said about them in their absence as they are of what they directly reveal about themselves. The image of Penthesilea as a Fury is present in the text long before she makes any such direct reference herself. The rhetorically ornate form of reporting the play establishes in the opening speeches provides abundant opportunities for the sowing of metaphors in the dialogue, which then undergo an autonomous development in other scenes and in the mouths of other characters.

Just as the metaphor of the hunt may be seen as a trap waiting to close on Achilles in his last moments, so the images of non-human savagery that surround Penthesilea in the words of others wait to turn into fact when, having brought Achilles down with her bow, she joins her dogs in tearing his corpse to pieces.[10]

But not all such images are negative. There is a strand of metaphor, evoking the descent of divine powers to earth, that serves to illuminate a contrary aspect of Penthesilea's figure in a moment when the dialogue between her and Achilles takes on a ritual formality:

> O du, die eine Glanzerscheinung mir,
> Als hätte sich das Ätherreich eröffnet,
> Herabsteigst, Unbegreifliche, wer bist du?
> Wie nenn ich dich, wenn meine eigne Seele
> Sich, die entzückte, fragt, wem sie gehört?   (SW I, 384)

---

10 Cf. Volker Klotz, 'Tragödie der Jagd. Zu Kleists *Penthesilea*,' *Kurze Kommentare zu Stücken und Gedichten*, Darmstadt, 1962, pp. 14-21.

The question 'Wie nenn ich dich?' is a familiar one in Kleist's work, and, as Gerhard Neumann has indicated, signals the characters' quest for a genuine language of intimacy among the formulaic approximations of the language of others.[11] Here, the image of an epiphany is neither more nor less apposite in its application to Penthesilea than the metaphors of destruction. Penthesilea is genuinely incomprehensible to the other characters, since the interpretations they place on her are partial or partisan. This is also the answer to Achilles' question as to how he should name her, since the text showers designations of one kind or another upon her without exhausting the complexity of her character in its interaction with a set of circumstances that are bound to bring out those contradictions that have been contained until the moment she falls in love with Achilles.

The chaos of the battlefield is a highly structured chaos in its textual realization. What maintains the unease, indeed confusion, of any audience or reader, even after repeated readings, is the refusal of the text to privilege any single perspective or level of metaphoric reference with that dominance usually accorded to 'reality' within fictional frameworks. Towards the end of the play, Meroe's bloody account of Penthesilea's desecration of Achilles' corpse is interrupted by two priestesses, one of whom says of her:

> Sie war wie von der Nachtigall geboren,
> Die um den Tempel der Diana wohnt.
> Gewiegt im Eichenwipfel saß sie da,
> Und flötete, und schmetterte, und flötete,
> Die stille Nacht durch, daß der Wandrer horchte,
> Und fern die Brust ihm von Gefühlen schwoll.   (SW I, 414)

After these speeches, Meroe resumes her description of the scene by Achilles' corpse. The text here demands an opposite response from that required by most other scenes. In those scenes, we are meant to be mindful of the chaos of war as a constant counterpoint to the polished rhetoric of most dialogues; in this scene, the image of Penthesilea as the embodiment of natural innocence is meant to superimpose itself on that of her as a beast of prey with blood dripping from her jaws.

In terms of dramatic technique, Kleist is at his most ambitious in his attempt to offset the linear momentum of the tragic action by forcing the reader or audience to accept the simultaneity of such conflicting perspectives. It was too much to ask of a dramatic convention in which the sequential unfolding of events was still so dominant. Kleist also makes

11 Gerhard Neumann, 'Hexenküche und Abendmahl,' pp. 23f.

this task harder through his reliance on narrative, that most pronouncedly sequential of literary forms. This not only brings events into the text
that could not be shown on a conventional stage, but also magnifies the
figures of the two main characters by their taking on larger-than-life
attributes in the reports of others. A further effect is to saturate a text that
strives toward a simultaneous presentation of contrary views with the
sequential unfolding of actions in addition to those occurring on stage.
There is nothing unusual about the use of expository narratives or the
reports of offstage action as such; rather, it is the degree to which these
guide the action and extend the fields of imagery, another fundamental,
structural principle of the text.

The use of metaphor tends to counteract linearity. It is a characteristic of Kleist's texts, from *Die Familie Schroffenstein* onward, that
metaphors become independent of the characters who employ them, and
that the figurative dimension gains ascendancy over what it designates.
Penthesilea takes these trends to an extreme. Emotions between
Penthesilea and Achilles are often clothed in the imagery of the hunt,
anticipating the manner in which Achilles will eventually find his death.
Stemming in all likelihood from Kleist's reading of Euripides' *Bacchae*,
this complex of metaphors has the great advantage that agent and object
may be human and animal by turn. It is entirely consonant with the
play's climax that Penthesilea, pursuing Achilles on the battlefield,
should take on the guise of a beast of prey, as in these lines from the
play's opening scene:

So folgt, so hungerheiß, die Wölfin nicht,
Durch Wälder, die der Schnee bedeckt, der Beute,
Die sich ihr Auge grimmig auserkor,
Als sie, durch unsre Schlachtreihn, dem Achill.   (SW I, 327)

But another report of the battle in the very same scene reverses the
roles and has Achilles, as the hound, so intent on killing his prey that he
ignores the hunter's commands:

Denn wie die Dogg entkoppelt, mit Geheul
In das Geweih des Hirsches fällt: der Jäger,
Erfüllt von Sorge, lockt und ruft sie ab;
Jedoch verbissen in des Prachttiers Nacken,
Tanzt sie durch Berge neben ihm, und Ströme,
Fern in des Waldes Nacht hinein: so er,
Der Rasende, seit in der Forst des Krieges,
Dies Wild sich von so seltner Art, ihm zeigte.
Durchbohrt mit einem Pfeilschuß, ihn zu fesseln,

Die Schenkel ihm: er weicht, so schwört er, eher
Von dieser Amazone Ferse nicht,
Bis er bei ihren seidnen Haaren sie
Von dem gefleckten Tigerpferd gerissen.   (SW I, 328f)

Metaphors are thus more a property of the text as a whole than of any individual figure. Through their anticipatory function, the pursuit and slaughter of Achilles by Penthesilea, and indeed of Penthesilea by Achilles, has been evoked many times before the catastrophe. Were the role of beast of prey exclusively Penthesilea's, the effect of this imagery would be purely convergent and enhance feelings of tragic inevitability. But the plurality of metaphorical roles beyond those of hunter and hunted, and the movement of the two main characters among them, have a number of significant effects.

❦ One is to suggest a symmetry of attributes between the heroine and hero. Both freely confess to wanting to do to each other what Achilles has already done to the Trojan hero Hector, and in their dialogue Penthesilea insists on Achilles explicitly confirming this:

Sprich, wer den Größesten der Priamiden
Vor Trojas Mauern fällte, warst das du?
Hast du ihm wirklich, *du*, mit diesen Händen
Den flüchtgen Fuß durchkeilt, an deiner Achse
Ihn häuptlings um die Vaterstadt geschleift? –
Sprich! Rede! Was bewegt dich so? Was fehlt dir?   (SW I, 384)

It is thus not only the image of the bloody conclusion of a hunt, but also the ghost of Hector that overshadows any moment of tenderness between the two. The dead Hector becomes for both of them the projection of their aggression toward each other. The symmetry is, in turn, indicative of another important effect of the metaphors in the text. This is to contribute to the blurring of conventional gender roles implicit in the very idea of the Amazon state, which is discussed often in the text and is an indication of an underlying conviction that the full and complete human being is androgyne.[12]

A further effect of the play's metaphors is to add ambivalence to the dominant thematic movement in the text, which is that of a descent into death. The motif appears in the opening scene, when it is reported of Penthesilea that she has spared Achilles' life in a moment when she might have killed him. Had she not intervened, he would have died: 'Er

---

12 On the significance of the figure of the androgyne among Kleist's German contemporaries, see Achim Aurnhammer, *Androgynie. Studien zu einem Motiv in der europäischen Literatur*, Cologne and Vienna, 1986, pp. 161-76.

stieg zum Orkus, wenn sie ihn nicht hielt' (SW I, 327). Evocations of downward movement are never far from the surface of the text, whether they be real or imagined plunges from a height, or Penthesilea's calling down the Furies to join in her final pursuit of Achilles. It is Kleist's genius to divest them of single meaning and thus enlarge the scope of the tragic process.

In counterpoint to the negative force of the motif, there is an occasional glimpse of a more benign descent, namely that of divinities or blessed spirits to earth, as in Penthesilea's words:

Nun dann, so mögen alle Seligen
Daniedersteigen, unsern Sieg zu feiern,
Zur Heimat geht der Jubelzug, dann bin ich
Die Königin des Rosenfestes euch!– (SW I, 350)

It is not clear whether 'alle Seligen' are the Olympian gods in a benevolent aspect, or whether the text is fleetingly adopting the confused syncretism, in divine matters, of *Amphitryon*. What is clear is that this positive image of a descent immediately follows one of the more frequent destructive shadings of the motif. For Penthesilea has just envisaged bringing down Achilles as she might shoot a splendidly plumed bird out of the air:

Nicht eher ruhn will ich, bis ich aus Lüften,
Gleich einem schöngefärbten Vogel, ihn
Zu mir herabgestürzt; doch liegt er jetzt
Mit eingeknickten Fittichen, ihr Jungfraun,
Zu Füßen mir, kein Purpurstäubchen missend. . . . (SW I, 349f)

The effect is not for the images to cancel one another out, but rather to suggest that descents need not always have the same meaning. A further illustration of this is the skillful blending of the motif with connotations of erotic fulfilment:

Ists meine Schuld, daß ich im Feld der Schlacht
Um sein Gefühl mich kämpfend muß bewerben?
Was will ich denn, wenn ich das Schwert ihm zücke?
Will ich ihn denn zum Orkus niederschleudern?
Ich will ihn ja, ihr ewgen Götter, nur
An diese Brust will ich ihn niederziehn! (SW I, 361)

It is characteristic of the metaphors in the text that the clearest articulation of this blending comes in words that are neither spoken by

Penthesilea nor have any direct reference to violence. They are part of a narration by one of the young girls who has been sent to pick roses:

Auf eines Felsens Vorsprung wagt ich mich,
Um eine einzge Rose dir zu pflücken.
Und blaß nur, durch des Kelches Dunkelgrün,
Erschimmerte sie noch, ein Knösplein nur,
Für volle Liebe noch nicht aufgeblüht.
Doch greif ich sie, und strauchl' und sinke plötzlich
In einen Abgrund hin, der Nacht des Todes
Glaubt ich, Verlorne, in den Schoß zu sinken.
Mein Glück doch wars, denn eine Rosenpracht
Stand hier im Flor, daß wir zehn Siege noch
Der Amazonen hätten feiern können.   (SW I, 351)

Coming in Scene 6, this may be read as anticipating the end. The dialogues with Achilles in Scenes 14 to 18 are to be the only 'Rosenfest' that Penthesilea experiences, but there will be no sexual fulfilment on her way to death. The body will assert itself in a way anticipated in other metaphors, such as the hunt, when she slaughters Achilles. The establishing of a line of sensuous imagery in the earlier scenes of the play is important, as sensuality plays so little part in her dialogues with Achilles. If one focuses too closely on her representation of herself in these speeches, she appears to be a heroine in the mold of German Idealism, scarcely capable of the atrocity of Achilles' end. The transition has always worried interpreters of the play – with good reason, for it is hard to reconcile the lucidity of Penthesilea's discourse in these scenes with the violence of her speech during her descent into madness and subsequent savagery.[13]

But surely such extremes within the one figure are intelligible only in terms of the play's whole imagery. The course of action Penthesilea ultimately pursues becomes visible as an involuntary selection from among a much wider range of potentiality. Earlier in the play, Penthesilea proclaimed the force of her sexual desires, but then solely in the context of the institutionalized antitheses of Amazon sexuality:

13 As an example of the mystifications into which interpretative argument can descend in order to endow the figure of Penthesilea with the appearance of unity, one may take the following assertion by Gerhard Kaiser, 'Mythos und Person in Kleists *Penthesilea*,' *Geist und Zeichen. Festschrift für Arthur Henkel zu seinem 60. Geburtstag*, eds. H. Anton, B. Gajek and P. Pfaff, Heidelberg, 1977, pp. 177f: 'Penthesilea muß Achill töten, weil sie anders nicht fähig werden, einander unbedingt anzugehören; sie muß ihn töten, weil er anders nicht Person in der Liebe zu werden vermag. Sie muß die Antwort aus ihm herausbeißen, die er sonst nicht gibt. Hier ist die Notwendigkeit im Zufall seines Todes; er beruht auf einem Mißverständnis, das erst Verstehen als Kategorie möglich macht.'

Verflucht, im blutumschäumten Mordgetümmel,
Mir der Gedanke an die Orgien!
Verflucht, im Busen keuscher Arestöchter,
Begierden, die, wie losgelaßne Hunde,
Mir der Drommete erzne Lunge bellend,
Und aller Feldherrn Rufen, überschrein!　　(SW I, 362)

The greatest problem for an audience or a reader is that the the play does not indicate a progressive unfolding of an intelligible character, but presents tangential approaches to something that remains irreducible to a simple set of polarities, and is not encompassed by any dialectical synthesis. There are two clear lines of causality for the tragic action. One extends from the prophecy of Penthesilea's dying mother, naming Achilles as the warrior her daughter will defeat and crown with roses; the other begins with the foundation of the Amazon state. It is Penthesilea's misfortune to become Queen, thus embodying the contradictions inherent within this social order and condemned to experience those contradictions as part of her personal tragedy.

The question of inevitability is one for which there is no single answer. Viewed one way, the movement of the work is inexorably downward into death, and any positive moments are merely delays; viewed another, the wide range of potentialities in the figure of Penthesilea makes alternative endings thinkable. If there is a clear dislocation between her eminently rational converse with Achilles and her later madness, then other dislocations within this figure are surely possible. It is, in a sense, arbitrary that Achilles chooses the worst possible strategy for continuing their relationship in terms of the reaction it provokes from her.

The oppressiveness of the Amazon state is something we have to gather from the imagery rather than from Penthesilea's exposition of its origins in Scene 15. The Amazons are both 'Arestöchter' and 'Marsbräute,' children and spouses of the one god. Penthesilea's first speech in the play also situates Achilles within this frame of reference:

Den jungen trotzgen Kriegsgott bändg' ich mir,
Gefährtinnen, zehntausend Sonnen dünken,
Zu einem Glutball eingeschmelzt, so glanzvoll
Nicht, als ein Sieg, ein Sieg mir über ihn.　　(SW I, 343)

Mars presides over the sexual economy of the Amazons, but he is equally the 'Vertilgergott' (SW I, 405), the deity of complete annihilation. The Amazon law thus inherently has a negation more drastic than anything Lacan envisaged as the 'nom du père.' It seems an ironic comment by Kleist on recent European history that this order of things, in Penthesilea's own account, results from an act of revolution:

Frei, wie der Wind auf offnem Blachfeld, sind
Die Fraun, die solche Heldentat vollbracht,
Und dem Geschlecht der Männer nicht mehr dienstbar.
Ein Staat, ein mündiger, sei aufgestellt,
Ein Frauenstaat, den fürder keine andre
Herrschsüchtge Männerstimme mehr durchtrotzt,
Der das Gesetz sich würdig selber gebe,
Sich selbst gehorche, selber auch beschütze:
Und Tanaïs sei seine Königin.
Der Mann, des Auge diesen Staat erschaut,
Der soll das Auge gleich auf ewig schließen;
Und wo ein Knabe noch geboren wird,
Von der Tyrannen Kuß, da folg er gleich
Zum Orkus noch den wilden Vätern nach.   (SW I, 388f)

After all this, the incestuous bond to Mars is clearly one of the contradictions of the Amazon state, for the dominant power in its pantheon remains oppressively masculine. Mars' female counterpart is Artemis, in the precinct of whose temple the 'orgies' take place, but it is unclear what relationship exists for the Amazons between the two divinities, beyond the fact that Artemis is *not* Mars' consort. The imperatives attributed to both gods seem entirely consonant, so that one might well ask what need there is for Mars in the Amazon scheme of things, unless it be to signal that this state has not overcome the principles of patriarchal society at all, but merely reversed gender roles with limited success.

In Meroe's narration of Achilles' death, Kleist plays on Artemis as the destroyer of Actäeon, comparing the fleeing hero to a deer. The destructiveness of Mars seems merely an intensification of this, indicating that there is no clear distinction, in the world of the play, between female and male authorities. For all that, the founders of the Amazon state use gender distinctions to set it apart from all others. It is also quite possible, as Hinrich C. Seeba suggests, that the Amazons' view of Artemis is a conscious reversal on Kleist's part of the benevolent and rational image of the same deity in Goethe's *Iphigenie auf Tauris*.[14]

If Artemis is patron of the very restricted sexuality the Amazons permit themselves to replenish their numbers with female children,

14 Cf. Hinrich C. Seeba, KW II, 749f.

Aphrodite must stand for sexuality without restraint. For her sole appearance in the text is in conjunction with the motif of universal destruction, which is later designated the province of Mars:

Daß der ganze Frühling
Verdorrte! Daß der Stern, auf dem wir atmen,
Geknickt, gleich dieser Rosen einer, läge!
Daß ich den ganzen Kranz der Welten so,
Wie dies Geflecht der Blumen, lösen könnte!
– O Aphrodite!   (SW I, 362)

From an Amazon perspective, unrestrained sexuality might well seem synonomous with the destruction of all order. Paradoxically, Penthesilea's desire for Achilles is both within and outside the Amazon law, just as it encompasses the contradictory goals of preserving his life and killing him. Even as she perceives Achilles as an incarnation of the god of war whom she, as a 'Marsbraut,' will set out to conquer and wed, she is, at the same time, full of a preoccupation with the *person* of Achilles, which is quite contrary to the Amazon ethos and derives from her mother's dying words. As she subsequently relates to Achilles, in the moment of her coronation she feels more loyalty to the wishes of her dead mother than to the god of war, a dangerous beginning for the head of a state that survives only through full obedience to an inflexible code that enjoins repeated warfare:

Ich erschien,
Wehmütig strebender Gefühle voll,
Im Tempel Mars', den Bogen gab man mir,
Den klirrenden, des Amazonenreichs,
Mir war, als ob die Mutter mich umschwebte,
Da ich ihn griff, nichts schien mir heiliger,
Als ihren letzten Willen zu erfüllen.
Und da ich Blumen noch, die duftigsten,
Auf ihren Sarkophag gestreut, brach ich
Jetzt mit dem Heer der Amazonen auf,
Nach der Dardanerburg – Mars weniger,
Dem großen Gott, der mich dahin gerufen,
Als der Otrere Schatten, zu gefallen.   (SW I, 394f)

Amazons are forbidden to pursue individuals in battle. Rather, their sexual partners and hence the fathers of their children are to be decided entirely by the fortunes of war. There is no clear motivation for

Penthesilea's mother to prophesy that her daughter will find and overcome Achilles, but because Penthesilea admits she loved Otrere, the act is profoundly subversive both of the Amazon state and of Penthesilea's continued ability to embody its values, the more so as Otrere links her naming of Achilles to a command of Mars: 'Mars ruft dich!/ Du wirst den Peleïden dir bekränzen' (SW I, 394). A double bind, if ever there was one.

In this way Achilles becomes Penthesilea's dream – 'Mein ewger Traum warst du!' (SW I, 395) – before she ever sees him, and, as she freely admits, part of this dream is the death of Hector and the desecration of his corpse. Unhappily for Penthesilea, she identifies by turns with the killer and his victim:

Laßt ihn kommen.
Laßt ihn den Fuß gestählt, es ist mir recht,
Auf diesen Nacken setzen. Wozu auch sollen
Zwei Wangen länger, blühnd wie diese, sich
Vom Kot, aus dem sie stammen, unterscheiden?
Laßt ihn mit Pferden häuptlings heim mich schleifen,
Und diesen Leib hier, frischen Lebens voll,
Auf offnem Felde schmachvoll hingeworfen,
Den Hunden mag er ihn zur Morgenspeise,
Dem scheußlichen Geschlecht der Vögel, bieten.   (SW I, 363)

The reason why Penthesilea admires Achilles' barbarous treatment of Hector's corpse and refers to it more than once is that she has already made it part of her fantasies of self-destruction. To ask why she has such fantasies is to venture into the genuinely incomprehensible area of her character, for which all the causal explanations the play offers tend to be correct in a limited sense, but inadequate as global explanations. Kleist seems, in *Penthesilea*, to have been intent on creating a character who would be much less reducible by formulaic judgements than any of his other main characters.

A solution of tantalizing simplicity for Penthesilea is to abandon all allegiance to the Amazon state and revert to a conventional female role as Achilles' wife. Certainly, in cursing her rescue by the Amazons in Scene 19, she embraces the object-role for herself that this implies:

War ich, nach jeder würdgen Rittersitte,
Nicht durch das Glück der Schlacht ihm zugefallen?
Wenn das Geschlecht der Menschen unter *sich*,

Mit Wolf und Tiger nicht, im Streite liegt:
Gibts ein Gesetz, frag ich, in solchem Kriege,
Das den Gefangenen, der sich ergeben,
Aus seines Siegers Banden lösen kann?
– Neridensohn!   (SW I, 400)

Appealing to a 'law of war,' which is defined neither here nor elsewhere in Kleist's works, to support her emotional opposition to the very
clearly defined law of the Amazon state, indicates Penthesilea's need to
be justified in terms other than her own individuality. This leads, in turn,
to the question of whether placing herself outside the law is a real possibility. When she does proclaim it as her final decision at the end of the
tragedy – 'Ich sage vom Gesetz der Fraun mich los,/ Und folge diesem
Jüngling hier' (SW I, 426) – then the irony is that following Achilles
into death will indeed set her outside all social contexts and also terminate the rule of the 'law of women.'

Her long dialogue with Achilles, before the Amazons counter-
attack and free her, ends with the lovers disagreeing as to who should
follow the other, and it is pointless to conjecture whether simply turning her back on the Amazon state for a life in Greek society is a genuine option for Penthesilea. All that one can say is that there are a
number of indications of a longing in her to be free of the constraints
of being an Amazon, so that, when her warriors recapture her from
the Greeks, she reacts by projecting herself back into the situation of
a prisoner of war, just as in Scene 9 she has reacted to her failure to
overcome Achilles on the battlefield by projecting herself into the
role of the dead Trojan hero, Hector. So many of the stances she proclaims are spontaneous reactions to circumstances that have frustrated her that it is impossible to hold her to one or another set of words.

If one still persists in asking why self-destruction features so
prominently in her fantasies, then a conventional explanation would
be that she has an intuitive awareness that the conflicts set up by her
contradictory feelings toward the law of the Amazons are such that
they can be resolved solely by her own death. There is little disagreement that the gods she invokes have, within the play's fictional world,
little reality outside the characters' feelings and the prohibitions society imposes on itself. Penthesilea has internalized her gods, and may
well experience the imperatives she names Mars and Aphrodite in
such absolute terms that a collision between them makes it impossible
for her to live.

A less conventional explanation makes use of Jacques Lacan's concept of desire. In his terms, human desire is not for the other as object,

but for the desire of the other.[15] From very early in the play, Penthesilea knows that, whatever else Achilles may desire, he desires to treat her as he has treated Hector, and proclaims it so that all can hear. One of the speeches that she clearly does listen to is that of Asteria in Scene 5:

Ja jener junge Nereïdensohn,
Den deine Hand mit Rosen schmücken sollte,
Die Stirn beut er, der übermütge, dir;
Den Fußtritt will er, und erklärt es laut,
Auf deinen königlichen Nacken setzen:
Und meine große Arestochter fragt mich,
Ob sie den Siegesheimzug feiern darf? (SW I, 347)

In desiring Achilles' desire of herself, Penthesilea can scarcely escape an awareness that she is reaching toward something of which her own destruction is part. This may help account for the otherwise puzzling fact that, when she does finally speak with Achilles, one of the first things she asks of him is explicit confirmation that he is indeed the slayer of Hector, although the act is already notorious and she can scarcely doubt who the man before her is. The expression of Penthesilea's death-wish is thus one of the most finely crafted aspects of Kleist's drama, since it is subtly and inextricably interwoven with her desire for love and life.

Her own fantasies of conquest also tend to be contradictory, implying at times that she desires to slaughter Achilles without really taking his life. Such confusion is evident in the following words from Scene 5:

Ich nur, ich weiß den Göttersohn zu fällen.
Hier dieses Eisen soll, Gefährtinnen,
Soll mit der sanftesten Umarmung ihn
(Weil ich mit Eisen ihn umarmen muß!)
An meinen Busen schmerzlos niederziehn.   (SW I, 349)

---

15 Cf. Jacques Lacan, *Écrits*, Paris, 1966, p. 268: 'Pour tout dire, nulle part n'apparaît plus clairement que le désir de l'homme trouve son sens dans le désir de l'autre, non pas tant parce que l'autre détient les clefs de l'objet du désir, que parce que son premier objet est d'être reconnu par l'autre.'; p. 691: 'La béance de cette énigme avère ce qui la détermine, dans la formule la plus simple à la rendre patente, à savoir: que le sujet comme l'Autre, pour chacun des partenaires de la relation, ne peuvent se suffire d'être sujets du besoin, ni objets de l'amour, mais qu'ils doivent tenir lieu de cause du désir.'; cf. also Elizabeth Grosz, *Jacques Lacan. A Feminist Introduction*, London, 1990, p. 64. A different Lacanian reading of *Penthesilea* in terms of the 'discourse of the hysteric' is offered by Helga Gallas, 'Kleists *Penthesilea* und Lacans vier Diskurse,' *Kontroversen, alte und neue. Akten des VII. Internationalen Germanisten-Kongresses Göttingen 1985*, vol. 6, eds. Inge Stephan und Carl Pietzcker, Tübingen, 1986, pp. 203-12.

The question has been asked whether 'schmerzlos' can imply anything other than Achilles' death,[16] since it is hard to imagine any other circumstance in which the embrace of a swordblade would cause no pain, and such a reading is quite plausible in conjunction with Penthesilea's words at the beginning of Scene 9:

> Hetzt alle Hund' auf ihn! Mit Feuerbränden
> Die Elefanten peitschet auf ihn los!
> Mit Sichelwagen schmettert auf ihn ein,
> Und mähet seine üppgen Glieder nieder! (SW I, 360f)

Penthesilea's fantasies of pain are by no means limited to her own suffering. The insuperable difficulty for any interpretation is that her character does not unfold in a linear progression, so that processes of critical thought that see characters developing, internal conflicts being mediated, and enigmas clarified in the course of a work will be largely frustrated. The temptation to opt for one clear direction has been too strong for many critics, and the result is usually to identify the lucid and rational Penthesilea of the dialogues with Achilles as her 'real' self, implying everything else is an aberration.[17] This is at odds with Penthesilea's acknowledgement of the death of Achilles as her own act in the final scenes of the play, but it does make the work more intelligible within the context of German Idealism, for all that Kleist's text makes clear again and again that it is precisely this mold that he has set out to break. There is no place in the feelings of an Idealist heroine for 'Begierden, die, wie losgeklaßne Hunde,/ . . . aller Feldherrn Rufen, überschrein!' (SW I, 362)

In her final speeches, Penthesilea rejects the factual consequences of her feelings, but does not explicitly disown the desires themselves. Instead, she gives a chilling rationalization of her act of cannibalism in terms, precisely, of her desire for Achilles. But once more, in terms Lacan would approve, his death does not satisfy her in the slightest, but rather redirects her unfulfilled desire 'in das Unendliche hinaus' (SW I, 414), a region into which her own suicide allows her to pursue it, this being the sense in which she is finally resolved to 'follow' Achilles.

---

16 Cf. Albrecht Sieck, *Kleists 'Penthesilea.' Versuch einer Interpretation*, Bonn, 1976, p. 150.

17 Cf. Walter Müller-Seidel, '*Penthesilea* im Kontext der deutschen Klassik,' *Kleists Dramen*, ed. Walter Hinderer, p. 155: 'Gleichermaßen beunruhigend wie das manchmal ununterscheidbare Ineinander von Traum und Wirklichkeit ist der Übergang von der Wirklichkeit zum Wahn. Keine Frage, daß es Psychopathologisches im Verhalten Penthesileas gibt und daß ihr Verhalten in einigen Szenen so auch verstanden werden soll. . . . Im Text Kleists wird Penthesileas Tun und Verhalten wiederholt als krankhaft bezeichnet.'

The beginning of her desire is ultimately as incomprehensible as its end. Many times she, as a royal princess, has been excluded from the orgies of the 'Rosenfest,' since her own sexuality is a matter for the state religion and outside her personal choice, as she explains to Achilles in Scene 15:

> Denn die
> Prinzessinnen, aus meinem Königshaus,
> Sie mischen nie aus eigener Bewegung,
> Sich in der blühnden Jungfrau Fest; der Gott,
> Begehrt er ihrer, ruft sie würdig auf,
> Durch seiner großen Oberpriestrin Mund.　　(SW I, 393)

The official summons reaches Penthesilea as she holds her dying mother in her arms. Her mother names Achilles with her last breath, and only Penthesilea hears her. But this is sufficient to make her obsessed with him, and she describes her first seeing him in the field as a vision of her own father and future spouse, the god of war:

> Wie aber ward mir,
> O Freund, als ich dich selbst erblickte –!
> Als du mir im Skamandros-Tal erschienst,
> Von den Heroen deines Volks umringt,
> Ein Tagsstern unter bleichen Nachtgestirnen!
> So müßt es mir gewesen sein, wenn er
> Unmittelbar, mit seinen weißen Rossen,
> Von dem Olymp herabgedonnert wäre,
> Mars selbst, der Kriegsgott, seine Braut zu grüßen!
> Geblendet stand ich, als du jetzt entwichen,
> Von der Erscheinung da –　　(SW I, 396)

Her desire is thus, quite literally, born of her mother's death and of the imperative to replace her as her father's bride. Seeing Achilles for the first time confirms its direction and intensifies its strength, but desire precedes the physical encounter:

> Mein ewiger Gedanke, wenn ich wachte,
> Mein ewger Traum warst du! Die ganze Welt
> Lag wie ein ausgespanntes Musternetz
> Vor mir; in jeder Masche, weit und groß,
> War deiner Taten einer eingeschürzt,
> Und in mein Herz, wie Seide weiß und rein,
> Mit Flammenfarben jede brannt ich ein.

Bald sah ich dich, wie du ihn niederschlugst,
Vor Ilium, den flüchtgen Priamiden;
Wie du, entflammt von hoher Siegerlust,
Das Antlitz wandtest, während er die Scheitel,
Die blutigen, auf nackter Erde schleifte;
Wie Priam flehnd in deinem Zelt erschien –
Und heiße Tränen weint ich, wenn ich dachte,
Daß ein Gefühl doch, Unerbittlicher,
Den marmorharten Busen dir durchzuckt. (SW I, 395f)

Penthesilea's tears at the thought that Achilles might have been
moved by the grief of Hector's father surely relate to her own fantasies
in which she identifies with the slain Trojan. Would Mars, the father she
knows only as a set of commands and prohibitions, be moved to grief if
she, his child, were to be killed, like Hector, by Achilles as Mars' own
incarnation?

It may not be too fanciful to place Mars in the ranks of the actually or
potentially murderous fathers in Kleist's work, at least within the perspective of Penthesilea's perceptions. Why else should she weep at the
mere conjecture that Achilles, as Mars' living presence, might feel a
fleeting compassion at the grief of another bereft father? Logic has
severe limits in a world ruled by such intense and complex feelings, but
it is significant that, in the rapid transition from uncertainty to murderous rage after she receives Achilles' challenge to a renewed battle, her
last rhetorical questions return to Achilles' brutality and his apparent
incapacity for feeling:

Der mich zu schwach weiß, sich mit ihm zu messen,
Der ruft zum Kampf mich, Prothoe, ins Feld?
Hier diese treue Brust, sie rührt ihn erst,
Wenn sie sein scharfer Speer zerschmetterte?
Ein steinern Bild hat meine Hand bekränzt? (SW I, 403)

Her response to Achilles' apparent lack of compassion eventually
becomes an absolute refusal of compassion on her part when he pleads
with her as she kills him. In between, she has invoked Mars in his aspect
of the 'Vertilgergott,' and in Meroe's account of the death of Achilles a
curious reversal of roles becomes apparent. It is as if Penthesilea is now
the embodiment of callous destruction and Achilles – like Pentheus in
Euripides' *Bacchae* – the incarnation of vulnerability, assuming the role
Penthesilea has claimed for herself shortly before. We know from an
intervening scene that Achilles' submissiveness is purely a stratagem,
rather than being indicative of any change of heart. Acting out a defeat

in battle is a means to follow Penthesilea to the temple of Artemis, enjoy the orgies, and take his leave together with the Amazon's other sexual partners. It is, however, curious that he remains locked in this role once the fury of Penthesilea's attack makes it clear his strategy has lost all value. Thus he dies as a willing victim, offering only reproaches:

> Er, in dem Purpur seines Bluts sich wälzend,
> Rührt ihre sanfte Wange an, und ruft:
> Penthesilea! meine Braut! was tust du?
> Ist dies das Rosenfest, das du versprachst?   (SW I, 413)

It is as if there is a limited number of roles available to the two protagonists, so that once Penthesilea completes her identification with Mars as the ruthless destroyer, Achilles is held fast in that of the helpless victim. Since Artemis seems merely a shadow of Mars, one might equally see Penthesilea, as the goddess bent on vengeance, compelling Achilles into the role of Actaeon:

> Stutzt er, und dreht den schlanken Hals, und horcht,
> Und eilt entsetzt, und stutzt, und eilet wieder:
> Gleich einem jungen Reh. . . .   (SW I, 412)

Penthesilea's words immediately before drawing her bow on him are, significantly: 'Ha! Sein Geweih verrät den Hirsch . . .' (SW I, 413). There is a good deal of psychological implausibility in all of this. From Achilles' earlier dialogues with his fellow Greeks, his strategy of surrendering to Penthesilea on the expectation that, after the erotic interlude in the temple of Artemis, she may well wish to follow him, is quite credible. That he does not revert to his usual, aggressive self once he sees his plan has misfired, but instead hides among the branches of a pine and waits for Penthesilea to arrive with her hounds so that he can sink in submission at her feet,[18] is not prepared for psychologically. Rather, it needs to be explained in terms of what roles the mythical framework makes available and how they are exchanged between the two protagonists.

Another role the text appears to hold ready for Penthesilea is that of Fury. To the Greeks, she appears as early as Scene 3 in the guise of 'die rasende Megär' (SW I, 334). It is not until Scene 20 – 'Die Furien auch

---

18 Cf. SW I, 412f: 'Er ruft: Odysseus! mit beklemmter Stimme,/ Und sieht sich schüchtern um, und ruft: Tydide!/ Und will zurück noch zu den Freunden fliehn;/ Und steht, von einer Schar schon abgeschnitten,/ Und hebt die Händ empor, und duckt und birgt/ In eine Fichte sich, der Unglücksel'ge,/ Die schwer mit dunkeln Zweigen niederhangt.-'

ruf ich herab . . .' (SW I, 404) – that Penthesilea calls on them herself, and the scene ends with her setting off with her entire army to find Achilles, rejecting all attempts to delay her with the words: 'Nein, hier sind noch die Furien nicht versammelt' (SW I, 406). She thus identifies the place where the Furies *are* gathered as her only appropriate destination.

Throughout the play, the words of others have frequently associated Penthesilea with the Furies, and her invocation of them at the end is an act of conforming to a particular demand of the text. All such roles that are foreshadowed in the imagery, whether they be that of the victorious hunter, the savage beast of prey, the vengeful Artemis, or the Fury, have in common a drastic simplification of Penthesilea's character.

They have the advantage, for the other characters, of being clichés and thus readily intelligible, which Penthesilea herself is not. Their frequency in the text is due to the repeated pattern of other characters searching for words to mask the inadequacy of language and settling on something that fits a pre-existing rhetorical or mythical pattern. Even Achilles, despite the close affinities between Penthesilea and himself and the long dialogue they have had, reverts to clichés in his last conversation with his fellow Greeks: 'Dies wunderbare Weib,/ Halb Furie, halb Grazie, sie liebt mich – ' (SW I, 406). Lost somewhere behind the plethora of epithets that make her both more and less than human is the full human complexity of this figure, which is not amenable to being reduced to one of the social roles available to her.

In some scenes, one has an impression of Penthesilea begging for time in which to be herself, before the tide of others' rhetoric sweeps her away again. This may be the sense of the appeal she makes in Scene 14:

> O laß mich, Prothoe! O laß dies Herz
> Zwei Augenblick in diesem Strom der Lust,
> Wie ein besudelt Kind, sich untertauchen;
> Mit jedem Schlag in seine üppgen Wellen
> Wäscht sich ein Makel mir vom Busen weg.   (SW I, 379f)

As Penthesilea has yet to speak with Achilles and thus encounter directly the temptation to abandon the law of the Amazons, it is impossible to fix a referent, for the 'pollution' she feels is being washed away by a 'stream of pleasure.' The very opacity of the speech does, however, raise the problem of emancipation, which is a major theme of the play.

As in these lines, Penthesilea's speeches often display a longing for respite from the pressures upon her, but the violence of her reactions usually obscures whatever she might envisage as her liberation. There are various reasons for this. First, she is living the conflicts that it is left to others to diagnose. When she tells Achilles of her mother's dying words, it falls to Prothoe to indicate with a question – 'So nannte sie den Namen dir, Otrere?' (SW I, 394) – that her personal fixation on the Greek hero is contrary to Amazon law. Second, emancipation makes visible the limits of language. Penthesilea's desires are articulated in such disparate and violent terms because the vocabulary of Amazon life leaves no middle ground between conquered and conqueror. The gruesome death of Hector is seized on because it offers this familiarly restricted choice of roles. The only middle way leads through the regimented sexuality of the 'Rosenfest,' and it is impossible to say at what point Penthesilea becomes uneasy about the final separation from Achilles this would mean. In Scene 15 he asks her: '– – Und auch mich denkst du also zu entlassen?' To which she can only reply: 'Ich weiß nicht, Lieber. Frag mich nicht' (SW I, 392). Their dialogue ends with each still proposing to the other the role acceptable in their respective societies and involving subordination.

Penthesilea's preferred outcome must lie somewhere between or beyond the roles that are pre-formed for her in the language of the play, but in moments of extreme stress she falls into one familiar pattern or another, or else simply contradicts herself. In the course of Scene 9, she goes through emotions from murderous rage to fantasizing her own death as Hector. At one point, she betrays an awareness of the extent to which she is influenced by the images of herself contained in the words of her fellow Amazons:

> – Die Hand verwünsch ich, die zur Schlacht mich heut
> Geschmückt, und das verräterische Wort,
> Das mir gesagt, es sei zum Sieg, dazu.
> Wie sie mit Spiegeln mich, die Gleißnerinnen,
> Umstanden, rechts und links, der schlanken Glieder
> In Erz gepreßte Götterbildung preisend. –
> Die Pest in eure wilden Höllenkünste!   (SW I, 364)

As is so often the case in Kleist's texts, the insight brings no direct benefit to the character who puts it into words. For Penthesilea to realize that she is describing a general problem of the power of words over feelings, she would need to gain some distance from her obsession with being either the victor or the vanquished. But as we have seen, nothing in the play allows her a period of calm. She is summoned into battle from the side of her dying mother, and the chaos of war is sustained until her enforced confrontation with the corpse of Achilles. In Scene 9, her own response to her giddy course from one predictable role to another is to lose consciousness for some time.

Fainting is not uncommon in Kleist's works, and usually signifies an incapacity of the individual consciousness to deal with the contradictions of experience. I have suggested elsewhere that the motif of a hiatus in experience, marked by a sudden loss of consciousness, is one Kleist seems to have developed from Rousseau in order to mark a contemporary crisis in the concept of individualism – one that had not been foreseen by thinkers and writers of the German Enlightenment, but which points to the fragmentation of the self so common in 20-century fictions.[19]

In Kleist's first drama, Graf Sylvester is so shocked by the false accusation that he is a murderer that he faints, and on awakening, seems possessed by a blissful amnesia. He has no awareness of the tensions that have led to his loss of consciousness and proclaims: 'Mir ist so wohl, wie bei dem Eintritt in/ Ein andres Leben' (SW I, 81). This is the first of a long series of such moments in Kleist's works. Awareness of reality becomes so oppressive that a sudden dislocation of consciousness produces the effect of a fresh beginning, often with overtones of the afterlife or the Elysian Fields.

Yet Kleist, as an inveterate ironist, consistently reveals these promises to be illusory. Sylvester is soon overtaken by the complications of the plot once more, and his ultimate state of mind seems no better for his glimpse of 'another life.' As Penthesilea is forced to live through more violent contradictions than most of Kleist's main characters, it is by no means surprising that a suspension of awareness provides, more than once, her only respite from acute tension, a momentary unification of the divided self before its conflicts re-assert themselves. In her first encounter with Achilles, she is described as losing all expression from her face until she suddenly catches sight of him:

Und Glut ihr plötzlich, bis zum Hals hinab,
Das Antlitz färbt, als schlüge rings um ihr
Die Welt in helle Flammenlohe auf.   (SW I, 325)

A little later, a similar hiatus of consciousness precedes her rescue of Achilles in battle:

Die Königin, entfärbt, läßt zwei Minuten
Die Arme sinken: und die Locken dann
Entrüstet um entflammte Wangen schüttelnd,
Hebt sie vom Pferdesrücken hoch sich auf. . . . (SW I, 328)

19 Anthony Stephens, '"Wie bei dem Eintritt in/Ein andres Leben",' pp. 200f.

These scenes anticipate her total loss of consciousness in Scene 9, when, after she has articulated, one by one, all the contrary passions that work within her, she attempts to plunge after the reflection of the sun in a river: 'Da fällt sie leblos,/ Wie ein Gewand in unsrer Hand zusammen' (SW I, 368). This in turn may be seen as a preparation for the episode in which she slaughters Achilles. She emerges from it, in Scene 24, by going through the phases of the earlier incidents: lack of facial expression and awareness of those around her; a loss of speech and slow recovery of it; an initial blissful amnesia as to what has gone before. This time, the irony of illusion is excessively cruel:

> O sagt mir! – Bin ich in Elysium?
> Bist du der ewig jungen Nymphen eine,
> Die unsre hehre Königin bedienen,
> Wenn sie von Eichenwipfeln still umrauscht,
> In die kristallne Grotte niedersteigt?   (SW I, 420)

What awaits Penthesilea is the realization that she has not only slain Achilles, but also mutilated his corpse. In the forgetfulness of her awakening, she appears to project her feelings of wholeness and harmony onto the world around her, so that she mistakes her friend Prothoe for an immortal nymph and sees reality as transfigured.

Just as in the more chaotic scenes the strife of war appears as an objective correlative of her inner turmoil, so here the solipsistic quality of her world produces, by an ironic reversal, a fleeting vision of Elysium to supplant an horrific reality. It is then left to Prothoe, in her reply, to invert this perspective once more: 'Es ist die Welt noch, die gebrechliche,/ Auf die nur fern die Götter niederschaun' (SW I, 421).

With these words, it is as if a world that has momentarily assumed the shape of Penthesilea's desire for freedom from the conflicts that beset her reverts to its familiar imperfection and separation from the divine. In it, no new beginning is possible outside delusion, and the distance between desire and fulfillment is similar to that between mundane experience and the distant gods. Such episodes surely express scepticism on Kleist's part toward grandiose views of the creative powers of the individual that, originating in the Enlightenment, had been further mythicized in the work of Novalis and other German Romantics. If conflicts are suddenly banished by an illusion of re-birth or of translation to another life, both self and world may share a fleeting simplicity and wholeness, but the more intense the relief, the more devastating is the return to a confrontation with Achilles' corpse and her own past actions.

The parallels between self and world in this play are social as well as cosmic. As Queen, Penthesilea is meant to incarnate the values of the Amazon state, and it has long been recognized that some of the contradictions she must suffer through derive from it.[20] Not a great deal is gained by stressing that this society is 'unnatural,'[21] for nature, from *Die Familie Schroffenstein* onward, is an inconstant and insubstantial authority in Kleist's works. What is important is that the founding of this state is as spurious a new beginning as Penthesilea's first return to self-awareness in Scene 24. We have seen that Penthesilea's account of its origin portrays it as a successful overthrow of male authority that, paradoxically, preserves Mars as its supreme deity. Emerging from a bloody revolt against invaders, the Amazon state claims to be emancipation personified, but yet can exist only by the most rigid of institutions, which include self-mutilation and the killing of all male children. Far from banishing patriarchal oppression, the Amazons enshrine Mars as the 'god of annihilation' whom Penthesilea will later invoke in her destructive frenzy. It is possible to see Mars, the 'Vertilgergott,' among other guises, as the most extreme of Kleist's demonizations of Napoleon, whom he brands in a letter of 1805 'der böse Geist der Welt.'[22]

The analogy to Kleist's views of post-Revolutionary France is inescapable, for Amazon society seems condemned to replicate the illusory fresh starts he perceived in contemporary history and ironized, in terms of individual experience, through the motif of a hiatus in self-awareness followed by a brief and false renewal.[23] Whatever acts of liberation may have led to the establishment of the Amazon state in the first place, they have long been overtaken by history and remain, as if petrified, in an order that subjugates sexual desire to a regimented code of procreation, making this, in turn, dependent on the state's total isolation, except when at war. While the first appearance of the Amazons seems to confront the Greeks with something outside the realm of nature,[24] later events tend to stress the similarity between

---

20 Cf. Müller-Seidel, 'Kleists *Penthesilea* im Kontext der deutschen Klassik,' pp. 149f.

21 Cf. Gerhard Kaiser, 'Mythos und Person in Kleists *Penthesilea*,' p. 169f.

22 'Warum sich nur nicht einer findet, der diesem bösen Geiste der Welt die Kugel durch den Kopf jagt.' SW II, 761.

23 Cf. Yixu Lü, *Frauenherrschaft im Drama des frühen 19. Jahrhunderts*, Munich, 1993, pp. 182f.

24 Cf. SW I, 326: 'So viel ich weiß, gibt es in der Natur/ Kraft bloß und ihren Widerstand, nichts Drittes./ . . . Doch hier/ Zeigt ein ergrimmter Feind von beiden sich/ Bei dessen Eintritt nicht das Feuer weiß,/ Obs mit dem Wasser rieseln soll, das Wasser,/ Obs mit dem Feuer himmelan soll lecken.'; see Müller-Seidel's commentary on this in 'Kleists *Penthesilea* im Kontext der deutschen Klassik,' pp. 150f.

Greek and Amazon society,[25] once one has allowed for obvious reversals and the fact that what the Amazons have created is, in any terms, an extreme version of the consequences of revolution. The Greeks' confidence in knowing what is 'natural' – an arrogance shared equally by the Enlightenment, Weimar Classicism, and Romanticism – is indeed one of the pillars of contemporary ideology Kleist's play sets out to subvert, just as it presents an aggressive confrontation with the very selective portrait of Classical Antiquity in Goethe's *Iphigenie auf Tauris*.

If, on the one hand, the Amazon state is an efficient war-machine, on the other it partakes of the precariousness of its Queen's existence. Penthesilea's last command is to scatter the ashes of the first Queen, Tanaïs, thus negating the state's foundation: 'Und – – – im Vertraun ein Wort, das niemand höre,/ Der Tanaïs Asche, streut sie in die Luft!' (SW I, 426). It seems clear that the state ends with Penthesilea's suicide, and this points up once more the solipsistic quality of the fictional world Kleist has created. If German Romanticism delighted in spinning fantasies about the power of the individual psyche to be a whole cosmos unto itself, Kleist shows the grim obverse of such wishful thinking. By containing a good part of all the emotional forces of this world within herself, Penthesilea must embody the conflicts within a bizarre social construct that lives and dies with her. The consequent effect on her psychology is to produce that hectic movement from one pre-formed role to another that I have already shown.

For the remainder of my discussion, it is necessary to allow that narcissism is not merely a theme in this tragedy, but defines the relation of the figure of Penthesilea to the whole text. It is impossible to discuss Penthesilea as a dramatic 'character' in the conventional sense, for the text sets no limits as to where her psyche begins and ends. As we have seen, in one respect she is very much a creation of others' language in a manner that recalls Alkmene in *Amphitryon*. In another, her emotional rhythms, which vary from pure aggression to extreme sensibility, often pursue a course of their own, independent of the plot, which repeatedly leaves dumbfounded those who know her best. When she kills herself by an act of will, without any weapon, her death becomes an expression of an autonomy that she has vainly pursued throughout the action, since the main obstacle to attaining it has been her own inner dividedness. But this, in turn, is only insuperable until her last moments because she faithfully reflects the fragmented nature of the human world she inhabits.

25 Cf. ibid., pp. 157f.

As Sigrid Lange has rightly pointed out, the Amazon state compels its citizens to alternate between conventional gender roles,[26] but beyond this, Penthesilea's extremes of tenderness and aggression are equally *threats* to the maintenance of the Amazon order. There are indications that her feelings for Achilles are too strong to be contained within the strictly regulated sexuality the state prescribes, while her savagery is equally menacing to this 'order,' for it holds up a mirror in which the other Amazons are forced to recognize the full destructiveness implicit in their regime. The mirroring effect also pervades the relationship between Penthesilea and Achilles, making it difficult to see the latter as a unified figure in conventional dramatic terms. Just as the complexities of Penthesilea are reflected and refracted in the words of others, so Achilles – both literally and metaphorically – mirrors aspects of herself, as the image in the following lines indicates:

> Ist das die Siegerin, die schreckliche,
> Der Amazonen stolze Königin,
> Die seines Busens erzne Rüstung mir,
> Wenn sich mein Fuß ihm naht, zurückespiegelt?　　　(SW I, 343)

Transposing attributes onto herself of Achilles as the 'terrible' slayer of Hector, she creates an exaggerated image, of which her own self-perception falls short. The note of doubt indicates that such reflections may also contain an element of distortion, which explains why Achilles and Penthesilea thoroughly understand one another in Scene 15, while totally misread each other immediately afterwards.

Just as Penthesilea may change from one pre-formed role to another, so Achilles seems to alternate between the Greek stereotype shared by the male minor characters and roles that reflect, instead, aspects of Penthesilea. On the one hand, he is the brutal killer of Hector who openly vows to treat her similarly; on the other, he three times lays aside his weapons in the play and assumes a role that corresponds to the more tender aspects of Penthesilea. His failure to escape or defend himself before she kills him strains the credibility of the scene, because he appears locked into a conventionally 'feminine' behavior pattern at the expense of his own survival (SW I, 412f).

---

26 Sigrid Lange, 'Kleists *Penthesilea*. Geschlechterparadigmen. Die Frau als Projektionsfigur männlicher Identität – oder doch nicht?,' in *Weimarer Beiträge*, vol 37 (5), 1991, p. 709: 'Somit wäre die Identität dieses Staates in der Leerstelle zwischen einem Nicht-Mehr und Noch-Nicht zu beschreiben, die die Zerreißprobe bis in das Individuum hinein radikalisiert: mit einer Brust als "Sitz der jungen, lieblichen Gefühle" (2013) und einer fehlenden, die dem Bogen Platz schafft, sind die Amazonen halb liebende Frau, halb tötender Mann und führen darin ein Leben zwischen Zukunft und Vergangenheit, das seinen Ort in der Gegenwart nicht festhalten kann.'

Achilles thus seems, at best, a hybrid figure, lacking the consistency of both the male and female minor characters. He and Penthesilea seem linked by a bond, of which neither is clearly aware, that has about it something of the futility of Narcissus' desire for his own reflection. Penthesilea's cannibalism, which may be read as an attempt to assimilate the imagined object of desire directly into the body when all other communication has failed, is thus lamented by her in retrospect, when she addresses Achilles' corpse, as a failure of language:

> Du Ärmster aller Menschen, du vergibst mir!
> Ich habe mich, bei Diana, bloß versprochen,
> Weil ich der raschen Lippe Herr nicht bin;
> Doch jetzt sag ich dir deutlich wie ichs meinte:
> Dies, du Geliebter, wars, und weiter nichts.
>   *Sie küßt ihn.*   (SW I, 425 f)

From this it is not easy to extract one generalized statement about gender roles in the play. The moments of intense communication between Achilles and Penthesilea in Scene 15 strongly suggest that Kleist posits an ideal of human relationships outside both social frameworks in which the one is subordinate and 'follows' the other. But this is placed in no clear relation to the extreme savagery of which both are capable, whose Leitmotiv is, from the early scenes of the play, the death of Hector. Penthesilea's obsession with it may be linked to the destructiveness inherent in a state that has institutionalized self-mutilation and the killing of all male children born to the Amazons; but within her own self-representations, the humane and the destructive seem to exist side by side without any mediation, just as she is depicted in the early scenes as exhibiting, at one moment, all the savagery of a beast of prey in her pursuit of Achilles, while in another she spares his life for no apparent reason.

In his essay 'Goethe and the Avoidance of Tragedy,' Erich Heller writes of *Iphigenie auf Tauris* that 'Iphigenie simply embodies the belief that the gods cannot fail her by contradicting her own convictions of what is good and necessary. Thus she stands for the impossibility of tragedy.'[27] Since the text of Kleist's *Penthesilea* alludes to that of Goethe's drama, and since it is generally recognized that this intertextuality is linked to an intention on Kleist's part to reverse the terms in which Classical Antiquity is presented, we must ask, by way of conclusion, in what terms Kleist renders his own tragedy possible? I have

27 Erich Heller, 'Goethe and the Avoidance of Tragedy,' *The Disinherited Mind*, Cambridge, 1952, p. 45.

argued elsewhere against the view of *Iphigenie auf Tauris* as a drama of intellectual liberation that progresses from myth to rationality, and shown that the mythical discourse is sustained till the end.[28] The contrast to *Penthesilea* is not that the world of Goethe's drama forsakes the structures of myth, whereas Kleist reinstates them, but that reconciliation is for Goethe an acceptable variant of the mythical discourse, whereas Kleist's text excludes from the outset all possibilities of mediation. Moreover, Goethe has confined gross violence to the history of the house of Atreus, whereas Kleist not only sets his play on a battlefield, but enshrines violence both in the divine realm and in the society that has formed Penthesilea. Whether one regards the gods as conflicting imperatives that she has internalized or as the distant spectators of whom Prothoe speaks (SW I, 421), their significance for human action must include the uncompromising destructiveness of Mars as 'Vertilgergott,' whose brides and daughters the Amazons proudly name themselves.

Kleist's mythical discourse is not *qualitatively* different from Goethe's. The significant distinctions consist, first, in the fact that Kleist makes violence all-pervasive, setting no area of experience aside where reconciliation may be permanent; and second, that he eschews the extreme selectivity of Goethe's dramatic world. While Goethe's Iphigenie evinces no sexual desires at all, Penthesilea confesses to 'Begierden, die, wie loßgelassne Hunde,/ . . . aller Feldherrn Rufen, überschrein!' (SW I, 362). Whilst Iphigenie's Olympians can be imagined as a crew of fair-dealers, Kleist lends Mars a truly frightening presence in his text and leaves the reader or audience to speculate on the enigmatic tension between him and Aphrodite. While there is no obstacle to Iphigenie's embodying only truth in her own person, Penthesilea is made to embody so many conflicting values and energies that she is driven from one representation to another by inner 'enemies' or 'contradictions.' I suggest that this restless movement is essential to create correspondences between her divided self and the heterogeneous world of the play that will cease to exist with her suicide.

George Steiner's criticism of the text is that this leads to excesses that lessen the dramatic effect, and in this he is not far from Goethe's criticism of the play.[29] But in Kleist's terms, excess is realism. The selectivity that allows Iphigenie to relegate violence to the background and

---

28 Cf. Kathryn Brown and Anthony Stephens, '"Hinübergehn und unser Haus entsühnen." Die Ökonomie des Mythischen in Goethes *Iphigenie*,' in *JbSchG* XXXII, 1988, pp. 94-115.

29 George Steiner, *The Death of Tragedy*, pp. 227f.: 'But the play has the vices of its great power. It cries havoc so relentlessly that it turns into an exalted piece of *grand guignol*. Like much of German romantic art, it carries too far the conceit that love and death are kindred.'

affirm a divine order free of conflict, deception, and cruelty, thus effectively making the world of the play adapt itself to her preferred vision of it, is rejected by Kleist, who insists that if an individual truly is to mirror a whole world, then theirs is not the choice as to what it will contain or exclude. For Kleist, in contradiction to both Weimar Classicism and the Romanticism of writers such as Novalis, an individual who mirrors a whole world will do so at a terrible cost, for the only cosmos Kleist deemed credible could not exclude the incoherence of contemporary European history, as he saw it in his letters. This, in turn, must transfer itself to a psyche already riven by its own conflicts. To such a vision, tragedy was not merely possible – it was inevitable. Where Kleist left realism behind was in expecting Goethe to accept a critique of what he had created in his *Iphigenie* that was couched in such uncompromising terms.

6

Das Käthchen von Heilbronn

Penthesilea was the last play Kleist was to designate a tragedy. The next play he completed, *Das Käthchen von Heilbronn*, was begun by late autumn 1807 and finished by June the following year.[1] It was first performed in Vienna and then published as a book in Leipzig in 1810. The very factors that made it the most popular of Kleist's works on the 19th-century German stage render it the most difficult of his dramas to interpret today. Given the sheer incomprehension that largely determined the reception of *Penthesilea* for roughly its first century as a published work, this claim may appear, at first sight, unlikely, but there is a fundamental difference in the problems each text presents to a reader or audience. *Penthesilea* directly challenges most of the dramatic conventions prevailing at the time through its radical innovations, and the negative ending reverses a basic principle of tragedy, namely the affirmation of a world order despite the fall of the tragic hero or heroine.

Penthesilea also tends to challenge our understanding by the heterogeneity of its frames of reference, but all of this is contained and rendered assimilable by the fact that the direction of the text is perfectly clear throughout: it begins as a new kind of tragedy, anticipates its own conclusion in a variety of ways, and carries this tragic intention through rigorously. There is none of the mingling of genres that marks Kleist's other plays, and his persistent tendency to subvert the convention within which he is working is, in this case, limited to a sustained attack on the conventional expectations of tragic form in contemporary Germany.

Das Käthchen von Heilbronn poses the problem that its frames of reference are, if anything, more heterogeneous than those of *Penthesilea*, while this effect is multiplied, rather than contained, by its mixing genres to a greater extent than any of Kleist's other dramas. Perhaps as a reaction to the puzzlement and rejection that greeted *Penthesilea,* Kleist returned to the idea of writing a popular success, as he had once intended *Die Familie Schroffenstein* to be. Certainly the

1 KW II, pp. 859-65.

overtly 'Romantic' trappings and various other concessions to contemporary fashion made the play seem accessible in a sense that *Penthesilea* clearly was not.[2] However, the then fashionable aspects of the work are only the beginning of the problems it presents to a modern interpretation. For Kleist's penchant for mingling genres, as a means of subverting the ostensible intention of a text, is taken even further in *Das Käthchen von Heilbronn* than it is in *Die Familie Schroffenstein*. The result has been a prolonged debate on how the play may best be labelled.[3] There is more at stake in this than mere classification, for on the decision hinges an implicit coding of the whole text into dominant and subordinate aspects. This, in turn, establishes global understandings that may be quite insensitive to specific transitions within the work, leading to fundamental disagreements as to whether the main character is ovecome with happiness or simply crushed by the weight of events in the closing moments of the play.[4]

The chief difficulty with *Das Käthchen von Heilbronn* is that the text does not establish an internal criterion that might help to discriminate among a number of alternative readings. Rather, it may be seen as a work that remains in suspension in two senses: first, in its lack of firm allegiance to any specific genre, so that even the stamp placed on the text by its ending need not be regarded as a final determination; and second, in terms of the image of humanity it offers, since, as Gerhard Schulz has observed, this ultimately hovers in a field of tension created by several clear polarities.[5]

Once more, the metaphor of a palimpsest, which I have used to indicate the layering effect achieved in other plays by Kleist, may illustrate

2 Cf. Kleist's letter to the publisher Johann Friedrich Cotta of 7 June 1808: 'Ich würde, in diesem Jahre, das *Käthchen von Heilbronn* dazu bestimmen, ein Stück, das mehr in die romantische Gattung schlägt, als die übrigen' SW II, 813.

3 A summary of such designations is given by Fritz Martini, '*Das Käthchen von Heilbronn* – Heinrich von Kleists drittes Lustspiel?,' in *JbSchG* XX, 1976, pp. 420-9.

4 Cf. Fritz Martini, ibid., pp. 445f: 'Käthchens Ohnmacht des Leidens kehrt wieder als Schwindel der Beglückung. . . . Die wütende Enttäuschung der Thurnecks, der Fluch Kunigundes und der Fluch des Grafen über die "Giftmischerin", die Überwältigung Käthchens in der Ohnmacht grenzenloser Seligkeit geben dem Lustspielschema des glücklichen Abschlusses, der über die Bösen richtet und die Guten nach Leiden und Täuschung zu paradiesischem Triumph führt, die letzten kräftigen Spielakzente.'; for a contrary view, cf. Lilian Hoverland, *Heinrich von Kleist und das Prinzip der Gestaltung*, Königstein/Ts., 1978, p. 87.

5 Gerhard Schulz, *Die deutsche Literatur. Zweiter Teil*, p. 654: 'Nirgends in Kleists Werk ist wohl die Zwischenstellung des Menschen zwischen Göttlichkeit und Animalität oder Marionettenhaftigkeit mit so vielen Bildern und in so vielen Variationen dargestellt wie in diesem Drama. Himmel und Erde, Kaiser und Waffenschmied, Engel und Teufelin, Feuer und Wasser schließlich . . . weisen allesamt auf diese Dualitäten hin, zwischen denen die Menschen sich bewegen müssen und aus denen als letzter sicherer Ausweg allerdings nur der Tod erscheint.'

the problems of reading this text. Just as *Die Familie Schroffenstein* is, superficially, a chivalric melodrama in the popular style, so *Das Käthchen von Heilbronn* presents itself first as a variation on the same convention, enriched by many elements which had since become popularly 'Romantic.' Contiguous to this is the level on which some, but not all, of these modish elements are exaggerated into parody. Beyond these lie the dimensions with which recent interpretations concern themselves and which elicit more serious consideration, such as the potential for a tragic outcome, similar to that of Alkmene in *Amphitryon*, which is present in Käthchen's situation, but only partially explored. A single field of reference may occupy more than one level. Thus, in some respects, the 'fairytale' aspects of the work may be taken as parodistic; in others, Kleist uses them as a means to access states of consciousness and feeling that eluded traditional dramatic conventions. It is probably this latter technique that accounts for E. T. A. Hoffmann's enthusiasm for the play and his linking it with 'the essence of Romanticism.'[6] His words also suggest an ability to experience the vagaries of the plot and gaps in the motivation of characters positively, as a dream-logic enjoyed in a state of 'somnambulism.' This is a pleasure denied most critical readings of the text today, which deploy the whole arsenal of discursive logic in a vain effort to force it to cohere on at least one of its levels.

The more serious dimensions of the text are sustained by the suffering of Käthchen herself. No matter how bizarre or hyperbolical the action or language may become, the presentation of the main character contains a substrate of suffering, which is presented without undue embellishment or exaggeration and to which the text always recurs. This clearly relates *Das Käthchen von Heilbronn* to *Penthesilea*.

For critical studies of the work, *Das Käthchen von Heilbronn* has been indissolubly linked to *Penthesilea* by two statements in Kleist's letters.[7] In the wealth of exegesis these remarks have attracted, it is rarely observed that both statements are defensive, seeking to use the recipient's capacity to accept one work to counteract in advance a possi-

---

6 E. T. A. Hoffmann, *Briefwechsel*, ed. Friedrich Schnapp, vol. 1, Munich, 1967, p. 335: 'Sie können denken, wie mich das "Käthchen" begeistert hat; nur drei Stücke haben auf mich einen gleichen tiefen Eindruck gemacht – das "Käthchen", "Die Andacht zum Kreuze" und "Romeo und Julie" – sie versetzten mich in eine Art poetischen Somnambulismus, in dem ich das Wesen der Romantik in mancherlei herrlichen leuchtenden Gestaltungen deutlich wahrzunehmen und zu erkennen glaubte!'

7 To Marie von Kleist in late autumn 1807: 'Jetzt bin ich nur neugierig, was Sie zu dem Käthchen von Heilbronn sagen werden, denn das ist die Kehrseite der Penthesilea, ihr andrer Pol, ein Wesen, das ebenso mächtig ist durch gänzliche Hingebung, als jene durch Handeln.' SW II, 797; to Heinrich Joseph von Collin on 8 December 1808: 'Denn wer das Käthchen liebt, dem kann die Penthesilea nicht ganz unbegreiflich sein, sie gehören ja wie das + und – der Algebra zusammen, und sind ein und dasselbe Wesen, nur unter entgegengesetzen Beziehungen gedacht' SW II, 818.

bly hostile reception of the other, and that in each case a different work is defended. Therefore, it is false to assume that Kleist's remarks are sovereign, final verdicts on both plays. It is equally misguided simply to set out to prove in what respects they are right. For Penthesilea is not the only one of Kleist's heroines whom Käthchen resembles. There are clear similarities to others in earlier plays who are, at first glance, more credible. Like Agnes in *Die Familie Schroffenstein*, Eve in *Der zerbrochne Krug*, and Alkmene in *Amphitryon*, Käthchen is at the mercy of pronouncedly masculine power figures, and her capacity to withstand the force of their manipulative strategies is equally doubtful.

Like Agnes, she is reduced to silence for long stretches of the play and ends it very much as a puppet directed by her lover. Like Eve, her innocence at times verges on a caricature of social inferiority, whilst all sophistication passes to those male figures in whom power resides. Like Alkmene, she is subjected to interrogations and ordeals, against whose cruelty she protests. The ending of both plays is ostensibly a masculine apotheosis that leaves the main female character unconscious or speechless.

From this perspective, Käthchen's kinship to Penthesilea may not be immediately obvious, and Kleist's description of both figures as 'mächtig' is in itself puzzling. It is easy to see Penthesilea as a driven victim of the conflicting forces within her and of the rapid course of events. For most of the play, she does not so much 'act' as react, and her slaying of Achilles takes place in 'madness.' Käthchen, moreover, is not incapable of making initiatives, as demonstrated in Act III, Scene 6, when she very sensibly takes it upon herself to seek out Graf Wetter vom Strahl to warn him of an impending attack on the castle of Thurneck. If 'mächtig' in Kleist's letter is meant to indicate merely the potential power of a figure over an audience or reader, it is easier to accept at face value than any attribution of power within the fictional world. But many questions remain.

The sentence in the letter to Collin, which appears to assign Käthchen to the positive pole and Penthesilea to the negative, has been endlessly interpreted to no very conclusive result.[8] Käthchen's frequent lapses into passivity or incomprehension make elaborations of this reading hard to swallow. Penthesilea's feelings are in no way less strong than those of Käthchen's, and her urgent hunger for emancipation from the stereotyped roles the text forces on her is surely as 'positive' as anything in *Das Käthchen von Heilbronn*. Moreover, Penthesilea's suicide is, paradoxically, understandable as a belated winning through to auton-

---

8 For some examples see Valentine C. Hubbs, 'The Plus and Minus of Penthesilea and Käthchen,' in *Seminar*, vol. 6 (3), 1970, p. 194; Albrecht Sieck, *Kleists Penthesilea*, p. 84; Dennis Dyer, '"Plus and Minus" in Kleist,' in *Oxford German Studies*, 2, 1967, pp. 75-86.

omy, thus a resolution of the conflicts that have tended to make her an object throughout the action. It is negative in the sense that her world dies with her, leaving nothing but a helpless appeal to a humanism that is conspicuously lacking among the authorities of the play, but the noisily creaking machinery of the contrived ending to *Das Käthchen von Heilbronn* is scarcely any more 'positive,' once one begins to scrutinize its terms.

Kleist's statement to Collin may mean no more than that Käthchen and Penthesilea are extreme examples of the female psyche, as he conceived it, and complementary by virtue of their extremity. Kleist's subtitles for the printed version of the play, 'Die Feuerprobe/ ein großes historisches Ritterschauspiel,' may equally be taken with a pinch of salt, for they seem intended mainly to enhance the play's popular appeal. 'Ordeal by fire' is, ultimately, the least of Käthchen's trials, since an angel conveniently appears to rescue her, and the episode adds very little to what has already been shown of her character. The interrogations and other abuses to which Graf Wetter vom Strahl subjects her are more harrowing and, appropriately, elicit Käthchen's loud protests. As Hinrich C. Seeba summarizes in his commentary, the 'historical' dimension of the play is riddled with anachronisms that distribute the action over a period between the 13th century and the end of the 17th.[9] Source studies have produced equally disparate results, and the play is no more 'historical' than Shakespeare's *A Midsummer Night's Dream*. The social and family structures, like those in Kleist's other dramas, reflect contemporary preoccupations, and he seems to have gone out of his way to make his version of Medieval Germany as diffuse as possible.

Kleist could make very precise historical allusions when he wanted to. The scattering of historical allusions over several centuries is surely a sign that the medieval decor is a setting for experiments with characterization in the terms of Kleist's own age, just as the inconsistencies in the internal chronology of the action are rightly seen as an indication that the important events of the play occur in a psychological frame of reference that is not governed by strict temporality.[10] In attaching the label 'historisch' to a play whose plot has no confirmed sources, Kleist was doing nothing extraordinary for the practices of the time, since Clemens Brentano was to include the epithet 'historisch-romantisch' in

9 KW II, 1050.
10 Cf. Hinrich C. Seeba's commentary on the chronology, KW II, 1050. As a final discouragement for readers concerned with making things add up, a monastery of the Augustinians in Act III, Scene 1, (SW I, 478) turns Dominican in Act III, Scene 4, (SW I, 484). Despite William C. Reeve's recent interpretation, '"O du – wie nenn ich dich?": Names in Kleist's *Käthchen von Heilbronn*', in *German Life and Letters*, vol. 41 (2), 1988, pp. 83-98, I think much the same applies to the mixture of 'significant' and ordinary names for the characters.

the subtitle of his drama *Die Gründung Prags*, which freely varies its source material.

While it was possible for Wilhelm Grimm to praise the work's being 'aus *einem* Gusse' without mounting a long defense of the apparent inconsistencies,[11] modern interpretations often fall into the trap of engaging in an excess of special pleading so as to bring the text much closer to logical discourse than is really the case. Shoring up the evident dislocations in the play with discursive scaffolding seems to me to work against this text's elusive uniqueness. If Kleist had wanted the dramatic form to be as convergent as that of *Penthesilea*, he would surely have made it so. Not every disparity in the text can be glossed over as an unfortunate concession to popular taste. Rather, the improbabilities and discontinuities seem to take on a life of their own, thrusting themselves on the reader or audience in a manner that demands they be accepted for what they are, rather than be briskly explained away. I suggest that the essence of the text lies in the tension it maintains between its conventional and experimental aspects.

One innovative interpretation, which has been influential in the last decade, is that of Gerd Ueding's.[12] Like many of his predecessors, Ueding concedes the parodistic, ambiguous, and labyrinthine quality of the world of the play, but breaks new ground by finding its unity in a 'world of imagery' for which Kunigunde, not Käthchen, is the model.[13] There is a lot to be said in favor of this view, not least its paradoxical blending of the dissonances usually registered in the text into a new kind of unity, that of aesthetic artifice. Ueding is quite right to locate the 'core' of this 'world of imagery' in the dream that Käthchen and Graf Wetter vom Strahl experience in different places on the same night, long before the play's action begins.[14] He also correctly stresses the power that traditional 'idols,' such as Eve, Helen of Troy, and Cleopatra, exert within the text.[15]

I differ with Ueding on two fundamental issues. First, having defined the 'world of imagery' as one lacking both 'security' and 'objective

11 KN, 303f.

12 Gerd Ueding, 'Zweideutige Bilderwelt: *Das Käthchen von Heilbronn,*' *Kleists Dramen*, ed. Walter Hinderer, pp. 172-87.

13 Ibid., pp. 174f: 'Daher ist das teuflische Fräulein Kunigunde von Thurneck auch mehr als das abermals kolportierte Hexenbild des Märchens; sie ist eine poetologische Figur, an der Kleist sowohl sein Verfahren wie auch die Zweideutigkeit des Produkts demaskiert . . . Kleist konstruiert ein ganzes Weltbild, doch es hat nichts mit dem des Mittelalters zu tun, ist ihm sogar schroff entgegengesetzt: es repräsentiert die Welt als eine Welt von Bildern, als menschliches Kunstprodukt, dem jegliche Sicherheit mangelt und keine objektive Wahrheit zukommt.'

14 Ibid., p. 177.

15 Ibid., p. 179.

truth,' Ueding reverses his own position in order to present Käthchen as 'liberating' her future husband from 'illusion' at the end,[16] by illogically re-installing the criterion of truth.[17] Against this is the fact that Graf Wetter vom Strahl goes out of his way at the end of the drama to confuse Käthchen once more about his intention to marry her, so that she appears in the final scene not as any liberating agent in her own right, but as a victim of patriarchal structures. The conclusion renders her inarticulate, and she loses consciousness before reviving for the final procession. I have difficulty seeing this as a 'victory for clear awareness and the start of a new world-history.' Moreover, to regard the ending as an apotheosis of truth, even one qualified by being 'im schönen Schein,' creates an aura about the most embarrassing aspects of the plot, such as the miraculous cure of the Emperor's amnesia. I find it preferable to see the closing moments of the play as strongly marked by a tension between Käthchen's being crushed by her awareness that Graf Wetter vom Strahl may indeed want to marry her – but is still no more sparing of her feelings than in the scenes before the secret court – and the power exerted by the stereotype of the ceremonial procession.

The second major issue on which I differ from Ueding relates to his assertion of a simple dominance of the 'world of imagery' over the rest of the play.[18] There is, in fact, a 'polar opposite' to the metaphorical dimension of the play within the thematics. It is in no sense the world of dream, but the simple fact of Käthchen's suffering, which no amount of extravagant imagery can disguise. That she should be reduced, in the final scenes, to a helplessness similar to that of Alkmene at the end of *Amphitryon* suggests that the tension between these antitheses persists from her first interrogation by Graf Wetter vom Strahl before the court to beyond the conclusion.

Ueding implies that the quasi-autonomous quality of the imagery is a poetological innovation Kleist first introduced in *Das Käthchen von Heilbronn*, but the difference between the imagery here and in *Die Familie Schroffenstein* is purely one of degree. The discrepancy between figurative discourse and any factual substrate is an explicit theme in Kleist's first drama, as is the tendency for images to assume dominance, in the minds of the characters, over their concrete situation.[19] But this does not mean that metaphor obliterates all else.

16 Ibid., p. 183.
17 Ibid., p. 185: 'Im märchenhaften Ausgang des Stückes wird das Ergebnis dieser Bilderlehre vorweggenommen: es feiert die Erkennbarkeit des Wahren im schönen Schein, den Sieg des hellen Bewußtseins und den Anfang einer neuen Weltgeschichte.'
18 Ibid, p. 175: 'In diesem Drama Kleists fehlt aber der Gegenpol zur Bilder- und Scheinwelt völlig, auch der Traum ist in ihr aufgehoben, und so geht ihm jede Sicherheit ab.'
19 See above p.34ff.

For all the transformations the language of the play works upon the figure of Agnes, she regains in death her factual identity as the daughter of Sylvester. Similarly, the Käthchen who has been elevated by imperial decree to Katharina von Schwaben and the Emperor's own daughter is, at the end of the play, in no way immune to the manipulations of Graf Wetter vom Strahl. There is a grim irony in the fact that his final pretence that she is to have herself dressed for someone else's wedding, only to reverse this deception in the final scene, repeats the pattern of humiliation followed by a forcible rise in status established in Act I, Scene 2. There, the president of the secret court, Graf Otto, accuses Graf vom Strahl of gratuitous cruelty. The latter justifies himself with the words: 'Ihr Herrn, was ich getan, das tat ich nur,/ Sie mit Triumph hier vor euch zu erheben!' (SW I, 448). The same sequence recurs at the conclusion of the drama, with Käthchen's expressions of bewilderment and incomprehension replacing Graf Otto's direct accusation. This surely signifies that the ending does not entirely dissolve 'im schönen Schein,' but is at best a deeply flawed resolution.

I have dwelt on Ueding's interpretation because his premises, if not his conclusions, are apposite, and because the issues he raises lead into the reading of the play I offer here. At the outset, I must emphasize that it is very difficult, in a discursive analysis, to preserve the essential looseness of plot and motivation for two reasons: first, Kleist shapes individual sequences of *Das Käthchen von Heilbronn* so that they cohere, and tends to set the dislocations of the plot *between* such segments. It is thus the progressive overview of the action that becomes blurred, while the focus on particular scenes may remain quite sharp; second, critical argument tends to impose its own convergent effect on the objects of discussion with the result that it is hard to preserve the full, suspensive ambiguity of a text such as *Das Käthchen von Heilbronn*.

In considering Act I, it is first necessary to ask what guidelines the text establishes to direct the response of an audience or reader. The *coup de théâtre* produced by a secret court, meeting in an underground cave, with hooded judges and ample opportunity for impressive lighting effects, is sustained, indeed magnified, by the hyperbolical language in which the 'Vehmgericht' presents itself:

Wir, Richter des hohen, heimlichen Gerichts, die wir, die irdischen Schergen Gottes, Vorläufer der geflügelten Heere, die er in seinen Wolken mustert, den Frevel aufzusuchen, da, wo er, in der Höhle der Brust, gleich einem Molche verkrochen, vom Arm weltlicher Gerechtigkeit nicht aufgefunden werden kann: wir rufen dich, Theobald Friedborn, ehrsamer und vielbekannter Waffenschmied aus Heilbronn auf, deine Klage anzubringen gegen Friedrich, Graf Wetter vom Strahle. . . .   (SW I, 431)

The effect of the metaphors is to heighten the solemnity of the visual representation and, at the same time, to open the frame of reference for what follows to include the cosmic mythology of the Last Judgement. This is a recurrent motif throughout Kleist's work, emerging in such disparate guises as in one of Adam's red herrings in *Der zerbrochne Krug*[20] or in the tableau at the gruesome conclusion of *Der Findling*.[21] In a sense, every inquest in Kleist's work is a simulacrum of the Last Judgement, since this expansion of the frame of reference enables him to experiment with those tensions between absolute principles and their becoming relative in practice, which he found of lasting fascination. Here, the hyperbole creates a setting in which the absolute quality of Käthchen's devotion to Graf Wetter vom Strahl becomes plausible, precisely because the self-representation of the court, Theobald's accusation, and the accused's response are all couched in equally extreme terms.

At the same time, the parodistic dimension is opened in Theobald's first speeches by one of the many passages in the play in which the text calls sceptical attention to itself:

Wenn ihr mich gleichwohl reden lassen wollt, so denke ich es durch eine schlichte Erzählung dessen, was sich zugetragen, dahin zu bringen, daß ihr aufbrecht, und ruft: unsrer sind dreizehn und der vierzehnte ist der Teufel! zu den Türen rennt und den Wald, der diese Höhle umgibt, auf dreihundert Schritte im Umkreis, mit euren Taftmänteln und Federhüten besäet.   (SW I, 432)

An audience can be reasonably expected to perceive that what follows is anything but 'a simple narrative.' Theobald's language creates an aura around Käthchen: 'als ob der Himmel von Schwaben sie erzeugt, und, von seinem Kuß geschwängert, die Stadt . . . sie geboren hätte' (SW I, 433) – and continues to embellish this with rhetorical bravura for some time before he describes her encounter with Graf Wetter vom Strahl. Moreover, Theobald's narrative is ineffective. Far from producing the bizarre behavior in the judges that he fantasizes, it merely leads them to hand over proceedings to the accused, who not only crushes Theobald but also arrogates to himself, in the course of his interrogation of Käthchen, all the authority of the court. Finally, the

---

20 'Gib Gotte, hörst du, Herzchen, gib, mein Seel,/ Ihm und der Welt, gib ihm was von der Wahrheit./ Denk, daß du hier vor Gottes Richtstuhl bist,/ Und daß du deinen Richter nicht mit Leugnen,/ . . . betrüben mußt' SW I, 214.

21 'Hier stand ein Priester und schilderte ihm, mit der Lunge der letzten Posaune, alle Schrecknisse der Hölle, in die seine Seele hinbzufahren im Begriff war; dort ein anderer, den Leib des Herrn, das heilige Entsühnungsmittel in der Hand, und pries ihm die Wohnungen des ewigen Friedens' SW II, 214.

excessive detail of what Theobald envisages the judges doing as a result of his story signals a parodistic effect, one often employed elsewhere in the text.[22] In all of these instances, the abundance of rhetoric and imagery, far from altering events, loses all instrumental function and may even seem an end in itself. The excessive quality of such speeches is easily recognized, since the language of the text as a whole is not uniformly dysfunctional in this manner, but, as Graf Wetter vom Strahl's interrogation of Käthchen shows, can be an extremely effective weapon.

Käthchen's first appearance has thus been thoroughly prepared by narratives that are extravagant both in what they say and in how they say it. The world of the play's first scene is one of angels and devils, miracles and curses, wild beasts and witches, but, above all, rhetoric:

> rinnt, ihr Säfte der Hölle, tröpfelnd aus Stämmen und Stielen gezogen, fallt, wie ein Katarakt ins Land, daß der erstickende Pestqualm zu den Wolken empordampft; fließt und ergießt euch durch alle Röhren des Lebens, und schwemmt, in allgemeiner Sündflut, Unschuld und Tugend hinweg! (SW I, 440)

Innocence and virtue, however, seem safely embodied in Käthchen from her first entrance. Having survived what Gerhard Schulz rightly denotes as a virtual death in her leap from a window, 'dreißig Fuß hoch, mit aufgehobenen Händen, auf das Pflaster der Straße nieder' (SW I, 436),[23] and emerging from such an other-worldly context, the very normalcy of her suffering throughout the Graf's interrogation may come as something of a shock. Stranger still, the fact that the judges of the secret court largely abstain from rhetoric after Graf Otto's first two speeches comes to display its appositeness, for these sinister figures reveal themselves as adherents of a down-to-earth humanism that is an echo of the ethical conventions of the German Enlightenment.

The theme of inhumane treatment is introduced by Käthchen before the interrogation has really commenced: ' – Du quälst mich grausam, daß ich weinen möchte!' (SW I, 442). It is taken up again by the presiding judge when Käthchen shows distinct signs of distress: 'Ihr quält das Kind zu sehr' (SW I, 447). Another judge reinforces this immediately: 'Das nenn ich menschlich nicht verfahren.' When Graf Wetter vom Strahl objects, the reprimand becomes even stronger:

22 Further examples are the verbosity of Graf Wetter vom Strahl's monologues in Act II, Scene 1, and Act IV, Scene 2; the Rheingraf's over-ornate statement of his intentions in Act III, Scene 3; the absurdly circumstantial fire-alarm given by the Nachtwächter in Act III, Scene 7.

23 Gerhard Schulz, *Die deutsche Literatur, Zweiter Teil*, p. 654.

Ihr sollt das Kind befragen, ist die Meinung,
Nicht mit barbarischem Triumph verhöhnen.
Seis, daß Natur Euch solche Macht verliehen:
Geübt wie Ihrs tut, ist sie hassenswürdger,
Als selbst die Höllenkunst, der man euch zeiht.   (SW I, 448)

In the strange transfer of power from the judges to Graf Wetter vom
Strahl that occurs in the course of the interrogation, it is left to Käthchen
– 'Du stießest mich mit Füßen von dir' (SW I, 449) – to maintain an
awareness of the cruelty of the hero's conduct. At the conclusion of the
scene, Graf Otto, the presiding judge, reasserts the court's authority
when he requests Graf Wetter vom Strahl to adjust the balance of power
he has swung in his own favor:

Ihr zeigtet
Von der Gewalt, die Ihr hier übt, so manche
Besondre Probe uns; laßt uns noch eine,
Die größeste, bevor wir scheiden, sehn,
Und gebt sie ihrem alten Vater wieder.   (SW I, 452)

This confirms, first, that Graf Wetter vom Strahl has absorbed not
only the power of the court, but also all the paternal authority that might
be present in the situation; and second, that the judges still see their role
as defending the mean of Enlightened human values, a balance between
the extremes which the text has so far brought out so strongly. It also
emphasizes that there are two kinds of language at work in the play's fictional world: the highly ornate and metaphorical discourse of the beginning, which has a very tenuous hold on what actually happens but
conveys a wealth of associative meaning, and the discourse of power
whose efficacy these words and Graf Wetter vom Strahl's reply confirm.
   The tension between these modes of discourse is essential to the play
as a whole, and is maintained to the end. The Graf's monologue at the
commencement of Act II marks a fresh access of rhetorical elaboration,
but, in the same act, Kunigunde reveals skills in manipulating others
through language that are initially as effective as Graf Wetter vom
Strahl's takeover of the court. The Emperor's decree, read aloud by Graf
Wetter vom Strahl in Act V, Scene 11, wrenches the course of the plot
into the path required for the final pageant, and demonstrates to the
point of caricature that there is an instrumental mode of language that is
the antithesis of the autonomy toward which the text's figurative dimension tends.
   Thus there are so far two 'polar opposites' to what Ueding calls the
'Bilderwelt': a thematic level on which Käthchen's suffering is present-

ed neither in metaphorical nor cosmic terms, but rather within the framework of Enlightenment convention, and a linguistic mode in which words function perfectly as a means of exerting and transferring power. The two are not synonomous, since instrumental discourse is not bound to any specific contents, but both clearly contrast with the wealth of imagery pursued apparently for its own sake within the text. The tensions set up by these dual contrasting effects help maintain in suspension the semantics of the whole text, so that no one thematic area or mode of discourse achieves lasting dominance.

The remaining enigmas posed by the first act are the figure of Käthchen herself and the nature of the emotional bond between her and Graf Wetter vom Strahl. The narratives that precede Käthchen's first entrance achieve two main effects, for all their rhetorical overload. First, they suggest she is less at home in her role as Theobald's daughter than she is in a mythical realm. For she not only seems to be a 'child of heaven,' but also an inhabitant of an earthly paradise: 'gesund an Leib und Seele, wie die ersten Menschen . . ., ein Kind recht nach der Lust Gottes' (SW I, 432f.). Part of this incongruity with her social context anticipates her final elevation to the peak of the nobility: 'die Ritter, die durch die Stadt zogen, weinten, daß sie kein Fräulein war' (SW I, 433). Second, her behavior on first encountering Graf Wetter vom Strahl makes her the respository of a secret: 'und leichenbleich, mit Händen, wie zur Anbetung verschränkt, den Boden mit Brust und Scheitel küssend, stürzt sie vor ihm nieder, als ob sie ein Blitz niedergeschmettert hätte' (SW I, 435). This is intensified by the account of her leap from the window, miraculous survival, and subsequent fixation on the Graf. Significantly, Theobald's imagery here expands the frame of reference to suggest that her otherness may be not only more than human, but also less: 'wie ein Hund, der von seines Herren Schweiß gekostet, schreitet sie hinter ihm her' (SW I, 437).

Kleist employs the same technique as he used to introduce Penthesilea, although the worlds of the two plays are otherwise quite dissimilar. The Queen of the Amazons is first presented through long narratives, which establish her as a mystery before she appears on stage. One of the Greeks asks: 'Und niemand kann, was sie uns will, ergründen?' (SW I, 327) – to which the answer is negative, and will remain so for conventional modes of understanding, even beyond her suicide in the last moments of the play. Theobald presents the mystery of Käthchen in almost identical terms: 'kein Mensch vermag das Geheimnis, das in ihr waltet, ihr zu entlocken' (SW I, 436), and it is again the case that no matter what the text reveals about her, the secret remains, and it is still cloaked in her inarticulate helplessness as she is marched to the altar in the play's final pageant. There is, for example,

nothing in the subsequent accounts of the dream she has shared with her
future husband that offers a discursive explanation of her suicidal leap
from the window. All connections between the dream and this event
remain essentially conjecture. A secret that is, paradoxically, both
known and intact had already been the object of Jupiter's interrogation
of Alkmene in *Amphitryon*; other female characters created by Kleist,
such as Elvire in *Der Findling*, continue this theme, even with similar
accompanying motifs.[24]

The latency of the secret is central to the interrogation in Act I, Scene
2, and is used to introduce a further ambivalence into the presentation of
Käthchen. She declares the court's intrusion on her secret to be inhumane, just as she has previously accused Graf Wetter vom Strahl of cruelty, thus linking the two kinds of power of which she is a victim:

KÄTHCHEN *in Staub niederfallend.*
Nimm mir, o Herr, das Leben, wenn ich fehlte!
Was in des Busens stillem Reich geschehn,
Und Gott nicht straft, das braucht kein Mensch zu wissen;
Den nenn ich grausam, der mich darum fragt! (SW I, 443f.)

Preserving the secret also leads her into an area that literature on the
play has ignored when delineating her character, namely duplicity.
Whilst a reader or audience is never told the reason for her suicidal
plunge, her setting off after Graf Wetter vom Strahl once her fractured
thighs have healed is clearly accounted for by her memory of the dream.
For unlike her amnesiac lover, she has apparently forgotten or repressed
nothing of it. Always prone to forgetting details of significance, Graf
Wetter vom Strahl seems to have lost touch with his own interrogation
of Käthchen before the secret court, since her reply is clearly quite different from the one he quotes later:[25]

Mein hoher Herr! Da fragst du mich zuviel.
Und läg ich so, wie ich vor dir jetzt liege,
Vor meinem eigenen Bewußtsein da:
Auf einem goldnen Richtstuhl laß es thronen,
Und alle Schrecken des Gewissens ihm,
In Flammenrüstungen, zur Seite stehn;
So spräche jeglicher Gedanke noch,
Auf das, was du gefragt: ich weiß es nicht.   (SW I, 444)

24 Cf. SW II, 212.
25 Cf. SW I, 504: 'So oft ich sie gefragt habe: Kathchen! Warum erschrakst du doch
so, als du mich zuerst in Heilbronn sahst? hat sie mich immer zerstreut angesehen, und
dann geantwortet: Ei, gestrenger Herr! Ihr wißts ja!'

While Käthchen may not 'know' the full significance of her dream, she does know whom she has seen in it, and she has Mariane's assurance that she is destined to marry a knight.[26] To withhold this information from the very person she recognizes from the dream is intelligible, in terms of guarding the secret at all costs, but contrary to her earlier protest that she will reveal all, if only Graf Wetter vom Strahl asks her: 'Wenn *du* es wissen willst, wohlan, so rede,/ Denn dir liegt meine Seele offen da!' (SW I, 444). Critics have been so eager to dilate upon the suggestions elsewhere in the text that she exists in a state of grace before the Fall, that no account has been taken of this inconsistency.[27]

Yet Käthchen's words present a clear image of a divided self, with parallels not only in *Penthesilea*, but also, surprisingly, in Adam's dream at the beginning of *Der zerbrochne Krug*.[28] Withholding the truth after agreeing to disclose it thus contributes to her distress throughout the interrogation, which ends with her fainting, and this can only be aggravated by the fact the the Graf's inquisitorial technique produces no less than four accusations that she is lying:

Du lügst mir Jungfrau? Willst mein wissen täschen?   (SW I, 444)

Nun seht, bei meiner Treu, die Lügnerin!   (SW I, 447)

Da schwört sie und verflucht
Sich, die leichtfertge Dirne, noch und meint,
Gott werd es ihrem jungen Blut vergeben!   (SW I, 447)

Nun denn! Da ists heraus! Da hat sie nun
Der Seelen Seligkeit sich weggeschworen!   (SW I, 447)

Ironically, this is all bluff and intimidation to extract from Käthchen details that have nothing to do with her dream at all, and thus form no part of the secret. Graf Wetter vom Strahl is intent on usurping the power of the court before which he stands accused, and demonstrating his power over Käthchen is chiefly a means to this end, but the weight of these words must oppress her because of what she *is* keeping back, namely her reason for following him.

26 '– Als ich zu Bett ging, da das Blei gegossen,/ In der Sylvesternacht, bat ich zu Gott,/ Wenns wahr wär, was mir die Mariane sagte,/ Möcht er den Ritter mir im Traume zeigen./ Und da erschienst du ja, um Mitternacht,/ Leibhaftig, wie ich jetzt dich vor mir sehe,/ Als deine Braut mich liebend zu begrüßen' SW I, 506f.

27 Cf, Gerd Ueding, 'Zweideutige Bilderwelt,' p. 182: 'Auch im Käthchen lebt das Bild der Eva fort, freilich der paradiesisch-unschuldigen, ganz im Stande der Natur lebenden.'; Hinrich C. Seeba's commentary: 'Käthchen's Weigerung, den Rock auch nur einen Millimeter anzuheben, unterstreicht das Paradox, daß sie zwar ein Wesen vor dem Sündenfall, aber doch nicht mehr ohne Scham ist.' KW II, 1034.

28 '– Mir träumt,' es hätt ein Kläger mich ergriffen,/ Und schleppte vor den Richtstuhl mich; und ich,/ Ich säße gleichwohl auf dem Richtstuhl dort . . .' SW I, 187.

If we now ask the vexed question of how best to describe the emotional bonds between Graf Wetter vom Strahl and Käthchen, then we have, in the foreground, the apparent simplicity of her complete devotion.[29] Yet even within the Romantic stereotype, things are not quite so clear, for there is no indication as to why the love itself may be freely confessed, whilst its origin in the dream must not be disclosed. A wealth of conjecture is possible here, depending on what brand of psychology, literary or clinical, one prefers. Käthchen may be patiently waiting for Graf Wetter vom Strahl – quite literally – to wake up to himself and link the girl who follows him with his own dream.[30] She may, alternatively, be willing to disclose the secret to him alone and refuse to share it with the court, thus revealing all he needs to suborn his accuser and his judges, but no more.

I suggest it is essential to the play's psychology that such questions should always have a plurality of answers, for Kleist could surely have made his motivations much more simple and explicit had he wanted to. As it is, an audience or reader is offered the Romantic trope of an absolute love, which precedes even a first meeting and is prefigured in a dream, and may accept it without enquiring further. Kleist's irony is then revealed in that attempts to go beyond this simplicity do not confirm the original impression, but rather encounter an unsuspected mixture of motives. This is even more the case with Graf Wetter vom Strahl.

The first act clearly brings out his incomprehension of Käthchen's behavior, but still more strongly his brutality toward her – 'Du stießest mich mit Füßen von dir' (SW I, 449) – and his strategic cruelty during the interrogation: 'Ihr quält das Kind zu sehr' (SW I, 447). I have elsewhere looked at this scene from the perspective of the theme of cruelty in Kleist's whole work, drawing parallels to the writings of de Sade and Baudelaire.[31]

It is hard to escape the conclusion that Kleist's counterpointing of Enlightenment humanism, through the protests against Graf Wetter vom Strahl's treatment of Käthchen, with an absolute love in Romantic terms

---

29 'DER GRAF VOM STRAHL. Du liebst mich?/ KÄTHCHEN. Herzlich!' (SW I, 452).

30 This would correlate with her reported words in Act IV, Scene 2: 'Ihr wißts ja!' (SW I, 504).

31 Anthony Stephens, '"Das nenn ich menschlich nicht verfahren". Skizze zu einer Theorie der Grausamkeit im Hinblick auf Kleist,' *Heinrich von Kleist*, ed. Dirk Grathoff, pp. 10-39. One passage from Baudelaire's *Journaux intimes* seems still particularly relevant as indicating the negative obverse of Romantic love: 'Je crois que j'ai déjà écrit dans mes notes que l'amour ressemblait fort à une torture ou à une opération chirurgicale . . . Quand même les deux amants seraient très épris et très pleins de désirs réciproques, l'un des deux sera toujours plus calme ou moins possédé que l'autre. Celui-là, ou celle-là, c'est l'opérateur, ou le bourreau; l'autre, c'est le sujet, la victime.' Charles Baudelaire. *Œuvres complètes*, ed. Claude Pichois, vol. 1, Paris, 1975, p. 651.

is meant to be subversive of *both* ideologies. The Graf wins, but the protests are not dismissed. His own justification: 'Ihr Herrn, was ich getan, das tat ich nur,/ Sie mit Triumph hier vor euch zu erheben!' (SW I, 448) does not silence the judges – nor should it, for it makes explicit the manipulative ruthlessness of the interrogation.

Käthchen is later to experience a further 'elevation' in the play through the decree of her newly discovered father, the Emperor, and we should be aware not only of the paternal flavor of the power Graf Wetter vom Strahl wields over her, but also of the ambiguities it may contain. Theobald has posed a question that reminds one of the destructive power of paternal authority in *Die Familie Schroffenstein*:

> Mußt ich vor dem Menschen nicht erbeben, der die Natur, in dem reinsten Herzen, das je geschaffen ward, dergestalt umgekehrt hat, daß sie vor dem Vater, zu ihr gekommen, seiner Liebe Brust ihren Lippen zu reichen, kreideweißen Antlitzes entweicht, wie vor dem Wolfe, der sie zerreißen will? (SW I, 440)

This is very much the language of Kleist's first drama, invoking a nature turned on its head, and associating human malevolence with beasts of prey. It may be overlooked among Theobald's many tirades, but, once recognized, it points to a kinship between the world of *Das Käthchen von Heilbronn* and the much more readily intelligible chaos of *Die Familie Schroffenstein*. It may, if nothing else, serve to make us sceptical about the unity and wholesomeness of nature in the later drama.[32]

To enquire further into Graf Wetter vom Strahl's motives in Act I is to embark on a sea of conjecture. It may well be that he unconsciously recognizes Käthchen as resembling the figure in his dream, and that his excessive treatment of her is explained by his suppressing this knowledge. It may equally be that his main concern is with putting Theobald and the 'Vehmgericht' in their places, and that he, incidentally, exhibits the same disregard for Käthchen's feelings as marks Adam's behavior toward Eve in *Der zerbrochne Krug* and Jupiter's toward Alkmene in *Amphitryon*. If we seek an explanation purely in terms of social inferiority and ascendance, then we must not forget that his deception of Käthchen at the end of Act V, after he has read the proclamation making her Katharina von Schwaben, is equally inconsiderate of her feelings. Tormenting Käthchen-become-princess with the same gratuitous callousness with which he tormented Käthchen the middle-class daugh-

---

32 The idea of Käthchen as a 'Naturwesen' has most recently been invoked by Hinrich C. Seeba, KW II, 950f.

ter may be Graf Wetter vom Strahl's closest approach to social impartiality.

I suggest Kleist's focus in this first act is on the tension between the readily acceptable trope of an honest nobleman, who has genuinely no idea why Käthchen is following his every step, and the dissonances set up by the cruel and excessive aspects of his actual behavior. In a framework so rich in hyperbole that virtually anything appears possible, Graf Wetter vom Strahl may strain the credibility of the convention he embodies without causing it to collapse entirely. The transition to the second act immediately places fresh strains on an audience's capacity to accept the character as plausible, for the savage inquisitor vanishes as if by magic, replaced by a man of sentiment, who opens the scene by hurling himself to the ground and weeping (SW I, 453).

The 'fairytale' aspect of the drama may be evident in this change. Folk tales are full of unmotivated cruelty, such as has occurred in the first act, and they also tend to ignore psychological coherence in favor of assembling sequences of narrative stereotypes.[33] Here, the outpouring of emotion in solitude is indeed a stereotype, not of genuine folk tales but of conventional dramatic sensibility, and thus the very abrupt transition may be assimilable in terms of Kleist's seeking feasible dramatic equivalents for 'fairytale' structures.

Yet what follows slides visibly into self-parody. Graf Wetter vom Strahl laments his incapacity to claim Käthchen as his own – 'Warum kann ich dich nicht mein nennen?' – and, incidentally, his own lack of a language to express his true feelings, but he does this in a torrent of rhetoric that makes Theobald's impeachment of him seem almost taciturn.[34] Language deploring the inadequacy of language is itself a familiar rhetorical trope, but the element of excess in this monologue shifts it clearly toward the absurd. All of Graf Wetter vom Strahl's imagery is secondhand. Even his venture into eroticism is straight from the Book of Esther:[35]

Warum kann ich dich nicht aufheben, und in das duftende Himmelbett tragen, das mir die Mutter daheim im Prunkgemach, aufgerichtet hat? Käthchen! Käthchen! Käthchen! Du, deren junge Seele, als sie heut nackt vor mir stand, von wollüstiger Schönheit

33 Cf. Vladimir Propp, *Morphologie du conte*, Paris, 1965, pp. 32f.
34 Cf. Gerhard Neumann, 'Hexenküche und Abendmahl,' p. 22.
35 Esther, II, 12-13: 'Now when every maid's turn was come to go in to King Ahasuerus, after that she had been twelve months, according to the manner of the women, (for so were the days of their purifications acomplished, to wit, six months with oil of myrrh, and six months with sweet odours, and with other things for the purifying of the women;)/ Then thus came every maiden unto the King; whatsoever she desired was given her to go with her out of the house of the women unto the King's house.'

gänzlich triefte, wie die mit Ölen gesalbte Braut eines Perserkönigs,
wenn sie, auf alle Teppiche niederregnend, in sein Gemach geführt
wird! (SW I, 454)

Graf Wetter vom Strahl's metamorphosis from the brilliant and
unscrupulous strategist of the previous act into the tearful would-be poet
of this scene places the same strain on the credibility of the characterization, in conventional terms, as do the sudden shifts in the behavior of the
two main characters in *Penthesilea*. Indeed, Kleist appears to be experi-
menting precisely with the degree of tension he may create between the
expectations aroused by the stereotype of the knightly hero, destined to
marry the heroine, and what the figure actually does and says.

The plot of Käthchen is essentially a middle-class fantasy: the elevation of a beautiful daughter of the respectable 'Bürgertum' to Princess of
Swabia and an aristocratic marriage, assisted by her being revealed as a
child of the Emperor's loins.[36] I suggest that Kleist is little concerned
with either endorsing or satirizing the ideology of this literary trope, for
all that his text appears to do both in different places. Rather, he seems
fascinated with the power the clichés of popular taste can exert on the
surface of the work, and with testing this power by opening the characterization to such dislocations and anarchic forces as Theobald's
rhetoric invokes at the play's beginning.

Theobald alleges so much and so wildly that an audience or reader
may soon begin to discount his invectives and hyperboles. But, as we
have seen, figurative language in Kleist, from *Die Familie
Schroffenstein* onward, is never used for mere decoration. Rather, the
metaphorical dimension of a text tends to create a fictional reality of its
own that then interacts on equal terms with the mechanics of the plot. It
is thus significant that Theobald is not the slightest convinced, as are the
judges, by Graf Wetter vom Strahl's demonstration that he has done
nothing to seduce Käthchen, but instead reiterates his original charge:

Ihr hochverehrten Herrn, ihr sprecht ihn schuldlos?
Gott sagt ihr, hat die Welt aus nichts gemacht;
Und er, der sie durch nichts und wieder nichts
Vernichtet, in das erste Chaos stürzt,
Der sollte nicht der leidge Satan sein? (SW I, 451)

It is surely worth considering, in the light of Graf Wetter vom
Strahl's astonishing transformation between the first and second acts,

---

36 Cf. Hans Mayer, *Heinrich von Kleist. Der geschichtliche Augenblick*, Pfullingen,
1962, pp. 15f. and Chris Cullen and Dorothea von Mücke, 'Love in Kleist's *Penthesilea*
and *Käthchen von Heilbronn*,' in *DVjs* 63, 1989, p. 492.

whether it is not the intention of the work to admit an element of 'das erste Chaos' into the psychology of the characters – under the cover of the so readily intelligible stereotypes of this fairytale of social elevation – in order to see what genuinely new facets of the human psyche are thus revealed. One of these could be the co-existence of desire and aggression in Graf Wetter vom Strahl's feelings toward Käthchen. Another could be the tension between her apparently complete subservience to him and her obstinate protection of her 'secret.' Thus the hero's ostensible chivalry may be seen as masking sexual impulses we would today term sadistic, while Käthchen's spurious 'openness' masks a strong reluctance to be penetrated in this manner.

Describing Käthchen's slow recovery from her injuries and her refusal to account for her action, Theobald says:

Hier liegt sie nun, auf dem Todbett, in der Glut des hitzigen Fiebers, sechs endlose Wochen, ohne sich zu regen. Keinen laut bringt sie hervor; auch nicht der Wahnsinn, dieser Dietrich aller Herzen, eröffnet das ihrige; kein Mensch vermag das Geheimnis, das in ihr waltet, zu entlocken. (SW I, 436)

Within the conventional plot, Käthchen certainly has a secret, the content of her dream and its link to the person of Graf Wetter vom Strahl, and we have seen how she perjures herself before the secret court to guard it. Beyond the purely conventional, there are many questions as to what motivates her actions, which the text simply leaves unanswered.

I suggest that Theobald's references to 'chaos' and 'madness' might encourage us to see the unconventional and genuinely mysterious aspects of the characterization as the unfolding of a subtext of psychic anarchy, kept under control by the stable sequences of a 'fairytale' plot. The resulting tensions give this experiment its lasting fascination, and may account for what Wilhelm Grimm described as the 'audacity' of the work.[37]

As further evidence for an experimental approach on Kleist's part, we may consider the two published versions of Graf Wetter vom Strahl's monologue at the beginning of the second act. In early 1809 Kleist published a substantial fragment of the play in his short-lived journal, *Phöbus*, while a full text was published in the autumn of 1810.[38] In the fragment, the soliloquy is even longer than in the first edition, and it is interesting to see what Kleist edited out.

---

37 'Schon aus dieser allgemeinen Andeutung läßt sich auf die Kühnheit dieser Dichtung schließen, die auch, wenn nicht alles Vorhergehende außerordentlicher Art wäre, und auf etwas Höheres die Erwartung spannte, in das gemein Abenteuerliche fallen und sich keinen Glauben erwerben würde.' LS, 304.
38 Cf. KW II, 854f.

Both versions begin with Graf Wetter vom Strahl throwing himself to the ground and weeping. They then express his dual frustrations at not being able to claim Käthchen as his own and having no adequate language to convey his feelings. Both end with his vision of the portraits of his male forebears expressing disapproval at the mere thought of his marrying a commoner, a prohibition to which the Graf, after a brief display of rebellion, acquiesces. Before the ancestors are invoked, the earlier version has a long passage, missing in the full text, which includes the following:

> War's nicht, als sie sich da, in ihrer lieblichen Unschuld, vor mir entfaltete, als ob ich, diese Verbindung von Eisen und Fleisch und Blut, die gegen die Erde drückt, gänzlich zu Gesang verwandelt worden wäre; als schwäng' ich mich, wie ein Adler, kreisend und gewälzt und kopfüber, in's Reich unendlicher Lüfte empor, immer jauchzend und wieder jauchzend: ich bin geliebt! daß die ganze Welt, wie ein großer Resonanzboden, wiederhallte: ich bin geliebt! – ich bin geliebt! ich bin geliebt! schwachher der Nachhall lispelnd von den äußersten Sternen, die an der Grenze der Schöpfung stehn, zu mir herüber zitterte.[39]

If ever there were doubts about the element of self-parody in the text, then the image of this knight in shining armour as an eagle cartwheeling through the sky would surely settle them. The motif of emotions expanding to fill the whole cosmos is, as we have seen, part of the world of *Penthesilea*. Here it is purely hyperbolical, for the Graf is in no sense the center of the world of the play, while it is quite arguable that Penthesilea has a whole fictional world constructed around her as a faithful reflection of her inner conflicts. The most significant omission in the later version of *Das Käthchen von Heilbronn* is Graf Wetter vom Strahl's rhapsody on the discovery that Käthchen loves him. She has confessed as much before the court, but there the Graf simply uses it to get her to agree to return to Theobald. As the play stands in its complete version, he remains preoccupied with his own feelings and does not enlarge at all on what Käthchen might feel for him. In the earlier version, these words are no more excessive than anything else in his monologue, but they do present an awesome obstacle to the credibility of Graf Wetter vom Strahl's abrupt switch of attention from Käthchen to Kunigunde in the scenes that follow.

For if he is not only aware of Käthchen's feelings for him, but is thrown into ecstasy by the revelation, then his infatuation with

---

39 KW II. 285f.

Kunigunde risks breaking the conventional mold of the honest and steadfast knight. Kleist's excision of this from the later version may represent an awareness that his experiment in suppressing causal motivations was in danger of getting out of control. As the text stands, it is fair to ask whether the gullible Graf Wetter vom Strahl of his early scenes with Kunigunde is recognizably the same character as so skilfully manipulates all the others in Act I. If the *Phöbus* text had been retained in full, then the dislocation of the Graf's feelings would become much more obtrusive in retrospect.

As a further indication of what concerns may have guided the redaction of the later text, we may compare the two versions of the Graf's invocation of his forebears, for having excized his luxuriating in the awareness he is loved, Kleist intensifies the imagery of patriarchal imperatives in the later text:

Nein, nein, nein! sag' ich; das war beschloßne Sache, noch eh ihr kamt: ich werd' eurem stolzen Reigen mich anschließen. Dich aber, Winfried, der ihn führt, Erster meines Namens, dich frag' ich, ob die Mutter meines Geschlechts war, wie diese: von jeder frommen Tugend strahlender, makelloser an Leib und Seele, mit jedem Liebreiz geschmückter, als sie?[40]

Nein, nein, nein! Zum Weibe, wenn ich sie gleich liebe, begehr ich sie nicht; eurem stolzen Reigen will ich mich anschließen: das war beschloßne Sache, noch ehe ihr kamt. Dich aber Winfried, du Erster meines Namens, Göttlicher mit der Scheitel des Zeus, dich frag ich, ob die Mutter meines Geschlechts war, wie diese: von jeder frommen Tugend strahlender, makelloser an Leib und Seele, mir jedem Liebreiz geschmückter, als sie?   (SW I, 454f)

Just as Theobald has previously invoked 'Hekate, Fürstin des Zaubers, moorduftige Königin der Nacht' (SW I, 440) in this bizarre travesty of the Christian Middle Ages, so Graf Wetter vom Strahl dignifies the first of his line in the later version with the epithet 'Göttlicher mit der Scheitel des Zeus.' All incongruity aside, the effect is to endow his fixation on his lineage, and hence on an appropriate marriage, with something of the divine authority that apparently guides Käthchen through her ordeals. Kunigunde entraps him, it seems, because an angel has told him in his dream that the woman he sees is an emperor's daughter; she is herself 'vom Stamm der alten sächsschen Kaiser'; and he has a conversation with his mother in Act II, Scene 13 in which the latter makes the connection to his dream: 'Und der Silvestertraum spricht für sie?/ Nicht? Meinst du nicht?' (SW I, 477).

40 KW II, 286.

Although Graf Wetter vom Strahl has narrated his dream so often to so many that its content is common knowledge, he most implausibly fails to make any visual connection with the appearance of Käthchen. He does, however, retain a firm grip on the idea that he is destined to marry a 'Kaisertochter.' Building up 'Winfried, du Erster meines Namens' to a divine authority in the text of the later version is clearly an adjustment on the author's part to make his hero's behavior a little more plausible than the *Phöbus*-fragment promised, especially in conjunction with the editing out of the passage in which he dwells on Käthchen's love for him.

Kunigunde is certainly the first, and perhaps the only femme fatale in European literature to be introduced to an audience by her false teeth.[41] She is borne on stage as a trussed bundle, and is to undergo many more transformations before she is firmly rejected in favor of Käthchen by Graf Wetter vom Strahl. Freiburg is to complete his description of her illusory physical charms at the end of the play, in a speech that interpretations usually treat as the last word on Kunigunde.[42] For Ueding, her falsity is a model of the 'world of imagery,' but I believe one can go further and say that the heterogeneity that lurks behind her image in others' eyes and words has some significance for the psychology of the play as well.

Kunigunde herself is remarkably consistent in what she says and does, but characters such as Theobald, the Emperor, and, most glaringly, Graf Wetter vom Strahl reveal inconsistencies and discrepancies of behavior that might suggest that their roles have been cobbled together from disparate parts. This is all the stranger since the play may be read – naively – as a celebration of patriarchal authority.

Hans Mayer described Kunigunde as 'einfach eine Hexe, die sich allerdings im Feudalstaat gut auskennt.'[43] Certainly, she uses language to impose her will in a way reminiscent of Graf Wetter vom Strahl himself before the secret court. If Käthchen is meant to embody the text's preferred version of the feminine, and she is sufficiently idealized to have led many to this conclusion, then there seems something distinctly

---

41 'Sie liegt, wie tot, zu des Pferdes Füßen da. FREIBURG. Ei, Possen! Das tut sie bloß, um ihre falschen Zähne nicht zu verlieren. Sagt ihr, ich wäre der Burggraf von Freiburg und die echten, die sie im Mund hätte, hätte ich gezählt. – So! bringt sie her' SW I, 458.

42 'So will ich es dir sagen. Sie ist eine mosaische Arbeit, aus allen drei Reichen der Natur zusammengesetzt. Ihre Zähne gehören einem Mädchen aus München, ihre Haare sind aus Frankreich verschrieben, ihrer Wangen Gesundheit kommt aus den Bergwerken in Ungarn, und den Wuchs, den ihr an ihr bewundert, hat sie einem Hemde zu danken, das ihr der Schmied, aus schwedischem Eisen, verfertigt hat' SW I, 520.

43 Hans Mayer, *Heinrich von Kleist*, p. 41f.

'masculine,' in the terms the text establishes, about Kunigunde's actions, if not her image in others' eyes.[44]

The real problem surrounding Kunigunde is very similar to that posed by the character of Graf Wetter vom Strahl. In his case, one cannot help asking: If he is really the Machiavellian strategist of Act I, why does he spend so long in Act II mouthing nonsense and fall such easy prey to Kunigunde? Concerning her the question arises: If she can mobilize so many high nobles in her campaign against Graf Wetter vom Strahl and then make him putty in her hands, why is her rivalry with Käthchen marked by so many crude blunders?

It is hard to answer this meaningfully because of the complex game played by the text with its own idealizations. Graf Wetter vom Strahl begins the play as the stereotype of noble masculinity in a Romanticized version of the Middle Ages. The first act reveals him to be, in addition, a figure of power whose hegemony over Käthchen has distinct marks of what the 20th century calls sadism. The second act blurs this image by superimposing on it the helpless sentimentalist and the witless victim of Kunigunde. The remainder of the action switches the portrayal of the character among these roles, much as Penthesilea and Achilles seem to shift between a small selection of possible modes of behavior. The Graf reverts to the stereotype of decisive action often enough, in his rescue of Kunigunde or his duel with Theobald before the Imperial court, to maintain a bare credibility for the masculine ideal for readers or audiences who have no wish to look beyond it. Equally, those aspects of the figure that contradict the stereotype re-emerge in other scenes or sequences in a manner that produces dislocations within the mode of what an audience expects of a readily identifiable idealization.

The result is not a 'fully rounded' character in conventional terms, but a set of characterizations that hovers on the brink of incoherence, for the transitions between them are too abrupt and puzzling to allow the kind of synthesizing paraphrase by which audiences or readers usually assimilate complex fictional characters. The text constantly tempts us into making judgements on the figure, by appearing to enact judgements itself, but then refutes these in a manner that remains arbitrary and provisional.

Much the same is true of the paired female characters, Käthchen and

---

44 Cf. Chris Cullen and Dorothea von Mücke, 'Love in Kleist's *Penthesilea*,' p. 487: 'The important thing about Kunigunde, however, is that she seems to understand this situation, and exploits it to the utmost, unlike Käthchen, who serves as the passive – and therefore, all the more attractive – object of male erotic phantasies.' I disagree with them however on their claim: 'she constitutes her being only in and through the gaze of men' (ibid.), since this is based on their adherence to the idea that *Das Käthchen von Heilbronn* must correspond to Lacan's concept of the Imaginary, rather than on the text. Kunigunde 'constitutes' her being both as a deceptive image and through manipulative language.

Kunigunde. The narratives that precede Käthchen's first appearance produce such a wealth of idealization, while also strongly emphasising the inaccessibility of her 'secret,' that there seems to be much less uncertainty about her than about Graf Wetter vom Strahl. But one may argue that the text permits Käthchen a relatively high degree of consistency only *because* she is paired with Kunigunde, as the negative Other of the stock feminine ideal, while Graf Wetter vom Strahl is compelled to contain both the positive stereotype and its own anti-figure, being 'doubled' in the sense of the three main characters in *Der Findling*.[45] Whatever ordeals the plot inflicts on Käthchen, the appearance on stage of an angel to protect her and guide her out of the burning castle in Act III, Scene 14, confirms that the text will sustain her idealization at any price, for all that her 'secret,' in the sense of what motivates specific actions, remains intact even after she has disclosed the content of her dream.

It is in this perspective that Kunigunde may assume a function in the text beyond being a mere amalgam of 'fairytale' witch and femme fatale. As we have seen, her behavior is much more like that of Graf Wetter vom Strahl in his Machiavellian mode than like that of Käthchen. Kleist subverts his own idealization of the latter by occasionally exaggerating her passivity and incomprehension. This may be read as a parody of such delineations of the middle-class female stereotype as are familiar from Fichte's writings on marriage.[46] However, the amount of sympathy Käthchen arouses through her suffering in the court scene tends to work against any awareness of parody becoming dominant. Kunigunde is then introduced as a rival and anti-figure to Käthchen, with conventionally 'masculine' attributes, and has an instant success in capturing the affections of Graf Wetter vom Strahl. The audience knows, from the way she is introduced, that her allure is deceptive, but the Graf does not, and promptly succumbs to it, especially as she offers what Käthchen at this point cannot, namely a marriage in conformity with the patriarchal imperatives he has internalized as 'divine.'

It is quite open to a reading of the text that recognizes there are dissonances in all the play's stereotypes to locate a more credible female role somewhere *between* the extremes of Käthchen and Kunigunde. In a similar way, the text of *Penthesilea* seems to invite the reader to allow for an androgynous ideal between the negative extremes of the Amazon female and the Greek male, although it is never delineated.[47] Given Kunigunde's 'masculine' aspects, an amalgam of herself and Käthchen

45 See below, p. 230-3.
46 See above, p. 21.
47 See above, p. 104.

would tend toward an androgyne figure, which was, in turn, a Romantic emblem of, among other things, 'absolute social equality.'[48]

In these terms, the crudity of the middle-class fantasy of social elevation might be tempered by a critique of the whole ideology of social class. It is tempting to see this as a genuine ideal, glimpsed through all the improbabilities of the plot, and hence as a subversion of both the aristocratic values Kleist had absorbed through his upbringing and also of the middle-class values that were dominant among contemporary German readers and audiences.

Such a reading is possible, but utopian. To uphold it, we must discount a good deal of the text's treatment of Kunigunde, which is aimed, quite literally, at destroying her credibility. As Chris Cullen and Dorothea von Mücke have pointed out in their Lacanian interpretation, the text seems to exact vengeance on Kunigunde for venturing outside prescribed female roles.[49] At the height of her ascendancy, the noble hero appears to have entirely forgotten the feelings for Käthchen he expressed with such fervour at the beginning of Act II. This is ostensibly motivated by class prejudice, but his inconstancy may equally be read as indicating that his – or the text's – preferred female image lies somewhere between the two extremes.

Kunigunde then inaugurates her own decline as a figure of power by sending Käthchen into the burning castle to retrieve a document, thus directing the hero's sympathies toward her middle-class rival. The plot ensures that her equally clumsy attempt to poison Käthchen is discovered, and that the Graf sees her without all her cosmetic props, which destroys his image of her. Graf Freiburg has, somewhat gratuitously, anticipated her demolition by enumerating, two scenes earlier, the source of all her appurtenances. The play then ends with her and Graf Wetter vom Strahl exchanging curses before the triumphal procession forms to conduct Käthchen to her marriage ceremony.

Given the power endings conventionally have to determine the most probable interpretation of the whole action, Kunigunde is not merely defeated, but, quite literally, disassembled by the convolutions of the plot. That the ending is so patently contrived does nothing to rehabilitate Kunigunde, for there is not enough of her left to maintain that grudging respect in the eyes of the audience that unsympathetic characters may still enjoy in comedy endings. Her own ineptitude in dealing with Käthchen has finished her as a figure of cunning, and the dissolution of her physical beauty has completed the process.

48 A. J. L. Busst, 'The Image of the Androgyne in the Nineteenth Century,' *Romantic Mythologies*, ed. Ian Flechter, London, 1967, p. 9.
49 Cf. Chris Cullen and Dorothea von Mücke, 'Love in Kleist's *Penthesilea*,' p. 486.

We may thus see her as a figure created by the patriarchal order, personified by Käthchen's multiple fathers, to embody what the often passive heroine is patently *not*, but then disqualified by an excess of the very attributes that make her powerful to begin with. This takes her a long way beyond the clichés combined to make her intelligible in terms of the popular theatre of the time. Kleist has indeed attempted something quite audacious with Kunigunde; how much of this will be apparent in a performance will depend on whether the clichés are played up or played down.

The center of the plot is the dream shared by Käthchen and Graf Wetter vom Strahl, the narrations of which he describes as fitting together 'like the two halves of a ring.'[50] There is no sign that Käthchen ever forgets any of her dream – indeed, the Graf claims she expects him to know why she is following him (SW I, 504), although she denies knowing this before the secret court. He finally coaxes the details from her by interrogating her, while no one else is present and she is in a kind of trance, in Act IV, Scene 2.[51] It is tempting to generalize that the trance removes the barriers to communication that apparently exist whenever Graf Wetter vom Strahl and Käthchen are alone together, but the play's inconsistencies make this no more than a conjecture.

Käthchen could presumably terminate the hearing before the secret court by recounting the Graf's dream to him in the same detail as she does later, and spare herself considerable pain. That she does not may be explained in a variety of ways, and if the words of the Graf in Act IV, Scene 1, are to be believed, she is given to telling him that he knows the reason anyway in scenes to which the audience is not a witness. One possibility is that the secret has a value in itself, as a poetological model for the entire text, and is thus in no way exhausted by what Käthchen narrates in her somnambulistic state. If we consider all levels of the text, and not just the plot, then the secret may appear as an overreaching metaphor for all those things that are *not* disclosed, for whatever suppresses causal links and produces dislocations and improbabilities. Once Graf Wetter vom Strahl is made to recall his dream, he greets it as a total revelation:

50 'Ein Märchen, aberwitzig, sinnverwirrt,/ Dir darzutun, das sich das Volk aus zwei/ Ereignissen, zusammen seltsam freilich,/ Wie die zwei Hälften eines Ringes, passend,/ Mit müßgem Scharfsinn, an einander setzte' SW I, 516. It is not unusual for the Graf's selective memory to omit the fact that he has first himself, in Act IV, Scene 2, to elicit from Käthchen the details of her dream before he can begin to match it with his own. That he here imputes making the connection to 'das Volk' may be explained as mendacity, embarrassment, or another of the dislocations to which his conscious mind is prone.

51 On Kleist's interest in 'somnambulism,' as recorded by Gotthilf Heinrich Schubert, cf. KW II, 872f.; also Uwe Henrik Peters, 'Somnambulismus und andere Nachtseiten der menschlichen Natur,' in *KJb* 1990, pp. 135-52.

Das Käthchen von Heilbronn

Was mir ein Traum schien, nackte Wahrheit ists:
Im Schloß zu Strahl, todkrank am Nervenfieber,
Lag ich danieder, und hinweggeführt,
Von einem Cherubim, besuchte sie
Mein Geist in ihrer Klause zu Heilbronn!   (SW I, 509)

This does not lessen his preoccupation with marrying a 'Kaisertochter,' but it does help Käthchen on the way toward her aristocratic apotheosis, since he now refers to her by her surname – 'die Friedborn' – and sends her to be looked after by his mother, thus along the same path as he had once led the noble Kunigunde. How much credence may be placed in his proclamation of 'nackte Wahrheit' is, once more, problematical. For no clear reason, he misrepresents it before the Emperor and his whole court in Act V, until Theobald provokes him with a torrent of abuse that includes the bizarre epithet 'Vatermördergeist,' which Kleist was later to apply to Napoleon.[52] Graf Wetter vom Strahl now declares the secret of Käthchen's paternity to be 'Wissenschaft,/ Entschöpft dem Himmelsbronnen' (SW I, 517); the Emperor recovers his memory, to the extent of even recalling Käthchen's mother's name (SW I, 519); and issues a decree that adopts her as his daughter and elevates her to 'Katharina von Schwaben' (SW I, 525).

The superabundance of 'truth' does not prevent Graf Wetter vom Strahl from playing on Käthchen the cruel deception that she is to dress herself for his wedding with Kunigunde, nor, stranger still, does it prevent her from believing him and weeping, just as she has wept under his interrogation in the first act (SW I, 447). The repetition of such cruelty from the beginning of the play could be read as parodistic, were Käthchen's suffering not one of the very few things that remains free of both irony and exaggeration. Parody is, however, not to be lightly dismissed at this point, since the Emperor's behavior is a travesty of the moral superiority of adoptive over natural fathers in the drama of the Enlightenment. Having denied his natural paternity with such vehemence before the whole court, the Emperor saves face by adopting Käthchen with the consent of Theobald, although his courtiers may well inquire as to why he bothers and an audience may well wonder why Theobald does not object. The tension between physical and moral parenthood, so important in the late 18th century, is thus dissolved by a stroke of the Imperial pen, and the very ease with which this is achieved may well be meant parodistically by Kleist.

---

52 Cf. *Katechismus des Deutschen*, SW II, 354. Given Graf Wetter vom Strahl's reverence for his own male forebears, SW I, 454f, he may find this especially provoking.

The 'truth' that wins out in the end of the play is thus a matter of contrivance, and quite likely an object of literary satire. It is put together out of disparate elements and offered to an audience who may choose to find it credible or not, much as the reaction of Kleist's contemporaries to the play varied between enthusiastic acceptance and contemptuous rejection. Graf Wetter vom Strahl's final cruelty to Käthchen is preceded by a declaration of love, whose terms also suggest that not a great deal has changed since the beginning of the play:

> Zuerst, mein süßes Kind, muß ich dir sagen,
> Daß ich mit Liebe dir, unsäglich, ewig,
> Durch alle meine Sinne zugetan.
> Der Hirsch, der von der Mittagsglut gequält,
> Den Grund zerwühlt, mit spitzigem Geweih,
> Er sehnt sich so begierig nicht,
> Vom Felsen in den Waldstrom sich zu stürzen,
> Den reißenden, als ich, jetzt, da du mein bist,
> In alle deine jungen Reize mich.
>
> KÄTHCHEN *schamrot.*
> Jesus! Was sprichst du? Ich versteh dich nicht.   (SW I, 527)

The image in Graf Wetter vom Strahl's speech is a parodistic elaboration of the beginning of the 42nd Psalm.[53] It also recalls the sadistic quality of his sexual impulses elsewhere in the text. Substituting Käthchen's body for the presence of God would be no more bizarre than many other metaphors in the play, were he to show any respect for her in the remainder of the scene, but he goes on to reduce her to tears by the pretense that he is still intending to marry Kunigunde. Whilst Käthchen has had a sight of Kunigunde without her cosmetic props in the first Gothic bath scene in German literature,[54] she does not know that Graf Wetter vom Strahl is privy to the secret of her rival's unimproved appearance. Thus it is just barely plausible that she is taken in by his deception, especially if she has ceased trying to understand anything her future husband says to her.

---

53 'As the hart panteth after the water brooks, so panteth my soul after thee, O God./ My soul thirsteth for God, for the living God: when shall I come and appear before God?' Luther's translation, with which Kleist would have been most familiar, uses the word 'Hirsch.'

54 '*Szene: Garten. Im Hintergrunde eine Grotte, im gotischen Stil.* . . . ELEONORE. Ei, ich will mich mit Käthchen, dem kleinen, holden Gast, den uns der Graf ins Schloß gebracht, weil die Luft so heiß ist, in dieser Grotte baden. ROSALIE. Vergebt! – Fräulein Kunigunde ist in der Grotte' SW I, 511.

Das Käthchen von Heilbronn

This is not the only dissonant note in Graf Wetter vom Strahl's declaration. Whereas he had used a biblical allusion in his only other profession of sexual desire in the play to assimilate his own status to that of Ahasuerus, the 'Perserkönig' (SW I, 454), he now uses another to transpose himself into the animal realm. This holds the promise of more violence to come in his relation to Käthchen, discrediting his apparent change of heart in Act III, Scene 7, when he ostentatiously throws away his whip as a sign that he will cease treating her as if *she* were an animal.[55] Once more: the imagery of the play as a whole suggests such heterogeneous fields of reference that a reader or audience may not blink at the implications of this speech. Taken together with Käthchen's inarticulate helplessness in the closing scene, however, they should forestall such descriptions of her fainting as a 'Schwindel der Beglückung.'[56]

Das Käthchen von Heilbronn is not the first of Kleist's dramas to develop a potential for tragedy and then negate it, as the clear parallels between its ending and that of *Amphitryon* show. It is, however, the first since he had, in *Penthesilea*, taken tragic form to an innovative and extreme conclusion that resulted in widespread incomprehension among contemporary readers. The text of *Das Käthchen von Heilbronn* is no less innovative and daring than *Penthesilea*, but its experimental aspects are overlaid with a readily assimilable veneer that ensured the acceptance that was denied *Penthesilea* until the 20th century. Since Kleist's experiments include, among other things, a dramatic psychology based on disjunctions of consciousness and an intensification of the tendency for metaphors in the text to work at variance with any factual substrate, any evaluation of his success in terms of conventional criteria of 'unity' or an 'aesthetic whole' is likely to miss the point.

The opening scene establishes a tension between a familiar template for the plot of a 'Ritterschauspiel' and exaggerated actions on the part of the stock characters. Not every indignant father presents his grievance in Theobald's outlandish rhetoric; not every noble knight accused of seduction supplants his own judges and torments his alleged victim before them; not every middle-class girl in love with an aristocrat hurls herself from a high window after their first encounter, especially if she has to last until Act V. A further tension is then created between such barely credible modes of conduct and the Enlightened, if sceptical,

---

55 'Hab ich hier Hunde, die zu schmeißen sind?/ *Er wirft die Peitsche, daß die Scherben niederklirren, durchs Fenster; hierauf zu Käthchen:* / Pferd' dir, mein liebes Kind, und Wagen geben,/ Die sicher nach Heilbronn dich heimgeleiten' SW I, 490. The Graf's whip is established as an emblem of his treatment of Käthchen in the court scene: 'Als du die Peitsche, flammenden Gesichts,/ Herab vom Riegel nahmst, ging ich hinaus,/ Vor das bemooste Tor, und lagerte/ Mich draußen, am zerfallnen Mauernring/ Wo in süßduftenden Holunderbüschen/ Ein Zeisig zwitschernd sich das Nest gebaut' SW I, 450.
56 See above note 4.

humanism of the judges, reinforced by its consonance with Käthchen's own protests. While the 'Vehmgericht' fades from the action of the play, Käthchen's suffering does not. An expectation of ethical behavior derived from the Enlightenment is thus never absent from the work, although it remains very much at odds with the apparent celebration of patriarchal power at the play's conclusion.

This, in turn, ensures the maintenance of a permanent conflict between a human order defined at the outset in terms perfectly intelligible to a contemporary audience and the 'chaos' Theobald quite accurately evokes after the court scene. Were the text to take up the option of a conventional comic plot, which it certainly contains, it would then have little choice but to return to the values propounded by the 'Vehmgericht.' That it does not, but rather moves toward an ending so full of dissonances as to appear quite arbitrary, surely suggests that Kleist's main interest is, after *Penthesilea*, in a renewed exploration of the 'chaos' that occupies the foreground of that work.

I think many of the enigmas of the text of Käthchen derive from the fact that Kleist found the interaction between this exploration and his efforts to write a popular success very hard to control, resulting in the 'Mißgriffe' he later deplored in his letter to Marie von Kleist of summer 1811.[57] The power of clichés is made explicit in the self-referential aspects of the text, but, in a sense, it leaves the author as a kind of sorcerer's apprentice who has let loose too many of them for his own good. For this and other reasons, I have tried to avoid giving a too convergent reading of *Das Käthchen von Heilbronn*, since the text ultimately seems to thrive on its own stubborn incapacity for a convincing resolution.

---

57 'Es war von Anfang herein eine ganz treffliche Erfindung, und nur die Absicht, es für die Bühne passend zu machen, hat mich zu Mißgriffen verführt, die ich jetzt beweinen möchte' SW II, 874.

7

Die Hermannsschlacht

If the difficulties that beset an adequate understanding of *Penthesilea* and *Das Käthchen von Heilbronn* stem chiefly from complexities within the texts that permit, indeed encourage, a plurality of alternative readings, the problems posed by *Die Hermannsschlacht* are primarily ideological. With this play, finished in one or another version by December 1808, Kleist was aiming for a different kind of success from that intended by either of the two preceding dramas.[1] *Penthesilea* was his final attempt to achieve recognition in the most prestigious of genres in contemporary German literature, high tragedy, while *Das Käthchen von Heilbronn* set out to conduct an equally radical experiment with dramatic form within a guise congenial to popular taste.

Die Hermannsschlacht was designed to arouse popular feeling against Napoleon's occupation of much of Germany in terms familiar to the circle of Prussian officers and intellectuals around Gneisenau, Scharnhorst, and vom Stein.[2] It was read aloud and circulated in manuscript in Dresden from the end of 1808, but Kleist's attempts to have it produced failed. It remained unpublished until 1821, and had its first performance in 1860. Kleist insisted that it was written for one particular historical moment, when the popular insurgency against the French in Spain awoke hopes in Germany that a war of insurrection against Napoleon might well succeed where the German armies had conspicuously failed, but the moment passed with the French victory at Wagram in July 1809.

The ambiguities surrounding the play began in 1810, when Kleist wrote to Joseph von Collin, who was preparing *Das Käthchen von Heilbronn* for its first performance in Vienna, to enquire whether *Die Hermannsschlacht* stood any chance of being produced.[3] For if the play

---

1 For a summary of information available on the composition and sources of the work see KW II, 1070-87.

2 Cf. Richard Samuel, 'Kleists *Hermannsschlacht* und der Freiherr vom Stein,' *JbSchG* V, 1961, pp. 64-101; Wolf Kittler, *Die Geburt des Partisanen aus dem Geiste der Poesie*, pp. 218f.

3 'Jetzt aber, da sich die Verhältnisse wieder glücklich geändert haben, interessiert es mich, zu wissen: ob sich das Manuskript noch vorfindet? ob daran zu denken ist, es auf die Bühne zu bringen? und wenn nicht, ob ich es nicht nach Berlin zurück erhalten kann?' SW II, 831.

was as closely linked to radical ideas about a specific moment of history as Richard Samuel and others have argued, following Kleist's own letters of 1809, what might he expect of a production in Vienna once it was evident that, whatever action Austria and various other German states might undertake against Napoleon, there would be no German version of the Spanish *guerilla*?

Obviously, a strengthening of feeling against Napoleon and in favor of the creation of a single 'Germania,' but in what terms and with what hopes of success? With these questions, the controversies concerning *Die Hermannsschlacht* began, and are still very much with us in the present, for the play lent itself very readily to the nationalistic fervor of both Wilhelmenian Germany and the Third Reich. In 1875, as Theodor Fontane recorded, a production in Berlin heightened the German euphoria that lingered after the war of 1870, and in 1933-34 the play was produced no less than 146 times in Hitler's Germany.[4] Did these audiences cheer a play that did not exist? No more than those who applauded in *Das Käthchen von Heilbronn* a sugary fairytale of a German never-never land.

The reception of *Die Hermannsschlacht* clearly shows that the palimpsest of the text contains something beneath the surface of a drama aimed at the political climate of 1808-9, but just what this is remains a matter of critical dispute. After 1945, interest in the play, not surprisingly, was greatly diminished, and Walter Müller-Seidel's influential study of 1961 expressed reservations as to whether it could be included among Kleist's 'poetic' works.[5] Claus Peymann's production of 1982 gave the work a fresh lease on life by revealing that the text contained its own anti-play to the drama of chauvinist enthusiasm offered to audiences in the Third Reich.[6] His Hermann added a dimension of neurotic isolation to the figure of the national hero, which in no way deformed the text, but had the great virtue of clearing away the more offensive clichés whose accretion began with the shaping of an icon of nationalistic theatre from 1860 onward.

Contemporary audiences might expect to enjoy a whole tribe of neurotic and isolated Hermanns for just a little longer. Certainly, all the ideological problems surrounding the work were already, by the time of Peymann's production, alive and well in critical writing on the play, and they have remained so. The debate ultimately devolves upon an overall

---

4 KW II, 1097f.
5 Walter Müller-Seidel, *Versehen und Erkennen*, pp. 52f.
6 For details of the production and the ideas behind it see Heinrich von Kleist, *Die Hermannsschlacht. Ein Drama. Programmbuch Nr. 38*, Bochum, 1982; also Claus Peymann, Hans Joachim Kreutzer, 'Streitgespräch über Kleists *Hermannsschlacht*,' in *KJb* 1984, pp. 77-97.

judgement of Kleist as a writer. Adherents of a general interpretation of his work in terms of liberal humanism find there is much in *Die Hermannsschlacht* that needs explaining; writers who hold that the savagery so often depicted in his works reflects the essential Kleist are contemptuous of such apologias.[7] A variant of the first is Lawrence Ryan's re-interpretation of the play in terms of German Idealism, which flatly contradicts its own premises, as I have shown elsewhere.[8]

What makes *Die Hermannsschlacht* exceptional is not that more characters die violent and gruesome deaths on and off stage than elsewhere. *Penthesilea, Der Findling*, and *Michael Kohlhaas* all contain conspicuous violence, and cruelty that stops short of bloodshed is amply evident in *Amphitryon* and *Das Käthchen von Heilbronn*, yet without making necessary a debate on whether Kleist advocates these forms of behavior. The main reason for this is the sheer complexity of Kleist's other texts and their tendency to undermine any firm ideological stance as soon as it is enunciated. For all the horror of the ending of *Penthesilea*, the text repeatedly asks what *is* inhumane behavior in terms that resist a simple answer. When Achilles calls the Amazon ritual of self-mutilation 'barbaric,' we may reflect that many of his own actions or words are equally inhumane, but at least the question as to *what* is humane has been asked – and received no simple answer. Much the same applies to Alkmene's and Käthchen's protests against the cruelty of the treatment they endure. Neither Jupiter nor Graf Wetter vom Strahl is punished for it, but neither does the text as a whole do anything to defuse the issue: the enigmatic pairing of desire and aggression occurs within a critique of inequality between conventional gender roles and thus does not become an end in itself, as does *jouissance* in the writings of de Sade.[9]

Most of the moral dilemmas posed by Kleist's fictions are intelligible in terms of his critical scrutiny of values upheld by the German Enlightenment or Weimar Classicism, but this, in turn, does *not* result in a conviction that the debate itself is not worth having. The conclusion of Wolf Kittler's treatment of *Die Hermannsschlacht*, however, precisely

7 For an example of the apologetic gesture, cf. Peter Michelsen, '"Wehe, mein Vaterland, dir!" Heinrichs von Kleist *Die Hermannsschlacht*,' in *KJb* 1987, p. 120: 'der deutsche Held, den Kleist in diesem Drama als Befreier- und Führer-Figur empfiehlt, ist ein undeutscher Held'; for the contrary stance, cf. Wolf Kittler, *Die Geburt des Partisanen*, p. 254: 'Da es immer noch Literaturwissenschaftler gibt, die ihn als den großen Liberalen feiern, sei ein letzter Text zitiert, der seine antiliberale Gesinnung in aller Deutlichkeit bezeugt [*Über die Rettung von Österreich*].'

8 Lawrence Ryan, 'Die "vaterländische Umkehr" in der *Hermannsschlacht*,' *Kleists Dramen*, ed. W. Hinderer, pp. 188-212; Anthony Stephens, 'Gegen die Tyrannei des Wahren', pp. 176-80.

9 For a fuller treatment of this issue cf. Anthony Stephens, 'Das nenn ich menschlich nicht verfahren,' pp. 31f.

implies that this discussion is idle: 'Kleists politische Haltung, daran führt kein Weg vorbei, ist eindeutig ständisch-antiliberal. Nur im Interesse des totalen Krieges gegen den nationalen Feind war er zu Lebzeiten bereit, sich mit bürgerlich-liberalen Männern zu liieren.'[10] Statements such as these are possible, if not particularly credible, because *Die Hermannsschlacht* gives every appearance of lacking the constant counterpointing of violent transgressions of contemporary norms of conduct with reinforcements of conventional moral expectations that many regard as the essential Kleistian technique. Put another way, no reader can doubt that the text of *Die Hermannsschlacht* presents itself as bloody-minded, but the question remains: is it simple-minded as well?

Answering this question involves asking whether the main character's perspective is also the work's perspective. Hermann is unique among the figures Kleist had so far created for the stage in the degree to which he exclusively dominates both the action and the other characters. Even Jupiter in *Amphitryon* has to see his omnipotence mocked by Alkmene's prolonged refusal to give him the answers he demands, whereas Hermann progressively takes charge of the play, to the point of ending it with an ascendancy over the other characters that is uncannily reminiscent of that of an omniscient narrator over the plot of a story. The temptation to make of him an authorial figure is thus very strong, and only his lack of humanity gives most critics pause.

Surprisingly perhaps, the first epithet applied to Hermann before his appearance in Act I is 'spielend':

> Und Hermann, der Cherusker, endlich,
> Zu dem wir, als dem letzten Pfeiler, uns,
> Im allgemeinen Sturz Germanias, geflüchtet,
> Ihr seht es, Freunde, wie er uns verhöhnt:
> Statt die Legionen mutig aufzusuchen,
> In seine Forsten spielend führt er uns,
> Und läßt den Hirsch uns und den Ur besiegen.   (SW I, 535)

The whole first act is, indeed, a game in which Hermann exerts considerable histrionic talents to manipulate the German princes, first into thinking him a defeatist with a strong death-wish, then – with a well timed volte face – into hailing him as their saviour: 'Hermann soll, der Befreier Deutschlands, leben!' (SW I, 546). It is characteristic of his

10 Wolf Kittler, *Die Geburt des Partisanen*, p. 255.

ascendancy to complete dominance that he need do nothing but talk in order to effect this transformation.[11]

A second aspect of the game-playing theme is that all of Hermann's strategies are part of one successful gamble. At the outset, his position with regard to the Romans is precarious. The German princes are divided by mistrust and rivalries, and the Romans sucessfully play them off against each other. To unify the Germans, Hermann must take risks, such as sending his two sons as hostages to Marbod in full awareness that the Romans have offered him the same treaty as Hermann himself pretends to accept from Varus, but, most unusually for Kleist's fictions, he wins every trick.[12] At the point where he sees himself in danger of losing, because the Roman army he has allowed into his land has not committed enough atrocities to inflame his people's rage and his henchmen, disguised as Romans to do the job, have apparently failed (SW I, 566), Hermann's solution is to raise the stakes by setting fire to his own territory:

> Verflucht sei diese Zucht mir der Kohorten!
> Ich stecke, wenn sich niemand rührt,
> Die ganze Teutoburg an allen Ecken an!
>
> EGINHARDT. Nun, nun! Es wird sich wohl ein Frevel finden.
>
> HERMANN. Komm, laß uns heimlich durch die Gassen
> schleichen,
> Und sehn ob uns der Zufall etwas beut.   (SW I, 586)

The third aspect of Hermann's game becomes evident at the end of the drama when all of his ploys have succeeded and his control over the other figures is like that of a puppeteer over his marionettes. While the work itself verges at times on a comedy of the absurd, there is no humor to be extracted from Hermann's manner, for he takes himself very seriously, and any character who contradicts him is swiftly proven wrong. In no other work by Kleist does such infallibility go unchallenged, but Hermann is permitted to exhibit a self-sufficiency that has overtones of solipsism.

His own homeland seems to have a very tenuous reality for him. He affirms allegiance to a vision of 'Germania,' a mythical construct popu-

---

11 On Hermann as the producer of a play see Jeffrey L. Sammons, 'Rethinking Kleist's *Hermannsschlacht,*' *Heinrich von Kleist-Studien*, ed. Alex Ugrinsky, Berlin, 1980, p. 35: 'Hermann not only thinks out his rebellion, he *stages* it . . . he arouses the emotions of the population by directing a theater of cruelty charged to the Roman account.'

12 Hans Joachim Kreutzer makes this point in 'Streitgespräch,' p. 91.

lar in Kleist's time in Romantic political writing, but a chilling indifference to its inhabitants:

> Cheruska, wie es steht und liegt,
> Kommt mir, wie eingepackt in eine Kiste, vor:
> Um einen Wechsel könnt ich es verkaufen.
> Denn käms heraus, daß ich auch nur
> Davon geträumt, Germanien zu befrein:
> Roms Feldherr steckte gleich mir alle Plätze an ...   (SW I, 592)

The thought does not distress him, for soon afterward he counters Eginhardt's protest that the Romans he is leaving behind will destroy his home with the reassurance:

> Kämpf ich auch für den Sand, auf den ich trete,
> Kämpf ich für meine Brust?
> Cheruska schirmen! Was! Wo Hermann steht, da siegt er,
> Und mithin ist Cheruska da.   (SW I, 599)

This is fortunate for the Cheruskans, as the battle with the remaining Romans results in complete devastation. Hermann dismisses the news:

> Doch hier, o Herr, schau her! Das sind die Folgen
> Des Kampfs, den Astolf mit den Römern kämpfte:
> Ganz Teutoburg siehst du in Schutt und Asche!
>
> HERMANN. Mag sein! Wir bauen uns ein schönres auf.
>   (SW I, 626)

When Hermann, at the play's conclusion, prevents Aristan from making a speech to the German princes before he is led off to execution, he justifies his command by saying that he already knows what the obstinate renegade will say: 'Führet ihn hinweg!/ Was kann er sagen, das ich nicht schon weiß?' (SW I, 628)

In a sense, the same applies to all the other characters in the play; Hermann knows what they will say before they say it. He is the only one to be consistently a puzzle to others, and his clairvoyance as to everyone else's motives and actions, coupled with his complete disregard for the fate of his own people, makes him appear both monstrous and omniscient. If, as writing on the play frequently asserts, the dominant idea is 'freedom,'[13] then we must ask: freedom for whom, and has such free-

13 Most recently by Hans Joachim Kreutzer, 'Die Utopie vom Vaterland. Kleist's politische Dramen,' in *Oxford German Studies*, vol. 20/21, 1991-1992, p. 78: 'Der zentrale Begriff in Kleist's *Hermannsschlacht* ist der Begriff "Freiheit".'

dom any meaning outside Hermann's solipsistic fantasy? Hermann himself is prone to apocalyptic forebodings, and the lines with which he concludes the play make it plain that any positive image of liberty for 'Germania' pales beside his preferred vision of complete destruction:

> Und dann – nach Rom selbst mutig aufzubrechen!
> Wir oder unsre Enkel, meine Brüder!
> Denn eh doch, seh ich ein, erschwingt der Kreis der Welt
> Vor dieser Mordbrut keine Ruhe,
> Als bis das Raubnest ganz zerstört,
> Und nichts, als eine schwarze Fahne,
> Von seinem öden Trümmerhaufen weht!   (SW I, 628)

Interpretations that try to render Hermann himself more acceptable by making him the inspired avenger of an outraged 'Nature,' as does Lawrence Ryan, or the reluctant executor of an 'inverted categorical imperative,' as does Peter Michelsen, import into the text philosophical apparatus that Kleist excluded.[14] Nature is no more an absolute moral authority here than it is anywhere else in Kleist; Hermann does not have to force himself to victory, since victory means destruction, and destruction is both his goal and chief source of pleasure. His concluding vision is not of a flourishing German empire, but of annihilation, and this has been fully prepared for in advance.[15] If we wish to gain a critical perspective on the play, the way does not lead through remodelling Hermann after Hölderlin or Kant. That merely anchors the critical discourse more firmly within the perspective of the dominant character, and then distorts it. It is necessary to move outside the perspective of Hermann himself.

The retrospective prophecy in the last lines of the play, normally read as anticipating the sacking of Rome by the Goths in the 5th century, raises the question of what kind of world the play presents beyond the mechanisms of Hermann's game. It is similar to Kleist's other 'histori-

---

14 Cf. Lawrence Ryan, 'Die "vaterländische Umkehr",' p. 204: 'wird der deutsche Befreiungskampf zum Aufstand der geknechteten Natur gegen die Anmaßungen eines universellen Herrschaftsanspruchs . . .'; Peter Michelsen, 'Wehe, mein Vaterland, dir!', p. 130: 'Hermanns Haß ist keine Natur und entspringt keiner Erfahrung. Er ist eine . . . selbst auferlegte Pflicht, ein . . . pervertierter, umgekehrter kategorischer Imperativ, dem zu gehorchen Hermann sich . . . künstlich zwingen muß.'

15 In addition to his blithe acceptance of the devastation of Cheruska, see Hermann's ecstatic vision of the war to come (SW I, 545); his pleasurable fantasy of his own dying 'den schönen Tod der Helden' and his encouraging the princes to burn their own crops and kill their own cattle (SW I, 546); his instructions to his disguised henchmen to burn and loot in his own lands (SW I, 566).

cal' settings by being full of obtrusive anachronisms. The historical Arminius was born in 17 BC, but Kleist's Hermann twice insists on having taken part in a battle 40 years before that date.[16] Varus, the Roman general, shows a surprising knowledge of the Hebrew scriptures (SW I, 603); Celtic 'bards' have a vital role in Germanic society, a borrowing from Klopstock; Hermann sees his warriors as wielding a medieval 'Morgenstern' (SW I, 544). The usual effect of Kleist's avoidable anachronisms is to set the work in question adrift in period and locality, and this obviously has some point in a play intended to arouse resistance to the French hegemony over various German states in Kleist's own time.

The play we now read, whose immediate historical context must be laboriously reconstructed if it is to be visible at all, has many elements that suggest black comedy. There is a farcical element in the confusion of names that accompanies Varus and his legions as they are being led in a circle through swamps at the beginning of Act V. Fust's and Hermann's duel over who should have the honor of murdering Varus has gruesome comic potential. Ventidius' death at the claws of Thusnelda's bear is narrated by the victim himself with parodistic elaboration – 'Zeus, du, der Götter und der Menschen Vater,/ Sie schlägt die Klaun in meine weiche Brust!' (SW I, 620) – while the imagery lightly puns on 'Hirsch' and 'Brunst.'[17] Viewed from a distance, Hermann's direction of the other characters may appear as a grim pastiche of the Duke's role in Shakespeare's *Measure for Measure*.

That these aspects were also visible to contemporaries is attested by Clemens Brentano, who attended a private reading of the manuscript in 1816, five years before it was published. He found it bizarre, yet 'ungemein lustig,' and observed of the author: 'Er denkt sich alle Personen halb taub und dämlich, so kommt dann durch Fragen und Repetieren der Dialog heraus.'[18] He may have had in mind such moments as Act III, Scene 6, when Thusnelda demands and receives an explanation from Septimius as to what the Roman legions' eagle-standards are for. Even in the depths of a German forest, questions and answers as to the function of the one symbol of Roman power with which the victims of Roman aggression would be familiar have a comic improbability. Were Thusnelda given to frivolous banter, we might imagine her to be pulling

---

16 Cf. KW II, 1118.

17 'Thusnelda! Komm und lösche diese Glut,/ Soll ich, gleich einem jungen Hirsch,/ Das Haupt voran, mich in die Flut nicht stürzen! – . . . THUSNELDA. Im Park, dem Wunsch gemäß, den du geäußert,/ Und heißer Brunst voll harrt sie schon auf dich!' (SW I, 618). The image of the stag also parodies the death of Achilles in *Penthesilea* (SW I, 412f.) and Graf Wetter vom Strahl's marital expectations in *Das Käthchen von Heilbronn* (SW I, 527).

18 KN, 80.

the Roman's leg, but all of her other dialogues are intensely serious, thus lending credence to Brentano's observation.

The cumulative effect of these discordant elements is to allow a reading or production a margin of alienation from Hermann's convergent vision. Nationalist interpretations that remain fixated on seeing Kleist as an advocate of 'total war' will ignore them, and they receive no mention in Wolf Kittler's discussion of the play.[19] They are neither sufficiently frequent nor consistent to afford relief from the usurpation of the whole perspective by Hermann's apparent infallibility, but their presence is sufficient to skew the presentation of the play world away from any realism that his obsessive 'Realpolitik' might suggest.

Working against any comic leavening and reinforcing the oppressive perspective of the main character, however, is the absence of any credible antagonist to Hermann. I have pointed out elsewhere that Hermann is much more like Kleist's vision of Napoleon than any historical personage on the German side.[20] In structural terms, Hermann and Ventidius present a further example of the paired characters so frequently found in Kleist, and the effect here is to make Hermann's enemy a pale reflection of himself. Ventidius' pretended passion for Thusnelda is presented as a cruel game that mirrors not only Hermann's duping of the German princes, but also his manipulation of his wife. Hermann progressively exhibits all the falsity and lack of scruple he quite correctly attributes to his enemy, so that he reveals himself as more and more 'Roman' in the course of the action. Given this affinity between Roman and German, Thusnelda's careful planning of Ventidius' murder, using a bear as a deadly weapon, and her explicit identification with the animal – 'Er hat zur Bärin mich gemacht!' (SW I, 616) – may suggest that she also cherishes certain aggressions toward Hermann.

She is the only character to criticize Hermann with any degree of insight. She rightly accuses him of using her as a decoy (SW I, 555), and variations of the word 'Spiel' in her dialogues with him imply that she is aware that he treats her as a plaything. Her diagnosis of his hatred is equally telling:

Dich macht, ich seh, dein Römerhaß ganz blind.
Weil als dämonenartig dir
Das Ganz' erscheint, so kannst du dir
Als sittlich nicht den Einzelnen gedenken.   (SW I, 557)

19 Cf. Wolf Kittler, *Die Geburt des Partisanen*, p. 230: 'Was Kleist in seiner "Hermannsschlacht" propagiert, ist also der totale Krieg, der nicht einmal haltmacht vor der Zerstörung der Ordnung im eigenen Land.'

20 Anthony Stephens, 'Kleist's Mythicisation of the Napoleonic Era,' *Romantic Nationalism in Europe*, ed. J. C. Eade, Canberra, 1983, p. 168; Peter Michelsen repeats the point in 1987, cf. 'Wehe, mein Vaterland, dir!,' pp. 119f.

She is correct, from a perspective that includes moral convictions, to perceive something lacking in Hermann's view of other human beings, even if they are Roman. She is wrong to think he shares her concern for what is 'sittlich' and what is not. An integral part of Hermann's game, and one that makes his world view oppressively monotonous, is his complete moral indifference. In a later scene, he loses patience with Thusnelda's scruples when she objects to his planning to massacre all of the Romans who have been living as their guests:

> Die Guten mit den Schlechten. – Was! Die Guten!
> Das sind die schlechtesten! Der Rache Keil
> Soll sie zuerst, vor allen andern, treffen!   (SW I, 593)

Thusnelda reacts by calling him 'Unmenschlicher!,' and her strictures against him might fulfill – for a reader or audience – a role similar to the reprimands of Graf Wetter vom Strahl by the secret court in *Das Käthchen von Heilbronn*, were she not to undergo a conversion to Hermann's way of seeing things in the wake of his revelation that Ventidius has planned to send her hair and teeth as a gift to the Empress in Rome. Hermann retrieves the lock of hair Ventidius has sent back by intercepting his messenger, or conceivably steals another lock while she sleeps, forges the letter,[21] and confronts Thusnelda with irrefutable evidence derived from her own body, a parallel to the use he has made of the body of the unfortunate Hally in a previous scene.

The stages of Thusnelda's capitulation to Hermann's way of thinking are instructive. She first exacts a promise from him that he will spare Ventidius (SW I, 595). He then produces a lock of her hair with a letter to the Empress Livia that reduces Thusnelda to speechlessness. Two of his henchmen appear and he breaks his oath to treat Ventidius as 'sacred,' instructing Astolf to kill him: 'Den Rest des Haufens fällst du, gleichviel, wo?/ Auch den Ventidius empfehl ich dir' (SW I, 598). Thusnelda, having recovered from her shock, then claims for herself the privilege of murdering Ventidius, and Hermann comments significantly: 'Nun denn, so ist der erste Sieg erfochten' (SW I, 599).

His 'victory' has an important but profoundly negative effect on the text as a whole. For Thusnelda's conversion to his grossly simplified view of his opponents as prey and her subsequent acting out one of his fantasies of destruction in lurid detail – Hermann consistently brands other people as animals – nullifies her previous line of resistance, and, with her renunciation of moral scruples, these effectively disappear

---

21 Cf. Norbert Miller, 'Verstörende Bilder in Kleists *Hermannsschlacht*,' in *KJb* 1984, p. 99.

from the play. She ensures the bear is starved in expectation of Ventidius, turns a deaf ear to her maid's pleas for compassion for the Roman, and fights with her and the bear's keeper to prevent them from seizing the key which might still release the Roman.[22] The text offers a last ironic comment on her act, when Astolf appears in response to Ventidius' screams:

> Was gibts, ihr Fraun? Was für ein Jammerruf,
> Als ob der Mord entfesselt wäre,
> Schallt aus dem Dunkel jener Eichen dort?   (SW I, 620)

For murder has indeed been let loose in this world, and there is no longer any resistance to its continuing on its way, as shown by Hermann's vision of carnage to come in the final lines of the play.

As I have argued elsewhere, the most significant casualty in this play is the criterion of truth itself.[23] In all his works, Kleist is profoundly sceptical of the ability of truth to become tangible in the fictional worlds he devises, and it is possible to see this as an aspect of his sustained critique of the tenets of Weimar Classicism, especially as exemplified by Goethe's *Iphigenie auf Tauris*. Characters in Kleist's fictions who believe themselves in possession of the truth, or preceive it embodied in others, are usually in for an unpleasant shock. This in no way weakens the imperative to seek truth, as the abundance of forensic dialogues and rituals in his works attest. Interrogations, whether between two lovers or before a court, are so much a part of Kleist's fictional worlds as to require no further comment. That truth may be found too late to be of any help, or that an apparent truth misleads entirely, makes no difference to the urgency of the quest, with the sole exception of *Die Hermannsschlacht*. No other work by Kleist sets out to discredit systematically the criterion of truth itself. Elsewhere, it remains the *Deus absconditus* of a tragic world – unverifiable, but reverenced none the less.

Hermann's indifference to truth extends to being free of any tabus concerning it. In his discourse, when he sets out to dupe the German princes in Act I, 'Wahrheit' is simply one piece among others he moves on the board, its function identical to falsehood (SW I, 545). His most spectacular perversion of truth is the use he makes of the body of the

---

22 A refreshing breath of self-parody is introduced by Peter Michelsen, 'Wehe, mein Vaterland, dir!,' p. 134: 'Die Tatzen der Bärin dringen nicht nur in das Fleisch des Ventidius, tiefer noch in das Mark Thusneldas ein.' Much is made of the fact that Thusnelda faints after ensuring Ventidius' gruesome end, but the murder requires so much premeditation that I am inclined to see her swoon as a parody of other, similar instances in Kleist's own work.

23 Anthony Stephens, 'Gegen die Tyrannei des Wahren,' pp. 181f.

dead girl, Hally, in Act IV. She is first raped by Romans, and a Roman officer summarily executes three of his soldiers for the offense. Hally is then brought on stage unconscious and covered with a cloth. Her father and two male cousins murder her in sight of the audience to expunge her dishonor: 'Stirb! Werde Staub! Und über deiner Gruft/ Schlag ewige Vergessenheit zusammen!' (SW I, 589). Hermann, searching for something to incite the German tribes to action, happens by, perceives his chance, and orders the father to cut his daughter's corpse into 15 pieces and despatch them to each of the 15 German tribes to inflame their anger. Act V, Scene 23, confirms the complete success of his deception.

There is a biblical model for this, but Kleist's immediate source was probably Rousseau's *Essai sur l'origine des langues,* where the same example from the Book of Judges is cited to show the superior eloquence of corporeal proofs over persuasive language.[24] Kleist's point is that the currency of truth has become so debased that it makes no difference that the crime against Hally has already been punished by the Romans, and that it is her own father who has murdered her. The value of proofs no longer has anything to do with their origin, but resides entirely in their power to incite action. Had Hally not provided a means to this end, Hermann would have reverted to his earlier stated intention of setting his own people's tents on fire and blaming it on the Romans (SW I, 586).

With the abolition of the criterion of truth, no matter how elusive it may have been, the play loses the characteristic tension of Kleist's other fictional texts. The world is reduced to the monotony of Hermann's simple equation of success with violence and destruction, in the name of a 'liberty' that is too intangible to enjoy in the present, but calls for further bloodshed until Rome itself is extirpated – 'Als bis das Raubnest ganz zerstört' (SW I, 628) – a conclusion Hermann admits he is unlikely to witness.

The nihilism of the play's conclusion is thus, if we entirely share the perspective of the main character, unrelieved, for even the most

---

24 Jean-Jacques Rousseau, *Essai sur l'origine des langues,* Paris, 1969, pp. 502f: 'Quand le Lévite d'Ephraïm voulut venger la mort de sa femme, il n'écrivit point aux tribus d'Israël; il divisa le corps en douze pièces, et les leur renvoya. A cet horrible aspect, ils coururent aux armes en criant d'une voix: *Non, jamais rien de tel n'est arrivé dans Israël, depuis le jour que nos pères sortirent d'Egypte jusqu' à ce jour.* Et la tribu de Benjamin fut exterminée. De nos jours, l'affaire, tournée en playdoyers, en discussions, peut-être en plaisanteries, eût traîné en longueur, et le plus horrible des crimes fût enfin demeuré impuni. Le roi Saül, revenant du labourage, dépeça de même les boeufs de sa charrue, et usa d'un signe semblable pour faire marcher Israël au secours de la ville de Jabès.'

nationalistic of audiences must be aware that Rome's empire was to outlive this defeat on its furtherst frontier by several centuries. Indeed, the text even points this up by having Varus, in despair, pronounce an epitaph for Rome that is entirely congruent with Hermann's ultimate desires, but absurd for all that: 'Da sinkt die große Weltherrschaft von Rom/ Vor eines Wilden Witz zusammen' (SW I, 622).

If the text as a whole can still adumbrate such correctives to Hermann's dominant perspective, but give his blood-lust the final word, what conclusion can we draw about the work's meaning beyond that of a piece of propaganda that failed to reach its intended audience in 1809? What it emphatically does *not* do is open any perspective onto a dialectical view of history.[25] Kleist's other fictional worlds are conspicuously lacking in the enforced harmonies of a dialectical world view. Rather, they derive their tensions and thus their shape from their problematical dependency on an elusive ideal of truth in human experience. Nullify that, and a perspective opens onto the featureless wasteland of Hermann's closing words: ultimate destruction and nothing in its place.

I suggest, by way of conclusion, that the nihilism of the play's ending is meant to be provocative. Kleist's personal vision of Napoleonic Europe was of a hiatus between the abolition of an old order and the emergence of a new one, a no-man's-land dominated by the carnage of recent battles and the figure of Napoleon, whom he had thoroughly demonized.[26] One of his scathing commentaries on post-Revolutionary French society, written in Paris in 1801, stresses the indifference of that state, which had established itself in the wake of the great upheavals and in the name of ideals Kleist also shared, to truth as a value.[27]

In writing *Die Hermannsschlacht*, Kleist initially wanted to achieve a specific effect on readers or audiences. Clearly, he went beyond this to create a mirror for his own age, but one which, through its reductionist savagery, could shock the beholder into a recognition of the underlying nihilism of a Europe in which truth had become purely a plaything of expediency, and expediency, in turn, a function of Napoleon's progress toward total dominance. Kleist was not to wit-

25 I disagree on this point with Dirk Grathoff, 'Heinrich von Kleist und Napoleon Bonaparte.' *Der Furor Teutonicus und die ferne Revolution, Schreckensmythen – Hoffnungsbilder. Die Französische Revolution in der deutschen Literatur*, ed. Harro Zimmermann, Frankfurt/M, 1990, p. 101.

26 See above p.5

27 'Warum verschwendet der Staat Millionen an alle diese Anstalten zur Ausbreitung der Gelehrsamkeit? Ist es ihm um *Wahrheit* zu tun? Dem *Staate*? Ein Staat kennt keinen andern Vorteil, als den er nach Prozenten berechnen kann' SW II, 681.

ness the collapse of this empire. Underlying all the patriotic bathos of this drama is a vision of Napoleonic Europe so bleak that it is as if the author were saying to a reader or audience: this cannot possibly be the last word on politics in the present age! *Die Hermannsschlacht* thus contains all the bitterness of a helpless act of provocation, adressed to whatever forces might – despite all appearances – be active in history, as a corrective to facile optimism. But it was a provocation that failed to impinge upon either its immediate or more distant interlocutors.[28]

---

28 Oppressed by the political climate of Napoleonic Europe, Kleist invokes a conventional Deism in a letter to the Freiherr vom Stein of August 1806: 'Es kann kein böser Geist sein, der an der Spitze der Welt steht: es ist ein bloß unbegriffener!' SW II, 766.

8

Prinz Friedrich von Homburg

Kleist's last play may best be described as a tragedy encapsulated in, and to some extent neutralized by, a fantasy of Prussia as it never had been, nor was to be. A version was completed by March 1810 and its composition had probably occupied the whole of the previous year.[1] Kleist's hopes for a positive reception of the play by the Prussian court – indeed, that its complex patriotic message might reach the King, Friedrich Wilhelm III, and provide an antidote to his chronic vacillation in his policies toward Napoleon – were unrealistic and duly disappointed. By taking a theme from the history of the ruling house of Brandenburg and freely embroidering it, by including tendentious references to contemporary Prussia, and finally by presenting a well known figure from the 17th century in the guise of a modern, Romantic somnambulist, Kleist had once again overshot the expectations of his chosen audience. That the Kurfürst of Brandenburg was a main figure who could not readily be disguised, as the Emperor in *Das Käthchen von Heilbronn* had been turned, to placate the censor, into the Duke of Swabia for the first production in Vienna, provided an obstacle to performing the play. That the hero, Prinz Friedrich von Homburg, should shatter the stereotype of military valor by exhibiting not only a desperate fear of death, but also a lack of scruple in his efforts to remain alive, was distasteful to the very people to whom Kleist wished to appeal, and so the play was not published until 1821, and it received only private readings until its first performance in 1828.[2]

The play suffered as much as *Penthesilea* from the tendency of contemporaries to judge fictitious characters as real people. There seemed no way around the personality of the main character, and even such a sophisticated observer as Theodor Fontane was, in 1872, to damn the play because its hero was no Prussian hero, but belonged to a common category of undesirables: 'Es sind eitle, krankhafte, prätentiöse Waschlappen, aber keine Helden, Kerle, die in Familie, bürgerlicher Gesellschaft, staatlichem Leben immer nur Unheil gestiftet haben und die immer nur in kranker Zeit oder von kranken Gemütern gefeiert wor-

1 Cf. KW II, 1158f.
2 Cf. KW II, 1179f.

den sind.'[3] Prince or no Prince, this is not someone a Prussian father would be happy to see going steady with his daughter.

Kleist had not improved prospects for his play by providing a beloved and bride for his hero, Prinzessin Natalie, who had no place in Prussian history, but who might be understood as an allusion to women of the contemporary ruling family, and by drastically rejuvenating the historical Prinz Friedrich von Homburg who, at the time of the battle of Fehrbellin, was 42 years of age, married for the second time, and had an artificial leg. Writing on the play is still dominated by a tug-of-war between the historicists, who continue to tease out the text's contemporary references, and the literary analysts who happily apply the most disparate critical paradigms.

The conviction that, despite the history of the play's reception, there can be one, definitive reading of the text is stronger in the writing on *Prinz Friedrich von Homburg* than on Kleist's other dramas. I suggest there are two main factors that explain this. First, Kleist keeps the dramatic form under more harmonious control than in any other play, so that there is a strong temptation to believe that the neatly integrated plot must yield one equally integrated reading. Second, once German audiences had become reconciled to Prinz Friedrich's conduct unbecoming, the play was readily intelligible in terms of two compatible stereotypes: the celebration of Prussian heroism and the plot of the 'Bildungsroman,' in the course of which an immature main character is educated in the ways of the world. Often those critics who are determined to discard both clichés still begin from a traditional understanding that is markedly convergent, and may cast their own readings in its image, rather than question its structural, as distinct from thematic, premises.

Both stereotypes are still alive and well in critical writing of the last decade. On the one hand, there is the awesome crudity of Wolf Kittler's reading of the play as a longer version of *Die Hermannsschlacht*.[4] On the other, and in the same year, Hinrich C. Seeba reformulates the understanding of the plot as a process by which Prinz Friedrich is educated, without expressing any reservations about this view.[5] Pleas for a

---

3 KN, 473.

4 Wolf Kittler, *Die Geburt des Partisanen*, pp. 267f: 'Nur im Moment des totalen Krieges kann das Volk auf einen Offizier wie den Prinzen von Homburg nicht verzichten. Denn er ist, nachdem er alle Tiefen und Höhen der Liebesleidenschaft und Todesangst durchlitten hat, wie kein anderer gestählt für einen Krieg, der keine Grenzen kennt. . . . Der Konflikt zwischen Homburg und dem Kurfürsten hat also die gleiche Funktion wie das Duell zwischen Hermann und den Germanenfürsten Fust und Gueltar.' Of course, Hermann duels only with Fust, *not* Gueltar, in Act V, Scene 22.

5 KW II, 1224: 'Insofern folgt . . . "die Erziehung des Prinzen von Homburg: aus schwärmerischer Gefühlsanarchie zum Preußentum" (Lukács) der Struktur eines Entwicklungsromans: als Bewährungsprobe, deren wichtigste Aufgabe die Integration des rebellischen Individuums in die – durch seine Rebellion zu reformierende – Gesellschaft scheint.'

pluralistic, indeed ironic reading of the work are much less frequent, though no less valuable for that, and Erika Swales' insistence on a 'text whose impulses are both integrative and subversive' and one 'poised on the point of parody' is a refreshing exception to the various mainstreams of writing on the play.[6]

The problem with a reading in terms of parody is the lack of consensus on what major aspects of the text, let alone what lines or even words, can thus be fairly understood.[7] I suggest that the difficulty should not be taken as an excuse to ignore this dimension altogether. *Prinz Friedrich von Homburg* not only offers a text that is as complex as any other Kleist wrote, but its dramatic technique shows a degree of sophistication that should never be understated. Its continued success on stage, in the most varied of cultural climates, not only militates against the idea that it has a simple message to convey,[8] but also demonstrates that the dramaturgical factors that still render *Penthesilea* extremely hard to stage, or else oblige a contemporary production of *Das Käthchen von Heilbronn* to reverse those effects which ensured its popularity in the 19th century, are here maintained in a fine balance.

Since it has become more fashionable to comment on affinities between *Prinz Friedrich von Homburg* and the drama written immediately before it, *Die Hermannsschlacht*, than with other plays by Kleist,[9] it may be time to look at the limits of this comparison and at the text's relation to other works, such as *Das Käthchen von Heilbronn*. While the last words of *Prinz Friedrich von Homburg* appeal to the spirit of Prussian militarism – 'In Staub mit allen Feinden Brandenburgs!' (SW I, 709) – it is easy to exaggerate the consistency of this strand of the text, for, as Helmut Arntzen has shown in detail, many contradictions beset both the ideological and the psychological

6 Erika Swales, 'Configurations of Irony,' pp. 419 and 429.

7 See, for example Klaus Lüderssen's discussion, 'Recht als Verständigung unter Gleichen in Kleists *Prinz von Homburg* – ein aristokratisches oder ein demokratisches Prinzip?,' in *KJb* 1985, pp. 27f, on whether Homburgs lines: 'Recht wacker, in der Tat, recht würdig!/ Recht, wie ein großes Herz sich fassen muß!' (SW I, 689) are meant sarcastically or not.

8 Thus Walter Müller-Seidel, 'Kleist. Prinz von Homburg,' *Das deutsche Drama vom Barock bis zur Gegenwart*, ed Benno von Wiese, Düsseldorf, 1964, p. 390, comments on a highly successful production in Paris in 1951, hence at a time that could scarcely be less propitious for a German drama of patriotism: 'Daß man unerachtet dieser störenden Faktoren das Drama um diese Zeit in Paris aufführen konnte und daß die Aufführung gelang, setzt Unbefangenheit und Vorurteilslosigkeit in der Aneignung der Dichtung voraus. Es spricht zugleich für ihre Größe, wenn sie sich derart über die Mißgunst der Stunde behauptet.'

9 Cf. Wolf Kittler, *Die Geburt des Partisanen*, p. 268; Hinrich C. Seeba, KW II, 1223; William C. Reeve, 'Die Hermannsschlacht: A Prelude to *Prinz Friedrich von Homburg*,' in *The Germanic Review*, vol. 63 (3), 1988, pp. 121-32.

aspects of the play.[10] The world of *Die Hermannsschlacht* is, by contrast, simple. Hermann's goals are clear in his mind before the action commences, and he achieves them by manipulating the other characters, with no effective antagonists and a minimum of dramatic tension. Thusnelda's initial resistance to his view of things, or any doubt as to whether Marbod will accept his gambit, are factors the action summarily sweeps away. Hermann does not agonize, because he is uninterested in moral issues, except to the extent they may be used in manipulative strategies.

Prinz Friedrich von Homburg confronts us with a much more complex world. The hero's course is marked by repeated transgressions, of which his disobeying his battle orders is only one. From the moment when, at Hohenzollern's instigation, the Kurfürst tries an experiment on Prinz Friedrich in his somnambulistic state, the protagonist is very much at the mercy of his own reactions to the consequences of transgressions he has not foreseen, let alone planned. This gives his actions the same driven quality that marks Penthesilea, and recalls Alkmene's question to Jupiter in *Amphitryon*: 'Kann man auch Unwillkürliches verschulden?' (SW I, 291). Like Penthesilea, he achieves a state of rest only by unifying his divided self about a clear resolve to die.

If there is to be a meaningful comparison with Hermann, then the figure in question must be the Kurfürst von Brandenburg, who has been interpreted as a sovereign puppetmaster.[11] But this interpretation, in turn, has been questioned with good reason.[12] The Kurfürst, in several speeches, rejects despotism, but acts despotically. Like the Queen of Hearts in *Alice in Wonderland*, he adheres to the principle of 'sentence first – verdict afterwards,' condemning Prinz Friedrich to death before a court martial can pronounce on his guilt.[13] Still, he shows a genuine concern for the problematic relations between power and morality, which is in complete contrast to Hermann's cynicism. Both Hermann and the Kurfürst have to face a threatened rebellion of their commanders, but

10 Helmut Arntzen, '*Prinz Friedrich von Homburg* – Drama der Bewußtseinsstufen,' *Kleists Dramen*, ed. Walter Hinderer, p. 221 'Ganz anders als im Drama Schillers kann hier von Konsequenz des Dargestellten nicht die Rede sein. Widerspruchsvoll ist die Kriegswelt der dargestellten Gesellschaft Brandenburgs in sich selbst . . . .'

11 Walter Müller-Seidel, '*Prinz Friedrich von Homburg*,' p. 407: 'Er ist in diesem Drama die überlegene Figur schlechthin. Dem Gott im Faustprolog vergleichbar, scheint er zu wissen, daß er seinen "Knecht" noch in die Klarheit führen wird.'

12 Cf. Helmut Arntzen, 'Drama der Bewußtseinsstufen,' pp. 220f; Klaus Lüderssen, 'Recht als Verständigung,' pp. 72f.

13 Lewis Carroll, *The Annotated Alice*, ed. Martin Gardner, Harmondsworth, 1970, p. 171; 'DER KURFÜRST. Wer immer auch die Reuterei geführt,/. . . Der ist des Todes schuldig, das erklär ich,/ Und vor ein Kriegsgericht bestell ich ihn./ . . . Wers immer war, der sie zur Schlacht geführt,/ Ich wiederhols, hat seinen Kopf verwirkt,/ Und vor ein Kriegsrecht hiemit lad ich ihn' SW I, 663.

Hermann has deliberately provoked his chieftains into disowning his apparent inactivity so that he can more securely bind them to him when he produces another strategic volte face and announces he will attack the Romans after all – whereupon one of his dupes embraces him, crying: 'Du Lieber, Wackrer, Göttlicher – !' (SW I, 546). The Kurfürst, by contrast, is in genuine trouble until he receives a note from Homburg assuring him he will accept the verdict of death (SW I, 694).[14] This enables the Kurfürst to manage the following scene by producing Homburg as a living refutation of the arguments mounted against his authority and actions, so that the parallel to *Die Hermannsschlacht* is, once more, trivial. Hermann is always self-sufficient, and needs only the gullibility of the other characters in order to win.

Hermann's family is of interest to him only as pawns in his strategic game – there is no sign that Thusnelda ever learns that Hermann has sent their sons off to Marbod as hostages. By contrast, the father-son relationship between Prinz Friedrich von Homburg and the Kurfürst is the most significant mythical complex in the drama, making the question of who won the battle of Fehrbellin of secondary interest. Whilst in *Die Hermannsschlacht* everything is ultimately a pretext for the main character's self-aggrandizement in the name of a liberty he shows no sign of wishing to enjoy, in *Prinz Friedrich von Homburg* the ambiguities in the contest between an at times murderously hostile adoptive father and a son, who, at one point, is indecently eager to usurp the place of the father he believes is dead (SW I, 657), are so finely balanced that no interpretation can reasonably claim to be definitive.

The sudden transitions and dislocations between the emotional states exhibited by Prinz Friedrich von Homburg are much more similar to the behavior of Graf Wetter vom Strahl in *Das Käthchen von Heilbronn* than to anything in *Die Hermannsschlacht*. Just as one may ask whether the sentimentalist of Act II, Scene 1, is recognizably the same character as the master courtroom strategist of Act I, so the same question can be raised with regard to Prinz Friedrich. The dislocations between Homburg's successive attitudes and emotional states are reminiscent, as well, of the world of *Penthesilea,* in which both major characters have a limited number of pre-formed roles at their disposal, and tend either to change abruptly from one to another or to activate the theme of 'chaos' by vacillating between incompatible positions.[15]

Recalling his dream in a dialogue with Hohenzollern, Homburg includes the Kurfürst among those dearest to him – 'Menschen, die mein Busen liebt' (SW I, 637) – and idealizes him in his memory as 'der

---

14 Cf. Hasso Hoffmann, 'Individuum und allgemeines Gesetz. Zur Dialektik in Kleists *Penthesilea* und *Prinz von Homburg*,' in *KJb* 1987, pp. 157f.
15 See above pp. 116-8.

Kurfürst mit der Stirn des Zeus' (SW I, 638). In Act II his resolve to replace the Kurfürst, believed to be dead, expresses itself, with no trace of grief for the 'father' he has claimed to love, as a delusion of grandeur: 'Ein Engel will ich, mit dem Flammenschwert,/ An eures Throns verwaiste Stufen stehn!' (SW I, 657). At the end of the act, he turns on the 'father' who has had him arrested and, in the Kurfürst's hearing, converts his previous adulation into contempt, attributing to him the meanest possible motives:

> Mein Vetter Friedrich will den Brutus spielen,
> Und sieht, mit Kreid auf Leinewand verzeichnet,
> Sich schon auf dem kurulschen Stuhle sitzen:
> Die schwedschen Fahnen in dem Vordergrund,
> Und auf dem Tisch die märkschen Kriegsartikel.
> Bei Gott, in mir nicht findet er den Sohn,
> Der, unterm Beil des Henkers, ihn bewundre. (SW I, 666)

The other main object of Prinz Friedrich von Homburg's affections, Natalie, receives equally inconsistent treatment. Having declared his love for her in Act II, in Act III he denies it to the Kurfürstin and in the hearing of a tearful Natalie:

> Nataliens, das vergiß nicht, ihm zu melden,
> Begehr ich gar nicht mehr, in meinem Busen
> Ist alle Zärtlichkeit für sie verlöscht.   (SW I, 676)

The affinity to Graf Wetter vom Strahl's unexplained swings of attitude toward Käthchen is much clearer than any parallel to *Die Hermannsschlacht*. Once again, Kleist's interest seems focused on evoking emotional states that are not causally linked in the manner of conventional dramatic exposition. The dream that underlies the plot of *Das Käthchen von Heilbronn*, described as a 'Märchen' in which two events – 'Wie die zwei Hälften eines Ringes, passend' (SW I, 516) – unite to yield meaning, is a clear prototype of the sequences with which *Prinz Friedrich von Homburg* begins and ends. In both instances, the fantasy ending presents itself as a celebration of paternal authority, but the gratuitous cruelty of the mock-execution, on which the Kurfürst insists even after he has announced he will pardon Homburg, echoes the dissonances in the ending of *Das Käthchen von Heilbronn*.

This raises the problem, already encountered in discussing Kleist's earlier 'fairytale' drama, of how critical discourse may best deal with a psychology that gives every appearance of having been devised to resist rational paraphrase. Explanations of Prinz Friedrich von Homburg's behavior are predicated on the assumption that there is a set of concepts that will unify his motivation, but, as in the case of Graf Wetter vom Strahl, I incline to the view that discursive unification misses the point. An example of this practice is Dieter Liewerscheidt's attempt to read the play as a comedy.[16] Beginning from the correct, but far from novel observation that there are a great many contradictions and inconsistencies in the text, Liewerscheidt sets out to deflate the 'emphatische Ehrfurcht, die einem der Protagonisten oder gar beiden aus der Rezeptionsgeschichte entgegenschlägt.'[17] Well and good, but the price he pays is yet another reductionist unification of Homburg's behavior, making him 'nichts anderes als personifizierte Ruhmbegierde' and simplifying the Kurfürst to a representation of 'eines engherzigen und kurzsichtigen Patriarchalismus.'[18] Within these categories there is no place for the strange mixture of adulation and aggression in Prinz Friedrich's attitudes to the Kurfürst, his struggle to be accepted as a son, or the Kurfürst's equivocal stances toward the role of adoptive father. For Homburg has other preoccupations besides fame, and the Kurfürst's behavior is much more inscrutable than these labels suggest.

The world of the play is remarkable for its wealth of doubling-effects, and I suggest that this may also extend to the characterization to a degree that makes the search for single motivations futile. The dream sequence that begins the play and is then re-enacted at the end signals other kinds of doubling within the text. The 'historical' dimension doubles the battle of Fehrbellin in 1675 with references to events in contemporary Prussia, such as the insubordination of Major Ferdinand von Schill in April 1809.[19] This amalgam is, in turn, doubled by a pseudo-historical fantasy, in which a Prinz Friedrich von Homburg, who has already lost the Kurfürst two victories by his impetuousness, is condemned to death; a Prinzessin Natalie is not only the ruler's niece and 'daughter,' but commands her own regiment of dragoons; and an envoy, Graf Horn, tries to negotiate a marriage between Natalie and the Swedish King – none of which corresponds to history.

Some of Kleist's pseudo-historical liberties are clearly functional. At the time of the battle of Fehrbellin, the difference in age between Prinz Friedrich von Homburg and the Kurfürst was only 13 years. The emphasis on Prinz Friedrich's youth throughout the play lends credibility to his insistence that the Kurfürst be his 'father,' in terms that have more in common with middle class ideals of intimacy at the beginning of the

---

16 Dieter Liewerscheidt, '"Ich muß doch sehn, wie weit ers treibt!" Die Komödie in Kleists *Prinz Friedrich von Homburg*,' in *Wirkendes Wort*, vol. 43 (3), 1990, pp. 313-23.
17 Ibid., p. 320.
18 Ibid., p. 321.
19 Cf. Hinrich C. Seeba, KW II 1172f.

19th century than with the austere dignity of an absolute ruler as 'Landesvater.' Other fictional additions seem gratuitous and intended to endow the world of the play with the quality of being adrift in time that is so marked in *Das Käthchen von Heilbronn.*

From this earlier drama we may also derive the idea of the doubling of characters in the same figure, which is a variation on the pairing of characters we have observed in most of Kleist's dramas. When Graf Wetter vom Strahl finally coaxes the narration of Käthchen's dream from her in her somnambulistic trance, he is obliged to recognize that he is both the predestined lover of the girl he has seen in his own dream and the aristocratic figure of power who has treated Käthchen, quite literally, as if she were one of his dogs. His perception, fleeting as it is, is contained in the words: 'Nun steht mir bei, ihr Götter: ich bin doppelt!/ Ein Geist bin ich und wandele zur Nacht!' (SW I, 509). I suggest that this principle is relevant to the characterization of both Prinz Friedrich von Homburg and the Kurfürst, and means that there can never be one, linear reading of either figure.

Although one may dispute endlessly just how capable a soldier Kleist's Prinz Friedrich is, since the Kurfürst harps on his having already lost two battles and there are indications that the battle of Fehrbellin may be won before his intervention, part of his conduct seems to fit the appellation 'junger Held,' and his fellow commanders, at the end of the play, are enthusiastic about keeping him on the team.[20] Conversely, Hohenzollern introduces him to both the court and audience, in the play-within-a-play of the opening scene, as a somnambulist lost in a fantasy of narcissistic fulfilment:

> Als ein Nachtwandler, schau, auf jener Bank,
> Wohin, im Schlaf, wie du nie glauben wolltest,
> Der Mondschein ihn gelockt, beschäftiget,
> Sich träumend, seiner eignen Nachwelt gleich,
> Den prächtgen Kranz des Ruhmes einzuwinden.   (SW II, 632)

Hohenzollern himself is paired with Homburg as his at times malevolent alter ego, but Prinz Friedrich, in his first aside to the audience, confirms that he is given to experiencing such trances: 'Daß mich die Nacht verschläng! Mir unbewußt/ Im Mondschein bin ich wieder umgewandelt!' (SW I, 636).

The opening scenes thus show the figure of Prinz Friedrich as doubled in two senses: he embodies both the erratic, but functioning army

---

20 Cf. the Kurfürst's address: 'Sprich, junger Held! Was ists, das du begehrst?' (SW I, 705) and the reactions of the commanders SW I, 706f.

commander and the 'Nachtwandler' who exists mainly in visions of future fulfilment. At the same time, he is doubled in the sense of being a subject to himself and the object of others' language, as Erika Swales has shown.[21]

Hohenzollern's presentation of Homburg as a spectacle for the amusement of the court could not be more vindictive if he were his worst enemy. Homburg's somnambulism, in Hohenzollern's words, is introduced not as a harmless eccentricity, but as a transgresssion of a personal order from the Kurfürst: 'Befehl ward ihm von dir, hier länger nicht,/ Als nur drei Füttrungsstunden zu verweilen. . . .' (SW I, 631). Whatever the source of Hohenzollern's knowledge of what is occurring in Prinz Friedrich's consciousness – the text remains silent on the matter – he compounds Homburg's disobedience by the worst possible insinuations, given that his 'friend' has a responsible command in the army:

> Schade, ewig schade,
> Daß hier kein Spiegel in der Nähe ist!
> Er würd ihm eitel, wie ein Mädchen nahn,
> Und sich den Kranz bald so, und wieder so,
> Wie eine florne Haube aufprobieren.   (SW I, 633)

The motivation for Hohenzollern's action is as cursory, indeed as fragmentary, as anything in *Das Käthchen von Heilbronn*. It would have been simple to render Hohenzollern intelligible, in conventional terms, as a rival by having him share an infatuation with Natalie, similar to that of the half-brothers Johann and Ottokar for Agnes in *Die Familie Schroffenstein*. Since neither Natalie nor Hohenzollern have historical counterparts, there was no obstacle to this among Kleist's sources. But one looks in vain for any comprehensible basis for bitter rivalry with Prinz Friedrich. Later in the play, whether from malice or ignorance, he encourages Homburg in the delusion that the latter's desire to marry Natalie is behind the Kurfürst's hostility, whereas the Kurfürst has twice pronounced the sentence of death before he has any chance to learn of Homburg's understanding with Natalie. Ironically, Hohenzollern uses the occasion to proclaim his own fidelity as a friend: 'Du unbesonnener Tor! Was machtest du?/ Wie oft hat dich mein treuer Mund gewarnt?' (SW I, 672).

On the one occasion when Hohenzollern does suit the function of a friend, re-interpreting the actions of the Kurfürst in the opening scene to demonstrate the latter's complicity in Homburg's transgressions, his eloquent defense is superfluous, since the Kurfürst has already read

21 Erika Swales, 'Configurations of Irony,' pp. 409f.

Homburg's letter in which he agrees to his own execution. The figure of Hohenzollern, therefore, makes most sense if he is seen not as an autonomous character, but as a further doubling of Homburg himself. His lack of intelligible motivation ceases to be a puzzle once one realizes that he functions as an aspect of Homburg that is, in any given moment, *absent* from the latter's own self-representation. Thus, in the opening scene, Hohenzollern exhibits all the contempt toward Homburg's neglecting orders and being immersed in narcissistic fantasies of unwon prizes that one might expect of Prinz Friedrich's own waking self, the battle-tried colleague of Kottwitz and the other generals.

When, in Act III, Homburg is trying to puzzle out the Kurfürst's behavior in terms of family intimacy – 'Ich bin ihm wert, das weiß ich,/ Wert wie ein Sohn' (SW I, 668) – Hohenzollern, whether consciously or not, plays devil's advocate by suggesting the political explanation of a dynastic marriage, which is so immediately obvious to Homburg the general and aristocrat that he leaps at it:

> Arthur, sei mir nicht böse, wenn ich zweifle.
> Graf Horn traf, der Gesandte Schwedens, ein,
> Und sein Geschäft geht, wie man mir versichert,
> An die Prinzessin von Oranien.
> Ein Wort, das die Kurfürstin Tante sprach,
> Hat aufs empfindlichste den Herrn getroffen;
> Man sagt, das Fräulein habe schon gewählt.
> Bist du auf keine Weise hier im Spiele?   (SW I, 672)

Up to this point, Hohenzollern seems to function as an alter ego of Prinz Friedrich, but one who ensures that the worst of all outcomes available in a given moment will, in fact, occur, by manifesting an aspect of Homburg's composite figure that is hostile to his present helplessness. In this sense, Sylvester's henchman, Theistiner, observes of Rupert in the final act of *Die Familie Schroffenstein*:

> Sein Teufel ist ein Beutelschneider,
> Und führt in eigener Person den Sünder
> In seiner Henker Hände.   (SW I, 147)

Thus, Hohenzollern functions as Prinz Friedrich's 'devil,' until Homburg's own change of stance renders him an unnecessary 'angel' in the dispute with the Kurfürst. Once Homburg has resolved that, rather than contest the Kurfürst's verdict, he will die willingly, Hohenzollern's function as adversary loses its point. Hence he can, in Act V, Scene 5, change to being a 'helper' in terms of the restricted roles offered within fairytales,[22] and mount an eloquent plea for Homburg in precisely those terms Homburg might use to defend himself were he in possession of all the facts:

> Vom Sieg des nächsten Tages mocht er träumen,
> Und einen Lorbeer hielt er in der Hand.
> Du, gleichsam um sein tiefstes Herz zu prüfen,
> Nahmst ihm den Kranz hinweg, die Kette schlugst du,
> Die dir von Hals hängt, lächelnd um das Laub;
> Und reichtest Kranz und Kette, so verschlungen,
> Dem Fräulein, deiner edlen Nichte, hin.　　(SW I, 700)

The Kurfürst is not slow to point out that, by implicating him, Hohenzollern also convicts himself (SW I, 702). This reveals the pointlessness, in terms of the text's own parameters, of asking why Hohenzollern behaves, by turn, as Homburg's worst enemy and best friend, with a complete absence of causal motivation. For Hohenzollern's function is simply to draw out the full complexity of the dramatic constellations by revealing what is missing from Homburg's image in any given moment, specifically those aspects the Kurfürst and Prinz Friedrich potentially share, for, again in schematic terms, they more than once exchange the roles of adversary and helper.

It is, from the first scene of the play, Homburg's ironic lot to be a creation of the language of others in those very moments when he appears most to unfold an autonomous subjectivity. His fantasy of 'Natalie! Mein Mädchen! Meine Braut!' and 'Friedrich! Mein Fürst! Mein Vater!' (SW I, 633) is at once his own subjective epiphany and part of a spectacle that Hohenzollern instigates and the Kurfürst takes over and conducts as an experiment: 'Bei Gott! Ich muß doch sehn, wie weit ers treibt!' (SW I, 633). The manipulation of Homburg's dream to satisfy the Kurfürst's curiosity and entertain the court suggests a parody of the Romantic postulate of a subjectivity so sufficient unto itself that it can dispense with the external world altogether. Homburg's doubling is thus not that of a division of 'higher' and 'lower' selves, explored in the writings of Novalis, but becomes visible in the tension between the illusory perfection of a Romantic narcissism, on the one hand, and the harsh opposition of a world of other's perceptions of him, on the other. There is the further ironic twist that Hohenzollern supplies the hostile, external perspective on Prinz Friedrich's subjectivity – a view that the latter ulti-

---

22 For the relevance of the stereotyped roles codified in Propp's, *Morphologie du conte*, to the plot of Kleist's other major fantasy, *Das Käthchen von Heilbronn*, see above p.143 :

mately espouses with that part of himself that emerges to condemn his own transgressions:

> Ruhig! Es ist mein unbeugsamer Wille!
> Ich will das heilige Gesetz des Kriegs,
> Das ich verletzt, im Angesicht des Heers,
> Durch einen freien Tod verherrlichen!　　　(SW I, 704)

Homburg is never to escape from this doubling of his role, so that he is, throughout the play, at once both subject and object. Even his final monologue – 'Nun, o Unsterblichkeit, bist du ganz mein!' (SW I, 707) – is ironized by the fact that, in the scene immediately before, the Kurfürst has finally torn up the document condemning him to death, with the result that Homburg's intensely private farewell to this world is perceived by the audience as another misprision of the 'reality' he shares with the other figures of the play.[23] He becomes, once more, the object of a play staged by the Kurfürst, with the tacit agreement of Natalie, Hohenzollern, and the rest.

It is just as pointless to ask why the Kurfürst insists on this last cruelty as it is to debate whether it is curiosity or something more sinister that prompts his actions in the first scene of the play. For just as the doubling of Homburg makes any single discursive account of his actions inadequate, so the same applies to the figure of the Kurfürst. Rosemarie Zeller provides some insight into the doubling of the figure of the Kurfürst by identifying the conventional expectations of the figure of a ruler in German dramas of the 18th century as involving a choice between the figures of 'tyrant' or 'father.'[24] She opts to read the Kurfürst as a benevolent father figure, but this is surely to miss the whole point, namely that he straddles both conventional roles and becomes a doubled and discrepant figure in the process.

It is significant that the Kurfürst defends himself against the charge of tyranny, brought in diplomatic – if somewhat comic – terms by Natalie: 'Das wäre so erhaben, lieber Onkel,/ Daß man es fast unmenschlich nennen könnte' (SW I, 679). A further comic element lies in the fact that he must be aware of his own despotic action in twice condemning Homburg to death in the hearing of his officers before delegating the matter to a court martial:

---

23 Cf. Erika Swales, 'Configurations of Irony,' pp. 423 and 427f.
24 Rosemarie Zeller, 'Kleists *Prinz Friedrich von Homburg* auf dem Hintergrund der literarischen Tradition,' *JbSchG* XXX, 1986, p. 412.

Mein süßes Kind! Sieh! Wär ich ein Tyrann,
Dein Wort, das fühl ich lebhaft, hätte mir
Das Herz schon in der erznen Brust geschmelzt.
Dich aber frag ich selbst: darf ich den Spruch
Den das Gericht gefällt, wohl unterdrücken? –
Was würde wohl davon die Folge sein?   (SW I, 679)

The Kurfürst has had to listen to Homburg accuse him of behaving like a tyrant of Antiquity in Act II, Scene 10, and he is sensitive enough to the issue to begin his soliloquy in Act V, Scene 2, with yet another disclaimer, referring to a proverbial oriental despot: 'Seltsam! – Wenn ich der Dei von Tunis wäre,/ Schlüg ich bei so zweideutgem Vorfall, Lärm' (SW I, 692). In a manner once more reminiscent of the apparently haphazard shifts of attitude by Graf Wetter vom Strahl in *Das Käthchen von Heilbronn* and of his own incapacity to convert insights into action, the Kurfürst still insists on putting Prinz Friedrich through the cruel charade of the mock execution at the end. The protest by Homburg at the delay of his execution may be read – by extension – as an indictment of every occasion his feelings have been the playthings of others, and this is more relevant to the Kurfürst's treatment of him than to those to whom his words are immediately addressed:

Tyrannen, wollt ihr
Hinaus an Ketten mich zum Richtplatz schleifen?
Fort! Mit der Welt schloß ich die Rechnung ab!   (SW I, 706)

If the Kurfürst is, in one of his guises, a tyrant who is eloquent on the iniquities of tyranny, in another guise he becomes a parody of the benevolent, adoptive father whom Lessing's dramas had celebrated and who was thoroughly familiar to contemporary audiences and readers.[25] In Kleist's reversal of the Enlightenment trope, adoptive paternity is not offered by the father as an act of philanthropy, prompted by the voice of reason, but has to be bought by the 'son' at the price of a willingness to die at the father's hands. From the moment in the opening scene when, in his somnambulistic trance, Homburg exclaims: 'Friedrich! Mein Fürst! Mein Vater!' (SW I, 633), a tension is created that lasts until, in Act V, Scene 7, the Kurfürst twice kisses him and addresses him for the first and only time as 'mein Sohn' (SW I, 705), but then ends the scene by ordering that he be marched back to prison.

In between, the role of son is very much alive in Homburg's fantasies, traversing the whole gamut of affirmation and denial. But the role

25 Peter Horst Neumann, *Der Preis der Mündigkeit*, pp. 21f.

has no presence in the discourse of the Kurfürst, who seems much more preoccupied with fending off suspicions of tyranny and with clarifying his own role vis-à-vis the 'law,' as he chooses to define it, and an ethical, indeed religious ideal of the 'Vaterland,' which he fails to live up to.

It is instructive to consider the phases of this very one-sided, father-son relationship in terms of the doubling of both characters and of the parody of conventional tropes. I have drawn attention above to the fact that Homburg the dreamer is presented, at the opening of the play, by Hohenzollern, his alter ego fully in tune with the values of the court of Brandenburg, as being in breach of an order issued by the Kurfürst. Homburg's claim, still in his dream, of a filial relationship to the Kurfürst is made within the framework of Hohenzollern's insinuations of narcissistic self-indulgence, a further transgression of the prevailing code. Worse still, his response to the Kurfürst's experiment produces a violent rejection from the figure of authority he claims as 'father': 'Ins Nichts mit dir zurück, Herr Prinz von Homburg. . . .' (SW I, 634). Prinz Friedrich's confusion, in the scene in which the battle orders are dictated, over Natalie's glove and its apparent confirmation of his dream, puts him once more at odds with his role as cavalry commander, and the Kurfürst ends the scene with words that deny all intimacy and stress the seriousness of any further transgressions:

Herr Prinz von Homburg, dir empfiehl ich Ruhe!
Du hast am Ufer, weißt du, mir des Rheins
Zwei Siege jüngst verscherzt; regier dich wohl,
Und laß mich heut den dritten nicht entbehren,
Der mindres nicht, als Thron und Reich, mir gilt!   (SW I, 647)

Prinz Friedrich is now so surrounded with potential breaches of the officer's code and with prohibitions that he resembles nothing so much as an accident waiting to happen. A very significant prohibition is that of the Kurfürst to Hohenzollern that he must reveal nothing to Prinz Friedrich of the 'jest' the ruler has allowed himself to play. A page conveys the instruction:

Der Kurfürst schickt mich her!
Dem Prinzen möchtet Ihr, wenn er erwacht,
Kein Wort, befiehlt er, von dem Scherz entdecken,
Den er sich eben jetzt mit ihm erlaubt!   (SW I, 635)

As the Kurfürst can have no real idea what consequences withholding this knowledge from Homburg will have for his conduct in a battle on which, as he himself states, the future of his throne and realm depends, interpretations of this figure as, consistently, a strict but fair pedagogue overseeing the unruly prince's education in the ways of war are in serious difficulties from the third scene of the first act. Hohenzollern's consistent obedience to this prohibition not only neutralizes him in his ostensible role of friend and confidant, but has further implications for Homburg's conduct, which the Kurfürst cannot possibly foresee, rendering this forbidding one more act of that caprice – 'Willkür' – that he later protests to have no part in his own actions.[26]

In the battle itself, it is the apparent death of the Kurfürst, not his own intitial neglect of orders, that drives Prinz Friedrich to victory (SW I, 656), leaving it open to interpret his heroic action, as does von Mörner's narrative of the battle, in terms of grief at the loss of his beloved ruler or – given his strange absence of mourning in the following scene with Natalie – in terms of an eagerness to replace an oppressive father-figure with himself. There is certainly no modesty or regret in the words in which he sees himself continuing what the Kurfürst has left undone:

Ich, Fräulein, übernehme eure Sache!
Ein Engel will ich, mit dem Flammenschwert,
An eures Throns verwaiste Stufen stehn!
Der Kurfürst wollte, eh das Jahr noch wechselt,
Befreit die Marken sehn; wohlan! ich will der
Vollstrecker solchen letzten Willens sein!   (SW I, 657)

All of this is illusion, but it is fascinating to observe the way in which Homburg, who has a penchant for seeing reality in terms of tableaux vivants, rearranges the constellation of the play's opening scene so as to have himself and Natalie looking up to a Kurfürst, who is now safely dead, to receive his blessing on their marriage:

O Gott, wär er jetzt da, den wir beweinen,
Um diesen Bund zu schauen! Könnten wir
Zu ihm aufstammeln: Vater, segne uns!   (SW I, 658)

His next visualization of the Kurfürst, literally as a scene 'mit Kreid auf Leinewand verzeichnet' (SW I, 666), has him as the Roman consul Brutus, who condemned two sons to death for conspiracy against the state, but demoted suddenly to 'Vetter Friedrich' and with Prinz Friedrich rejecting a filial role that he imagines – with no evidence – that

26 Cf. SW I, 680: 'Meint er, dem Vaterlande gelt es gleich,/ Ob Willkür drin, ob drin die Satzung herrsche?'; SW I, 694: 'Da müßt ich noch den Prinzen erst befragen./ Den Willkür nicht, wie dir bekannt sein wird,/ Gefangen nahm und nicht befreien kann. –'

the Kurfürst has offered him: 'Bei Gott, in mir nicht findet er den Sohn,/ Der, unterm Beil des Henkers, ihn bewundre' (SW I, 666).

It is at this point that conventional explanations of what is transacted between Prinz Friedrich von Homburg and the Kurfürst tend to break down, for the end of the play reveals these words to have a strange clairvoyance about them. To attain recognition as son and receive a fatherly kiss, Prinz Friedrich does indeed have to profess complete support for the Kurfürst's actions while under imminent sentence of death. All that is required for the bestowal of the filial role he has pursued from the opening of the play, and indeed beyond the supposed death of the father, is his affirmation of what he here indignantly and contemptuously rejects – and most interpretations, for different reasons, reject with him. No matter how one may rationalize the relation between these two divided figures in terms of legality, patriotic fervour, and the Prussian officer's code, they are distinctly acting out a variant of the myth of Abraham and Isaac, which, as I have suggested elsewhere, Kleist likely encountered in Wieland's verse epic *Die Prüfung Abrahams*, of which there are many echoes in *Prinz Friedrich von Homburg*.[27]

The myth is based on the paradox that the dynastic principle stands or falls with a father who is willing to sacrifice his son and a son who is willing to die for no reason he can comprehend. Wieland had explored the various ways in which this offended the Enlightenment's concepts of a benevolent deity and a paternal authority based on humanity and reason. In adapting the myth to the terms of his Prussian fantasy, Kleist, as always in his dramas, reveals the premises of rationalism to be inadequate to the situation he creates. This does not mean that he advocates the full savagery of atavistic sacrificial rites, but that he allows the mythical and rationalist discourses to interact in his text so as to produce an effective critique of each other. That this disunifies the protagonists, in terms of conventional motivation, goes without saying, but at least it offers an alternative to both the endless ethical hair-splitting that is endemic in attempts to reduce their words and actions to complete consistency and the primitive chauvinism that holds 'In Staub mit allen Feinden Brandenburgs!' to be the clear and final message of the play.[28]

One may identify a genuine tragic blindness in Homburg's conduct, in that he chooses to pursue reconciliation with the Kurfürst in terms of the code of family intimacy, whereas the key to an acceptance of the filial bond is to be found outside it. Each code manifests itself in Homburg as an alternative way of being, and tragic irony is evident in the fact that his acting out of certain incompatibilities between the two codes is,

27 Cf. Anthony Stephens, 'Der Opfergedanke bei Heinrich von Kleist,' pp. 188-94 and 223-31.

28 Cf. Wolf Kittler, *Die Geburt des Partisanen*, p. 267.

quite logically, experienced as a fragmentation of the identity that has assumed them to be one and the same. For Kleist has devised the mythical discourse of the text, which ultimately includes the Kurfürst's acceptance of Prinz Friedrich as 'mein Sohn,' to operate, first, in terms of the aristocratic, military code of unquestioning self-sacrifice, and only second, in terms of 'die lieblichen Gefühle,' to which Natalie appeals (SW I, 680), echoing words previously spoken by Homburg.[29] Kleist's variations on mythical archetypes always have a commercial dimension,[30] and the acceptance of Homburg's filial bond has to be bought by his willingness to die and, incidentally, to save face for the Kurfürst, whose actions have been openly challenged by both his officers and Natalie.

As I have shown elsewhere, the threefold appellation that Homburg addresses to the Kurfürst in his dream – 'Friedrich! Mein Fürst! Mein Vater!' (SW I, 633) – raises, at a moment when all dramatic conflicts are still latent, the question as to where the center of power in this fictional world resides.[31] Homburg shares with the Kurfürst the name Friedrich, and one aspect of his dilemma is his early belief, stemming from his dream, that fulfilment lies in a simple, narcissistic identification with an idealized self. This underlies his monologue at the end of Act I, which is full of misplaced conviction of his own infallibility.

The second appellation – 'Mein Fürst!' – activates the code of military obedience, which Homburg breaches at his own peril, while 'Mein Vater' reveals itself in the course of the action as opening a dimension of family intimacy, which has nothing to do with the traditions of Prussian aristocracy, but rather correlates with middle-class celebrations of sentiment that were fashionable in German literature at the time Kleist was writing. Homburg's error is not to realize, once the illusion of narcissistic splendor has been banished by his sentence of death, that the sole means of activating the code of intimacy lies in and through the code of aristocratic formality, with which he is thoroughly familiar and which the Kurfürst expects him to follow. It is therefore not necessary for him to 'learn' anything, as interpretations that see the work as a dramatized 'Bildungsroman' would have it, but merely to revert to defining himself in terms that, until his present crisis, have been familiar and, indeed, habitual.

This explains the Kurfürst's confusion in Act IV, Scene 1, when Natalie tells him that Homburg, far from behaving in these terms, is

---

29 SW I, 668: 'Der Kurfürst hat getan, was Pflicht erheischte,/ Und nun wird er dem Herzen auch gehorchen.'

30 See below p. 228f. and p. 256f.

31 Anthony Stephens, 'Name und Identität bei Kleist und Kafka,' in *Jahrbuch des Freien Deutschen Hochstifts*, 1985, pp. 241-6.

pleading for his life and has become, from the *aristocratic* perspective of the woman who loves him: 'ganz unwürdig,/ Ein unerfreulich, jammernswürdger Anblick!' (SW I, 681). For the expectation is that, whatever the Kurfürst addresses to him, he will respond in the terms in which the latter, as ruler, has chosen to define their relationship, namely as 'Herr Prinz von Homburg' (SW I, 647).

The discrepant codes in the text thus reflect the transitions, in Kleist's lifetime, within the makeup of fictional German families. Much in *Prinz Friedrich von Homburg* testifies to the displacement of the clearly prescribed behavior of the aristocratic code by a much less disciplined, middle-class version of intimacy – and nowhere more clearly than in Homburg's helpless attempts to save himself. In his dialogue with Hohenzollern, when both know the court martial has confirmed the sentence of death, he bases his confidence in a pardon on the code of family intimacy: 'Ich bin ihm wert, das weiß ich,/ Wert wie ein Sohn' (SW I, 668) and on his derivation of personal worth from the proofs of affection he has received, since earliest childhood, from the Kurfürst: 'Bin ich nicht alles, was ich bin, durch ihn?' (SW I, 669). The tragic irony of this misreading is clear from two pieces of information Hohenzollern brings. The first is that the Kurfürst has had Homburg's name formally announced as the victor in the battle:

Und auf des Herrn ausdrücklichem Befehl,
Ward deines, als des Siegers Namen –
Erwähnung von der Kanzel her getan.   (SW I, 668)

The second is that he has formally requested the court martial's sentence of death to be sent to him for signature:

Der Marschall hat, höchst seltsam ists, soeben
Das Todesurteil im Schloß ihm überreicht;
Und er, statt wie das Urteil frei ihm stellt,
Dich zu begnadigen, er hat befohlen,
Daß es zur Unterschrift ihm kommen soll.   (SW I, 670)

Both pieces of news make clear that the Kurfürst is bent on remaining within the formal code of state and military affairs, and indicate, were Prinz Friedrich only able to read the signs, that it is in these terms that a resolution must be sought. Instead, he misreads the Kurfürst in two different ways, which are, strategically, disastrous for him, although both are marked by that perceptiveness that, ironically, emerges from his discourse whenever he thinks the worst of his 'father.' The first contains an intuition that there is indeed an element of pleasure – 'Lust' – in the Kurfürst's treatment of him, which correlates with his admission, in the page's instruction to Hohenzollern, that his behavior in the first scene has been indulgence in a jest – 'Scherz':

Nein, Freund, er sammelt diese Nacht von Wolken
Nur um mein Haupt, um wie die Sonne mir,
Durch ihren Dunstkreis strahlend aufzugehn:
Und diese Lust, fürwahr, kann ich ihm gönnen!   (SW I, 669)

Prinz Friedrich is quite correct in guessing that the Kurfürst enjoys directing charades, indeed his own mock execution will be another of them. He is wrong to think that there is no price attached to a happy outcome.

His second misreading revives the theme of tyranny. It contains a whole catalogue of legendary despots (SW I, 671), and, once more, the Kurfürst has, in fact, much more in common with a tyrant than either he or Homburg is ready to believe. Were Homburg to realize that there is more accuracy in his outburst than he suspects, then he might also realize that the Kurfürst might be ready to reverse his sentence of death if it can be done without losing face.

But Homburg persists in reading his own situation in terms of the code of intimacy, which the Kurfürst is as yet unwilling to apply, and so turns to the Kurfürstin, appealing to her three times as 'Mutter' (SW I, 674f). She does not deny him the appellation 'Mein Sohn!,' but Prinz Friedrich, evoking another of his implausible tableaux vivants, insists on her seeing him as a helpless infant:

Dir übergab zu Homburg, als sie starb,
Die Hedwig mich, und sprach, die Jugendfreundin:
Sei ihm die Mutter, wenn ich nicht mehr bin.
Du beugtest tief gerührt, am Bette knieend,
Auf ihre Hand dich und erwidertest:
Er soll mir sein, als hätt ich ihn erzeugt.   (SW I, 676)

He then compels Natalie to envisage adopting a child – 'einen Knaben, blondgelockt wie ich' (SW I, 677) – in place of marrying himself. What is remarkable about these two visions is not their pathos, so much as the fact that Homburg objectifies himself as a helpless infant, implying a murderous father in the background, to wring both women's maternal feelings for all they are worth. This is an ironic reversal of the 'jest' both Hohenzollern and the Kurfürst play on him in the opening scene. There, his worth as an individual is demeaned by being made the plaything of others' language and pretense; here, he reduces himself to a pitiable object out of a misapprehension that he can manipulate the Kurfürst through the medium of the code of intimacy that both women, in maternal guise, accept. Through all this infantile imagery gleams the faint irony that a Prussian hero is struggling to be born, from the nothingness to which the Kurfürst has consigned him in the opening scene, but cannot, as it were, find the right path.

It is thus no surprise that Natalie adopts the same code in her opening plea the Kurfürst:

> Den wirst du nicht mit Füßen von dir weisen!
> Den drückst du um die Mutter schon ans Herz,
> Die ihn gebar, und rufst: komm, weine nicht;
> Du bist so wert mir, wie die Treue selbst! (SW I, 679)

It is equally unsurprising that the Kurfürst responds to the suggestion that he treat Homburg like a puling infant with a discourse on avoiding tyranny and the true nature of the 'Vaterland.' In all his guises, he is uninterested in any form of adoptive paternity that does not predicate the code of intimacy on where he has chosen to locate the ultimate center of power, namely, not in himself as father, but in a deified 'Vaterland':

> Kennst du nichts Höhres, Jungfrau, als nur mich?
> Ist dir ein Heiligtum ganz unbekannt,
> Das in dem Lager, Vaterland sich nennt? (SW I, 680)

While he and Natalie dispute the nature of this supreme authority, it has the great advantage for the Kurfürst that he can define it however he likes, being an absolute ruler, while his own willing subordination to it is an excellent defense against any charge of tyranny by others – a contradiction in terms, but dramatically effective. Never one to show all his cards at once, he saves for his refutation of Kottwitz in Act V the definition of this highest authority which permits its reconciliation with the code of intimacy:

> Den Sieg nicht mag ich, der, ein Kind des Zufalls,
> Mir von der Bank fällt; das Gesetz will ich,
> Die Mutter meiner Krone, aufrecht halten,
> Die ein Geschlecht von Siegen mir erzeugt! (SW I, 697f.)

There is no need to resort to Freudian parlance to integrate the code of state with that of intimacy. In the terms the Kurfürst chooses, Prinz Friedrich has gone a fair way toward being a bastard. If he wishes to be a legitimate son, he must align himself with the 'Mutter meiner Krone' and become a 'son of the law' by accepting the death penalty which, as the Kurfürst knows from his letter, he has by this point already done. Homburg's pleading to the Kurfürstin and Natalie is thus revealed, ironically, as an appeal to the wrong mothers.

His response to the Kurfürst's offer of pardon in the words: 'Pah! Eines Schuftes Fassung, keines Prinzen. – (SW I, 688) means he must phrase his reply not in the code of intimacy, but in that in which princes speak to their sovereign rulers. In doing so, he sanctifies the law, just as the Kurfürst has previously sanctified the 'Vaterland': 'Ich will das heilige Gesetz des Kriegs,/ . . . Durch einen freien Tod verherrlichen!' (SW I, 704). One may fairly regard this process as the birthing of a Prussian hero in terms that effect a complete tragic action. Kleist thus may have realized in this work the fantasy of autogenesis that is foreshadowed in the fragment of *Robert Guiskard*. I have suggested, when interpreting that text, that the highly problematic imagery of marriage and procreation may signal an insoluble dramaturgical problem, which only here attains its resolution.[32] With this, the tragedy of Prinz Friedrich von Homburg is complete. He is ready to face his execution with the same unity of purpose and spiritual calm as is shown by the heroine at the conclusion of Schiller's *Maria Stuart*. What follows is a neutralization of the tragic effect by a fantasy ending that has much in common with those of *Amphitryon* and *Das Käthchen von Heilbronn*.

For all that they are complex, indeed composite figures, Prinz Friedrich and the Kurfürst achieve instant harmony, once the son understands in what code he must address his father in order to have his filial status confirmed:

> DER KURFÜRST *küßt seine Stirn.*
> Seis, wie du sagst! Mit diesem Kuß, mein Sohn,
> Bewillg' ich diese letzte Bitte dir!
> Was auch bedarf es dieses Opfers noch,
> Vom Mißglück nur des Kriegs mir abgerungen;
> Blüht doch aus jedem Wort, das du gesprochen,
> Jetzt mir ein Sieg auf, der zu Staub ihn malmt!
> Prinz Homburgs Braut sei sie, werd ich ihm schreiben,
> Der Fehrbellins halb, dem Gesetz verfiel,
> Und seinem Geist, tot vor den Fahnen schreitend,
> Kämpf er auf dem Gefild der Schlacht, sie ab!
> *Er küßt ihn noch einmal und erhebt ihn.*   (SW I, 705)

32 See above, p. 53f.

It is idle to ask what motivates these words and gestures. The whole play has its entelechy in this moment, in which a father kisses his son and, in the same breath, pronounces him dead. All the rest remains conjecture. Most interpretations agree that Homburg is less than delighted to be reprieved after his mock execution, and that Natalie's words when he loses consciousness: 'Himmel! die Freude tötet ihn!' (SW I, 708) may not be an exact description of what he feels. He may, indeed, resent rebirth into a world with which he has closed accounts and, like Wieland's Isaak, already anticipate a more prestigious incarnation.

That the words in his final monologue: 'Es wachsen Flügel mir an beiden Schultern,/ Durch stille Ätherräume schwingt mein Geist' (SW I, 707) take up the image of himself as an angel which he coined in the moment of his greatest delusion in Act II, Scene 6, may well mean that narcissism has the last word, but the essential point is that the text yields no unequivocal answers to questions of psychological motivation. One may conjecture a greater or lesser enthusiasm on Prinz Friedrich's part for sonship, militarism, or marriage, or for various combinations of all three, but at this point the intention of the text is to allow the rest to be silence – once the din of the final cannonade (SW I, 708) and the patriotic chorus has died away.

Throughout all his dramas, Kleist explored the role of violence within the family, a region which, in terms of contemporary middle-class sensibilities, should have been a domain of intimate harmony. Violence is made plausible by allowing his families to interact, and indeed merge, with the apparatus of a state. The linking of paternal power with a murderous hostility toward a child or children runs from *Die Familie Schroffenstein* to *Prinz Friedrich von Homburg*, and is evident in such stories as *Das Erdbeben in Chili* and *Der Findling*. While the temptation for critics is always to explain it away, it is one of the fundamental data of Kleist's fictional worlds, and the tableau in which the Kurfürst kisses the son whom he still holds under sentence of death – regardless of any conjectures about what he 'really feels' in this moment – is one the text has carefully selected, from among all other possible outcomes, as a balance of forces that cannot elsewhere be achieved.

Certainly, the violence within Kleist's families may be read as a critique of the somewhat facile celebration of the moral dignity of adoptive fathers in dramas of the Enlightenment. Anticipating Kafka, he shows that the hostilities within families, and especially between fathers and children, are no different in quality from those that produce wars and massacres. He also demonstrates, and nowhere more clearly than in *Prinz Friedrich von Homburg*, that mythical constellations have an economy of their own, and that a willingness to shed blood may be the price of paternal blessing, as the myth of Abraham sets forth. This does not mean that he advocates cruelty, or that savage patriotism is his solution for the dilemmas of the human condition. It does mean, and *Prinz Friedrich von Homburg* shows it, that a mythical discourse based on an economy of violence need be no less coherent than the discourse of humanity and reason so dear to both the Enlightenment and Weimar Classicism. It need be no more convincing either, and, with the sole exception of *Die Hermannsschlacht*, Kleist was, despite his scepticism, to allow the discourse of human values a strong presence in all of his texts. What we may conclude from *Prinz Friedrich von Homburg* is that the idols of reason have no inherent superiority over the darker gods of irrationalism when the prime aim of an aesthetic construct is to reveal the full complexity of the ways of power within human relationships.

9

Das Erdbeben in Chili – Die Verlobung in St. Domingo

Das Erdbeben in Chili was the first of Kleist's stories to be published, being completed by autumn 1806, and may well have been the first to be thought out. There is no way of knowing whether any experiments in narrative form preceded it, and source studies have been characteristically unrewarding as far as the main plot is concerned.[1] Kleist's control of complex narrative form in his first published story is even more astonishing than his precocity as a dramatist in *Die Familie Schroffenstein*, finished in 1802. By the time he wrote *Das Erdbeben in Chili*, he had been through the long battle to resolve the problems of tragic form in *Robert Guiskard* and had also completed *Der zerbrochne Krug*. His stories, as a whole, combine a penchant for tableaux, *coups de théâtre*, and 'set pieces' with a sophisticated control of perspective, and it is likely that his narratives benefited from his continual experiments in dramatic technique.

Das Erdbeben in Chili has attracted, and continues to attract, more critical exegesis than any other prose narrative of comparable length in German literature. Perhaps more tantalizing in its brevity and condensation than any other of Kleist's stories, it experiments with the masochistic gratification readers may derive from texts that do violence to genre-based expectations. It does this in three ways: first, it places the reader in the same situation as the fictional characters, forced to decipher a plethora of signs whose apparent meaning is misleading; second, it subjects the reader to an unreliable narrator who is by turns omniscient and partisan, inclusive and exclusive of the reader's position; third, it plays on the trope of a deferred ending in a way that has generated endless controversy and, properly, remains unresolved,

In 1979, John Ellis commented on the contradictory readings of this text that 'previous interpretations achieve a special interest for a story whose very theme is interpretation. This is because the point of the story

---

1 KW, II, 827f; the fullest documentation of possible sources is to be found in *Heinrich von Kleist. Das Erdbeben in Chili. Erläuterungen und Dokumente* eds. Hedwig Appelt and Dirk Grathoff, Stuttgart, 1986, pp. 36-75.

lies not in the meaning of the events themselves but in the attempts made by the narrator and the characters to give them meaning.'[2] This is a good summation, and has the further interest of placing 'the narrator and the characters' in the same predicament, raising the question of whether this is possible in terms of narrative structure. There are no accidental narratives, and to posit a narrator struggling with thematics in the same way as the figures of the plot has the logical corollary of positing a further narrator who ironizes the limited perspective of the figure whose 'attempts' are analogous to those of other 'characters.' Writing on the story indeed drew this conclusion as soon as the critical apparatus became available,[3] but, paradoxically, it has not meant an end to partisan or moralistic readings that imitate, at one or more removes, the attitudes taken by the foreground narrative persona to characters, actions, and events. Such interpretations still ignore the fact that this narrator, by imitating the attitudes of the characters, *at times* becomes one of them in a formal sense, and is thus subject to ironic treatment by the whole of the narrative structure. Most tantalizing to the reader is the fact that this effect is sporadic, rather than sustained, and I thus cannot agree with Bernd Fischer's simplification of the foreground narrator into a figure in consistent opposition to the text's 'deeper intentions.'[4] There would be less writing on the story if the narrative perspective were so predictable.

As with Kleist's first drama, the story begins with a family conflict that is heightened to yield violence on a cosmic scale. While *Die Familie Schroffenstein* begins as a variation on *Romeo and Juliet*, *Das Erdbeben in Chili* takes up the theme, familiar in German literature of the time and ultimately stemming from the story of Eloise and Abelard, of a tutor who falls in love with his pupil, thus calling forth the hostility of the family. In the case of Jeronimo and Josephe, Don Pedro Asteron responds by placing his daughter in a nunnery. Jeronimo scales the walls and gets her pregnant. The story opens at the moment Josephe is on the point of being executed and Jeronimo, in prison, on the point of suicide. The earthquake that supervenes, destroying the city of St. Jago and

2 John M. Ellis, *Heinrich von Kleist*, p. 37.

3 The decisive move in this direction was made by Wolfgang Kayser, 'Kleist als Erzähler,' *Die Vortragsreise*, Berlin, 1958, p. 169: 'Der Erzähler ist selbst ein Teil des Werkes, ist nicht etwa der Dichter, sondern eine erdichtete Gestalt, die mit und in dem Werk ihr unvergängliches Leben hat.'; cf. also Wolfgang Wittkowski, 'Skepsis, Noblesse, Ironie. Formen des Als-ob in Kleists *Erdbeben*,' in *Euphorion*, vol. 63, 1969, p. 257: 'Vielleicht aber liegt das Verwirrende und liegt zugleich die Erklärung der Erzählstruktur gerade darin, daß der Erzähler den Standpunkt des Dichters teils vermittelt, teils verhüllt, daß er teils sich irrt und teils allwissend ist. . .'

4 Bernd Fischer, 'Fatum und Idee. Zu Kleists *Erdbeben in Chili*,' *DVjs*, 58, 1984: 'In seiner allzu menschlich einfältigen, weltanschaulich borniertern Haltung wird er aber zugleich zu einer Figur, die der tiefer liegenden Erzählintention des Textes konträr gegenübersteht und von dieser fortwährend unterminiert wird.'

thousands of lives, unites the lovers and their child and defers the expected ending to this family tragedy.

In the aftermath, Jeronimo and Josephe are accepted by another aristocratic family, that of Don Ferando Ormez; they unwisely return to the city to join in a service of thanksgiving and are, together with Don Fernando's sister-in-law and infant son, massacred in a scene of mob violence. At the conclusion, Don Fernando has adopted their child in place of his dead son. Just as the plot falls into three clear divisions – events leading up to the earthquake and the destruction of the city; an idyllic interlude, with overtones of a utopian vision, among the survivors in the countryside; the return to the city, the massacre, and its aftermath – so the plot revolves around three families.

There is, first, Josephe's family of origin, the aristocratic household of Don Pedro Asteron into which Jeronimo, as an intruder from the lower classes, is denied acceptance and which asserts patriarchal authority to punish both the love affair across class barriers and, much more savagely, Josephe's motherhood. There is a strong parallel to *Die Familie Schroffenstein* in the theme of a paternal hostility to children that gets out of hand. When Josephe, walking as a novice in a religious procession, is overtaken by birth pains on the steps of the cathedral, the ensuing scandal results in her being subjected to torture on the command of the Archbishop and condemned to be burned alive. At this point, the text attributes the commuting of her sentence to beheading to 'die Fürbitte der Familie Asteron, noch auch sogar der Wunsch der Äbtissin selbst, welche das junge Mädchen . . . liebgewonnen hatte' (SW II, 144f).[5] The Archbishop takes over the role of Josephe's father as punitive authority and carries it to an excess of cruelty, while the family now joins in the humane intercession of the abbess, whose affection for Josephe contrasts with the savagery of the patriarchal church.

There is, in Don Pedro's initial rage and subsequent attempt to mitigate its full consequences, something of the helplessness of the two fathers at the end of *Die Familie Schroffenstein,* when confronted too late with the murderous effects of their own aggression. If all social power in Kleist's works may ultimately be seen as deriving from paternal authority, it is equally the case that such power is always likely to exceed the control of individual fathers. The alignment of the family with the Abbess, however, does something toward restoring to it a measure of ambivalence, which becomes significant when Jeronimo and Josephe are accepted by the family of Don Fernando.

5 For a discussion of protective female figures in the story see Dagmar Lorenz, 'Väter und Mütter in der Sozialstruktur von Kleists *Erdbeben in Chili,*' in *Etudes Germaniques,* 1978, pp. 270-81.

Philipp, Josephe's child, is conceived while she is still identified as the daughter of Don Pedro Asteron. His birth both makes her the victim of the violence inherent in the whole of Christian society, and places her in the center of a new family of her own with Jeronimo and the child, after all three survive the earthquake. While a Christian Archbishop has played a leading part in setting the destruction of this second family, Kleist's narrator appears to want to even the balance by giving the idyllic tableau of their reunion after the earthquake an equally religious aura by alluding to pictorial representations of Joseph, Mary, and Jesus – perhaps even to a 'Rest of the Flight to Egypt,' which Kleist may have seen in Dresden.[6] Within the idyllic framework of the second part of the narrative, the second family is kindly received by the third, that of Don Fernando Ormez, and the narrator enhances this sign of the reconciliation of Josephe's new family, social pariahs before the earthquake, with an established aristocratic clan by an evocation of a harmonious society outside the ruined city in which the divisions of property and social class no longer have force: 'als ob das allgemeine Unglück alles, was ihm entronnen war, zu *einer* Familie gemacht hätte' (SW II, 152). One of the chronic puzzles of motivation, so familiar from Kleist's dramas, is the question of whether Don Fernando's humane, and later heroic, conduct is simply to be read in terms of a code of aristocratic chivalry, or whether it represents one lasting effect of the utopian interlude.

The family of Don Fernando Ormez survives the catastrophe in the square in front of the cathedral, despite the murders of Donna Constanze and the infant Juan, for whom Josephe has been caring, and adopts Philipp in his place. In structural terms, the child Philipp connects the three families and thus the three segments of the story.[7] His birth in scandalous circumstances effectively places Josephe beyond the reach of the family Asteron, for good or ill. As a bastard begotten on a novice in a convent, he at first shares the pariah status deriving from both his parents being branded as criminals, but is then included in the reconciliations of the second part of the story. He survives his natural parents to be adopted by a family very like the one from which his mother was rejected, with the difference that his adoption is an act of conscious choice and not, like his birth, a consequence of sexual desire. His transmission from family to family thus unifies the plot in terms of narrative syntax. Here Kleist stops short of his usual satirical portrayal of the idealization of parentage by adoption in the German Enlightenment, leav-

6 Cf. KW III, 818 and Plate 2.
7 While varying it in what follows, I am indebted to the interpretation of David E. Wellbery, 'Semiotische Anmerkungen zu Kleits *Das Erdbeben in Chili,' Positionen der Literaturwissenschaft. Acht Modellanalysen am Beispiel von Kleists 'Das Erdbeben in Chili,'* ed. David E. Wellberry, Munich, 1985, pp. 69-87.

ing Don Fernando's words and thoughts in the concluding sentences of the story a genuine enigma, which invites the reader to embark on a decoding of the rest of the story so as to resolve it.

Thematically, Don Fernando's adoptive fatherhood is opposed not so much to natural as to destructive paternity. The text's patent hostility to the hypocrisy and inhumanity of a professedly Christian and Catholic society led to the volume of Kleist's stories containing it being banned in Vienna on its first publication.[8] Destructive paternity correlates with both the Christian church and mob violence, while natural paternity, in the person of Jeronimo, may take on the aura of a benign Christian icon in the scene beneath the pomegranate tree. Mob violence is unleashed by the sermon of the 'Chorherr' who, interpreting the earthquake as an anticipation of the Last Judgement, attributes it to God's vengeance on immorality, specifying Jeronimo and Josephe: 'und in einer von Verwünschungen erfüllten Seitenwendung, die Seelen der Täter, wörtlich genannt, allen Fürsten der Hölle übergab!' (SW II, 156). The consonance of religious authority and paternal vengefulness, which was first evident in the Archbishop's replacing Don Pedro Asteron as chief punitive agent, is quite deliberately restated in the massacre.

The mob violence turns the rhetoric of the sermon condemning Jeronimo and Josephe into actuality, and the sentence in which Jeronimo is killed reinforces this by having as its grammatical subject 'eine Stimme':

> Doch kaum waren sie auf den von Menschen gleichfalls erfüllten Vorplatz derselben getreten, als eine Stimme aus dem rasenden Haufen, der sie verfolgt hatte, rief: dies ist Jeronimo Rugera, ihr Bürger, denn ich bin sein eigner Vater! und ihn an Donna Constanzens Seite mit einem ungeheuren Keulenschlage zu Boden streckte. Jesus Maria! rief Donna Constanze, und floh zu ihrem Schwager; doch: Klostermetze! erscholl es schon, mit einem zweiten Keulenschlage, von einer andern Seite, der sie leblos neben Jeronimo niederwarf. (SW II, 157f)

The syntax renders the murderers anonymous, but at the same time makes two connections clear: the 'voice' that strikes down Jeronimo is an extension of the voice that delivers the sermon; the same voice makes an unverifiable claim to being Jeronimo's father. The 'Chorherr' thus revives and intensifies, in his consigning the souls of the two lovers to 'all the Princes of Hell,' the previous actions of the Archbishop, which, in turn, had magnified the paternal indignation of Don Pedro Asteron. The mob violence is doubtless a quotation from accounts of similar

8 Cf. KW III, 808.

scenes during the Terror in France,[9] but we must be aware that the behavior of the populace at large is not tied to any one political model, but simply echoes the constellation of family relationships dominant in each phase of the story.

In the first segment, popular reaction is entirely consonant with the vengefulness of Josephe's father and the Archbishop:

Man sprach in der Stadt mit einer so großen Erbitterung von diesem Skandal. . . . Man vermietete in den Straßen, durch welche der Hinrichtungszug gehen sollte, die Fenster, man trug die Dächer der Häuser ab, und die frommen Töchter der Stadt luden ihre Freundinnen ein, um dem Schauspiele, das der göttlichen Rache gegeben wurde, an ihrer schwesterlichen Seite beizuwohnen. (SW II, 144f)

The emergence of a humane vision of the family in the second segment, with the idealization of the reunion of Josephe and her child with Jeronimo and their acceptance by Don Fernando and his relatives, is echoed by the evocation of a general reconciliation with strong Rousseauistic overtones (SW II, 152). The third section is then introduced by a general movement of the surviving citizens back into the city for the thanksgiving service: 'Das Volk brach schon aus allen Gegenden auf, und eilte in Strömen zur Stadt' (SW II, 153). The mob that, after the sermon, turns on the group led by Don Fernando and including Jeronimo, Josephe, and both children, thus cannot help but include some of the same 'Volk' who appear to form one, harmonious family in the idyllic sequence. Kleist's Rousseauistic allusions are, in his poetic works, consistently critical or ironical. This is one such irony, though subtle enough to be a trap for readers.[10]

Political interpreters should always be aware that Kleist has given this 'Volk' a very different structural function from that of the identically named chorus in *Robert Guiskard*. There, the voice of the people is a consistent and distinctive expression of the needs of the whole community, as against the wrangling in the Ducal family and the evasions of Guiskard himself. In *Das Erdbeben in Chili*, this essential counterpoint is absent, and the populace, as chorus, simply enhances the prevailing emotional tone of whatever version of family relationships dominates the foreground of the story at any given time.

9 Cf. Helmut J. Schneider, 'Der Zusammensturz des Allgemeinen,' *Positionen der Literaturwissenschaft*, ed. David E. Wellbery, pp. 115f.

10 Thus Peter Horn, *Heinrich von Kleists Erzählungen. Eine Einführung*, Königstein/Ts, 1978, p. 118, seems to go even than further than the foreground narrator: 'Kleist bietet uns eine andere . . . Alternative: die völlige Befreiung des Menschen von Staat und Gesetz, die Rückkehr zur wahren Natur des Menschen, bevor sie durch den Gesellschaftsvertrag verdorben wurde, die Rückkehr zur Anarchie.'

Criticism has long recognized that the story quotes the philosophical debate on Divine Providence and the Lisbon earthquake of 1755.[11] There has been a strong tendency to see Kleist as continuing the debate as well. Certainly, the fictional characters restate the terms in which Voltaire, Rousseau, and Kant, to name only the most prominent contributors, had discussed the issue of how the terrible effects of the earthquake could be reconciled with the idea of a benevolent deity. What is missing from such interpretations is an awareness that Kleist, in *Die Familie Schroffenstein*, had already explored the work of art as a demiurgic creation, demonstrating that a fictional world could, on the one hand, exhibit all that symmetry characteristic of Newton's or Leibniz' vision of the cosmos, whilst, on the other, presenting nothing but meaningless destruction. I suggest, therefore, that Kleist quotes the debate in an ironic sense, fully aware that an aesthetic construct can offer a well-ordered appearance that in no sense satisfies a hunger for meaning in religious terms and in the real world.

In support of this, I draw attention to the fact that the two gestures toward calculating the effect of the earthquake on the sum of human happiness and suffering, which are most reminiscent of Rousseau's reply to Voltaire's poem on the Lisbon earthquake,[12] are enmeshed with Jeronimo's and Josephe's complete misunderstanding of the realities they confront:

> und waren sehr gerührt, wenn sie dachten, wie viel Elend über die Welt kommen mußte, damit sie glücklich würden! (SW II, 150)

> so war der Schmerz in jeder Menschenbrust mit so viel süßer Lust vermischt, daß sich, wie sie [Josephe] meinte, gar nicht angeben ließ, ob die Summe des allgemeinen Wohlseins nicht von der einen Seite um ebenso viel gewachsen war, als sie von der anderen abgenommen hatte. (SW II, 152f)

They do not consistently misunderstand these realities in the central segment of the text, for they agree on the prudent plan 'lieber nach La

---

11 Most recently discussed by Susanne Ledanff, 'Kleist und die "beste aller Welten". *Das Erdbeben in Chili* – gesehen im Spiegel der philosophischen und literarischen Stellungnahmen zur Theodizee im 18. Jahrhundert,' in *KJb* 1986, pp. 125-55.

12 Cf. *Correspondance de J.-J. Rousseau*, vol. 1, Paris 1839, letter to Voltaire of 18 August 1756, pp. 312f: 'De tant d'hommes écrasés sous les ruines de Lisbonne, plusieurs, sans doute, ont évité de plus grands malheurs; et malgré ce qu'une pareille description a de touchant et fournit à la poésie, il n'est pas sûr qu'un seul de ces infortunés n'ait plus souffert que si, selon le cours ordinaire des choses, il eût attendu dans de longues angoisses la mort qui l'est venu surprendre. . . . Mais il est difficile de trouver sur ce point de la bonne foi chez les hommes, et de bons calculs chez les philosophes, parce que ceux-ci, dans la comparaison des biens et des maux, oublient toujours le doux sentiment de l'existence indépendant de toute autre sensation . . ..'

Conception zu gehen, und von dort aus schriftlich das Versöhnungsgeschäft mit dem Vizekönig zu betreiben' (SW II, 153), but their speculations on the sum of human happiness, in the manner of the 'philosophers' criticized by Rousseau, correlate with their misreading reality in terms of a special providence that safeguards them.

Reality as text and the unforeseen consequences of conflicting readings are always in the foreground of the story. The earthquake is read in the first and third segments in the context of the Last Judgement; in the second it suggests a regeneration of society in which the institutions of property and class pale into insignificance. Jeronimo and Josephe's relationship is read differently by Don Fernando and his family in the second segment from the way in which society at large reads it in the first and third segments. We are left to wonder as to how Don Fernando saw things prior to the earthquake. Kleist has infused the text of reality with a 'demonic' quality, which reminds one of Goethe's summary of the concept in the phrase: 'Nemo contra Deum nisi Deus ipse.'[13] For the discourse of Divine Providence is only intelligible in such contradictory terms, thus leaving the question open as to whether this semantic axis, for all its insistent presence, yields any final sense at all.

Put another way, the fictional characters are steadily compelled to run the gauntlet of signs that encourage one or other reading. This is most blatant in the description of Josephe's progress through the ruined city:

Sie hatte noch wenig Schritte getan, als ihr auch schon die Leiche des Erzbischofs begegnete, die man soeben zerschmettert aus dem Schutt der Kathedrale hervorgezogen hatte. Der Palast des Vizekönigs war versunken, der Gerichtshof, in welchem ihr das Urteil gesprochen worden war, stand in Flammen, und an die Stelle, wo sich ihr väterliches Haus befunden hatte, war ein See getreten, und kochte rötliche Dämpfe aus. (SW II, 148f)

13 Cf. Johann Wolfgang von Goethe, *Aus meinem Leben. Dichtung und Wahrheit*, HA, vol. X, p. 175f: 'Er glaubte in der Natur, der belebten und unbelebten, der beseelten und unbeseelten, etwas zu entdecken, das sich nur in Widersprüchen manifestierte und deshalb unter keinen Begriff, noch viel weniger unter ein Wort gefaßt werden könnte. Es war nicht göttlich, denn es schien unvernünftig, nicht menschlich, denn es hatte keinen Verstand, nicht teuflisch, denn es war wohltätig, nicht englisch, denn es ließ oft Schadenfreude merken. Es glich dem Zufall, denn es bewies keine Folge, es ähnelte der Vorsehung, denn es deutete auf Zusammenhang. . . . Dieses Wesen, das zwischen alle übrigen hineinzutreten, sie zu sondern, sie zu verbinden schien, nannte ich dämonisch . . . Selten oder nie finden sich Gleichzeitige ihresgleichen, und sie sind durch nichts zu überwinden, als durch das Universum selbst, mit dem sie den Kampf begonnen; und aus solchen Bemerkungen mag wohl jener sonderbare aber ungeheuere Spruch entstanden sein: Nemo contra deum nisi deus ipse.'

The consistent pattern of the text is to present the characters with events that may also be meaningful signs, in the manner in which Josephe is here confronted with the visible destruction of all the patriarchal authorities that have conjoined to condemn her to death. The model for the way in which the semiotics of the text treat the characters is given early in the story in the description of how Jeronimo is pursued through the collapsing city:

> Besinnungslos, wie er sich aus diesem allgemeinen Verderben retten würde, eilte er, über Schutt und Gebälk hinweg, indessen der Tod von allen Seiten Angriffe auf ihn machte . . . Hier stürzte noch ein Haus zusammen, und jagte ihn . . . in eine Nebenstraße; hier leckte die Flamme schon . . . und trieb ihn schreckensvoll in eine andere; hier wälzte sich . . . der Mapochofluß auf ihn heran, und riß ihn brüllend in eine dritte. (SW II, 146)

The verbs produce a state in which Jeronimo entirely forgets Josephe and their child, loses consciousness once he is in safety, and has to be reminded of them by catching sight of a ring on his hand: 'Drauf, als er eines Ringes an seiner Hand gewährte, erinnerte er sich plötzlich auch Josephens" (SW II, 147). All this is signalled to the reader, in terms of the semantic patterns of the whole text, by the word 'besinningslos,' with which the narrative sequence begins, for it is to recur at significant points. Josephe is similarly thrown into panic: 'Ihre ersten entsetzensvollen Schritte trugen sie hierauf dem nächsten Tore zu; doch die Besinnung kehrte ihr bald wieder, und sie wandte sich, um nach dem Kloster zu eilen, wo ihr kleiner, hülfloser Knabe zurückgeblieben war' (SW II, 148). After rescuing the child, she undergoes much the same ordeal as Jeronimo, and indeed is on the point of succumbing to helplessness when a narrow escape from death has the effect of clarifying her thoughts rather than throwing her into further panic:

> Sie schritt, den Jammer von ihrer Brust entfernend, mutig mit ihrer Beute [the child] von Straße zu Straße, und war schon dem Tore nah, als sie auch das Gefängnis, in welchem Jeronimo geseufzt hatte, in Trümmern sah. Bei diesem Anblicke wankte sie, und wollte besinnungslos an einer Ecke niedersinken; doch in demselben Augenblick jagte sie der Sturz eines Gebäudes hinter ihr . . . durch das Entsetzen gestärkt, wieder auf; sie küßte das Kind . . . und erreichte . . . das Tor. (SW II, 149)

Through 'Besinnung' she converts panic into heroism, thus offering one of the few and sporadic instances of a successful resistance to the structural factors within the text of reality that press toward misreading. Despite the clear contrast to Jeronimo's lack of 'Besinnung' and the tendency for 'helper' figures to be female, the motif is not gender specific. A variant of the word returns in the text at the moment when Don Fernando tries to capitalize on the mob's momentary confusion by implementing a strategy to confuse them still further: 'so antwortete dieser, nun völlig befreit, mit wahrer heldenmütiger Besonnenheit: "Ja, sehen Sie, Don Alonzo, die Mordknechte! Ich wäre verloren gewesen, wenn dieser würdige Mann sich nicht . . . für Jeronimo Rugera ausgegeben hätte"' (SW II, 157).

The strategy is less than fully successful, but this semantic axis suggests that 'Besinnung' is the only alternative to violence the characters may successfully employ to deal with the breathless course of events. The most cynical reading of the story would insist that Josephe and Don Fernando are permitted just enough 'Besinnung' as is necessary to effect the rescue of the child and his transmission to a new family – but no more. Whether a reader will recognize such signals or not is a moot point, and brings us to the problem of the narrator's behavior toward the reader.

The narrator in the foreground is liberal with value judgements and emotional epithets, and is quite willing, at times, to include the reader within the fiction of omniscience: 'Aber wie dem Dolche gleich fuhr es durch die von dieser Predigt schon ganz zerrissenen Herzen unserer beiden Unglücklichen, als der Chorherr. . . .' (SW II, 155f). In the coda to the catastrophe, by contrast, the narrator retreats from both this prior complicity with the reader and the tendency to leave nothing to the imagination into an enigmatic terseness that has produced a welter of conjecture and paraphrase in writing on the story: 'Don Fernando und Donna Elvire nahmen hierauf den kleinen Fremdling zum Pflegesohn an; und wenn Don Fernando Philippen mit Juan verglich, und wie er beide erworben hatte, so war es ihm fast, als müßt er sich freuen' (SW II, 159).

The laconic conclusion invites the reader to re-examine the text for clues to a fuller understanding, but the problem is that there are too many of them. The reader tends to be inveigled into taking one semantic axis through the judgements of the characters and the narrator and aligning the conclusion with this, only to have a further reading choose another. Rather than pursue this course yet again, I prefer to consider the structural device of the deferral of endings in the text.

The earthquake itself forestalls the foreshadowed endings to a familiar tragedy: the execution of one lover and the suicide of the other. The pocket in narrative time that is thus created is captured in the following image: 'alle Wände des Gefängnisses rissen, der ganze Bau neigte sich . . . und nur der, seinem langsamen Fall begegnende, Fall des gegenüberstehenden Gebäudes verhinderte, durch eine zufällige Wölbung, die gänzliche Zubodenstreckung desselben' (SW II, 145f). Commentators usually point to other mentions of vaults or arches in Kleist's work, without realizing that these examples are purposely constructed to endure, whilst the whole point of the 'zufällige Wölbung' here is that it collapses in the next paragraph. Within the brief respite, which becomes the second segment of the story, the lovers have the opportunity to plan alternative endings for themselves, one of which is marked by a play on the word 'beschließen': 'Sie beschlossen . . . nach La Conception zu gehen, . . . von dort nach Spanien einzuschiffen . . . und daselbst ihr glückliches Leben zu beschließen' (SW II, 150). However, the story opts against such a closure.[14] The temptation of a reconciliation with the society of St. Jago is too strong; such 'Besinnung' as might be available in the warnings of Donna Elizabeth is ignored; and mob violence enacts the ending that the earthquake had deferred, with the sole difference that Philipp is preserved to be adopted by Don Fernando and his wife.

Some of the enigma of the deferred conclusion has been well described by John Ellis: 'The point of the ending is that even after so many attempts to construe the world in a positive way have failed, despair is impossible too. . . . Throughout, the story has moved us from one view of the world to the next; its ending serves not as a turn toward hope but as a reminder that the continual process of coming to terms with the world cannot ever stop. . . .'[15] Put in structural terms, the implication is that all endings are deferred or arbitrary.

The text here plays upon its own fictional quality, as it does elsewhere, most notably in the evocation of the idyll in the valley,[16] for it has already provided a 'set-piece' ending, full of pathos and taking up motifs from earlier in the text, in the tableau in the wake of the massacre:[17]

Hierauf ward es still, und alles entfernte sich. Don Fernando, als er seinen kleinen Juan vor sich liegen sah, mit aus dem Hirne vorquellenden Mark, hob, voll namenlosen Schmerzes, seine Augen gen Himmel. (SW II, 158)

---

14 We may recognise an ironic counterpoint of 'openings' and 'closures' throughout the story, beginning with Jeronimo: 'überall . . . stieß er auf Riegeln und Mauern' (SW II, 145) – as opposed to: 'Kaum befand er sich im Freien, als die ganze . . . Straße . . . völlig zusammenfiel' (SW II, 146).

15 John M. Ellis, *Heinrich von Kleist*, p. 51.

16 SW II, 149: 'Indessen war die schönste Nacht herabgestiegen, . . . wie nur ein Dichter davon träumen mag.'

17 The 'silence' here is a reversal of the moment of innocent religious fervour before the sermon begins: 'und Stille herrschte, da die Orgel jetzt schwieg' (SW II, 155); Don Fernando's gesture as a victim of mob violence reverses the sense of similar gestures in the context of the Last Judgement: 'hier stand ein anderer, bleich wie der Tod, und streckte sprachlos zitternde Hände zum Himmel' (SW II, 146).

That the text proceeds beyond this to Philipp's adoption and Don Fernando's enigmatic comparison of the dead child with the living suggests an interplay between two narrative authorities. There is one narrator who is consistently close to the characters and who, in the scene of the massacre, becomes excessively engrossed in the action, bestowing extravagant epithets left and right: 'dieser göttliche Held . . .; Sieben Bluthunde lagen tot . . .; der Fürst der satanischen Rotte' (SW II, 158). The tableau quoted above is this narrator's ending. But there is another narrator active in the text who appears to know better, or at least knows enough to regard omniscience as a sham and all endings as provisional, especially those that look like final tableaux. It is this narrator that restores ambiguity to the story.

It is tempting to see in this duality of narrative voices an analogy to that of Deity and Demiurge in Gnostic thought, for this offers the closest parallel I can see to Kleist's aversion to final authorities that are both unified and predictable. In his dramas, the fragmentation of paternal authority is, as I have shown, a recurrent theme. That his narrative authorities should succumb to the same malady produces structural effects in his stories that help account for their proverbial modernity. Readers who expect Kleist's narrators to keep to the rules are misled – or, to employ a term Ross Chambers has fruitfully applied to a series of 19th- and early 20th-century narratives, seduced.[18]

They are seduced into thinking the text of reality always signals its own preferred reading. Since the negative connotations of a successful seduction become apparent only when the event is seen in retrospect, Kleist's stories demand at least one re-reading for this effect to become visible. To provoke a re-engagement with the text, Kleist uses what might best be termed irritants. Even a cursory reading of *Das Erdbeben in Chili* will produce an awareness that Divine Providence is invoked by the characters, but conspicuously does not deliver the outcome it appears to promise. A re-reading may then reveal that the prime structural authority in the text, namely the narrative perspective, is, by analogy, as equivocal and inscrutable as 'das Wesen, das über den Wolken waltet' (SW I, 147). A similar irritant may be seen in the enigmatic terms of the story's final sentence, which has indeed sent readers back to the text in an effort to clarify its import. Readers may, of course, choose

18 Cf. Ross Chambers, *Story and Situation. Narrative Seduction and the Power of Fiction*, Manchester University Press, 1984, p. 212: 'I suggested at the outset that narrative seduction is a consequence of the alienation undergone by literary discourse in the text and a condition of its interpretability. But the further claim is now made that such seduction, producing authority where there is no power, is a means of converting (historical) weakness into (discursive) strength. As such, it appears as a major weapon against alienation, an instrument of self-assertion and an "oppositional practice" of considerable significance.'

to ignore such factors and reduce the text's ambivalences to a linear understanding – but at the ironic cost of exchanging an impartial overview for the blinkered vision of a character within the fiction.

Die Verlobung in St. Domingo is linked thematically to *Das Erdbeben in Chili* in a variety of ways, though there is no indication of their being composed in proximity to one another. At the most basic level, both texts suggest the ambience of *Die Familie Schroffenstein* by engaging our sympathies for two young lovers brought down by a combination of an imperfect emancipation from their social provenance and of their misreading of the text of reality. More significantly perhaps, both texts quote versions of the aftermath of the French Revolution. While *Das Erdbeben in Chili* chooses a highly stylized analogy, *Die Verlobung in St. Domingo* is set in 1803, and is the only one of Kleist's fictions to present a world whose connection to Revolutionary France is not metaphorical. Finally, there are related motifs, such as a play on the semantic complex formed by variations on 'sich besinnen.' The narrator, at the outset, attributes the outbreak of warfare on the island of Haiti to 'die unbesonnenen Schritte des Nationalkonvents' in Paris (SW II, 160), and Gustav, in his narration of the death of his first betrothed, Mariane Congreve, places his own guilt squarely on 'die Unbesonnenheit . . ., mir eines Abends Äußerungen über das eben errichtete furchtbare Revolutionstribunal zu erlauben' (SW II, 174). The first printed version of the story had Herr Strömli and his two sons call Gustav 'Du unbesonnener Mensch!' after he shot Toni, whilst this was amended in the collected edition to 'Du ungeheurer Mensch!' (SW II, 192).[19]

The recurrence of this motif leads us to expect that misreading the text of reality will be a dominant theme, since 'Unbesonnenheit' clearly implies in these contexts that an opportunity to pause and re-interpret the events of which the character is part has been missed. Indeed, the main shift of emphasis between *Das Erdbeben in Chili* and *Die Verlobung in St. Domingo* is in the degree of blindness that produces the tragic conclusion. Insight and misapprehension are more finely balanced in the former story, with Jeronimo and Josephe being lured away from prudent courses of action by an abundance of apparently encouraging signs.

Die Verlobung in St. Domingo, by contrast, derives much of its power from exploiting the device much used in horror fiction since Bram Stoker's *Dracula*, namely the stupidity of the good. Much of the story is narrated from the perspective of Gustav von der Ried, a Swiss officer in the French Army, and no effort is spared to deprive him of insight when he needs it most. Not only does his simple equation of

19 Cf. KW III, 854.

moral qualities with skin color consistently lead him into pitfalls, but he himself narrates two stories that are obvious metatexts to the main action without making the obvious connections which might neutralize the fatal 'Unbesonnenheit' that has already cost the life of one woman he loves. As Sigrid Weigel observes, the two stories may, together, have a profound effect on Toni, but Gustav can draw no conclusions from them for his own situation.[20]

At times, Gustav's obtuseness suggests that the text, over the heads of the characters and the foreground narrator, is signalling a parodistic intention to the reader. It is incautious, but plausible, that Gustav's first question to Babekan is: 'seid Ihr eine Negerin?' (SW II, 162). It is surely somewhat sinister that Babekan, even before she asks who he is, should demand to know: 'seid Ihr herein gekommen, um diese Wohltat, nach der Sitte Eurer Landsleute, mit Verräterei zu vergelten?' (SW II, 164), since this initiates the whole process of mutual accusations of betrayal that culminates in the catastrophe. If Gustav, ignoring the fact that Babekan has just accused whites as a whole of consistently repaying good with evil, then proclaims: 'Euch kann ich mich anvertrauen; aus der Farbe Eures Gesichts schimmert mir ein Strahl von der meinigen entgegen' (SW II, 164) – then the crudity of his perceptions borders on parody. It says much for Kleist's skill that he can multiply examples such as these throughout the text without the parodistic dimension becoming more obtrusive.

That the character of Gustav retains credibility is due to the amount of genuine confusion the text presents. In complete contrast to the schematic succession of dystopian and utopian settings in *Das Erdbeben in Chili*, *Die Verlobung in St. Domingo* creates a world of obscurity that persists till the catastrophe has been reached. Gustav emerges, literally, from the 'Finsternis einer stürmischen und regnichten Nacht' (SW II, 161), but remains metaphorically within the occlusion of his own racial prejudices and the chaotic situation on the island until he has killed Toni in a moment of extreme 'Unbesonnenheit.' Writing on the story has raised the question as to whether Kleist also had racial prejudices, to which the only sensible answer is that, if he had them, he did not have them here.[21] The blunders and cruelties committed as a result of racist thinking in *Die Verlobung in St. Domingo* are as negatively marked as the excesses of the Catholic Church in *Das Erdbeben in Chili*, and no critic has yet suggested that that story be read as an apologia for Catholicism in Latin America in Kleist's own time.

---

20 Sigrid Weigel, 'Der Körper am Kreuzpunkt von Liebesgeschichte und Rassendiskurs in Heinrich von Kleists Erzählung *Die Verlobung in St. Domingo*,' in *KJb* 1991, S. 209f.

21 Cf. Peter Horn, *Heinrich von Kleists Erzählungen*, pp. 134-47.

Kleist, in representing the opposing sides in the racial conflict, returns to a device first used in *Die Familie Schroffenstein,* namely, of making the perceptions, language, and actions of the opposing parties symmetrical with one another.[22] Both appeal to divine vengeance to annihilate the other; both pursue a futile kind of arithmetic of atrocity in trying to calculate who has most wrong on whose side; both sides prove able, after Toni and Gustav have died senselessly, to respect a pact involving hostages that ends this particular episode of bloodshed, whilst the war still continues.

This should have prevented critics from taking sides, yet part of Kleist's peculiar magic is to make literary scholars behave like characters in his stories, and so Ruth Angress has him siding with the blacks,[23] while Gonthier-Louis Fink has him justifying slavery as part of his aversion to the French Revolution.[24] But what Kleist is presenting, impartially, is the confusion that allows Gustav to condemn, in one breath, 'das Gemetzel der Schwarzen gegen die Weißen' (SW II, 169), while in the next he answers Toni's question as to why the whites have made themselves so hated by acknowledging it is 'das allgemeine Verhältnis, das sie, als Herren der Insel, zu den Schwarzen hatten' (SW II, 170). Gustav's attempt to extricate himself from this confusion by telling an anecdote of vengeance in a racial context only enmeshes him further, so that at the end he is reduced to invoking a vision of angels deciding the issue. But every mention of divine vengeance or providence in the story functions as a signal that the character speaking cannot attain any clarity about purely human affairs.

The pivotal figure in the story is Toni, who begins as the natural daughter of Babekan and the adopted daughter of Congo Hoango and ends as the dead betrothed of Gustav von der Ried, who commits suicide after killing her in error. Until Gustav changes her view of things by his narrative of the death of his first betrothed, Mariane Congreve, she has acted as decoy for Congo Hoango, luring whites to stay in the house by her sexual attraction, so that Hoango can kill them. Her change of alle-

---

22 'Warum nicht mein Gemahl? Denn es liegt alles/ Auf beiden Seiten gleich, bis selbst auf die/ Umstände noch der Tat. Du fandst Verdächtge/ Bei deinem toten Kinde, so in Warwand;/ Du hiebst sie nieder, so in Warwand . . .' SW I, 121.

23 Ruth K. Angress 'Kleist's Treatment of Imperialism: *Die Hermannsschlacht* and *Die Verlobung in St. Domingo,*' in *Monatshefte,* vol. 69 (1), 1977, p. 30: 'But her loyalty from the point of view of the whites is betrayal from that of the blacks. And there is no doubt that Kleist has represented the black side.'

24 Gonthier-Louis Fink, 'Das Motiv der Rebellion in Kleists Werk im Spannungsfeld der Französischen Revolution und der Napoleonischen Kriege,' in *KJb* 1988/89, pp. 70f: 'Kleist ist nicht für eine Revolution, sondern für eine Evolution, . . . wie er auch in *Die Verlobung in St. Domingo* erklärt. . . . Auf diese Weise wird aber nicht nur die bestehende Sklaverei, sondern auch der Sklavenhandel . . . gerechtfertigt.'

giances is abrupt and complete, and her fatal misreading is to expect Gustav to trust her despite all appearances.

Her position between the two fronts is an uneasy one, and nothing has prepared her for its ambiguities. The claims on her are symmetrical. The narrator concludes one of the last private exchanges between her and Gustav with the words: 'nannte er sie noch einmal seine liebe Braut, drückte einen Kuß auf ihre Wangen, und eilte in sein Zimmer zurück' (SW II, 176). The words reinforce their sexual bond and are not lost on Toni, as the narrator assures us: 'Denn sie sah den Jüngling, vor Gott und ihrem Herzen, nicht mehr als einen bloßen Gast, dem sie Schutz und Obdach gegeben, sondern als ihren Verlobten und Gemahl an' (SW II, 181). The irony that surrounds the word 'Gast' encompasses the whole tragedy of imperfect emancipation. For, as Babekan reminds her, she has been an accessory to the deaths of numerous white 'guests' in this household, and when Congo Hoango is deceived into thinking she has remained loyal to him, there is a disconcerting symmetry in the narration between his words and Gustav's farewell to her: 'und nannte sie sein liebes Mädchen; klopfte ihr die Wangen, und forderte sie auf, ihm den übereilten Verdacht, den er ihr geäußert, zu vergeben' (SW II, 186).

Toni, while much more perceptive and certain of her feelings than Gustav, fails to perceive that her conversion may be less visible to him than it is to herself. Indeed, there is an element of exaggeration in the narrator's molding her into a heroine whose natural medium of expression is suddenly Schilleresque rhetoric.[25] With a total lack of caution, she proclaims to her mother:

du hast sehr Unrecht, mich an diese Greueltaten zu erinnern! Die Unmenschlichkeiten, an denen ihr mich Teil zu nehmen zwingt, empörten längst mein innerstes Gefühl; und um mir Gottes Rache wegen alles . . . zu versöhnen, so schwöre ich dir, daß ich eher zehnfachen Todes sterben, als zugeben werde, daß diesem Jüngling . . . auch nur ein Haar gekrümmt werde. (SW II, 177)

Quite inadvertently, Babekan is doing Toni a favor by giving her an opportunity to re-read the text of her own experience in terms of her changed attitude to what now appears a criminal past. But conversions, in Kleist's work, involve dislocations of perspective, and the only unease Toni displays here is betrayed by swearing an oath before her mother, of all people, as if she needs to establish herself in her new role

---

25 Bernd Fischer, 'Zur politischen Dimension der Ethik in Kleists *Die Verlobung in St. Domingo,' Heinrich von Kleist,* ed. Dirk Grathoff, pp. 258f., draws a parallel to Luise in Schiller's *Kabale und Liebe,* but without considering the incongruity of Toni's language in this fictional situation.

by asserting it in absolute terms – 'zehnfachen Todes sterben' – and in the face of an embodiment of her own immediate past. I have elsewhere discussed the role of oaths and other formal declarations in the story in the context of the shifting quality of language as a means of ordering reality in Kleist's fictions.[26] Their ambivalence is here evident in the irony that, whatever inner strength Toni may draw from her own words, she has just endangered both Gustav and herself by making Babekan suspicious. The same words may stabilize Toni's inner turmoil, while having the opposite effect on her external situation.

The narrator in *Die Verlobung in St. Domingo* has attracted much less scrutiny than in *Das Erdbeben in Chili*, probably because the structure is less schematic and because the narrative perspective fulfills any expectations a reader might have of an appropriately dramatic ending, thus discouraging further enquiry in precisely the opposite manner to which the ambiguous ending of the other story provokes it. For the lovers are ceremonially united in death: 'nachdem man noch die Ringe, die sie an der Hand trugen, gewechselt hatte, senkte man sie unter stillen Gebeten in die Wohnungen des ewigen Friedens ein' (SW II, 194f). To ensure no cliché is omitted, they also receive a monument in Herr Strömli's garden in Switzerland: 'und noch im Jahr 1807 war . . . das Denkmal zu sehen, das er Gustav, seinem Vetter, und der Verlobten desselben, der treuen Toni, hatte setzen lassen' (SW II, 195). The only discord is the fact that the narrator seems to have forgotten that the story is set in 1803.

There are many dissonances in the narrative perspective once one goes looking for them. The frequent value judgements and emotional epithets are not consistent. Omniscience tends to fade and reappear like the Cheshire Cat in *Alice in Wonderland*, obtruding, in one moment, by a gratuitously inappropriate image to capture Gustav's innermost feelings – 'so legte sich ein Gefühl der Unruhe wie ein Geier um sein Herz' (SW II, 171) – while skilfully masking, in the next, the precise stages by which Toni frees herself from the role of decoy for a gang of murderers. Similarly, we are left in no doubt as to Gustav's confused attempts to reconcile his racial prejudices with an awareness that all wrong is not on the side of the blacks, whilst, from the moment he seduces Toni, we get only the most fragmentary glimpses of his motivations. His killing of Toni seems to involve one of those dislocations of consciousness that are common in Kleist's works, especially among his male protagonists, and the violence of his actions *after* he has shot her makes him as much of an enigma as Graf Wetter vom Strahl in *Das Käthchen von Heilbronn*: 'schleuderte er das Pistol über sie, stieß sie mit dem Fuß von

26 Anthony Stephens, 'Eine Träne auf den Brief', pp. 331f.

sich, und warf sich, indem er sie eine Hure nannte, wieder auf das Bette nieder' (SW II, 192).

There is thus no more reason to accept the narrative perspective at face value here than there is in any other of Kleist's stories. The foreground narrator is a piece on the board in a game the text plays with the reader. As in *Das Erdbeben in Chili*, there is no lack of axes along which the semantics of the text may be pursued, and it is arbitrary to opt for any single one. To indicate, by way of conclusion, a counterpoint to the narrator's professed indignation at the gruesome events he purveys, one may take the axis in the text that suggests that death is the entelechy of the main characters, rather than something they flee.

When, at the beginning of the story, Babekan embarks on her deception of Gustav, she says, with a biblical reference that is quite obtrusive in the context,[27] that if Congo Hoango were to learn that she and Toni were sheltering a white 'wir wären alle . . . Kinder des Todes' (SW II, 166). Shortly afterwards, Gustav makes the incongruous assertion to Toni: 'so hätte ich, auch wenn alles Übrige an dir schwarz gewesen wäre, aus einem vergifteten Becher mit dir trinken wollen' (SW II, 168). Babekan nearly obliges him shortly after by poisoning his food (SW II, 178). Toni's exalted state of feeling when she sets off to fetch Herr Strömli and his party to rescue Gustav explicitly embraces the thought of martyrdom: 'und sie frohlockte bei dem Gedanken, in dieser zu seiner Rettung angeordneten Unternehmung zu sterben' (SW II, 187). In view of the way both die, it is surely worth asking whether they may not be seen in a more esoteric sense as 'Kinder des Todes,' for Babekan is not lying when she elaborates how many whites Toni has seduced into being victims of murder, and Gustav has a guilt for the death of Mariane Congreve that may attract its own expiation. These motives would align themselves with the almost loving care that marks the narrator's evocation of their obsequies. I do not suggest that this is more than one possible code for reading the whole story, for there is so much death about that a reader might well miss the signals. It does, however, imply a dimension of the narrative, beyond the thematics of war and 'das . . . furchtbare Revolutionstribunal' (SW II, 174), which may contain its own intrinsic dread.

---

27 Cf.1. Samuel, 26, 16: 'Es ist aber nicht fein, was du getan hast. So wahr der Herr lebt, ihr seid Kinder des Todes, daß ihr euren Herrn, den Gesalbten des Herrn, nicht behütet habt.'

10

Die Marquise von O...– Der Findling

All of Kleist's fictional families risk destruction. It may, as in *Die Familie Schroffenstein*, be self-destruction, through the extinguishing of the future in the form of children; it may, as in *Das Erdbeben in Chili*, result from a consonance of the effects of patriarchal authority and external circumstance; it may, as in *Die Marquise von O...*, take the form of a threatened alienation of members one from another, a possibility Kleist had already explored in *Amphitryon*. The temptation to apply psychological models from the 20th century to Kleist's fictions is very strong, and there is no doubt that his stories answer questions phrased in Freudian or Lacanian terms. Given the strong element of intertextuality in Kleist's works, not merely between his own creations, but also with the works of other writers and with the conventions of popular literary forms, there is also an argument for preferring, in the first instance, to apply psychology in terms familiar to the author himself.[1] This cannot be turned into a restriction, as the sheer incomprehension that greeted *Penthesilea* shows to what extent Kleist was devising codes that resisted conventional readings. Where he stopped short of devising something entirely new, he usually achieved much the same effect by subverting a number of identifiable conventions from a standpoint that remains elusive – hence the wide consensus that there is plenty of parody in Kleist's writings, but disagreement as to which particulars are meant parodistically.

While an examination of Kleist's invented families inevitably engages in psychological conjecture in coming to grips with the many puzzles of individual motivation, there are some general factors which combine to threaten the existence of his families that derive from what we know of the author himself. First, there is his overriding pessimism toward contemporary history, his conviction, which nothing in his works refutes, that he was living in a time when one world-order had

---

1 In these terms, Curtis C. Bentzel, 'Knowledge in Narrative: The Significance of the Swan in Kleist's *Die Marquise von O...*,' in *The German Quarterly*, vol. 64 (3), 1991, pp. 296-303, opposes a reference to Kosegarten's poem *Die Unschuld*, first published in 1788, and G. H. Schubert's mentions of 'Vorahndungen' in oneiric states to 'psychoanalytic dream interpretation.'

collapsed and no new one had replaced it.[2] This makes the future of families in Kleist's fictions the domain of either despair or irony. *Der Findling* is a good example of the former, ending with the destruction of all members; *Die Marquise von O...* typifies the latter, since the positive ending is not achieved without an ironic critique of the terms that make such a conclusion possible.

Second, there is the changing nature of the family itself in Kleist's own lifetime: the sentimentalizing of family life as an aspect of increasing middle-class dominance in the areas of domestic and literary values,[3] and the redefinition of gender roles, of which Fichte's was the most radical known to Kleist.[4] This is particularly evident in *Die Marquise von O...*, where the ostensibly aristocratic family seems, in terms of its sensibilities and the ordeals its members undergo, to drift between the upper and middle classes.[5]

Third, there is the specific questioning of paternal and patriarchal authority as the basis of the social order. Rousseau had made a long debate in European philosophy on this topic more acute by his assertion that paternal power derived from society as a whole,[6] thus challenging the converse view that anchored Absolutism and, equally, Enlightened Despotism in the person of the ruler. Kleist's Rousseauism must always be seen in the perspective that, from his first visit to Paris in 1801, he had not one good word to say about post-Revolutionary French society. Without ever going so far as to blame Rousseau for what he found offensive in Napoleonic Europe, he could not help but cast a cold eye on much that had been done in Rousseau's name and, from there, to test severely many of Rousseau's dogmatic assertions in his own writings. *Die Marquise von O...* has as one of its strands the critical examination

---

2 See above p. 5.

3 Cf. Michael Mitterauer und Reinhard Sieder, *The European Family*, pp. 131f; Werner Krueger, 'Rolle und Rollenwechsel. Überlegungen zu Kleists *Marquise von O...*,' in *Acta Germanica*, vol. 17, 1984, p. 29.

4 See above p. 2 and Axel Laurs, 'Towards Idylls of Domesticity in Kleist's *Die Marquise von O...*', in *AUMLA*, vol. 64, 1985, pp. 179f.

5 Cf. Gerhard Schulz, *Die deutsche Literatur, Zweiter Teil*, p. 380: 'Zwei Formen des Zusammenlebens der Familie stehen einander gegenüber: das eine im Bilde der Festung und das andere im Bilde des bürgerlichen Wohnzimmers. Erstürmung, Eroberung und Waffen gehören zum ersteren, waffenlose, auf Gemeinsamkeit beruhende Intimität zum anderen. Darin spiegeln sich Übergänge von einer adlig-dynastischen zur bürgerlichen Familienstruktur.'

6 Jean-Jacques Rousseau, *Discours sur l'origine et les fondemens de l'inégalité parmi les hommes, Œuvres complètes*, vol. III, eds. Bernard Gagnebin and Marcel Raymond, Paris, 1964, p. 182: 'Au lieu de dire que la Société civile dérive du pouvoir Paternel, il falloit dire au contraire que c'est d'elle que ce pouvoir tire sa principale force: un individu ne fut reconnu pour le Pere de plusieurs que quand ils restérent assemblés autour de lui; les biens du Pere, dont il est véritablement le Maître, sont les liens qui retiennent ses enfans dans la dépendance. ....'

of paternal authority as embodied in the Kommandant. He is allowed to pursue his conventional literary role to the point where he becomes a tyrant in the eyes of his wife (SW II, 130), and has his power subverted by both his wife and daughter. His way back to being an acceptable father in a re-formed family constellation is one of the most bizarre social peregrinations in Kleist's works. It is indicative of his aversion to tyrants, whether domestic or regal, that the Kommandant's final place in the family is quite different from the position in which he begins.

Die Marquise von O... was Kleist's second story to be published, and was likely finished soon before its appearance in February 1808. It shocked conventional readers, since its plot was scandalous, and Kleist satirized this not altogether surprising course of events in an epigram mocking moralistic condemnations of the work.[7] Moralizing could hardly be expected to be absent from writing on the story, since the rape of an unconscious woman and the suffering she undergoes as a consequence constitute a provocation in any terms. Only Kleist could have taken such an event as the basis for what is essentially a comedy of manners that encapsulates a potential tragedy as stark as that of Alkmene in *Amphitryon.*

Alkmene's question to Jupiter, 'Kann man auch Unwillkürliches verschulden?' (SW I, 291), lies at the heart of the Marquise's dispute with society, as represented by the attitudes of her family, since she has no awareness of any guilt, but is nevertheless treated as a transgressor to the point where both her parents violently reject her. That she has nothing of which she can repent and be forgiven, in the tradition of the 'bürgerliches Rührstück,' only makes her suffering longer and more acute.[8] At the dénouement, after Graf F... has finally made his guilt apparent by appearing in the same uniform he wore when he raped the unconscious Marquise, he falls at her feet and weeps. Her mother pronounces the formula that *should* usher in the happy end: 'stehn Sie auf, Herr Graf, stehn Sie auf! Trösten Sie jene; so sind wir alle versöhnt, so ist alles vergeben und vergessen' (SW II, 141). But the Marquise surprises everyone by manifesting equal aggression toward her mother and Graf F...: 'Die Marquise blickte, mit tötender Wildheit, bald auf den Grafen, bald auf die Mutter ein; ihre Brust flog, ihr Antlitz loderte: eine Furie blickt nicht schrecklicher' (SW II, 141).

Writing on the story has focused on her rejection of the Graf in terms that allow metaphysical embroidery: 'gehn Sie! gehn Sie! gehn Sie! rief sie, indem sie aufstand; auf einen Lasterhaften war ich gefaßt, aber auf keinen – – – Teufel!' (SW II, 141). But the fact that her mother becomes

7 *'Die Marquise von O...* / Dieser Roman ist nicht für dich, meine Tochter. In Ohnmacht!/ Schamlose Posse! Sie hielt, weiß ich, die Augen bloß zu' SW I, 22.
8 Cf. Horst Albert Glaser, *Das bürgerliche Rührstück*, Stuttgart, 1969, pp. 27f.

equally the object of her hostility, after they have previously gone through a long process of making-up, sustains the tragic dimension of the story against the facile convention of reconciliation. One does not need metaphysics to see Graf F...'s failure to clarify the situation at the earliest opportunity as – from the Marquise's perspective – behavior of diabolical cruelty. One of the letters he proclaims his intention to write, but never does, would have sufficed. Her hostility toward her mother may in part be motivated by a renewed awareness of the treatment for which she has already forgiven her. But it is surely more likely that she rejects the injunction to 'forgive and forget' as an infringement of her human worth as grave as the original rape; hence she glares 'mit tötender Wildheit' at her mother as well. Not only has most of her suffering been avoidable, but it is now to be further discounted by the suggestion that a few tears shed by Graf F... are all that is required to make it as if it had never been.

The moment also has a metafictional quality, for the hostility of the Marquise as 'Furie' is directed past Graf F... and her family to the text itself. In violently rejecting an ending that would make everyone else, including the conventional reader, happy, she insists her suffering be taken seriously. In other words, her revolt is that of a fictional character against the narrative convention that apparently has her trapped. For it is undeniable that the text has played with her suffering, as it has played with the expectations of the reader. Just as she has been forced to exchange the role of a dutiful daughter and mother for that of a social outcast in order to remain herself, so she here refuses the role of object in a compact between Graf F... and the family, because to do so would expunge the self she has constituted by the autonomy her family's rejection has forced upon her.

Thus, the happy ending is deferred. Not forever, but for more than a year, until a second wedding – 'froher, als die erste' (SW II, 143) – can be celebrated as the result of her conscious choice. Since it is ostensibly the same narrator who concedes her the deferred ending and makes her suffer through the long humiliations of the central part of the story, we are once more confronted with narrative omniscience and omnipotence in dubious guises. But I suggest this motif may provide suitable access to the comic dimension of the text. In *Das Erdbeben in Chili*, it is in the service of a tragic plot, and serves, initially, to underline the inability of the characters to decipher their own situation. It is subsequently used to signal to the reader that all endings are, in a sense, arbitrary, even tragic ones.

In *Die Marquise von O...* a tragic ending is adumbrated very early on, but withdrawn in favor of a gruelling, but essentially comic elaboration of the consequences of Graf F...'s not dying of his wounds. The tragic conclusion is presented with every appearance of finality:

Die Familie dachte nun darauf, wie sie in der Zukunft eine Gelegenheit finden würde, dem Grafen irgend eine Äußerung ihrer Dankbarkeit zu geben; doch wie groß war ihr Schrecken als sie erfuhr, daß derselbe noch am Tage seines Aufbruchs aus dem Fort, in einem Gefecht mit den feindlichen Truppen, seinen Tod gefunden habe. Der Kurier . . . hatte ihn mit eignen Augen, tödlich durch die Brust geschossen, nach P . . . tragen sehen, wo er, wie man sichere Nachricht hatte, in dem Augenblick, da ihn die Träger von den Schultern nehmen wollten, verblichen war. Der Kommandant, der sich selbst auf das Posthaus verfügte . . . erfuhr noch, daß er auf dem Schlachtfeld, in dem Moment, da ihn der Schuß traf, gerufen habe: 'Julietta! Diese Kugel rächt dich!' und nachher seine Lippen auf immer geschlossen hätte.   (SW II, 108)

This is clearly a possible ending for the whole story, complete with enigmatic last words, and it is stressed that it is not merely the account of one unreliable messenger, since the Kommandant obtains independent corroboration. Like Josephe's execution and Jeronimo's suicide at the beginning of *Das Erdbeben in Chili,* it does not happen. The story takes up an alternative version, which even goes so far as to repeat the now erroneous formula 'tödlich durch die Brust geschossen' (SW II, 108) in Graf F. . .'s own account of his wounding and recovery, and there is indeed an ironic play on the force of such formulaic endings in the Marquise's parents' reproof to him for being still alive:

Der Graf F...! sagte der Vater und die Tochter zugleich; und das Erstaunen machte alle sprachlos. . . . Der Kommandant sprang sogleich selbst auf, ihm zu öffnen, worauf er, schön, wie ein junger Gott, ein wenig bleich im Gesicht, eintrat. Nachdem die Szene unbegreiflicher Verwunderung vorüber war, und der Graf, auf die Anschuldigung der Eltern, daß er ja tot sei, versichert hatte, daß er lebe; wandte er sich, mit vieler Rührung im Gesicht, zur Tochter, und seine erste Frage war gleich, wie sie sich befinde? Die Marquise versicherte, sehr wohl, und wollte nur wissen, wie *er* ins Leben erstanden sei?   (SW II, 109f)

The text calls attention to its own fictionality by various dissonances. To the Marquise, Graf F... appears 'schön, wie ein junger Gott,' and it is perhaps as well for their eventual marital felicity that he does. Her parents, for whom he does not possess the same appeal, turn on him as one with the accusation – 'Anschuldigung' – that he has no right to be in this part of their story. Thus the sentiment – 'Rührung' – of the 'set piece,' in which the heroic savior of their daughter returns from the dead and is welcomed effusively and joyously, cannot win out against stark amazement. Instead, it becomes displaced from what remains 'die Szene unbegreiflicher Verwunderung' and is transferred to Graf F...'s question to the Marquise: 'wandte er sich, mit vieler Rührung im Gesicht, zur Tochter, und seine erste Frage war gleich . . ..' There are good reasons for this, as the narrator knows. So there are too for everyone's being rendered 'sprachlos' by his appearance, since this motif attended his rescue of the Marquise from the soldiers who were about to rape her (SW II, 105). But these details will mean nothing on a first reading. What is clear is the comic effect of his having to reply to the parents' 'Anschuldigung . . ., daß er ja tot sei' with the assurance 'daß er lebe.'

If his demise has been deferred indefinitely, so also have the dual explanations that the narrator owes the reader and that Graf F... owes the Marquise and her family. The narrator's perfidy in concealing the rape of the Marquise behind a gap in the narrative and a punctuation mark is paralleled on the thematic level by Graf F...'s inability to provide the clarification that the other characters need. This is heightened by a remorseless play on the two meanings of 'Erklärung,' in the senses of an explanation and a formal statement of intent, in the episodes that follow.[9] Everything, on the surface of the text, revolves around the degree to which the family or the Marquise are prepared to commit themselves in an 'Erklärung' to a response to Graf F...'s formal proposal of marriage.

In the ironic dimension, all these are pretexts for the explanation he has several times intended to offer, but – for a variety of reasons – cannot: 'daß er mehrere Male die Feder ergriffen, um in einem Briefe, an den Herrn Obristen und die Frau Marquise, seinem Herzen Luft zu machen' (SW II, 111). After the Marquise has suffered all the rejections and humiliations her circumstances impose, he has still managed neither a written nor a verbal explanation, and the narrator observes with a truly gruesome irony: 'Er fühlte daß der Versuch, sich an ihrem Busen zu erklären, für immer fehlgeschlagen sei, und ritt schrittweis, indem er einen Brief überlegte, den er jetzt zu schreiben verdammt war, nach M... zurück' (SW II, 129f). For in the scene with the Marquise immediately before, he has kissed her on the breast, announced he feels 'als ob meine Seele in deiner Brust wohnte,' and declared he will defy the world – but explains nothing (SW II, 129). Moreover, the letter he now feels 'con-

---

9 The Kommandant replies to Graf F...'s proposal on behalf of his daughter with what the latter terms 'diese gütige Erklärung,' but requests 'eine bestimmtere Erklärung' (SW II, 111); the Kommandant stresses she must know him better 'bevor sie sich erkläre' and insists that at present they can give 'keine andere Erklärung, als die gegebene' (SW II, 112). A little later, on the mother's asking 'wie würdest du dich . . . erklären?,' the Marquise says she would feel obliged to marry him out of gratitude, and the mother has trouble 'ihre Freude über diese Erklärung zu verbergen' (SW II, 117) etc., etc.

demned to write' is still the same letter he knows he should have written several months ago, as soon as he became aware he would not die of his wounds.

Kleist had already made a play on the different senses of 'erklären,' a significant motif in *Die Familie Schroffenstein*.[10] Here, the subterfuge of what the narrator does *not* explain to the reader is echoed on the thematic level by what the characters do not explain to one another. One may speculate at length on why Graf F... cannot write the letter he knows he should write, or speak the words he knows he should speak, but the simplest explanation is that by doing so he would define himself out of his own social role. Critics have observed that the characters in the story are not only predominantly designated by their social status, rather than personal names, but that, as well, among the forms of violence sanctioned by the code that applies in the upper levels of society, *sexual* violence does not figure.[11] That is the province of the lower orders and animals. The common soldiers who are eventually shot for trying to rape the Marquise are 'die Hunde, die nach solchem Raub lüstern waren' (SW II, 105). But this is also the language her father uses of the Marquise, some time after he has disowned her and when he misconstrues her advertising for the father of her child as an attempt to veil her sexual misdemeanours by a cunning ploy: 'Zehnmal die Schamlosigkeit einer Hündin, mit zehnfacher List des Fuchses gepaart, reichen noch an die ihrige nicht!' (SW II, 132). The Marquise has no difficulty in conniving at an elaboration of her mother's fiction, in which the improbably named 'Leopardo, der Jäger' – a servant – might have raped her while she was asleep, but she does not suspect her saviour, Graf F....

Graf F... thus confronts the, for him, insuperable difficulty that what he has done defines him out of the categories that constitute his social role. Axel Laurs pertinently cites Fichte on rape, from a text with which Kleist elsewhere shows familiarity: 'Wer seiner selbst nicht mächtig ist, ist ein wütendes Tier; die Gesellschaft kann durch kein Mittel ihn zähmen, sonach ihn nicht in ihrer Mitte dulden.'[12] This does not mean

10 Cf. 'Wir haben viel einander zu erklären,/ Viel zu vertraun' (SW I, 99); 'Du hast gleich einer heilgen Offenbarung/ Das Unbegriffne mir erklärt' (SW I, 131).

11 On names and status, cf. Dirk Grathoff, 'Die Zeichen der *Marquise*': Das Schweigen, die Sprache und die Schriften. Drei Annäherungsversuche an eine komplexe Textstruktur,' *Heinrich von Kleist*, ed. Dirk Grathoff, pp. 212f; on violence, John M. Ellis, *Heinrich von Kleist*, pp. 25f: 'Thus the convention of the story is established: bombing, shooting, burning is aceptable, so gross an act as smashing a soldier in the face may even be gallant, but acts not covered by this agreement as to what will count as civilised violence are unacceptable and "viehisch."'

12 Axel Laurs, 'Domesticity in Kleist's *Die Marquise von O...,*' p. 179; he further points out that the later marriage contract 'fulfils to the letter Fichte's requirements for restitution' (p. 187).

Kleist believed Fichte had said the last word on such matters, but it does fit the parameters of a fictitious world that he consistently ironizes. If Graf F... can marry the Marquise without a confession, his role remains intact; if he confesses, he makes himself one with animals, servants, and 'Asiaten,' as the narrator mischievously suggests in an image that makes of Graf F..., immediately after the rape, almost a prodigy of phallic energy: 'Bald kletterte er, den Schlauch in der Hand, mitten unter brennenden Giebeln umher . . .; bald steckte er, die Naturen der Asiaten mit Schaudern erfüllend, in den Arsenälen, und wälzte Pulverfässer und gefüllte Bomben heraus' (SW II, 106).

The world of the Marquise's family is one of marked formality of manners, resolute denial of sexuality, and extreme rigidity of roles. Werner Krueger has provided the most comprehensive analysis of these roles and the changes to which they are subjected as a result of Graf F...'s doing the unspeakable.[13] As the symptoms of her pregnancy become evident and are confirmed, the Marquise appears to contradict her role as dutiful daughter in the eyes of her family. Her father dictates a letter expelling her from the house, and when she, faithful to literary convention, throws herself at his feet to beg mercy, he seizes a pistol from the wall: 'Sie warf sich ihm . . . eben zu Füßen, und umfaßte zitternd seine Kniee, als ein Pistol, das er ergriffen hatte, in dem Augenblick, da er es von der Wand herabriß, losging, und der Schuß schmetternd in die Decke fuhr' (SW II, 125). This description does two quite different things: like the dissonances in the scene of Graf F...'s reappearance from the dead, it subverts by its excess of violence the 'set piece' scene of the hard-hearted father denying the pleas of the disgraced daughter. All the Kommandant needs to do, in terms of the expectations of the contemporary reader, is utter a few well chosen words of rejection. It also begins the undermining of the father's role in the eyes of the mother, since the discharge of the pistol does not bring the Kommandant to his senses. Rather, he follows this action by an unlawful demand that the Marquise surrender her children to the family.

The mother, immediately before, has pronounced a formal curse on her daughter, usurping, in a sense, the father's privilege of doing so: 'Verflucht sei die Stunde, da ich dich gebar!' (SW II, 124). By going beyond even this, the Kommandant has breached the code and produces the first signs of rebellion in his wife:

13 Werner Krueger, 'Rolle und Rollenwechsel,' p. 45: 'Die Rollen haben in einer für alle ungemütlich werdenden Weise begonnen zu zirkulieren.'

Die Obristin war über die zerstörende Heftigkeit ihres Gatten und über
die Schwäche, mit welcher sie sich, bei der tyrannischen Verstoßung
der Tochter, von ihm hatte unterjochen lassen, äußerst erbittert. Sie
war, als der Schuß in des Kommandanten Schlafgemach fiel, und die
Tochter aus demselben hervorstürzte, in eine Ohnmacht gesunken . . .
Nachher, da von der Abforderung der Kinder die Rede war, wagte sie
schüchtern, zu erklären, daß man zu einem solchen Schritt kein Recht
habe; . . . doch der Kommandant erwiderte weiter nichts, als . . . vor
Wut schäumend: geh! und schaff sie mir!   (SW II, 130f)

The domestic tyrant has overplayed his hand, and the initiative has
passed to both women.[14] The Marquise is forced to embark on a process
of emancipation, since the role of daughter, to which she had reverted
after the death of her first husband, is closed to her. The mother, who has
previously accepted a fair degree of 'Unterjochung' as the proper way of
things, is provoked by the 'destructive violence' of her husband's
behavior into visiting her daughter, testing her innocence by the naive
ploy of having her pretense that 'Leopardo, der Jäger' has confessed to
violating the Marquise accepted, and effecting her own reconciliation.
This leaves the father stranded in an untenable position.

At the beginning of the story, his patriarchal authority is so absolute
that he does not hesitate to inform his family of their insignificance in
the scheme of things: 'Der Obrist erklärte gegen seine Familie, daß er
sich nunmehr verhalten würde, als ob sie nicht vorhanden wäre; und
antwortete mit Kugeln und Granaten' (SW II, 104f). It is from this
height of male autonomy that the text progressively lowers him to a parodistic exaggeration of lachrymose repentance:

Doch die Mutter erwiderte: Beruhige dich – denn eben hörte sie
jemand von weitem heranschluchzen . . . Der Kommandant stand in
der Stube und weinte. Er soll dir abbitten, fuhr Frau von G... fort. . . .
Und muß ich eine Wahl treffen, so bist du vortrefflicher, als er, und
ich bleibe bei dir. Der Kommandant beugte sich ganz krumm und
heulte, daß die Wände erschallten. . . . Hierauf erhob sich die
Marquise, umarmte den Kommandanten, und bat ihn, sich zu beruhi-
gen. . . . doch er antwortete nicht; er war nicht von der Stelle zu bringen . . . und stand bloß, das Gesicht tief zur Erde gebeugt, und
weinte.   (SW II, 137)

14 Cf. Werner Krueger, ibid., pp. 45f: 'Die Autorität des Kommandanten und
Patriarchen ist gebrochen. . . . Das seiner Frau auferlegte Verbot, sich mit der Marquise in
Verbindung zu setzen, ist nur eine Phrase. Sie fährt trotzdem zu ihrer Tochter hinaus. . . .
Das Ergebnis ist die Allianz der Weiber, die sich vor allem gegen den Vater und Mann,
den Obristen, richtet.'

Like many other scenes in the story, this offers much more than the convention demands. The Kommandant's own violence – 'Heftigkeit' – has resulted in his being so violently displaced from his role that there seems very little left of the staunch defender of the fortress at the story's beginning. The text may well be insinuating to the reader that Graf F... fears an equally violent demotion in the eyes of all if he confesses to having raped the Marquise. But worse is to follow. The reconciliation between father and daughter assumes, before the eyes of the mother, a clearly incestuous quality:

> Darauf endlich öffnete sie die Tür, und sah nun – . . . die Tochter still, mit zurückgebeugtem Nacken, die Augen fest geschlossen, in des Vaters Armen liegen; indessen dieser, auf dem Lehnstuhl sitzend, lange, heiße und lechzende Küsse, . . . auf ihren Mund drückte: gerade wie ein Verliebter! . . . Die Mutter fühlte sich, wie eine Selige . . . Sie nahte sich dem Vater endlich, und sah ihn, da er eben wieder mit Fingern und Lippen in unsäglicher Lust über den Mund seiner Tochter beschäftigt war, sich um den Stuhl herumbeugend, von der Seite an.   (SW II, 138f)

John Ellis embarks from this scene upon a long discussion of sexual rivalry between the father and Graf F..., but seems to forget that the Marquise, who has put the role of obedient daughter behind her for good, is a willing participant.[15] What is here transacted does not only concern the tensions between the two men, which have aroused ribald comment in the secondary literature.[16] For there is no sign that the Marquise, whose new found self-possession could rapidly stop her father's advances, ever returns after this scene to the total subjugation to her father that marked the early episodes of the story. The family re-creates itself around her new marriage, but she continues to take the decisive role that she discovered for herself as a result of being cursed and expelled.

If father and daughter together act out the unthinkable before the eyes of the mother, then the text implies two things: first, that here is yet another instance where a 'set piece' tableau is exaggerated to reveal elements that the narrative convention would normally bury in silence, but which are none the less potent; second, that the displacement of figures from roles, which had begun with the consequences of Graf F...'s rape of the Marquise no longer being susceptible to that code of denials upon

15 John M. Ellis, *Heinrich von Kleist*, pp. 23-35.

16 Cf. Dirk Grathoff, 'Die Zeichen der *Marquise*,' p. 219: 'Wenn die Schwiegersöhne in Kleists Werk dem Vater den Phallus abnehmen müssen, dann impliziert dies eine Art von phallischem Recht des Vaters auf die Tochter. Kleist bricht also auf unerhört skandalöse Weise das Inzesttabu.'

which this society is based, has advanced to the point where social roles appear – briefly – to be abolished altogether.

Kleist achieves this by a twofold parodistic reference to Rousseau. In the sixty-third letter of the first part of *La Nouvelle Héloïse*, Julie, as commentators on *Die Marquise von O...* have observed, recounts a mildly erotic reconciliation scene between herself and her father. It is not always noted that the reconciliation is preceded by a scene in which the father is excessively violent to his daughter for the first time in her life.[17] Two details mark Kleist's text as a reversal of Rousseau's. First, Julie regrets that her father's inhibitions prevent him from going further in erotic terms.[18] Second, it is she who takes the initiative and, pretending to slip, manages to cover her father's face in kisses.[19] As a final ironic reversal, Julie's father returns, the next morning, to his full patriarchal authority, forbidding her to see Saint-Preux ever again, while Julietta's father – in *Die Marquise von O...* – plays a useful but subdued role in arranging her first marriage to Graf F...: 'Der Vater . . . ordnete alles, nach gehöriger schriftlicher Rücksprache mit dem Grafen, zur Vermählung an' (SW II, 142).

The complete lack of inhibition in Kleist's scene goes so far as to suggest another allusion to Rousseau, namely to his depiction of the state of nature as set forth in his *Discours sur l'origine et les fondemens de l'inégalité parmi les hommes*. There Rousseau firmly rejects the imaginings of others that the state of nature is full of idyllic family scenes. Rather, in this state, there are no families at all. Sexual encounters are so casual that children never know their father, and separate from their mother so early that they are unlikely to recognize one another again.[20] There can be no prohibition against incest, especially as there

---

17 Cf. Jean-Jacques Rousseau, *Julie ou La Nouvelle Héloïse*, Paris, 1960, p. 149: 'A l'instant, mon père . . . s'élança sur ta pauvre amie: pour la première fois de ma vie je reçus un soufflet qui ne fut pas le seul; et, se livrant à son transport avec une violence égale à celle qu'il lui avait coûtée, il me maltraita sans ménagement . . . je tombai, et mon visage alla donner contre le pied d'une table qui me fit saigner.'

18 'Je ne sais quelle mauvaise honte empêchait ses bras paternels de se livrer à ces douces étreintes.'

19 'Je feignis de glisser; je jetai, pour me retenir, un bras au cou de mon père; je penchai mon visage sur son visage vénérable, et dans un instant il fut couvert de mes baisers et inondé de mes larmes . . . ma mère vint partager nos transports.'

20 'ce seroit commettre la faute de ceux qui raisonnant sur l'état de Nature, y transportant les idées prises dans la Société, voyent toujours la famille rassemblée dans une même habitation, et ses membres gardant entre eux une union aussi intime et aussi permanente que parmi nous . . .; au lieu que dans cet état primitif, n'ayant ni Maison, ni Cabane, ni propriété d'aucune espèce . . . les mâles, et les femelles s'unissoient fortuitement selon la rencontre, l'occasion, et le désir, sans que la parole fût une interprête fort nécessaire des choses qu'ils avoient à se dire: Ils se quittoient avec la même facilité. . . . Et comme il n'y avoit presque point d'autre moyen de se retrouver, que de ne pas se perdre de vûe, ils en étoient bientôt au point de ne pas même se reconnoître.'

is no language in which to enunciate one. Kleist has, perhaps for this reason, also included the absence of speech in his scene: 'Die Tochter sprach nicht, er sprach nicht; mit über sie gebeugtem Antlitz saß er, wie über das Mädchen seiner ersten Liebe, und legte ihr den Mund zurecht, und küßte sie' (SW II, 138). To a contemporary reader, the Kommandant's loss of speech could appear as a parodistic reversal of the verbosity of repentant fathers in reconciliation scenes in dramas of the Enlightenment. A glance at Sir William's speech of repentance in Act V, Scene 9, in Lessing's *Miss Sara Sampson* makes this clear.

As Jean-Louis Flandrin has pointed out, the emotional 'indecency' of writers such as Rousseau may appear crude, but was essential to the emancipation of middle-class sensibility at the end of the 18th century.[21] Kleist's was that much more shocking at the time, but the point was that he was not only parodying Rousseau as a predecessor he now saw with scepticism, but also permitting himself the only emancipatory discourse in his whole work that he carried through to a happy conclusion. Kleist's 'indecency' signifies that the price of a meaningful account of emancipation is to render explicit some of those factors that, within the acceptable literary and social conventions, work through silence.

The Marquise would have been spared her sufferings if the code of her society and family were not based on such a resolute denial of 'nature,' in the sense of sexuality. The tendency of social discourse, her own included, is to transpose anything unusual into the supernatural. Thus Graf F... initially appears to her first as 'ein Engel des Himmels' (SW II, 105), then as 'schön, wie ein junger Gott' (SW II, 110). Her mother employs the same hyperbole when she convinces herself her daughter is innocent: 'o du Reinere als Engel sind . . . nein, eher nicht von deinen Füßen weich ich, bis du mir sagst, ob du mir die Niedrigkeit meines Verhaltens, du Herrliche, Überidische, verzeihen kannst' (SW II, 135).

That such transpositions have their uses is shown by the way the Marquise exploits them in coming to terms with being an outcast from her family: 'Ihr Verstand, stark genug, in ihrer sonderbaren Lage nicht zu reißen, gab sich ganz unter der großen, heiligen und unerklärlichen Einrichtung der Welt gefangen' (SW II, 126). This is exactly the same 'order of things,' namely a disorder, that is invoked at the end of the

---

21 Jean-Louis Flandrin, *Famille. Parenté, maison, sexualité dans l'ancienne société*, Paris, 1976, p. 166: 'Il y a, dans le sentimentalisme de cette fin du XVIIe siècle, une impudeur qui gêne parfois notre sensibilité actuelle. Bernardin de Saint-Pierre, Greuze, voire Rousseau, provoquent chez beaucoup d'entre nous une sorte de répulsion. Mais s'y abandonner, réduire leur impudeur à une superficialité de sentiments, serait refuser de voir, de comprendre, une grande transformation historique. Leur impudeur est une forme d'agressivité. Elle combat un ancien ordre des choses qui n' était plus acceptable et avec lequel nous n'avons pas renoué . . . .'

story to enable the forgiveness of Graf F... : 'daß ihm von allen Seiten, um der gebrechlichen Einrichtung der Welt willen, verziehen sei' (SW II, 143), but it is of strategic value to the Marquise to be able to sanctify what has happened as a way of re-affirming herself, just as it helps her to speculate on a divine origin for the child she cannot remember conceiving (SW II, 126).

There is thus no need to take the metaphysical dimension of the text at face value, nor to agonize over why the Marquise, at the dénouement, calls Graf F... 'ein Teufel'. It is, in fact, to his advantage for the later course of events that he should be perceived as a devil – supernatural still, though negative – rather than as a dog: natural, but socially impossible, like 'Leopardo, der Jäger.' The breaking through of nature, in the most radical terms in which Rousseau had conceived it, in the incestuous eroticism between father and daughter, is thus the obverse of a whole social discourse founded on denial. It need only appear once to correlate with what Graf F... has done, and the mother takes care to dissipate it by humor: 'und machte der Rührung durch Scherzen ein Ende' (SW II, 139). For there is no place in society for *homo natura*,[22] and, whilst she and her daughter have devised an emancipatory alternative to the father's former tyranny, roles are essential, and care must be taken in their delineation and distribution: 'Die Mutter bemerkte die Unschicklichkeit der Rollen, die der Vater und der Bruder dabei zu spielen haben würden, bat die Tochter, die Entfernung der Männer zuzulassen, wogegen sie in ihren Wunsch willigen, und bei dem Empfang der Person gegenwärtig sein wolle' (SW II, 139f).

The element of literary parody, though not for purposes of amusement, also provides access to the world of *Der Findling*. If *Die Marquise von O...* showed the dissolution of a family, brought about because the fragility of stereotyped roles could not withstand the pressures created by a scandal without an obvious transgression, it also demonstrates that such roles have, as regulatory mechanisms, a capacity to modify and re-order themselves so as to assimilate the unassimilable. *Der Findling*, by contrast, takes the destruction of a family beyond any conceivable reconciliation. Once considered by critics to be one of Kleist's early stories, largely because of its supposed lack of ambiguities and sophisticated narrative techniques, it has, since Hans Joachim Kreutzer's examination of the issues, been recognized as one of the last

---

22 Cf. Friedrich Nietzsche, *Jenseits von Gut und Böse, Sämtliche Werke, Kritische Studienausgabe*, eds. Giorgio Colli and Mazzino Montinari, vol. 5, Berlin/New York, 1980, p. 169: 'Den Menschen nämlich zurückübersetzen in die Natur; über die vielen eitlen und schwärmerischen Deutungen und Nebensinne Herr werden, welche bisher über jenen ewigen Grundtext homo natura gekritzelt und gemalt wurden . . . .'

to be written.[23] An explanation for its negativity must therefore be sought elsewhere than in Kleist's setting out to master narrative form in the shadow of *Die Familie Schroffenstein.*
The idea that an explanation is required is itself a piece of critical mythology. For Kleist's technique is very much to opt for one variation of events among various possible sets, and to signal the arbitrariness of this to the reader. Thus, a few pages into the text of *Die Marquise von O...*, the reader is offered an ending to the story in which Graf F... simply dies of his wounds and the Marquise and her family are left to come to terms with her pregnancy without his interventions. The story then takes another path, but the illusory, though at first sight convincing, finality of the first ending reminds us that this choice is arbitrary. *Der Findling* may likewise be read as a variation that consistently takes the most negative of all the options offered. I suggest it is useful to consider what options the story does *not* take up, as a means of placing it in perspective.

In his dramas, Kleist shows himself aware of the Enlightenment's uncritical celebration of adoptive paternity, and takes a sceptical stance toward it as a panacea for all family conflicts.[24] Antonio Piachi sees one son die of a plague, and adopts another, only to declare, at the end of the story, that he wants to pursue his vengeance against the son whom he has murdered through an eternity of suffering in hell: 'Ich will nicht selig sein. Ich will in den untersten Grund der Hölle hinabfahren. Ich will den Nicolo, der nicht im Himmel sein wird, wiederfinden, und meine Rache, die ich hier nur unvollständig befriedigen konnte, wieder aufnehmen!' (SW II, 214f). Piachi's end is attended by certain elements of black humor that may be taken as dissonances signalling a parody. For this reversal of one of the Enlightenment's most cherished tropes has as its setting that least Enlightened of ambiences, the Papal States.[25] Kleist not only shows the social system of this 'Kirchenstaat' to be quite corrupt, but also invents a 'law' to the effect that criminals may not be executed before they have received absolution. This not only means that the Pope has to reverse his own law to make possible Piachi's execution, but it provides Kleist with the opportunity to present a tableau in which institutionalized religion and Piachi's denial of its consolations are equally tinged with absurdity:

23 Hans Joachim Kreutzer, *Die dichterische Entwicklung Heinrichs von Kleist*, pp. 186f.
24 See above p. 18.
25 It has been pointed out that the 'Kirchenstaat' no longer existed at the time Kleist wrote the story, cf. KW III 878.

Nachdem man vergebens alles, was die Religion an die Hand gab, versucht hatte, ihm die Strafwürdigkeit seiner Handlung fühlbar zu machen, hoffte man, ihn durch den Anblick des Todes, der seiner wartete, in das Gefühl der Reue hineinzuschrecken, und führte ihn nach dem Galgen hinaus. Hier stand ein Priester und schilderte ihm, mit der Lunge der letzten Posaune, alle Schrecknisse der Hölle, in die seine Seele hinabzufahren im Begriff war; dort ein anderer, den Leib des Herrn, das heilige Entsühnungsmittel in der Hand, und pries ihm die Wohnungen des ewigen Friedens. . . . Drei hinter einander folgende Tage machte man dieselben Versuche und immer mit demselben Erfolg. Als er am dritten Tag wieder, ohne an den Galgen geknüpft zu werden, die Leiter herabsteigen mußte: hob er, mit einer grimmigen Gebärde, die Hände empor, das unmenschliche Gesetz verfluchend, das ihn nicht zur Hölle fahren lassen wolle. Er rief die ganze Schar der Teufel herbei, ihn zu holen. . . . (SW II, 214f)

The idea of an eternity of punishment for offenses committed in a brief human life was an aspect of orthodox Christianity that the Enlightenment saw as particularly offensive, and Voltaire found ludicrous the idea of a supreme being who could occupy himself through infinite time roasting some poor miscreant.[26] Kleist's parodistic intention becomes evident in his contriving a scene, three times repeated, in which an adoptive father, one of the Enlightenment's favourite clichés of humane altruism, is to be punished for a gruesome murder, and now protests, with an indignation that faithfully echoes the tone of much Enlightenment criticism of religion, against 'das unmenschliche Gesetz' that, in the Church's terms, will *mitigate* his punishment. The repetition of the 'Versuche' on the part of the clergy drives Piachi to the point where he invokes the Satanic powers to come and rid him of these troublesome priests by dragging him off to eternal suffering. Neither dogmatic religion nor Enlightened humanism emerges from this tableau unscathed.

The parodistic element becomes clearer if we examine the terms in which Piachi comes to adopt Nicolo in the first place. He is on a journey with his young son Paolo when news of an epidemic in the city he is planning to enter makes him prudently stop to make further enquiries. Hearing that the city is about to be sealed off to prevent the plague from spreading, he decides to leave: 'so überwand die Sorge für seinen Sohn alle kaufmännischen Interessen: er nahm Pferde und reisete wieder ab'

---

26 Cf. John Mc Manners, *Death and the Enlightenment. Changing Attitudes to Death among Christians and Unbelievers in Eighteenth-century France*, Oxford, 1981, p. 178, who quotes a letter by Voltaire dated January 1761: 'Il est ridicule de penser que Dieu s'occupe pendant une infinité de siècles à rôtir un pauvre diable.'

(SW II, 199). This is the last unambiguous action Piachi is to carry out until his insistence that he be hung without absolution so that he can go to hell. For, soon after, he encounters the orphan Nicolo, who declares he is infected, and Piachi's response to him begins a series of fatally ambivalent gestures and attitudes that will lead to the destruction of all concerned:

Dabei faßte er des Alten Hand, drückte und küßte sie und weinte darauf nieder. Piachi wollte in der ersten Regung des Entsetzens, den Jungen weit von sich schleudern; doch da dieser, in eben diesem Augenblick, seine Farbe veränderte und ohnmächtig auf den Boden niedersank, so regte sich des guten Alten Mitleid: er stieg mit seinem Sohn aus, legte den Jungen in den Wagen, und fuhr mit ihm fort, obschon er auf der Welt nicht wußte, was er mit demselben anfangen sollte. (SW II, 199)

At first sight, we are confronted with a clear instance of Enlightened altruism: 'des guten Alten Mitleid.' Rousseau had praised pity, in his *Discours sur l'origine et les fondemens de l'inégalité parmi les hommes*, as 'the only natural virtue,' and insisted that even savages must feel it toward the helpless, especially children.[27] Kleist, in venturing into a parody of a simplistic view of pity, appears to contradict Rousseau's assertion that humanity, for all its moral principles, would have been nothing but monstrous if nature had not given it the capacity for pity as a support for reason.[28] For Piachi's act of pity drowns out reason, rather than complementing it. His first clear decision is to save Paolo by removing him from the area of infection. His act of pity for Nicolo involves putting an infected child in the same coach as his healthy one, and driving off with no clear idea of what he is to do with him. He is on the point of trying to get rid of Nicolo again when all three are arrested and transported into the plague-ridden city, where Piachi and Nicolo survive but Paolo dies.

A parody of Rousseau becomes very likely when we consider the passage in which the latter seems to forget the necessary complementarity of pity and reason and embarks on a eulogy in extravagant terms that

27 Jean-Jacques Rousseau, *Œuvres complètes*, vol. III, p. 154: 'Je ne crois pas avoir aucune contradiction à craindre, en accordant à l'homme la seule vertu Naturelle, qu'ait été forcé de reconnoître le Detracteur le plus outré des vertus humaines. Je parle de la Pitié, disposition convenable aux êtres aussi foibles, et sujets à autant de maux que nous le sommes ...'; p. 156: 'C'est elle qui détournera tout Sauvage robuste d'enlever à un foible enfant ... sa subsistance acquise avec peine, si lui-même espere trouver la sienne ailleurs.'
28 Ibid., p. 155: 'Mandeville a bien senti qu'avec toute leur morale les hommes n'eussent jamais été que des monstres, si la Nature ne leur eût donne la pitié à l'appui de la raison: mais il n'a pas vû que de cette seule qualité découlent toutes les vertus sociales qu' il veut disputer aux hommes.'

explicitly negate reflection and link pity with religious faith.[29] Kleist's point, in his ironic reference to Rousseau, is that pity may indeed be a virtue, but that Piachi is not living in the state of Nature, in which Rousseau's first humans enjoy not only natural goodness but also permanent amnesia, but in a *social* context in which all actions have a before and after. Thus Kleist lets his narrator, whose judgements turn out to be crude and fallible, celebrate 'des guten Alten Mitleid,' as the text will later persist in referring to Piachi as 'den redlichen Alten' after he has seized possession of a letter not intended for him 'halb mit List, halb mit Gewalt,' and forged a reply in order to humiliate Nicolo in the crypt of the 'Magdalenenkirche' (SW II, 205f). But there are no more actions in the story without their own ambivalence, and so dogmatism becomes the province of the narrative perspective, and, by this declension, of the secondary literature.

Thus Piachi's subsequent adoption of Nicolo is presented in terms that adulterate simple altruism in two significant ways:

> Piachi schickte ihn in die Schule, wo er Schreiben, Lesen und Rechnen lernte, und da er, auf eine leicht begreifliche Weise, den Jungen in dem Maße liebgewonnen, als er ihm teuer zu stehen gekommen war, so adoptierte er ihn, mit Einwilligung der guten Elvire, welche von dem alten keine Kinder mehr zu erhalten hoffen konnte, schon nach wenigen Wochen, als seinen Sohn. Er dankte späterhin einen Kommis ab, mit dem er, aus mancherlei Gründen, unzufrieden war, und hatte, da er den Nicolo, statt seiner, in dem Kontor anstellte, die Freude zu sehn, daß derselbe die weitläuftigen Geschäfte, in welchen er verwickelt war, auf das tätigste und vorteilhafteste verwaltete. (SW II, 201)

There is, first, the element of economic calculation in the adoption and of his rapidly finding a use for Nicolo in his business. Since Piachi is a 'Güterhändler,' there is nothing inherently sinister in this. Only the later course of events reveals a deep-seated malaise in family relations, which seems to relate to members being less concerned with each other's humanity than with their social function, a state of affairs familiar from the family of the Kommandant in *Die Marquise von O...* His reflection on the price he has paid for Nicolo could be a somewhat grotesque reminiscence of Sir Williams 'adoption' of the dying Mellefont at the end of Lessing's *Miss Sara Sampson*: 'Ich bin Vater,

---

29 Ibid., p.156: 'C'est elle, qui nous porte sans réflexion au secours de ceux que nous voyons souffrir: c'est elle qui, dans l'état de Nature, tient lieu de Loix, de mœurs, et de vertu, avec cet avantage que nul n'est tenté de désobéir à sa douce voix. . . .'

Mellefont, und bin es zu sehr, als daß ich den letzten Willen meiner Tochter nicht verehren sollte. – Laß dich umarmen, mein Sohn, den ich teurer nicht erkaufen konnte!'[30]

Second, the apparently innocuous aside concerning Elvire, 'welche von dem Alten keine Kinder mehr zu erhalten hoffen konnte,' is misleading in a number of senses. First, Piachi, in a story whose chronology is – unusually for Kleist – quite clear, is only about 50. Second, to conceive a child by Piachi is the last thing Elvire would want, since the rest of the story makes clear that her desires are directed toward the dead Colino. Third, even the *prospect* of sexual contact sets up conflicts within her that consistently result in 'fevers,' the last of which causes her death. Adoption is thus the only form of parenthood acceptable to her, and she is said to have loved Paolo, to whom she became step-mother, so that the only thing for which she can 'hope' is to continue to keep her erotic cult of the dead Colino isolated from the rest of the family.

With such ambiguities multiplying through the surface of the text, it is little wonder that writing on the story is polarized between those who condemn Nicolo and those who see in him a victim. Earlier interpretations simply took the narrator's judgements at face value, and saw Nicolo as an incarnation of evil, thus sparing the other participants all censure. This form of paraphrase still determines Denys Dyer's reading of 1977: 'Out of the goodness of his heart, a worthy middle-class tradesman, happily married with a wife and child, adopts a foundling. . . .'[31] We have already seen that Piachi's act of compassion may not be as simple as the narrator suggests; he does not adopt Nicolo until Paolo has been dead some time; how 'happily' he is married to Elvire is a moot point, since, from her perspective, she is united in a bond of erotic spirituality with the dead Colino; finally, Piachi is not a 'tradesman,' but a capitalist with a considerable fortune that he assigns to Nicolo and which plays a role in the complications of the plot.

In 1978, Peter Horn quite rightly recognized there was something wrong with approaches of this kind and shifted all the blame from Nicolo to an inhumane and corrupt society.[32] Certainly, the ambience of the Carmelite monks, of Xaviera Tartini, who seduces Nicolo when he is 15, and of a system of justice that can be perverted in Nicolo's favor once he promises to take Xaviera off the Bishop's hands, is anything but a school of morality. Horn's partisan approach, however, comes up against the fact that the only access we have to the events of the story is through an unreliable narrator – whereupon, instead of seeing this figure

---

30 *Lessings Werke*, vol. 3, Stuttgart, 1890, p. 209.
31 Denys Dyer, *The Stories of Kleist. A critical study*, London, 1977, p. 48.
32 Peter Horn, *Heinrich von Kleists Erzählungen*, p. 178.

as a character who is ironized along with the others, Horn concludes Kleist has misunderstood his own story.[33]

In 1985, Jürgen Schröder, in an article subtitled 'Ein Plädoyer für Nicolo,' makes acute observations in the course of once more representing Nicolo as victim, but reaches as empty a conclusion as does Horn.[34] For the story is neither disunified nor unintelligible. It is the assumption that it requires a linear, partisan reading that is wrong, for this only places the critic, as echo or opponent, in a subservient role to the judgements enunciated by the narrative perspective, some, but not necessarily all, of which are clearly at variance with other parts of the text.

I suggest that a recognition of parody in the story may be extended to a principle for grasping the text's ambiguities. A parodistic text is one that at each point has two meanings: one ostensible, and one referred. If a reader does not know the literary model, then there is little access to the referred meaning, and the ostensible one will stand unchallenged to the extent to which it is not patently absurd. There are good reasons for assuming Kleist was writing for a public to whom adoptive paternity and the theme of pity sent strong signals, and so Piachi becomes credible as a parodistic figure.[35] As such, it is not unusual for him to be ill at ease in his role. This comes out most clearly in the fact that, while assigning 'auf gerichtliche Weise' (SW II, 203) virtually all his fortune to Nicolo, thus rendering him autonomous in a society where his wealth duly attracts the predatory Carmelite monks, Piachi paradoxically assumes he can maintain all his paternal authority over a financially independent adult, and does not hesitate to humiliate him over his continued attachment to Xaviera Tartini. There thus appear to be two Piachis: one who finds the role of father an encumbrance and takes elaborate steps to free himself of it; another who clings to paternal authority and to whom it does not occur that he may be doing something dangerous by humiliating Nicolo so spectacularly in the 'Magdalenenkirche.' We may pursue this division in the figure back to the beginning of the

33 Ibid., p. 172: 'Das hieße aber ein Selbstmißverständnis von Kleist . . . zu übernehmen . . . Wenn man überlegt, wie radikal und neu diese Problematik ist, wird man verstehen, warum sich Kleist selbst dieser Problematik noch nicht *bewußt* war.'

34 Jürgen Schröder, 'Kleists Novelle *Der Findling*. Ein Plädoyer für Nicolo.' in *KJb* 1985, p. 127: 'Es handelt sich um eine pervertierte, negative Identitätsgeschichte. . . . Auch der Leser findet keinen Platz mehr in der Novelle. Er wird allmählich und immer schneller aus allen möglichen Identifikationen herausgedrängt und auf den bloßen Nachvollzug der Affektbewegungen beschränkt. Selbst am Ende der Geschichte kommt er nicht zur Ruhe, bleibt auch er obdachlos.'

35 For a summary of the importance of pity as a literary theme at this time, cf. Hans Jürgen Schings, *Der beste Mensch ist der mitleidigste Mensch. Poetik des Mitleids von Lessing bis Büchner*, Munich, 1980, p. 22: 'Die überragende moralische Bedeutung des Mitleids und ihre Übertragung auf das Trauerspiel – das ist die ursprüngliche Inspiration, von der Lessing sich leiten und nicht mehr abbringen läßt.'

story, where we find a prudent Piachi, who makes a clear decision not to risk Paolo's life in the plague-infected city, and a rash one who acts on impulse, has no idea how to deal with the consequences, and is trying to reverse his action when the law catches up with him.

The only difference between the divided quality of Piachi as a fictional character and a normal piece of literary parody becomes apparent when we ask: Which is the ostensible figure and which the model to which the former refers? In this story we cannot tell. The separation of attributes that is usual for an apprehension of parody is so thoroughly blurred in Kleist's text that the hierarchical relationship between ostensible and referred meaning, between parody and model, disappears. The narrator does much to stress Piachi's feebleness, to the point of implying he is impotent at 50, only to have him overcome the much younger Nicolo with his bare hands a decade later and murder him: 'und stark, wie die Wut ihn machte, warf er den von Natur schwächeren Nicolo nieder und drückte ihm das Gehirn an der Wand ein' (SW II, 214). Is Piachi *primarily* a decrepit old man, or a strong, violent one?

If we cast back through the text to identify the 'real' Piachi, then we find on the one hand a figure who is altruistic and generous, if confused as to his own motives, and, on the other, a calculating, loveless, domestic tyrant, whose unscrupulousness in forging letters and humiliating Nicolo anticipates his intransigence in the final tableau. Much the same applies to Elvire, to whom positive qualities are consistently attributed by the narrator and whose ambivalent existence within Piachi's household only gradually becomes apparent. On the one hand, she is the dutiful wife and step-mother; on the other, her life centers on a devotion to the dead Colino that involves undressing in front of his portrait and falling into an ecstasy – 'Verzückung' – in which she whispers his name (SW II, 207). In her case, there is a stronger temptation to see the 'real' Elvire as Colino's lover, but this should not make us overlook the fact that the existence she has chosen for herself takes place in two different spheres concurrently and depends on their remaining separate.

With hindsight, the 'fever' that afflicts her immediately after her marriage to Piachi is an indication that the sexual role expected of her is incompatible with her love for the dead Colino. Her next fever results from her catching sight of Nicolo in the disguise so similar to the portrait of Colino. No sexual contact is threatened by Nicolo at this point; rather, Elvire's illness results from the fact that a figure that belongs in one of her worlds has manifested himself in the other. She cannot live, isolated, in a continuous state of ecstasy before Colino's image, but her survival requires that one role not infringe on the other: the two worlds must remain separate. When Nicolo, a savagely parodistic embodiment of the dead Colino, first attempts to rape her and then, after Piachi has quit the scene, abandoning her, probably succeeds in raping her,[36] she suffers her third fever and dies (SW II, 214). Her two roles are thus interdependent but incompatible, and having them encroach on each other is fatal for her. The essential point for an understanding of the figure of Elvire is that her two worlds exist in parallel with one another, just as the benign Piachi does not become, once and for all, the tyrannous Piachi, but rather alternates between both roles.

Similarly, there is no point in either damning Nicolo – the narrator does it quite adequately – or attempting to exculpate him. This is not the point of the story. The point is that he too exists in two roles, one of which is indeed that of victim. It has been recognized that the story works by substituting one character for another, and it is impossible to deny that Nicolo exists for the others as the object of substitutions. This does not mean he does nothing on his own volition,[37] but it is apparent that he substitutes, from Piachi's perspective, for the dead Paolo and also for the incompetent assistant whom he dismisses. He makes himself into a substitute for the dead Colino in order to enjoy Elvire sexually and humiliate her. His parents marry him to Constanze Parquet, making her a substitute for Xaviera Tartini, with whom he has had a sexual relationship for five years, and Xaviera shows she feels displaced by his sudden fixation on Elvire, suffering 'das bittere Gefühl der Eifersucht' (SW II, 208).

In all of these substitutions, Nicolo's own identity seems divided between a childlike dependency, which persists after Piachi has made his fortune over to him, and an inhumane vengefulness, which one should not try to explain away. Even as an adult, he seems to fear punishment from both parents,[38] and his first aggressive feelings toward Elvire appear as hatred motivated by a kind of sibling rivalry:

36 Piachi abandons Elvire to Nicolo's mercies, and it is not clear how much time she then spends alone with him. It is clear that Piachi loses consciousness once he reaches the house of his friend, Dr Valerio, and that Elvire is received there 'later.' Nicolo thus has every opportunity to complete the rape.

37 Hence I disagree with Jürgen Schröder, 'Kleists Novelle *Der Findling*,' p. 124: 'Denn weil die Figuren wie elektrische Körper behandelt werden, fällt der gesamte menschliche Mittelbereich des Ethos, des Seelischen, der Gefühle bei ihnen aus. Was sie bewegt und reagieren läßt, anzieht und abstößt, sind unwillkürliche Affekte und Leidenschaften, über die sie mit zunehmender Aufladung des Spannungsfeldes alle Kontrolle verlieren.'

38 'so unterdrückte die Besorgnis, einen Verweis von ihm [Piachi] zu erhalten alle andere Rücksichten: er riß ihr, mit verstörter Beeiferung, ein Bund Schlüssel von der Hüfte. . . .' SW II, 204; 'doch ehe er sie noch gesammelt und geordnet hatte, ergriff ihn schon Furcht, von Elviren entdeckt und gestraft zu werden; er schloß, in nicht geringer Verwirrung, die Tür wieder zu, und entfernte sich' SW II, 207.

es schien ihm unglaublich, daß sie, bei so viel Lockungen dazu, nicht selbst zuweilen auf dem Wege wandeln sollte, dessen Blumen zu brechen er eben so schmählich von ihr gestraft worden war. Er glühte vor Begierde, ihr, falls dies der Fall sein sollte, bei dem Alten denselben Dienst zu erweisen, als sie ihm, und bedurfte und suchte nichts, als die Gelegenheit, diesen Vorsatz ins Werk zu richten.   (SW II, 206)

Lust comes later, and indeed seems to arise in him as a reaction to his witnessing Elvire's erotic devotions to Colino and to his mistaken belief that he himself is the object of her desires:

Der Gedanke, die Leidenschaft dieser, als ein Muster der Tugend umwandelnden Frau erweckt zu haben, schmeichelte ihn fast eben so sehr, als die Begierde, sich an ihr zu rächen; und da sich ihm die Aussicht eröffnete, mit einem und demselben Schlage beide, das eine Gelüst, wie das andere, zu befriedigen, so erwartete er mit vieler Ungeduld Elvirens Wiederkunft. . . . (SW II, 209)

One may argue that he proves which is the 'real' Nicolo by his carefully planned attempt to rape Elvire, but the tableau, in which he lies at Piachi's feet pleading for forgiveness and Piachi, seizing a whip that has no right to be hanging on Elvire's bedroom wall, wordlessly points with it to the door, is disconcertingly reminiscent of the image of an unloved child we may assemble from earlier parts of the text.

I therefore suggest that each of the three main characters becomes intelligible only once one ceases to demand causal consistency from their behavior, but recognizes instead that the dislocations of behavior and consciousness that are very common in both Kleist's dramas and stories in linear sequences should here be read as *alternations*. Piachi is, by turns, both a humane father in the tradition of the Enlightenment and a callous and unscrupulous tyrant; Elvire is both the domestic figure who mostly appears 'gleichgültig und ruhig' (SW II, 207) and the passionate lover of the dead Colino; Nicolo is both 'die Beute der Verführung einer gewissen *Xaviera Tartini*' (SW II, 201), the victim also of his adoptive parents' indifference, and the cruel rapist who knows right from wrong and deserves the various verdicts the narrator pronounces on him. The point is that the figures do not evolve or degenerate from one state to another, but shift back and forth between them.

There are various other semantic axes that unify the story in conventional terms, such as: displaced sexuality, the withholding of verbal communication, the formality of behavior within the family, and the confusion of moral values, which begins with Piachi's first act of compassion. It is therefore unnecessary to reject the text as disunified simply because Kleist chose it for a successful, if gloomy, experiment in divided characterization. If we enquire why the parodistic portrayal of character stops short of the normal assigning of dominance to one of the two meanings a text conveys, so that one Nicolo, for example, might appear as a parodistic shadow of another, then the answer may be found in the fact that the plot seems to revolve around a center that is blank. Jürgen Schröder has shown that one may construct 'triangles' of characters, in terms of conventional stories of adultery, if one assigns to Colino the status of a living person.[39] There is no problem in reading the patterns of relationships that result parodistically, since the dead do not usually commit adultery with the living. In this story, Colino does, however, disrupt Piachi's marriage both as himself and in his reincarnation as Nicolo. The text even hints at a parody of Christ's passion and resurrection.[40]

But if Colino is accorded, in this parodistic world, the status of a participant, he cannot be at the same time the occluded center around which the plot revolves. By definition, it remains undisclosed. But once more, there may be hints in the text. One of the zaniest interpretations of the story has Nicolo as the real son of Elvire.[41] For this to be correct, she would have, in terms of the story's chronology, to have given birth to him at the age of nine.

But we may read various aspects of the text as indicating that the real center of the story is a child who does not exist at all and for which all others are, from the perspective of the entire text, necessarily substitutes, namely the child of Elvire and Colino. It is thus of prime significance that the text so relentlessly pursues the motif of substitution, but that all substitutions are ultimately unsuccessful. Thus Nicolo is not this absent child, since Elvire is emotionally neutral to him. His physical resemblance to Colino hints that this may be an identity he pursues in the worst possible way, namely by usurping the place Elvire has reserved for her dead lover. Since there is no living substitute for the child whose absence is clearly alluded to, all human relationships within this family exist in a state of deficiency, which eventually attracts its own catastrophic resolution.

The narrator in *Der Findling* becomes more intelligible through a contrast with *Die Marquise von O...* There, the narrative perspective

---

39 Jürgen Schröder, 'Kleists Novelle *Der Findling,*' p. 120.

40 'Die mindeste Veranlassung, die sie auch nur von fern an die Zeit erinnerte, da der Jüngling für sie litt und starb, rührte sie immer bis zu Tränen. . . .' SW II, 203 – this quotes the Christian Creed as a preparation for Colino's terrible 'resurrection' as Nicolo at the conclusion.

41 Frank G. Ryder, 'Kleist's *Findling*: "Oedipus *manqué*?",' in *Modern Language Notes*, vol. 92, 1977, pp. 509-24.

remains close to the fictional characters' mode of perception, while, at a further remove, the text makes arrangements that enable an ironic reading of the narrator as well as the other characters. In *Der Findling*, the narrator is both more vehement and less consistent. The narrative perspective affects the stance of certainty in its judgements, but even a slightly critical re-reading reveals the narrator to be as bemused by the duality of the figures as any naive reader. If the narrator states of Piachi: 'und zog sich, mit seiner treuen, trefflichen Elvire, die wenige Wünsche in der Welt hatte, in den Ruhestand zurück' (SW II, 202) – then a most cursory appraisal must reveal this apparently unqualified statement to be ironized by the text on more than one count. 'Trefflich' Elvire may be, but her fidelity to Piachi is, at best, a technicality. She may have few desires 'in the world,' but the reader is soon to learn she has very strong ones outside it. Piachi's retirement is revealed as a sham, since he never relinquishes his claim to paternal dominance over Nicolo. Dissonances like these can scarcely be missed on reflection, and should serve as the point of departure for a reading of the story that does justice to it as the tour de force of experimental narration which indubitably it is.

11

Der Zweikampf – Michael Kohlhaas

Der Zweikampf and *Michael Kohlhaas* are linked, superficially, by settings that evoke a relatively distant German past. More significantly, they are related by their dependence on the device of the intrusive narrator and their use of legal processes to explore the tensions between written and other modes of communication. *Der Zweikampf* has been interpreted in the belief that it was Kleist's last completed story,[1] and it has attracted the usual partisan verdicts on the characters.[2] Partisan interpretation also surrounds the issues of whether the text is in harmony with or in contradiction to Enlightenment thinking,[3] and whether irony is fundamental to or entirely absent from the text. Like *Michael Kohlhaas*, *Der Zweikampf* has produced ample evidence of the unrequited love historians bear Kleist's texts, a phenomenon I shall briefly examine.

In choosing settings for his plays and stories, Kleist, for various reasons, with censorship being not the least, tended to avoid the present. *Die Verlobung in St. Domingo*, set in 1803, is his only longer fiction to be situated in his own time. But even here, Kleist chooses an exotic milieu far away from Prussia, while his other settings range from the explicitly mythical to the pseudo-historical. Kleist's addiction to

1 For a summary of such readings, see James M. McGlathery, 'Kleist's *Der Zweikampf* as Comedy,' *Heinrich von Kleist-Studien*, ed. Alexej Ugrinsky, pp. 87f.

2 Cf. Wolfgang Wittkowski, '*Die heilige Cäcilie* und *Der Zweikampf*. Kleists Legenden und die romantische Ironie,' in *Colloquia Germanica*, 1972, p. 52: 'Das ist die Vergöttlichung des Menschen, die sich bei Kleist allenthalben findet. Ihr Grundzug ist edle Noblesse. Sie bezeugt sich in Trotas vollkommener Einheit mit seiner tiefsten Überzeugung; in seiner Bereitschaft, sein Leben rückhaltlos, frei und leicht aufs Spiel zu setzen. . . .'; for a contrary verdict, see John Ellis, *Heinrich von Kleist*, p. 56: 'Once we have begun to notice Friedrich's inadequacy for the role in which he is cast by the plot outline, additional evidence piles up. His performance in the duel is conspicuously unheroic, and he defends until the spectators are so bored that they complain . . . .'

3 Cf. Peter Horn, *Heinrich von Kleists Erzählungen*, p. 209: 'Gerade die Fundierung der Rechtssprechung im Religiösen und Metaphysischen entlarvt Kleist aber . . . als ideologische Täuschung und Selbsttäuschung der handelnden Personen. . .'; Ernst Schubert, 'Der Zweikampf. Ein mittelalterliches Ordal und seine Vergegenwärtigung bei Heinrich von Kleist,' in *KJb* 1988/89, p. 304: 'Er wendet sich . . . gegen den so häufig zur Schau gestellten Juristenstolz der Aufklärung, die Zeiten des mittelalterlichen "Faustrechts" überwunden zu haben.'

anachronisms has, as its corollary, the effect that his texts are usually read as signalling references to contemporary political events or philosophical controversies. Thus, *Das Erdbeben in Chili* alludes both to 18th century philosophical debates about the Lisbon earthquake and to society in the aftermath of the French Revolution.

It was Kleist's consistent technique to improvise freely on whatever historical sources he may have used, adding and changing whatever suited his artistic purpose. In *Prinz Friedrich von Homburg*, for example, the hero is a young bachelor rather than a middle-aged married man, and Kleist invents Natalie to enrich the complications between Homburg and the Kurfürst. Plots that have a veneer of historicity abound in fictional modifications and slips in time. The most obvious reason for this lies in the fact that Kleist's approach to his plots was wholly experimental. He devised models that allowed the exposition of variations on his recurrent themes, and if the historical background did not suit the purposes of the experiment, he changed it.

Thus, in *Der Zweikampf*, set 'gegen das Ende des vierzehnten Jahrhunderts' (SW II, 229), Kleist has Graf Jakob der Rotbart declare an intention to embark on a 'Kreuzzug nach Palästina, auf welchem er die Sünden einer raschen Jugend . . . abzubüßen dachte' (SW II, 230), although Jerusalem had passed out of Christian hands in 1244 and crusading ceased around 1270. Moreover, the Church had taken a dim view of eliciting a divine judgement through a duel since 1215, so that, while the practice continued among the feudal aristocracy, the law, by virtue of which both Friedrich von Trota and Frau Littegarde are condemned 'auf dem Platz des Zweikampfs selbst, den schmählichen Tod der Flammen zu erleiden' (SW II, 254), is all Kleist's own work. Given such major anachronisms, which Kleist could have avoided by a modicum of research, it is not surprising that there are many minor ones as well in the text.

The condemnation of the two innocents and the subsequent burning of Graf Jakob's corpse in place of the live Friedrich and Littegarde have a clear function within the semantics of the text. Hence, it does not matter whether Kleist mentions this law out of ignorance; whether he knew there was no such law but wanted to make his narrator appear ignorant to readers versed in medieval history; or whether he did not care for historical accuracy and used the law to give the plot two more ironic twists.

But in writing on Kleist, the pursuit of historical details that might be coaxed into an appearance of accuracy or relevance is relentless. This would be harmless enough were it not that Ernst Schubert's essay on *Der Zweikampf*, which musters an impressive historical apparatus, typifies such exercises by reaching a dogmatic conclusion at variance with the simplest terms of the text: 'Von einer Verdächtigung oder gar von einer Ironisierung des Kampfrechts findet sich bei ihm [Kleist] keine Spur.'[4] By denying that the text presents its own setting ironically, Schubert presents Kleist as a straight-faced antiquarian – but at the expense of what the text actually does. For there is the first and most obvious irony that the duel *cannot* yield an intelligible answer to the question it is meant to resolve, namely, whether Frau Littegarde or Graf Jakob is lying. Graf Jakob is guilty of the murder of his half-brother, but genuinely believes he has spent the Eve of St. Remigius in bed with Frau Littegarde, whereas he has, in fact, been duped by Rosalie, her maid. Frau Littegarde, on the other hand, knows he has not spent the night with her. Hence neither has lied on the issue in question.

The second irony is that the outcome of the duel has none of the clarity expected from a 'Gottesurteil,' but is ambiguous in the style of the Delphic oracle. This ambiguity is promptly subjected to dogmatic *interpretations*, one of which nearly has two innocents burnt alive at the command of a well-meaning but dithering Emperor. A third irony is that the corpse of the *victor* in the duel is burnt instead of the losing parties, because he stands revealed as a criminal, but not without his first making some amends: 'eine Tat der Gerechtigkeit verübt zu haben' (SW II, 258).

This last irony has the incidental effect of also ironizing the narrator's limited view. Even though Graf Jakob's last moments on earth are spent clarifying the innocence of Littegarde and repenting the murder of his half-brother,[5] the narrator takes leave of him with the words: 'Bei dieser Erklärung sank er auf die Bahre zurück und hauchte seine schwarze Seele aus' (SW II, 260). Such dissonance is clearly reminiscent of the unreliability of judgements passed in *Das Erdbeben in Chili* and *Der Findling*, because the narrator is too caught up in the emotions generated by the text to be impartial. Graf Jakob gets no credit for his deathbed change of heart, while Littegarde's brothers, who have savagely maltreated her and obviously perjured themselves in the letter the Emperor receives, get off without a reprimand.

There is nothing in the pursuit of historical source-studies on Kleist's writings that intrinsically should promote neglect of the precise terms of the fictions, but Schubert is not alone in using a positivistic study as a springboard for misplaced dogmatism. For if irony is excluded from an understanding of the plot of *Der Zweikampf*, I am at a loss to know how it can be understood at all. The basic requirements of literary irony are that there be two different apprehensions of the same event, or set of events, and that one presents itself as superior to the other, whether the

4 Ernst Schubert, 'Der Zweikampf,' p. 304.
5 Cf. Timothy J. Mehigan, *Text as Contract*, p. 237: 'It is those conspicuously lower world figures, Jakob and Rosalie, who emerge to rescue order in the narrative.'

text finally vindicates this or not.[6] *Der Zweikampf* abounds in ambiguous events about which fictional characters draw conclusions that are subsequently exposed as misapprehensions, and neither the narrator nor the reader is exempt from being the victim of ironic ploys.

Der Zweikampf contains one of Kleist's most flagrant examples of a narrator's confounding the reader's expectations. At the point where Littegarde and Friedrich have been condemned to be burnt 'wegen sündhaft angerufenen göttlichen Schiedsurteils' (SW II, 254), while the apparent victor, Graf Jakob, has succumbed to 'ein äußerst verderbter Zustand seiner Säfte,' resulting in an arm's being amputated (SW II, 255), mystification within the plot is complete. It is here that the narrator abruptly chooses to reveal the details of a subplot that contains the elements of the dénouement. The manner of revelation reveals that the reader has been deliberately kept in the dark:

> Man muß nämlich wissen, daß der Graf schon lange, ehe seine Begierde sich auf Frau Littegarden stellte, mit Rosalien, ihrer Kammerzofe, auf einem nichtswürdigen Fuß lebte; fast bei jedem Besuch, den ihre Herrschaft auf seinem Schlosse abstattete, pflegte er dies Mädchen, welches ein leichtfertiges und sittenloses Geschöpf war, zur Nachtzeit auf sein Zimmer zu ziehen.   (SW II, 256)

Previous to this point, the reader has not even been told Rosalie's name, let alone received any inkling of her major involvement in the plot. The narrator's assertion that this knowledge is essential emphasizes, at the same time, that it has been arbitrarily withheld from the reader. Just as the outcome of the duel does not tell the fictional characters what they need to know in order to draw accurate conclusions, so the narrator has deprived the reader of the key to the central puzzle of the plot. Moreover, nothing that is central to the main action prompts the disclosure. Had Rosalie's pregnancy not resulted in her parents interrogating her until her connection with Graf Jakob became clear, and then promptly suing the count for maintenance of the child, Friedrich and Littegarde might have been burnt and Graf Jakob died of his septic humours, still believing he had spent a night with Littegarde.

The story could thus have reached a conclusion as grim as that of *Der Findling* had the narrator not arbitrarily decided to make the missing information available, first to the reader and subsequently in written form – 'einen Brief mit der gerichtlichen Aussage des Mädchens' (SW II, 258) – to the characters within the plot. We may conclude either that the narrator is omniscient, but absent-minded, or that, more probably,

6 Cf. D. C. Muecke, *The Compass of Irony*, London, 1969, pp. 34-9.

Kleist is making his game with the reader's expectations as explicit as the puzzlement of the fictional characters over the outcome of the duel. This brings us to the question of what the reader does expect of the story – for as long as the narrator still appears to be disclosing all relevant details. Bernd Fischer recognizes an experiment is in train and claims that the theme is an 'oppositionelle Struktur von romantischem und politischem Mittelalter' aimed at the subversion of the Romantic 'Kunstmärchen.'[7] Subversion is definitely afoot, but I doubt the target is as simple as Fischer maintains. For the 'fairytale' aspects of the story are a great deal less pronounced than in *Das Käthchen von Heilbronn*, and I would argue that the story is far too circumstantial from the beginning to allow this dimension to achieve enough presence to be subverted in a way readers might recognize.

For the plot begins with a murder that is investigated through the due processes of law, as the text chooses to define them. Fischer claims that Graf Jakob's use of a night spent with Littegarde as an alibi means leaving behind the 'Paradigmen mittelalterlicher Politik' and involving himself in the plot of a 'Kunstmärchen,'[8] but I fail to see any clear transition. 'Medieval' politics are as the story chooses to depict them, given all the anachronisms and the fact that the dukedom of the murder victim is entirely fictitious. The equivocal outcome of the duel is entirely congruent with this setting. A number of false judgements is made that reveals a belief in miracles, but they do not assemble themselves into a consistent 'fairytale.' The miraculous does not attain the autonomy it enjoys in *Das Käthchen von Heilbronn*, for any event that is claimed to be so has an alternative explanation in terms of ordinary causality.

When the Emperor exclaims at the end of the story: 'Nun, jedes Haar auf eurem Haupt bewacht ein Engel!' (SW II, 259), the reader and the other characters are fully aware that the deliverance of Littegarde and Friedrich owes more to Rosalie's parents' initiating a paternity suit against Graf Jakob for financial reasons than it does to any angelic intervention. While the two texts are similar to the extent that a somewhat haphazard patriarchal order asserts itself in the conclusion, there is nothing in *Der Zweikampf* as unambiguous as the meaning of the shared dream in *Das Käthchen von Heilbronn*, let alone the appearance of the 'Cherub' on stage in Act III, Scene 14.

What the story does conspicuously subvert is the judicial process it has itself instituted. At the beginning, Graf Jakob is accused on two points: that the arrow that kills his brother has been traced to him and

---

7 Bernd Fischer, 'Der Ernst des Scheins in der Prosa Heinrich von Kleists: Am Beispiel des *Zweikampfs*,' in *ZfdPh*, vol. 105 (2), 1986, pp. 215f.
8 Ibid., p. 218.

that he was absent from his castle on St. Remigius' Eve. The second point is pursued exhaustively, but the first is simply forgotten until the dying murderer confesses: 'der Bösewicht, der ihn mit dem Pfeil aus meiner Rüstkammer nieder warf, war sechs Wochen vorher, zu dieser Tat, die mir die Krone verschaffen sollte, von mir gedungen!' (SW II, 260). Since Graf Jakob has hired an assassin, his own whereabouts on the night of the crime are irrelevant, but the reader is firmly led from any further consideration of the evidence of the arrow, although no explanation for it is offered until the confession.

Why the Emperor's judiciary loses interest in the arrow is as enigmatic as the narrator's exclusion of all mention of Rosalie from earlier, relevant incidents in the plot. It is surely not beyond the 'medieval' forensic imagination to conceive that an alibi does not necessarily disqualify all other evidence, especially as there are allegations of more than one assassin being involved: 'wegen der Mörder ihres Gemahls, deren man im Park eine ganze Schar wahrgenommen haben wollte' (SW II, 230). Kleist has left the 'historical' background far behind in devising a world of elaborate written communications that makes much more sense when viewed in terms of the judicial procedures of his own time than it does as a depiction of law in the Middle Ages. Much the same applies to the world of *Michael Kohlhaas*. Within this framework, it is scarcely plausible that a judiciary, having found two instances requiring a response, is content simply to forget the first:

> Der Kaiser . . . setzte daselbst ein Gericht von drei Grafen, zwölf Rittern und zwei Gerichtsassessoren nieder; und nachdem er dem Grafen Jakob dem Rotbart . . . freies Geleit zugestanden hatte, forderte er ihn auf, sich dem erwähnten Gericht zu stellen, und demselben über die beiden Punkte: wie der Pfeil, der, nach seinem eigenen Geständnis, sein gehöre, in die Hände des Mörders gekommen? auch: an welchem dritten Ort er sich in der Nacht des heiligen Remigius aufgehalten habe, Red und Antwort zu stehen. (SW II, 234)

Peter Horn is quite right to say: 'Von Anfang an bestimmt die kriminalistische Ermittlung das Bild der Novelle mindestens ebenso stark wie das Gottesgericht,'[9] but it is necessary to add that the one is shown to be as ineffective as the other. The futile clash of interpretations within the story may be seen in parallel to the mystification of the reader by the text. Forensic incompetence, an arbitrary narrative intervention, and a duel that cannot decide the question it is meant to resolve are all indications that reality is chronically illegible within the fictional framework.

---

9 Peter Horn, *Heinrich von Kleists Erzählungen*, p. 204.

They further suggest that the text itself signals that it cannot be compelled to yield meaning – or if it concedes meaning, then it will do so only on its own terms.

This is where the imperfect communication of the 'Gottesurteil' becomes synonymous with the narrator's treatment of the reader. For the duel is to elicit a clear meaning from a recalcitrant world by obliging the deity, as author and editor, to make the text of reality legible in one of two senses. That it fails to do so may be explained in metaphysical, psychological, or forensic terms – as one pleases – but in end it comes down to a problem of hermeneutics common to all of Kleist's fictions, whether dramatic or narrative: characters who are forced into the situation of reading a text of which they themselves are part will lack detachment and oversight, and thus misinterpret that text.

The narrator – as elsewhere in Kleist's stories – is not quite adequate to the expectations of Olympian detachment a conventional reading will place in omniscience and omnipotence, and strews epithets with no more restraint than any of the fictional characters. Ironically, the Emperor is elevated to a semblance of the editorial role reserved for the deity and, after scarcely performing it with distinction, bows out with a textual amendment which says little more than that there is no guarantee such duels will ever perform the function for which they are intended, namely, to clarify *instantly* the meaning of a given set of events:

> Der Kaiser aber hing Herrn Friedrich, nach der Trauung, eine Gnadenkette um den Hals; und sobald er . . . wieder in Worms angekommen war, ließ er in die Statuten des geheiligten göttlichen Zweikampfs, überall wo vorausgesetzt wird, daß die Schuld dadurch unmittelbar ans Tageslicht komme, die Worte einrücken: 'wenn es Gottes Wille ist.'   (SW II, 261)

Needless to say, the ending has been read as 'Kaiserverherrlichung,'[10] but it surely makes more sense to conclude that the Emperor is merely making the best of a very bad job that nearly had him incinerate a couple of loyal and virtuous subjects.

There is a good deal of intertextuality between this and other fiction by Kleist, some of it significant, some trivial.[11] The treatment of Littegarde by her brothers takes up motifs from Graf Wetter vom Strahl's brutality toward Käthchen and from a tableau near the end of

---

10 Ernst Schubert, 'Der Zweikampf,' in *KJb*, p. 301.

11 Cf. Christian Grawe, 'Zur Deutung von Kleists Novelle *Der Zweikampf*,' in *Germanisch-Romanische Monatsschrift* (NF), vol. 27, 1977, pp. 420-5.

Der Findling.[12] There is also, in the abuse of Frau Littegarde at the hands of her brothers, an echo of the Kommandant's treatment of his daughter in *Die Marquise von O...*, which points, in turn, to the most interesting parallel with another story. For despite its also ending in a marriage, *Der Zweikampf* stops at a point where the earlier story continues, and thus refuses Littegarde entry to the emancipatory process that is forced on the Marquise.

Interestingly, the explanation for this lies in the constellation of gender roles. For the Marquise reaches a point where there is no male savior to whom she can turn. This, happily for her, coincides with a shift in her perspective that launches her on a series of initiatives of which the plot ultimately approves. Littegarde comes to a similar crossroads. The scene following the death of her father, which occurs while she is 'besinnungslos' (SW II, 236), and her maltreatment by her brothers, place her in a state that is familiar from *Das Erdbeben in Chili* and elsewhere in which she is too harried by unexpected catastrophes to know what she is doing, and loses consciousness. Villagers come to her aid, and her fainting turns out to be a blessing in disguise, since it restores to her a semblance of 'Besinnung': 'Sie erholte sich durch die Bemühungen dieser Leute gar bald, und gewann auch, bei dem Anblick der Burg, die hinter ihr verschlossen war, ihre Besinnung wieder. . . .' (SW II, 238).

After hesitating, she embarks on a sensible course, namely, to throw herself on the mercy of Herr Friedrich von Trota. If we read *Der Zweikampf* from the perspective offered by *Die Marquise von O...*, there is a clear irony in the fact that the availability of a male protector means that she takes no further initiative for herself. Herr Friedrich happens to be working on legal documents when she appears. She repeats before him the gesture of submission that had already proven ineffective with her bothers: 'und Frau Littegarden, bleich und entstellt, ein wahres Bild der Verzweiflung, vor ihm auf Knieen nieder sinken sah' (SW II, 239). Friedrich, however, responds by offering to be her advocate – 'Anwalt' – and indeed does his best to counteract the forces ranged against her. His best is, however, not enough, and Littegarde is sufficiently confused by the outcome of the duel to be brought to the edge of madness. Only the mercenary interests of Rosalie's parents and their surprising readiness, given their daughter's reputation and their own low social status, to bring a paternity suit against Graf Jakob manage to untie the knot of circumstance. Herr Friedrich does seem to benefit from his ordeal to the extent of realizing that reality is not obliged to yield clear answers as a result of the crude pressure the appeal to a 'Gottesurteil' applies:

12 Cf. SW I, 449f; SW II, 213.

Laß uns, von zwei Gedanken, die die Sinne verwirren, den verständlicheren und begreiflicheren denken, und ehe du dich schuldig glaubst, lieber glauben, daß ich in dem Zweikampf den ich für dich gefochten, siegte! . . . Wo liegt die Verpflichtung der höchsten göttlichen Weisheit, die Wahrheit im Augenblick der glaubensvollen Anrufung selbst, anzuzeigen und auszusprechen?   (SW II, 254)

The only thing wrong with Herr Friedrich's hermeneutics is a belief that the dice are *not* loaded against fictional characters in the games they play with whatever authority ultimately controls the text of which they are part. The narrator's behavior toward the reader, in concealing Rosalie's role in events for so long, shows plainly that, in this particular experiment, they are. Hence all Friedrich's insight cannot save him from nearly being burnt alive with Littegarde, and the story's only moral is to encourage a healthy distrust of the narrator.

One anachronism in *Der Zweikampf* that is strongly functional and which links this fictional world to that of *Michael Kohlhaas* is Kleist's bureaucratization of his pseudo-historical setting. It is no accident that Franz Kafka was to recognize in Kleist a 'blood relative,'[13] for in these two stories Kleist has transposed his own experience of the Prussian bureaucracy onto the fictional past, and created, in *Der Zweikampf,* a 'medieval' setting in which Kafka's castle might be just down the road. It is significant that Herr Friedrich is introduced to the reader in a scene that has him immersed in paperwork, rather than jousting or performing heroic rescues. His sisters lead Frau Littegarde 'zu ihrem Bruder hinauf, der in Akten, womit ihn ein Prozeß überschüttete, versenkt, an einem Tische saß' (SW II, 239). Herr Friedrich's skills as 'Anwalt' are pertinent, if not quite adequate, in a story in which the first significant event is the obtaining of a 'kaiserliche Legitimationsakte' and the last an amendment to the statutes in Worms. The disclosure of Rosalie's elaborate deception hinges not on any act of heroism, but on her parents taking Graf Jakob to court, and the victimization of Frau Littegarde by her brothers reaches a decidedly textual climax: 'Dabei trugen sie . . . darauf an, ihren Namen aus der Geschlechtstafel des Bredaschen Hauses auszustreichen' (SW II, 241), another anachronism that emphasizes that the text in question is the text of reality. This, in turn, should remind the reader that the story as text is hierarchically superior to any document that appears on a thematic level.

The world of *Michael Kohlhaas* is even more clearly dominated by formalized language. Some 90 different documents or classes of docu-

---

13 Cf. Franz Kafka, *Briefe an Felice*, eds. Erich Heller and Jürgen Born, Frankfurt/M, 1967, p. 460.

ments are mentioned on the thematic level. Figures of power, notably Luther and the Kurfürst of Saxony, are presented, like Herr Friedrich in *Der Zweikampf*, amid piles of documents:

> Luther, der unter Schriften und Büchern an seinem Pulte saß, . . . fragte ihn [Kohlhaas], wer er sei? . . . Luther, mit einem verdrießlichen Gesicht, warf die Papiere, die auf seinem Tisch lagen, übereinander, und schwieg. . . . Luther sagte, indem er unter mancherlei Gedanken, wieder zu seinen Papieren griff: er wolle mit dem Kurfürsten seinethalben in Unterhandlung treten. . . . und da der Famulus vergebens . . . an der Tür wirkte, Luther aber sich wieder zu seinen Papieren niedergesetzt hatte: so machte Kohlhaas dem Mann die Türe auf. . . . Am anderen Morgen erließ Luther ein Sendschreiben an den Kurfürsten von Sachsen. . . . (SW II, 44-9)

It is a document, damning Kohlhaas and published throughout Saxony, that has brought Kohlhaas to Luther in the first place. Their dialogue, which is a less than perfect communication, is marked by Luther's rummaging in his documents, as if to reassure himself of his own power in the face of Kohlhaas' considerable popular support. The day afterward, Luther sends a despatch to the ruler in which political pragmatism is dominant and which results in the conditional offer of amnesty to Kohlhaas.

Since irony surrounds the power of documents, as it does all other kinds of power in Kleist's works, it is to be expected that it might turn against those who wield it. This happens to the Kurfürst of Saxony in the final part of the story, when his desire to learn the contents of the message in the lead capsule Kohlhaas possesses makes him regret that he has lodged an accusation with the Emperor against Kohlhaas. The scene in which he learns it is too late to reverse the legal procedures in Vienna, which he himself has set in motion, implies a helpless resentment against the bureaucracy in which even figures of power are enmeshed:

> Der Kurfürst, indem er errötend an seinen Arbeitstisch trat, wunderte sich über diese Eilfertigkeit, indem er seines Wissens erklärt hätte, die definitive Abreise des Eibenmayer, wegen vorher notwendiger Rücksprache mit dem Doktor Luther, der dem Kohlhaas die Amnestie ausgewirkt, einem näheren und bestimmteren Befehl vorbehalten zu wollen. Dabei warf er einige Briefschaften und Akten, die auf dem Tisch lagen, mit dem Ausdruck zurückgehaltenen Unwillens, über einander. Der Prinz . . . versetzte, daß es ihm leid täte . . .; inzwischen könne er ihm den

Beschluß des Staatsrats vorzeigen, worin ihm die Abschickung des Rechtsanwalts, zu dem besagten Zeitpunkt zur Pflicht gemacht worden wäre. (SW II, 87)

I have suggested that the modes of written communication in *Michael Kohlhaas* provide a key to structuring this extremely complex text and to solving some of the dilemmas posed by its content.[14] While it has been claimed that the story has some affinity to a drama in five acts,[15] I propose that the narrative text falls clearly into three sections, if read along the axis of the thematics of the language of power.

The first section begins with Kohlhaas being challenged to furnish a 'Paßschein' that has no legal validity. Despite his obtaining an official, written confirmation of this in Dresden – 'einen schriftlichen Schein über den Ungrund derselben' (SW II, 13) – his efforts to set matters right through normal legal channels come to nothing. His wife undertakes to present a petition to the Kurfürst of Brandenburg in his stead, is injured trying, and dies. At her funeral, Kohlhaas receives an official document from Brandenburg that not only denies this petition, but forbids him, on pain of imprisonment, to make any more written submissions, thus rendering him dumb in the medium through which official power flows:

Der Geistliche hatte eben eine rührende Rede an ihrer Bahre vollendet, als ihm die landesherrliche Resolution auf die Bittschrift zugestellt ward, welche die Abgeschiedene übergeben hatte, des Inhalts: er solle die Pferde von der Tronkenburg abholen, und bei Strafe, in das Gefängnis geworfen zu werden, nicht weiter in dieser Sache einkommen. Kohlhaas steckte den Brief ein, und ließ den Sarg auf den Wagen bringen. Sobald der Hügel geworfen, das Kreuz darauf gepflanzt, und die Gäste . . . entlassen waren, warf er sich noch einmal vor ihrem verödeten Bette nieder, und übernahm sodann das Geschäft der Rache. (SW II, 31)

In this first part, Kohlhaas has been transformed from a successful merchant at ease with the world into a bereaved victim thirsting for revenge. The agent of transformation is the power that resides in the states of Saxony and Brandenburg, is subject to abuse and inconsistent application, and is transmitted through formalized, written language. Before the episode at his wife's grave, Kohlhaas has twice been discour-

---

14 Anthony Stephens, '"Eine Träne auf den Brief",' pp. 335-8.
15 First suggested by Charles E. Passage, '*Michael Kohlhaas*: Form Analysis,' in *The Germanic Review*, vol. 30, 1955, pp. 181-97, and since repeated by many.

aged from pursuing his cause in documentary form.[16] The tableau that makes abundantly clear to what extent the language of power is alienated from the feelings of a victim of such power occurs in a scene between Kohlhaas and the Stadthauptmann, Heinrich von Geusau, who also has an important role to play in the rehabilitation of Brandenburg in the final section of the story:

> Der Stadthauptmann, der, während er mit dem Arzte sprach, bemerkte, daß Kohlhaas eine Träne auf den Brief, den er bekommen und eröffnet hatte, fallen ließ, näherte sich ihm . . . und fragte ihn, was für ein Unfall ihn betroffen; und da der Roßhändler ihm, ohne ihm zu antworten, den Brief überreichte: so klopfte ihm dieser würdige Mann, dem die abscheuliche Ungerechtigkeit, die man auf der Tronkenburg an ihm verübt hatte . . . bekannt war, auf die Schulter, und sagte ihm: er solle nicht mutlos sein. . . . (SW II, 22f)

As I have argued elsewhere, Kleist's narrative technique plays on Rousseau's views of the negative relation between written and spoken language and spontaneous emotion, as set forth particularly in his *Essai sur l'origine des langues*.[17] Kleist differs from the Rousseauistic model in at least two important points: first, he reverses, in the light of the role of demagoguery in the French Revolution, Rousseau's conviction that the language of public discourse has lost all power; second, he qualifies Rousseau's view of written language as a decadent and alienated mode of communication by accepting the factor of estrangement, but adding to it a constant emphasis on documents as vehicles of power.

The second main episode of *Michael Kohlhaas* thus begins with the main character's arrogating to himself precisely that power which has progressively reduced him to silence in the first: 'Er setzte sich nieder und verfaßte einen Rechtsschluß, in welchem er den Junker Wenzel von Tronka, kraft der ihm angeborenen Macht, verdammte, die Rappen . . . binnen drei Tagen nach Sicht, nach Kohlhaasenbrück zu führen. . . .' (SW II, 31). As Hans Joachim Kreutzer points out, Kohlhaas' invocation of 'Macht,' rather than 'Recht,' takes the text at this point beyond the ethical dimension of Enlightenment debates on civil author-

---

16 'und schloß mit dem Gesuch, ihn wenigstens . . . mit ferneren Aufträgen in dieser Sache zu verschonen' SW II, 22; 'er möchte nach der Burg schicken, und sie holen, . . . die Staatskanzlei aber . . . mit solchen Plackereien und Stänkereien verschonen' SW II, 24.

17 Anthony Stephens, '"Eine Träne auf den Brief",' pp. 323-7.

ity.[18] There follows a series of incidents in which Kohlhaas' increasing power against the state is paralleled by the documents he writes and publishes. The 'Kohlhaasche Mandate,' four in number, make his power appear increasingly absolute. In the third, he proclaims himself "'einen Reichs- und Weltfreien, Gott allein unterworfenen Herrn'" (SW II, 36), and in the fourth "'einen Statthalter Michaels, des Erzengels, der gekommen sei, an allen . . . mit Feuer und Schwert, die Arglist, in welcher die ganze Welt versunken sei, zu bestrafen'" (SW II, 41).

Significantly, this excess of self-aggrandisement loses him the approval of the narrator, which anticipates a rapid decline of Kohlhaas' power on the thematic level:

> Dabei rief er . . . das Volk auf, sich zur Errichtung einer besseren Ordnung der Dinge, an ihn anzuschließen; und das Mandat war, mit einer Art von Verrückung, unterzeichnet: 'Gegeben auf dem Sitz unserer provisorischen Weltregierung, dem Erzschlosse zu Lützen.' (SW II, 41)

He luxuriates in the extent to which his 'Mandate' can apparently reverse the humiliation visited upon him through other documents in the first part of the story, and explicitly places himself beyond any temporal power. The reversal of his triumph occurs – with appropriate irony – through another document, namely, Luther's proclamation condemning him, which arrogates to itself the privilege of speaking in the name of the one authority Kohlhaas still does acknowledge:

> meinst du, Sünder, vor Gott dereinst, an dem Tage, der in die Falten aller Herzen scheinen wird, damit auszukommen? . . . dergestalt, daß wenn dereinst du vor Gottes Thron trittst, in der Meinung, ihn anzuklagen, er [der Landesherr], heiteren Antlitzes, wird sprechen können: diesem Mann, Herr, tat ich kein Unrecht, denn sein Dasein ist meiner Seele fremd? (SW II, 42f)

Not only does Kleist's Luther misrepresent the facts, but his subsequent, private letter to the Kurfürst of Saxony is wholly concerned with the pragmatics of statecraft, not at all with the Last Judgement. Ironically, these factors are irrelevant, since Kohlhaas, by becoming

---

18 Hans Joachim Kreutzer, 'Wann lebte Michael Kohlhaas? Über die ästhetische Einheit der Erzählung Kleists,' *Literatur und Geschichte 1788-1988*, eds. Gerhard Schulz and Tim Mehigan, Bern, Frankfurt/M, New York and Paris, 1990, pp. 75f: 'Ich fürchte, Kleist und sein Michael Kohlhaas gehen noch einen Schritt weiter. Die "Macht" als rechtssetzende Kraft setzt auch der Rechtsphilosophie ein Ende. . . . Michael Kohlhaas könnte Rousseau und Kant das Fürchten lernen.'

intoxicated with the rhetoric of power, has rendered himself vulnerable to a document carrying the prestige of Martin Luther and purporting to exert divine authority. In the midst of acting out a chiliastic fantasy, which is reminiscent of the Anabaptist reign of Bockelson in Münster,[19] Kohlhaas is, quite literally, disarmed by a written assertion of a power greater than his own in Luther's 'Plakat': 'Mehr als dieser wenigen Worte bedurfte es nicht, um ihn, in der ganzen Verderblichkeit, in der er dastand, plötzlich zu entwaffnen' (SW II, 44).

He passes from being the source of utterances of power to being once more their object. By accepting an ambivalent amnesty, he re-enters a world in which documents about his case multiply and he steadily loses the autonomy he achieved so rapidly by embarking on his campaign of vengeance. His final loss of power occurs through a parodistic doubling of his own situation. Johann Nagelschmidt, an unscrupulous member of his band, has continued a career of banditry after the amnesty, proclaiming himself 'einen Statthalter des Kohlhaas' (SW II, 65), issuing his own mendacious 'Mandate' (SW II, 67), and further undermining Kohlhaas' position in the eyes of the state of Saxony. In words that echo the episode between Luther and Kohlhaas, the text portrays Kohlhaas as trying to exert over Nagelschmidt the authority that had disarmed himself, when applied by Luther: 'Kohlhaas . . . setzte sich nieder, und erließ ein Sendschreiben an den Nagelschmidt, worin er das Vorgeben desselben . . . für eine schändliche und ruchlose Erfindung erklärte. . . .' (SW II, 68). But Kohlhaas has none of Luther's prestige, the von Tronka faction exploits the situation to its own advantage, and Kohlhaas compromises himself in a private letter of quite different content to Nagelschmidt, which is intercepted, copied, and published abroad in a manner that recalls, once more, the original 'Mandate' and Luther's 'Plakat':

Man machte ihm [Kohlhaas] auf den Grund dieses Briefes, der an alle Ecken der Stadt angeschlagen ward, den Prozeß; und da er vor den Schranken des Tribunals auf die Frage, ob er die Handschrift anerkenne, dem Rat, der sie ihm vorhielt, antwortete: 'ja!' zur Antwort aber auf die Frage, ob er zu seiner Verteidigung etwas vorzubringen wisse, indem er den Blick zur Erde schlug, erwiderte, 'nein!' so ward er verurteilt, mit glühenden Zangen von Schinderknechten gekniffen, geviertelt, und sein Körper, zwischen Rad und Galgen, verbrannt zu werden.   (SW II, 77)

19 Cf. Hartmut Boockmann, 'Mittelalterliches Recht bei Kleist. Ein Beitrag zum Verständnis des *Michael Kohlhaas*,' in *KJb* 1985, p. 102.

So ends the second and longest section of the story. Within the dimension of power and of the language that is its medium, Kohlhaas' career, in this second major section, has described a parabola. Beginning from a position of enforced impotence and silence, he usurps the discourse of the authority to which he is subject, much as Graf Wetter vom Strahl does of the 'Vehmgericht' in the first act of *Das Käthchen von Heilbronn*.[20] His stylizations of himself as 'Gott allein unterworfen' and 'Statthalter Michaels, des Erzengels' prepare, however, the ironic pitfall that he must succumb to a verbal attack by Luther that usurps the one authority Kohlhaas still admits above himself.

Once he has agreed to have his case heard by the courts in Dresden, he not only returns to acknowledging the authorities he had previously rejected, but he has also divested himself of the power that made Luther advise the Kurfürst to treat him carefully in the first place. Once more vulnerable to court intrigues, he suffers a further loss of credibility through the depredations of his alter ego, Nagelschmidt, and is finally obliged to recognize his own writing in a letter that amounts to criminal conspiracy. Nothing could be further from the exalted rhetoric of his original 'Mandate' than his monosyllabic statement at his trial that he has nothing to say in his own justification. In an unmistakable parallel to the end of the first section, he has once more been reduced to silence.

The third section is essentially a Prussian fantasy, similar to that which encapsulates the tragedy in *Prinz Friedrich von Homburg*.[21] It begins: 'So standen die Sachen für den armen Kohlhaas in Dresden, als der Kurfürst von Brandenburg zu seiner Rettung aus den Händen der Übermacht und Willkür auftrat, und ihn . . . als brandenburgischen Untertan reklamierte' (SW II, 77). It has been observed that the Kurfürst of Brandenburg is not developed as a character, as is the ruler of Saxony, but is presented schematically, a compendium of the qualities of a strict but just prince.[22] It has also been observed that the story changes its formal character as it nears its ending.[23] The problem is not simply that the horses, which were previously at the center of the dispute, disappear from view to be replaced by other objects, including, in one imaginative study, the 'Vorstellung vom Phallus der Mutter, bzw. vom Phallus des Vaters, den die Mutter in sich trägt'[24] – just as

---

20 See above p. 137.
21 See above p. 191.
22 Hans Joachim Kreutzer, 'Wann lebte Michael Kohlhaas?,' p. 72: 'Kleists brandenburgischer Kurfürst bleibt ohne persönliche Züge, gleichsam der abstrakte Inbegriff eines Herrschers.'
23 John M. Ellis, *Heinrich von Kleist*, p. 72, lists five significant aspects.
24 Helga Gallas, *Das Textbegehren des 'Michael Kohlhaas.' Die Sprache des Unbewußten und der Sinn der Literatur*, Reinbek, 1981, p. 87; cf. also, for a mild variant, Clayton Koelb, 'Incorporating the Text: Kleist's *Michael Kohlhaas*,' in *PMLA*, vol. 105 (5), 1990, p. 1099.

Kohlhaas' main adversary changes from Wenzel von Tronka to the Kurfürst of Saxony. For with the sounding of the Prussian trumpet, what has been a most scrupulously circumstantial narration with a minimum of improbabilities begins to signal the opposite to the reader.

Shortly after the intervention of the Kurfürst of Brandenburg on a thematic level, the text introduces an encapsulated narrative, which alters the plot as drastically as does that concerning Rosalie in *Der Zweikampf*, and which reaches back in time to the beginning of the second major section:

> Sieben Monden mögen es etwa sein, genau am Tage nach dem Begräbnis meiner Frau; und von Kohlhaasenbrück . . . war ich aufgebrochen, um des Junkers von Tronka . . . habhaft zu werden, . . . als . . . der Kurfürst von Sachsen und der Kurfürst von Brandenburg in Jüterbock, einem Marktflecken, durch den der Streifzug mich führte, eine Zusammenkunft hielten. (SW II, 82)

According to the earlier part of the narrative, he in fact waited *three* days after his wife's burial for a response from Wenzel von Tronka to his 'Rechtsschluß' (SW II, 31), but more significant is the fact that there has been no mention of his having stopped anywhere on his way to destroy von Tronka's castle, let alone had such a momentous encounter with two sovereign lords as is now revealed. The enclosed narrative unexpectedly places him in possession of a note in a lead capsule, written by a gypsy woman who resembles his dead wife and is later, in a further note, to sign herself 'Deine Elisabeth' (SW II, 101). This piece of writing dominates the end of the story, as it is supposed to contain the fate of the House of Saxony, and the Kurfürst's fixation on obtaining it at all costs has the effect of placing him at Kohlhaas' mercy:

> Wenn Euer Landesherr käme, und spräche, ich will mich . . . vernichten – vernichten, versteht Ihr, welches allerdings der größte Wunsch ist, den meine Seele hegt: so würde ich ihm doch den Zettel noch . . . verweigern und sprechen: du kannst mich auf das Schafott bringen, ich aber kann dir weh tun, und ich wills! (SW II, 86)

Mercy there is none. This Prussian fantasy is further marked by the sheer implausibility that the old woman, suborned to masquerade as the mysterious gypsy woman by Kunz von Tronka, turns out to be the gypsy woman herself, who is, in turn, in some mysterious way, Kohlhaas' dead wife. The narrator mimics a certain embarrassment over this blatant manipulation of the plot by intruding the comment:

und wie denn die Wahrscheinlichkeit nicht immer auf Seiten der Wahrheit ist, so traf es sich, daß hier etwas geschehen war, das wir zwar berichten: die Freiheit aber, daran zu zweifeln, demjenigen, dem es wohlgefällt, zugestehen müssen: der Kämmerer hatte den ungeheuersten Mißgriff begangen, und in dem alten Trödelweib, das er in den Straßen von Berlin aufgriff, um die Zigeunerin nachzuahmen, die geheimnisreiche Zigeunerin selbst getroffen, die er nachgeahmt wissen wollte.   (SW II, 96)

This gesture on the part of the narrator is a clear signal to the reader that the rules of the game have been changed arbitrarily – something that is always the prerogative of a narrative text. Just in case the reader is slow of understanding, the signal is repeated a little further on, when the narrator pretends to despair of making sense of the previous narratives on which this one is allegedly based: 'Wohin er eigentlich ging . . . lassen wir dahin gestellt sein, indem die Chroniken, aus deren Vergleichung wir Bericht erstatten, an dieser Stelle, auf befremdende Weise, einander widersprechen und aufheben' (SW II, 99).

To make quite sure that even a careless reader will grasp that the final episode is cast in a narrative mode that subverts the conventions of the first two, there is finally an obtrusive suspension of narrative omniscience: 'Ja, er [Kohlhaas] hatte noch die Genugtuung, den Theologen Jakob Freising, als einen Abgesandten Doktor Luthers, mit einem eigenhändigen, ohne Zweifel sehr merkwürdigen Brief, der aber verloren gegangen ist, in sein Gefängnis treten zu sehen. . . .' (SW II, 100). Not only has the narrator previously been able to specify the contents of the 90-odd documents that carry the plot of *Michael Kohlhaas*, but all the inner processes of the characters have also been immediately open to disclosure in a way that completely transgresses the pretense of narrating 'aus einer alten Chronik' (SW II, 9). To raise, at the very end of the story, the claim that here is a document whose content is not known because it has been 'lost,' is to bring home the fact that not only the fictional characters are the victims of irony, but that this also extends to the relation between reader, narrative perspective, and text.

That the narrative persona is *not* the final authority in the text is entirely congruent with Kleist's technique in other stories. His narrators, from *Das Erdbeben in Chili* onward, reveal themselves to be partisan, excitable, censorious, mistaken, or inconsistent by turns. In *Michael Kohlhaas*, the narrator's sympathies change, but subtly rather than schematically, and not in phase with the major divisions of the text. In the beginning, a verdict is enunciated that has an air of objectivity and, remarkably, anticipates Bradley's theory of 'tragic flaws' in Shakespeare's heroes: 'kurz, die Welt würde sein Andenken haben segnen müssen, wenn er in einer Tugend nicht ausgeschweift hätte. Das Rechtgefühl aber machte ihn zum Räuber und Mörder' (SW II, 9). Given the labyrinthine nature of the story that is to unfold, such a formula cannot help but be a simplification. In fact, its prime function is to tempt the reader into the belief that the world of the story *can* be encompassed by such formulaic judgements, for many are to follow.

At some point, most readers will realize that there are too many such judgements with too many shifts between them to be a reliable guide to deciphering this world, and some will begin making judgements on the narrator's judgements as a way of maintaining clarity. The change in the quality of the narrative after Kohlhaas' first being sentenced to death and the intervention of the Kurfürst of Brandenburg will initially create confusion, because the important textual axis of the narrator's sympathy for Kohlhaas or criticism of him does not coincide with the thematic divisions.

After initially enunciating a verdict on the main character before the story has begun, the narrator presents Kohlhaas' viewpoint sympathetically throughout the first section, and continues to do so beyond the death of his wife and his destruction of Wenzel von Tronka's castle. The first explicit withdrawal of sympathy occurs with the contents of the second 'Mandat,' in which Kohlhaas places himself beyond even the Emperor's hegemony. The narrator terms this:

eine Schwärmerei krankhafter und mißgeschaffener Art, die ihm gleichwohl, bei dem Klang seines Geldes und der Aussicht auf Beute, unter dem Gesindel, das der Friede mit Polen außer Brot gesetzt hatte, Zulauf in Menge verschaffte. (SW II, 36)

The tone of this passage is to recur in the text when Kohlhaas has his already precarious position further weakened by the banditry of his alter ego, Johann Nagelschmidt (SW II, 65f). In the episodes that follow, the narrator is either explicitly critical of Kohlhaas or allows violent epithets that present the perspective of Kohlhaas' enemies or victims to go unchallenged: 'Gleichwohl war die Bestürzung in der Stadt, über das Dasein des rasenden Mordbrenners, und den Wahn, in welchem derselbe stand, daß der Junker in Leipzig sei, unaussprechlich. . . .' (SW II, 41). It is only after Kohlhaas has had a conversation with the Großkanzler of Saxony, Graf Wrede, lasting two full hours, and, with the help of an eminent lawyer, has reconstructed his original suit against Wenzel von Tronka that the narrator resumes manifesting overt sympathy for him: 'das Unglück aber Herrn Wenzels, und noch mehr des ehrlichen Kohlhaas wollte, daß es der Abdecker aus Döbbeln war' (SW II, 58).

Two factors appear to be important for the narrator's regaining sympathy for Kohlhaas. First, the conversation with Graf Wrede rehearses all the details of the story to date, but without any interference from the multitude of documents that has already accumulated. It is one of the very few instances in the story where an important dialogue between two characters is not subordinated to written language and does not result in a fatal lack of communication. Another is the conversation between the Kurfürst of Brandenburg and Heinrich von Geusau in the third segment, which inaugurates the Prussian fantasy (SW II, 77). Graf Wrede has formed his own opinion of Kohlhaas, which is at variance with his status as 'Würgengel' and 'Mordbrenner' in the popular imagination, and thus receives him 'mit Milde und Freundlichkeit' (SW II, 55). This, presumably, allows a version of events to emerge in the conversation that evens out some of the distortions produced by reactions to Kohlhaas' reign of terror throughout Saxony. Second, by reconstructing the terms of his original complaint against Wenzel von Tronka within the legal system, Kohlhaas effectively revokes the stance of his 'Mandate,' the second of which had originally lost him the narrator's sympathy: 'eine Schwärmerei krankhafter und mißgeschaffener Art' (SW II, 36).

The irony that surrounds the reformulation of the original complaint and the narrator's regaining sympathy for Kohlhaas is, quite simply, that these changes are not enough to avert a catastrophic ending. Kohlhaas may well be prepared to go back to being a law-abiding citizen with a genuine grievance; the narrative persona may well be prepared to forgive him his excesses, as Graf F... is forgiven in *Die Marquise von O...* 'um der gebrechlichen Einrichtung der Welt willen' (SW II, 143), but neither change of heart is sufficient to prevent him from being condemned: 'mit glühenden Zangen von Schinderknechten gekniffen, gevierteilt, und sein Körper, zwischen Rad und Galgen, verbrannt zu werden' (SW II, 77).

The sense of the third section, which begins immediately after these words with Brandenburg's intervention and which signals its difference from the other two in the several ways already outlined, is that the nature of the fictional world itself must be changed in order to achieve a conclusion that entirely satisfies the main character: 'Demnach glich nichts der Ruhe und Zufriedenheit seiner letzten Tage. . . . (SW II, 100). In a world such as the text has originally created, two narrative cycles – or experiments – have led to the complete humiliation of Kohlhaas. Only by shifting the terms in which this fictional world is constituted, by admitting, in the note in the lead capsule, a piece of writing of a different status to all others; by interpolating a narrative that takes time back to the end of the first section and introduces a character, the gypsy woman, whose function is unlike that of all the rest; by stretching coincidence beyond all plausibility; and finally by narrative intrusions that call the text itself into question – only through these means can the *sense* of the ending of the second section be reversed.

In discussing other stories, I have shown Kleist's use of the trope of the deferred ending to vary the outcomes of his narrative experiments.[25] In the case of *Michael Kohlhaas*, it is essential to realize that the ending is deferred not once, but twice. The coincidence of the funeral of his wife with the receipt of the 'landesherrliche Resolution,' forbidding him on pain of prison to take his grievance any further, is an ending appropriate to a world in which the exercise of power is manifestly not congruent with such abstractions as 'justice.' This first ending is deferred in order to see, as it were, whether Kohlhaas, by seizing all that power which is normally denied an individual within a social context, can bring events to a different conclusion. A much more elaborate narrative ensues as a result. Ironically, the only final difference, in this second part, is that the violence Kohlhaas adds to the fictional world by arson and armed insurrection is mirrored in the violence of the sentence imposed upon him by the state of Saxony.

The third section, in turn, defers the second ending by the intervention of the Elector of Brandenburg, a figure in whom power and the abstraction of justice are made to coincide, as they clearly do not in the Elector of Saxony, nor, indeed, in Kohlhaas himself during his brief but spectacular career as an autonomous figure of power, as his parodistic doubling by the figure of Johann Nagelschmidt makes clear. But to stress that one just ruler does not alone suffice to change a whole world, the text additionally resorts to the narrative of the gypsy woman and various other devices to produce a final tableau in which all appears to come together.

That the apparent harmony veils a considerable incoherence is what the text has been persistently suggesting to the reader in the final section by calling its own plausibility into question. The effect of a narrative structure that rejects an initial ending, reworks the plot to produce – from the main character's perspective – an even more negative one, then withdraws this, and contrives one that leaves the same character entirely satisfied, is to signal a fundamental dissonance within the narrative discourse itself.

Put another way: *Michael Kohlhaas* can be read as testing the proposition that, within the framework the story initially creates, a narrative discourse which seeks to reconcile the desires of an individual such as Kohlhaas with *both* the exercise of power through the complex that con-

25 See above pp. 203ff. and 215ff.

stitutes a state *and* such abstract values as individual and state nominally espouse, is doomed to incoherence. An *apparent* coherence, which satisfies Kohlhaas' desires and replaces a state machinery, in which power and abstract values are *not* consonant, by one in which they, arbitrarily, coincide, may be contrived, but only at the visible cost of altering the original terms of the narrative, which initially excluded the kind of 'causality' the figure of the gypsy woman brings into the plot.

My description consciously avoids charges of aesthetic disunity against the text and moral verdicts on the characters, since both are far too common in writing on *Kohlhaas* to retain any interest. A narrative may change its own metaphorical contract with the reader in mid-course, though always at the risk of causing indignation;[26] the moral issues explored through the convolutions of a narrative may become so complex that a wide range of moral reactions to them, some mututally contradictory, is possible – and this is amply documented in the secondary literature.

What I have tried to do is describe a literary form that tests the coherence of its own discourse. That the result is ultimately negative is a thematic phenomenon that has nothing to do with a judgement of the text's literary quality. For the thematic incoherence is grounded in the terms of the original constellation of individual, state, and abstract values. None of the three, as originally defined, is sufficiently simple to yield a consistent result in interaction with the other two.

To begin with the individual: at one extreme, Kohlhaas has internalized a whole judiciary and is thus aptly described as 'rechtschaffen': 'Doch sein Rechtgefühl, das einer Goldwaage glich, wankte noch; er war, vor der Schranke seiner eigenen Brust, noch nicht gewiß, ob eine Schuld seinen Gegner drücke. . . .' (SW II, 14). At the other extreme, his desires take leave of moral principles entirely: 'ich aber kann dir weh tun, und ich wills!' (SW II, 86), and his last gesture in life is directed toward their satisfaction – hence there can be little objection to the label 'entsetzlich.' What contributes to the incoherence of the discourse is that, between the extremes, there are very many other nuances of this figure that stand in no logical relation to these clear opposites.

There is, for example, the Kohlhaas of the dialogue with Luther: 'Kohlhaas erwiderte, indem ihm eine Träne über die Wangen rollte: hochwürdiger Herr! es hat mich meine Frau gekostet; Kohlhaas will der Welt zeigen, daß sie in keinem ungerechten Handel umgekommen ist' (SW II, 46f). Passages like these enrich the story, but they also immedi-

26 Cf. Theodor Fontane's verdict, KN, 549: 'Diese bekannteste seiner Erzählungen ist nicht seine beste; sie nimmt nur den Anlauf dazu. Bis zur Mitte ist sie vollendet . . . in ihrer zweiten Hälfte aber sinkt die Kohlhaas-Erzählung zu etwas relativ Unbedeutendem herab.'

ately invite questions such as: What has profit and loss to do with principles of justice? In what terms does Kohlhaas envisage being recom-
pensed for his wife's death? What is the point of 'showing a world,' that
patently does not work according to moral principles, anything?

Similarly, the state, as a mechanism for distributing power, is not a
simple quantity. The abundance of differing legalistic interpretations of
the story shows that Kleist has been nothing if not eclectic in his variations of traditional or hypothetical structures of power. If the prevalence
of nepotism in Saxony were all that caused Kohlhaas' grief, the story
would be much simpler than it is. If the well-oiled machinery of justice
in Brandenburg in the third section were meant to be read as the norm,
then there would be no need to associate it with the note in the lead capsule, the mystery of the gypsy woman, or the narrative's questioning of
its own validity. The most striking emblem of the intricacies of the distribution of power is the obsessive multiplication of the documents that
act as its vehicles.

Finally, the simplicity of the values in which the text deals is deceptive. Just as the initial conflict between Kohlhaas and Wenzel von
Tronka resembles in some ways a traditional feud and in others differs
from whatever historical models Kleist might have envisaged,[27] and as
the amnesty offered to Kohlhaas is understood differently by different
characters,[28] so there is a great uneasiness in the text about the ways in
which justice can be understood. Is it primarily an individual enactment
for Kohlhaas? Or does it genuinely have the altruistic dimension he supplies by way of self-justification about halfway through the first section:

> Dagegen sagte ihm ein ebenso vortreffliches Gefühl, und dies Gefühl
> faßte tiefere und tiefere Wurzeln, in dem Maße, als er weiter ritt, und
> überall, wo er einkehrte, von den Ungerechtigkeiten hörte, die täglich
> auf der Tronkenburg gegen die Reisenden verübt wurden: daß wenn
> der ganze Vorfall, wie es allen Anschein habe, bloß abgekartet sein
> solle, er mit seinen Kräften der Welt in der Pflicht verfallen sei, sich
> Genugtuung für die erlittene Kränkung, und Sicherheit für zukün-
> ftige seinen Mitbürgern zu verschaffen.   (SW II, 16)

27 Cf. Malte Dießelhorst, 'Hans Kohlhase/ Michael Kohlhaas,' in *KJb* 1988/89, p.
352: 'Anders Michael Kohlhaas: An die Stelle der Fehde ist die Rache getreten. . . . Von
solchen persönlichen Gefühlssteigerungen hören wir beim historischen Kohlhase nichts,
hier liegt nur der (mehr oder weniger) äußere Verlauf der Fehde zutage.'; cf. also Hartmut
Boockmann, 'Mittelalterliches Recht bei Kleist,' in *KJb* 1985, p. 99.
28 Raymond Lucas, 'Die Aporie der Macht. Zum Problem der Amnestie in Kleists
Michael Kohlhaas,' in *KJb* 1992, p. 147: 'Daß überhaupt von der Amnestie gesprochen
wird, ist schon ein Fehler. Die Amnestie, die in Aussicht gestellt wurde, falls er seinen
Prozeß gewinnt, womit sein Einfall in Sachsen nachträglich "gerechtgertigt" würde,
gehört eigentlich in die Zukunft, solange der Prozeß nicht abgeschlossen ist.'

This is a very long way away from the simplicity of: 'ich aber kann dir weh tun, und ich wills!' (SW II, 86) in the final section, and the text invites readers to compare and contrast, leaving it open as to whether they begin from the *lex talionis* or from some more sophisticated view of law current in Kleist's own time. From such elements the text's thematic incoherence derives, for there are simply too many variables to be balanced against one another, in too many possible combinations, to yield one consistent set of answers. Hence the relative harmony contrived within the third section appropriately marks itself as one possibility among others. It asserts an aesthetic unity, but in such provocative terms as to invite contradiction.[29]

For the remainder of this chapter I shall be concerned with the recent fortunes of the text in the secondary literature, in hope of shedding some light on why there are so many divergent readings. The main problem with critical writing on *Michael Kohlhaas* is that the text's invitations to join in debate have been far too successful – often at the expense of a due and sustained recognition of its fictional quality. Besides the usual moral judgements on characters, writing on the story has been marked by implicit assumptions that it is an historical treatise, a legal case-study, a tract on late 18th and early 19th century political philosophy and – most ludicrously – a handbook of guerila warfare.[30]

It is astounding that essays of very recent vintage can become so immersed in the various ways the text does or does not accord with its supposed historical, jurisprudential, or philosophical sources as to completely ignore two essential aspects: first, the fact that the terms of the narration toward the conclusion are conspicuously different from the premises from which the story begins; and second, what consequences this has for understanding the text as fiction.[31] The tendency to de-fictionalize *Michael Kohlhaas* is a backhanded tribute to its power as fiction, since in these readings it has proven itself believable to the point where its fictionality vanishes altogether.

In some interpretations, Kohlhaas does not sell horses for a living, but studies philosophy. Thus, Monika Frommel has him sitting at the feet of Kant: 'Kohlhaas beherzigt Kants Verbot, man dürfe nicht um der Glückseligkeit willen seine Pflicht verletzen.'[32] Joachim Bohnert, on the other hand, has him receiving instruction from Fichte: 'Kohlhaas, von

---

29 Cf. Klaus-Michael Bogdal's view of 'eine Ästhetik des Heroismus,' *Heinrich von Kleist: 'Michael Kohlhaas,'* Munich, 1981, pp. 48-51.

30 Wolf Kittler, *Die Geburt des Partisanen*, p. 301: 'So wird der Text zum umfassenden Kompendium für den kleinen Krieg.'

31 Neither Malte Dießelhorst, 'Hans Kohlhase/ Michael Kohlhaas,' nor Monika Frommel, 'Die Paradoxie vertraglicher Sicherung bürgerlicher Rechte. Kampf ums Recht und sinnlose Aktion,' in *KJb* 1988/89, pp. 357-74, mentions the gypsy woman at all.

32 Monika Frommel, ibid., p. 368.

Fichte belehrt, tritt aus dem Gesamtvertrag aus, er beruft sich auf "das unveräußerliche Recht des Menschen, auch einseitig, sobald er will, jeden seiner Verträge aufzuheben".'[33] Such metaphors are infectious, since it is only a small step from having Kohlhaas learning from Fichte to having the authorial intention, as supposedly embodied in the Kurfürst of Brandenburg, also subordinate to that stern philosopher: 'Welche gewaltigen Anstrengungen unternimmt dieser wunderbare Mann, um einen Untertanen, der später von einem Gerichtspräsidenten als querulatorischer Terrorist eingeschätzt wurde, vom Tod des Vierteilens zum Tod durch Enthaupten zu bringen – nur um der Rechtsphilosophie Fichtes willen.'[34]

It is typical of non-literary approaches to the story that attributions of an ideological attitude to Kleist himself are scarcely ever supported by evidence from the text. The lack of success of Graf Wrede's initiative has been construed as signifying the *author's* disapproval of this figure. Yet, Graf Wrede does not lack his defenders,[35] and it is equally open to argue that the fact that Wrede is *dismissed* by the corrupt court of Saxony is a clear statement that Kleist, as author, enthusiastically supports whatever ideological position this figure may be seen to embody. The fallacy inherent in proceeding from whether an incident within this fiction turns out well or badly to deduce a dogmatic conviction on Kleist's part is that it makes the author of one of the most complex narratives in German literature appear simple-minded. Surely, if such a crude criterion were really applicable to the story, then the battle of the philosophers in the secondary literature would not have occurred in the first place.

I have tried to show that Kleist is adept at *quoting* in his fictions, whether narrative or dramatic, philosophical or ideological views current in his time without necessarily espousing them. Rousseau is the clearest case in point. In letters to Wilhelmine von Zenge of early 1801, Kleist gives a quite unreserved endorsement of Rousseau's philosophy[36]; wherever we encounter allusions to Rousseau in his fictional works, from *Die Familie Schroffenstein* onward, we find, however, that Rousseau's views are *quoted* within an experimental framework that varies their terms to make them less than authoritative. There is no rea-

33 Joachim Bohnert, 'Kohlhaas der Entsetzliche,' in *KJb* 1988/89, p. 426.
34 Ibid., p. 429.
35 Hartmut Reinhardt, 'Das Unrecht des Rechtskämpfers. Zum Problem des Widerstandes in Kleists Erzählung *Michael Kohlhaas*,' in *JbSchG* XXXI, 1987, p. 226: 'Am besten führe man wohl, wenn sich immer jemand wie Graf Wrede . . . durchsetzen könnte. In der Abwägung aller Umstände des Kohlhaas-Falles plädiert er für "ein schlichtes Rechttun". Aber das Einfachste wird in dieser gebrechlichen Welt oft zum Schwersten. Der Graf verliert sein Amt.'
36 SW II, 632 and 647.

son to assume this does not also happen to the views of Fichte, Kant, or Adam Müller[37] in the process of Kleist's devising a fictional world in which so many variables interact, as is the case in *Michael Kohlhaas*.

Kleist has in common with Shakespeare the talent to present emotional or ideological statements that convince a reader or audience, without committing the work in which they occur, to one point of view. At the same time, he is less Olympian than Shakespeare, in that he seems to vacillate chronically between subversion and commitment. Hence he offers the reader of *Michael Kohlhaas* a choice of final endings: one in which the central character is drawn and quartered with all his desires unfulfilled, or the alternative and opposite ending that is marked as fantasy.

There can be no doubt that the fantasy ending has its specifically Prussian aura for reasons deriving from Kleist's allegiance to the state that so little prized his devotion. The sympathetic figure of the Stadthauptmann, Heinrich von Geusau, who does not figure in the earlier version of the beginning published in the journal *Phöbus* in 1808,[38] is brought back in the final segment of the final version to have a conversation with the Kurfürst of Brandenburg. The result of this dialogue, which parallels that between Kohlhaas and Graf Wrede, is that the upright prince acts, the corrupt Erzkanzler is dismissed, the honest servitor is rewarded, and the arrangement of Kohlhaas' final tableau is expedited:

> Denn der wackere Stadthauptmann, Herr Heinrich von Geusau, hatte ihn, auf einem Spaziergange an den Ufern der Spree, von der Geschichte dieses sonderbaren und nicht verwerflichen Mannes unterrichtet, bei welcher Gelegenheit er von den Fragen des erstaunten Herrn gedrängt, nicht umhin konnte, der Schuld zu erwähnen, die durch die Unziemlichkeiten seines Erzkanzlers, des Grafen Siegfried von Kallheim, seine eigene Person drückte: worüber der Kurfürst schwer entrüstet, den Erzkanzler . . . ohne weiteres, mit mehreren Zeichen seiner Ungnade entsetzte, und den Herrn Heinrich von Geusau zum Erzkanzler ernannte.   (SW II, 77)

If the entire moral dimension of the story were as simple as this one, idyllic piece of statecraft, the plot of *Michael Kohlhaas* would be quite different from the story Kleist wrote. That so much writing on this text

---

37 Cf. Paul Michael Lützeler, *Geschichte in der Literatur*, Munich/Zurich 1987, p. 161; Monika Frommel, 'Die Paradoxie vertraglicher Sicherung,' pp. 358f.
38 Cf. KW III, 40-5.

is at odds with itself surely leads to the conclusion that this particular fantasy of virtue rewarded has its place within the mosaic of the work, but that the text's main thrust is to question such simplicity. One may examine the components of Kleist's eclecticism in light of any number of external frames of reference, and make any number of further conjectures as to which receives his particular support or criticism, but, while such partisan behavior reveals the writers as not merely willing, but even enthusiastic victims in the game played by the text with its readers, I fear it will continue to tell us very little we do not already know about *Michael Kohlhaas* as literature.

12

Die heilige Cäcilie – Das Bettelweib von Locarno

Die heilige Cäcilie and *Das Bettelweib von Locarno* are comparable in that they narrate incidents that have every appearance of the supernatural, but also in the respect that recent writing on them has tended to stress their metafictional dimension. Thus, Christine Lubkoll has most recently summarized *Die heilige Cäcilie* as a demonstration of the elusiveness of truth, while Timothy Mehigan has aptly, and wittily, remarked of the other: '*Das Bettelweib von Locarno* is . . . the tale of a ghost in search of a story.'[1] While I share this perspective, I should qualify it by pointing out that these stories are not any more preoccupied with the theme of narration itself than Kleist's other stories. Where they differ is by offering less impediment to a consistently poetological interpretation than, for example, *Die Verlobung in St. Domingo*, where the plot's inclusion of events in post-Revolutionary France invariably produces some comment on Kleist's understanding of history, or *Der Findling*, where the moral judgements of the narrative perspective are so obtrusive as to provoke interpretations that respond in the same terms. Whereas all of Kleist's stories are concerned with the exertion of power over the fictional world, as well as within it, the central importance of the fantastic in the plots of *Die heilige Cäcilie* and *Das Bettelweib von Locarno*, and their relative lack of extra-literary reference, have meant that writing on them focuses increasingly on the construction and subversion of narrative discourse.

This does not mean it has entirely escaped attempts to de-fictionalize it, as Bernd Fischer sees it in very literal terms as attacking Romantic Catholicism: 'Schlegel, Brentano, Görres und Müller könnten die Söhne der bürgerlich protestantischen Aufklärung heißen, die mit jugendlichem Eifer . . . durch die Lande ziehen und die Revolution der

1 Christine Lubkoll, 'Die heilige Musik oder Die Gewalt der Zeichen. Zur musikalischen Poetik in Heinrich von Kleists *Cäcilien-Novelle*', *Heinrich von Kleist*, ed. Gerhard Neumann, p. 362: 'auf der Ebene der Erzählstruktur dokumentiert und inszeniert der Text zugleich selbst die Nicht-Auffindbarkeit der Wahrheit'; Timothy J. Mehigan, *Text as contract*, pp. 192f.

Religion verkünden, um schließlich zu ideologischen Stützen ihrer Restauration zu werden.'[2] But, in general, recent interpretations have tended to see it as being subversive of its own ostensibly religious stance to the point of making the text a kind of black hole into which meaning disappears altogether.

It was not always so. Kleist's contemporaries recorded very mixed reactions to the text, although at least one devout reader, Joseph von Eichendorff, was affronted by its lack of true religiosity: 'in seiner [Kleists] einziger Novelle religiösen Inhalts . . . schlägt die Gewalt des religiösen Gefühls trostlos nur in spukhaften Wahnsinn aus.'[3] While a series of 20th century interpretations still has no difficulty in accepting the religious thematics at face value,[4] more recent readings in terms of irony began with Wolfgang Wittkowski's essay of 1972.[5]

There is, indeed, a choice of readings created by the intertextuality of *Die heilige Cäcilie* with Kleist's other stories. Wittkowski's line of argument tends to be suggested by the undoubted parallels with *Der Zweikampf*. At the end of that story, the Emperor opts for a miraculous reading of events – 'Nun, jedes Haar auf eurem Haupt bewacht ein Engel!' (SW II, 259) – but the text offers a much more mundane and probable alternative in the form of Rosalie's parents' paternity suit against Graf Jakob. Documents as vehicles of power figure in *Die heilige Cäcilie*, as they do in *Der Zweikampf* and *Michael Kohlhaas*, most conspicuously in the letter from the Pope, which confirms the miracle, and the clause in the Treaty of Westphalia, which disestablishes the convent some 50 years afterwards.

Readings that cast doubt on a rationalist explanation of events receive encouragement from the arbitrariness of the narrative perspective, which shows strong affinities to the final section of *Michael Kohlhaas*. For in *Die heilige Cäcilie*, Kleist permits his narrator a most high-handed intrusion: 'Dies und noch Mehreres sagte Veit Gotthelf, der Tuchhändler, das wir hier, weil wir zur Einsicht in den inneren Zusammenhang der Sache genug gesagt zu haben meinen, unterdrücken. . . .' (SW II, 224). The admission that elements of a potentially fuller narrative are being suppressed signals the possibility that other elements are being *added* to enhance the impression the narrative voice wishes to make, and thus the way stands open to a fully relativistic reading, which

2 Bernd Fischer, *Ironische Metaphysik*, Munich, 1988, p. 95. Brentano and Görres are, in 1811, surely most improbable 'Söhne der bürgerlich protestantischen Aufklärung.'
3 KW III, 883f.
4 Listed by Donald P. Haase and Rachel Freudenburg, 'Power, Truth and Interpretation: The Hermeneutic Act and Kleist's *Die heilige Cäcilie*,' in *DVjs* 60 (1), 1986, p, 90, note 3.
5 Wolfgang Wittkowski, '*Die heilige Cäcilie* und *Der Zweikampf*,' pp. 17-58.

may well begin with the story's subtitle: 'Eine Legende' (SW II, 216). In this way the text calls attention to its own seductive power. It can imply to the reader that the transmitted version is not the whole version, while still offering bait after bait to the reader's credulity.

For the ambivalence of the word 'Legende' in German, meaning originally an edifying tale of a saint's life and then acquiring the futher sense of a spurious account of events, may imply that an excess of meaning, in the form of a narrative that does not merely report events, but does so with the intention of strengthening the reader's faith, may well have the reverse effect – if it once begins to call its own veracity into question. Kleist's text does this more than once by inconsistencies. There is, for example, the discrepancy between the narrator's claim that the Imperial officer, 'ein Feind des Papsttums' (SW II, 217), refused to send guards to protect the convent, and the account of Veit Gotthelf, which has soldiers already in place by this officer's orders when the music begins:

> und da, auf Befehl des Kommandanten, in eben diesem Augenblick mehrere Arretierungen verfügt, und einige Frevler, die sich Unordnungen erlaubt hatten, von einer Wache aufgegriffen und abgeführt wurden, so bleibt der elenden Schar nichts übrig, als sich schleunigst . . . aus dem Gotteshause zu entfernen.   (SW II, 222)

A further ambiguity surrounds the use of the formula: 'Hier endigt diese Legende' (SW II, 228). It introduces the final paragraph of the story, as if to mark off what has gone before as something that might be treated with a certain scepticism. Yet the events that *follow* are a direct continuation of the main narrative, in tone as well as in content. Thus, the last word of the legend is not in the conclusion of the conversation between the Abbess and mother; rather, the ending is deferred so as to recapitulate, once more, the kernel of the mystery: 'die Söhne aber starben, im späten Alter, eines heitern und vergnügten Todes, nachdem sie noch einmal, ihrer Gewohnheit gemäß, das gloria in excelsis abgesungen hatten' (SW II, 228). One is therefore confronted with a text in which events and their interpretations are often doubled by their contraries.

The music of the miracle must be taken on trust; the singing of the four brothers, which the inhabitants of Aachen can hear regularly for many years, is, as its contrary, a kind of non-music:

> fangen sie, mit einer entsetzlichen und gräßlichen Stimme, das gloria in excelsis zu intonieren an. So mögen sich Leoparden und Wölfe anhören lassen, wenn sie zur eisigen Winterzeit, das Firmament

anbrüllen: die Pfeiler des Hauses, versichere ich Euch, erschütterten, und die Fenster, von ihrer Lungen sichtbarem Atem getroffen, drohten klirrend, als ob man Hände voll schweren Sandes gegen ihre Flächen würfe, zusammen zu brechen. (SW II, 223)

As I have elsewhere shown, Kleist heightens the discrepant and nonhuman effect of the voices in the second version of the story.[6] There are further contradictions surrounding the account of these vocalizations. Earlier, the 'Vorsteher' of the asylum, who appear to speak in chorus, have assured the mother of the four men that, for the last six years, her sons have performed the same ritual every night, but with effects that can scarcely be so often repeated: 'daß sie sich bloß in der Stunde der Mitternacht einmal von ihren Sitzen erhöben; und daß sie alsdann, mit einer Stimme, welche die Fenster des Hauses bersten machte, das gloria in excelsis intonierten' (SW II, 220). There is the further apparent contradiction that, apart from the *Gloria*, 'kein Laut über ihre Lippen käme,' while the 'Vorsteher' report in the same breath:

daß sie, wenn man sie für verrückt erklärte, mitleidig die Achseln zuckten, und daß sie schon mehr als einmal geäußert hätten: 'wenn die gute Stadt Aachen wüßte, was sie, so würde dieselbe ihre Geschäfte bei Seite legen, und sich gleichfalls, zur Absingung des gloria, um das Kruzifix des Herrn niederlassen.' (SW II, 220)

The text therefore insists on a singing that is not singing, intermitted by a silence that is not silence – all centering around a knowledge that is never known beyond the four converts, who are not about to tell.[7] In conformity with this, the source from which the brothers ultimately, if involuntarily, derive their esoteric 'knowledge' is 'eine uralte von einem unbekannten Meister herrührende, italienische Messe . . ., mit welcher die Kapelle mehrmals schon, einer besondern Heiligkeit und Herrlichkeit wegen, . . . die größesten Wirkungen hervorgebracht hatte' (SW II, 217). The brothers' singing effectively communicates nothing, and their existence in the asylum is marginal to the life of the city. It is thus appropriate that whatever has produced this situation should also have an unknown source. In consonance with both of these instances,

---

6 Anthony Stephens, '"Menschen/ Mit Tieren die Natur gewechselt",' p. 115f; on the differences between the two published versions of *Die heilige Cäcilie*, see Rosemarie Puschmann, *Heinrich von Kleists Cäcilien-Erzählung. Kunst- und literarhistorische Recherchen*, Bielefeld, 1988, pp. 9-17.
7 Critics have further pointed out that the music is alternately termed a mass and an oratorio; that, although a mass, it is apparently played on instruments only and not sung; that it also contains a *Salve regina*, which has no place in the Catholic mass.

the Abbess declares a final absence of knowledge, albeit one supported by a written testimony:

> Denn vernehmt, daß schlechterdings niemand weiß, wer eigentlich das Werk, das Ihr dort aufgeschlagen findet, im Drang der schreckenvollen Stunde, da die Bilderstürmerei über uns hereinbrechen sollte, ruhig auf dem Sitz der Orgel dirigiert habe. Durch ein Zeugnis . . . ist erwiesen, daß Schwester Antonia . . . während des ganzen Zeitraums seiner Aufführung, krank, bewußtlos, ihrer Glieder schlechthin unmächtig, im Winkel ihrer Klosterzelle darniedergelegen habe . . . (SW II, 227)

Out of these semantic blanks emerges the paradoxical certainty that sends the mother of the four would-be iconoclasts back into the bosom of Mother Church. But has a 'feminine principle' finally triumphed, as some critics suggest? It has been pointed out that there is an element of male sexual aggression in the behavior of the iconoclasts;[8] that the four brothers, through their mysterious conversion, are then effectively neutered;[9] and that the narrator – but should we trust the narrator? – is at pains to highlight the 'feminine' quality of the musical performance: 'wegen der weiblichen Geschlechtsart dieser geheimnisvollen Kunst' (SW II, 217).[10] The reader is thus tempted into reading the story as an aggressive discourse of female emancipation: a female saint triumphs over male iconoclasm.

But this could also be a false trail, for both the final establishment of the legend and the disestablishment of the convent only 50 years later come about through exertions of male authority, within the Church and outside it. It is the Archbishop of Trier who makes the pronouncement that attributes the miracle to St. Cecilia and on which the title of the narrative is based, and an even more remote male personage, the Pope, who confirms that a female saint has indeed intervened to save the nuns:

> Auch hat der Erzbischof von Trier, an den dieser Vorfall berichtet ward, bereits das Wort ausgesprochen, das ihn allein erklärt, nämlich, 'daß die heilige Cäcilie selbst dieses zu gleicher Zeit schreckliche und herrliche Wunder vollbracht habe'; und von dem Papst habe ich soeben ein Breve erhalten, wodurch er dies bestätigt.   (SW II, 227)

---

8 Cf. James M. McGlathery, *Desire's Sway: The Plays and Stories of Heinrich von Kleist*, Detroit, 1983, p. 143f; Donald P. Haase and Rachel Freudenburg, 'Power, Truth and Interpretation,' pp. 93 and 103.

9 Christine Lubkoll, 'Die heilige Musik oder Die Gewalt der Zeichen,' p. 350f.

10 Ibid., p. 352: 'Musikalischer Ausdruck gilt als höchste Form der Kunst, jedenfalls aus der Perspektive *schreibender* Männer; diese versuchen nun, sich der "weiblichen Geschlechtsart dieser geheimnisvollen Kunst" zu bemächtigen.'

This is, in turn, a statement by the Abbess, one of several narrative voices in the story, and a figure in whom conventionally male and female attributes seem to be fused. When she first learns of the threat to destroy the convent, her impulse is to seek male protection from the officer in command of Imperial troops in the city of Aachen. This is refused, and so she is left – in the narrator's version – exposed to the threat of more than a hundred armed iconoclasts: 'Niemand beschützte sie, als ein alter, siebenzigjähriger Klostervogt, der sich, mit einigen bewaffneten Troßknechten, am Eingang der Kirche aufstellte' (SW II, 217).

The Abbess' response to the lack of a male savior, in the material world, is not unlike that of the heroine in a similar moment in *Die Marquise von O....* For she displays an unswerving strength of will that more than makes up for the lack of a conventional masculine hero:

> Die Äbtissin, die am Abend des vorhergehenden Tages befohlen hatte, daß eine uralte . . . Messe aufgeführt werden möchte, . . . schickte, mehr als jemals auf ihren Willen beharrend, noch einmal zur Schwester Antonia herab . . . Aber die Äbtissin bestand unerschütterlich darauf, daß das zur Ehre des höchsten Gottes angeordnete Fest begangen werden müsse. . .   (SW II, 217f)

One might say that, read along one axis of the text, the Abbess' fixity of will is what produces the miracle. When she re-enters the story toward the conclusion, it is in a tableau that emphasizes her personal authority, later to be reinforced by the Archbishop's proclamation and the Pope's letter:

> Daselbst fand sie die Äbtissin, welches eine edle Frau, von stillem königlichen Ansehn war, auf einem Sessel sitzen, den Fuß auf einem Schemel gestützt, der auf Drachenklauen ruhte; ihr, zur Seite, auf einem Pulte, lag die Partitur einer Musik. Die Äbtissin, nachdem sie befohlen hatte, der Fremden einen Stuhl hinzusetzen, entdeckte ihr, daß sie bereits durch den Bürgermeister von ihrer Ankunft in der Stadt gehört. . . .   (SW II, 225f)

The dragon's claws have not lacked impact on the secondary literature, and the musical score has the same privileged status among the documents mentioned in *Die heilige Cäcilie* as does the note in the lead capsule in the final section of *Michael Kohlhaas*.[11] Appropriately, the

---

11 Cf. KW III, 894; Christine Lubkoll, 'Die heilige Musik oder Die Gewalt der Zeichen,' p. 359; for *Michael Kohlhaas*, see above p. 254f.

mother of the four brothers kisses both the Abbess' hand and the score with the same fervor. Endowed with this authority, the Abbess pronounces solemnly: 'Gott selbst hat das Kloster, an jenem wunderbaren Tage, gegen den Übermut Eurer schwer verirrten Söhne beschirmt' (SW II, 227). She is thus part of a chain of authorities, all male, that extends from the civil officials, who certify the four brothers as insane, and the mayor, who reports their mother's arrival, through the Archbishop, the Pope, and the Divinity, to the ultimate authority of the text itself – also male? – which causes all this to be narrated in just such a manner.

The text thus marks out distinct gender roles only to blur them again. The Abbess represents the point where what might appear to be a discourse of female emancipation merges back into the male chain of authorities, making her a kind of honorary male by virtue of her extreme strength of will – not a conventional female attribute in writing of the time. It is as if the text surrounds its inexplicable core with strands of interpretation that promise a clear reading, but then merge into their contraries. This makes it appropriate that reading itself should become prominent on the thematic level of the story. All of Kleist's fictions are concerned, to some extent, with deciphering situations and people as if they were texts. *Die heilige Cäcilie* plays on the tension between conviction and interpretation by contrasting differing modes of interaction between text and reader.

The apparent infallibility of the Abbess' declaration has been prepared by two acts of reading, which have contrary outcomes.[12] The Abbess, who is placed in this carefully composed tableau so as to convince, has no difficulty in assimilating the letter, which the mother carries from one of the four brothers to a friend in Antwerp, announcing their intention to destroy the convent on the feast of Corpus Christi. Since the Abbess knew of this intention before the iconoclasts reached the convent, and since their aggression was quite explicit, the function of the letter is that of a ritual confirmation. It tells her nothing new, but enables her to add another link to her chain of testimonies and authorities. The mother, who is there to be convinced, enacts a non-reading of the real document of power, the musical score. Her incomprehension of this text stands in an ambivalent relationship to both her sons' conversion and the citizens' lack of reaction to their regular singing, since the score seems to communicate, quite literally, everything and nothing to her. The sons have, allegedly, received a total knowledge, but it stops with them, communicating nothing beyond the walls of the asylum. The point of the mother's experience is that she arrives at a suitably devout *interpretation* as a result:

12 Cf. Timothy J. Mehigan, *Text as contract*, pp. 186f.

Sie betrachtete die unbekannten zauberischen Zeichen, womit sich ein fürchterlicher Geist geheimnisvoll den Kreis abzustecken schien, und meinte, in die Erde zu sinken, da sie grade das gloria in excelsis aufgeschlagen fand. Es war ihr, als ob das ganze Schrecken der Tonkunst, das ihre Söhne verderbt hatte, über ihrem Haupte rauschend daherzöge; sie glaubte, bei dem bloßen Anblick ihre Sinne zu verlieren, und nachdem sie schnell, mit einer unendlichen Regung von Demut und Unterwerfung unter die göttliche Allmacht, das Blatt an ihre Lippen gedrückt hatte, setzte sie sich wieder auf ihren Stuhl zurück. (SW II, 226f)

It is of most significance that the mother cannot read past the title of the *Gloria*, since this is firmly connected in her mind with her sons' bizarre condition, while the rest of the musical score, appropriately, suggests everything she has already heard and begun to believe, but conveys nothing concrete, as signalled by the qualifiers 'schien' and 'als ob.' Hence she improvizes meanings for the text that take her further in the direction in which the visit to her sons in the asylum and Veit Gotthelf's narration has already set her moving.

Conviction in the story is therefore not a sequential process, based on an accumulation of logical deductions, but seems to be arrived at momentarily and non-discursively. As the conversion of the sons and the mother's reaction to the score suggest, an epiphany of significance has something coercive, even violent about it. There is a significant parallel between *Die Verlobung in St. Domingo* and *Die heilige Cäcilie*, in that the former begins in a time of civil war, 'als die Schwarzen die Weißen ermordeten' (SW II, 160),[13] and produces, as ultimate meaning, the paradox of an oath without words: 'denn du warst mir durch einen Eidschwur verlobt, obschon wir keine Worte darüber gewechselt hatten!' (SW II, 193). The setting of *Die heilige Cäcilie* is equally violent to start with, 'als die Bilderstürmerei in den Niederlanden wütete' (SW II, 216), and its ultimate creation of meaning appears as a triumph of conviction that does violence to rationality, while still surrounding this event with all the trappings of discursive interpretation.

But all appearances can reverse themselves: the iconoclasts are originally bent on giving 'der Stadt Aachen das Schauspiel einer Bilderstürmerei' (SW II, 216); instead, they end up offering, till their life's end, an alternative spectacle, with unusual sound effects, but one in which the citizens of Aachen soon lose interest. The figure on whom the enactment of conviction is centered, the mother, is presented with a

---

13 Cf. ibid., p. 189: 'the creation of meaning is conceived of as a violent process which emands the capitulation of the intellect in order to be realized.'

series of tableaux and narratives that are, as it were, staged for her benefit, and much the same is true of the relation between text and reader.
The game played by the text is to coax the reader toward sharing the perspective of the mother, but at the same time, to build sufficient contrary
indications into what is staged, such as discrepancies in the plot and the
disestablishment of the convent after only 50 years, to make a sceptical
view of the 'Legende' equally available.

Christine Lubkoll has made the fine suggestion that the model of a
polyphonic score, heard simultaneously, may stand for the narrative
itself as a counterpoint of the narrator, Veit Gotthelf, and the Abbess.[14]
This has the advantage of giving due recognition to the fact that the text
is producing more than one message at a time. The metaphor of
polyphony still does not capture the effect of contraries that confront
one another, but do not cancel one another out, such as the miraculous
music and the brothers' terrible singing. I would therefore make two
qualifications: first, there are more than three voices; second, narrative
texts are limited to sequentiality, and thus fall short of a genuine
polyphony.

On the first point: there are voices within voices. The Abbess' insistence on proceeding with the mass in honor of Corpus Christi is clearly
audible through the first narrative sequence, as is also – in dissonant
contrast – the chorus of the 'Vorsteher' of the asylum, whose words are
given in a long passage of quoted speech (SW II, 220). Through Veit
Gotthelf's narration we hear the terrible voices of the four brothers, suggested by the extravagant sonic imagery of wild beasts and souls of the
damned, and evoked now much more vividly and non-musically than in
the words of the 'Vorsteher.' After the end of Veit Gotthelf's account,
the narrative perspective blends with the perceptions of the mother to
the point of making her devout confusion an appropriate counterpoint to
the certainty of the Abbess' declaration. Finally, there is the miraculous
music itself, evoked with none of the detail of the brothers' voices, but
reaching the reader as a curious blend of absence and presence. All this
is surely more like a cacophony than the masterpiece of an old Italian
composer.

There is admittedly a suggestion of harmony in some parts of the
text: the Abbess' production of meaning and the mother's reception of it
are clearly complementary. But, equally, other sections of the narrative
are harshly at odds with one another, and, unfolding in sequence, are
never given a chance to synchronize. In my view, the text brings out precisely the *imperfection* of narrative when contrasted with the sumultane-
ity of musical form. Whereas genuine harmony or polyphony combines

---

14 Cf. Christine Lubkoll, 'Die heilige Musik und Die Gewalt der Zeichen', p. 362.

different lines in the score into a single effect, narrative is obliged to resort to all kinds of subterfuges if it sets out to have the same effect on the reader as the miraculous music had on the four brothers. Hence it blends together sequences that do not quite fit; opens lines of interpretation that turn equivocal; and plays a series of tableaux of conviction off against the explicatory model of a forensic investigation. It need not do so, but Kleist has cast his text as a mutual subversion of *both* conventional senses of a 'Legende' – the edifying strengthener of belief and the fiction whose implausibility is patent.

The relation between whatever music may have been heard on the feast of Corpus Christi and the brothers' daily and discordant intoning of the Gloria is therefore something about which nothing can be said with any final claim. The narrative model remains in a *perpetuum mobile* about an undisclosed center, which is inexplicable in much the same way as the cliff at the end of Kafka's text *Prometheus*: 'Blieb das unerklärliche Felsgebirge. – Die Sage versucht das Unerklärliche zu erklären. Da sie aus einem Wahrheitsgrund kommt, muß sie wieder im Unerklärlichen enden.'[15] For this reason the story tantalizes the reader with its insistence on the motifs of truth and belief.

Much the same might be said of the import of *Das Bettelweib von Locarno*.[16] That such a brief narrative, which mimics the popular convention of the ghost story, has elicited the same kind of moralizing interpretations as *Der Findling* or *Michael Kohlhaas* indicates that responses to Kleist's stories are largely independent of whether the narrative perspective showers the reader with moral evaluations, or whether the plot plays fast and loose with extra-fictional controversies as to what constitutes lawful or unlawful conduct.

It is characteristic of Kleist's experimental technique to create situations whose entelechy appears to move toward a judgement, whether this be the result of the reader's sorting through the disparate strands of the plot or that simulacrum of the Last Judgement which his figures so often invoke. It is equally characteristic for the text to subvert this process, so that the verdict tends to evanesce in the act of its enunciation. In this, it has an affinity to the paradoxical epiphany of the 'wirkliche Freisprechung' in Kafka's *Der Prozeß*: 'Bei einer wirklichen Freisprechung sollen die Prozeßakten vollständig abgelegt werden, sie verschwinden gänzlich aus dem Verfahren, nicht nur die Anklage, auch der Prozeß und sogar der Freispruch sind vernichtet, alles ist vernichtet.'[17]

15 Franz Kafka, *Sämtliche Erzählungen*, ed. Paul Raabe, Frankfurt/M, 1970, p. 306.

16 For a recent summary of critical opinion on this story, see Bernd Fischer, *Ironische Metaphysik*, pp. 84f.

17 Franz Kafka, *Der Prozeß*, Frankfurt/M, 1976, p. 136.

Since an unequivocal judgement in Kleist is as elusive as a genuine acquittal in Kafka, readers and scholars opt for the understandable, if makeshift, solution of behaving like one of the fictional characters and privileging one semantic axis through the text at the expense of all others. As a superabundance of meaning is indistinguishable from an annihilation of meaning, there is some comfort to be found in readings that are reproducible at the price of being always partial and contestable.

The reticence of the narrator of *Das Bettelweib von Locarno* in apportioning blame seems, even after so many content-based interpretations, to have left some critics' appetite for guilt unslaked. Thus, Kevin Hilliard has written in an essay of 1991: 'What seems missing from the story is the clear articulation, in the consciousness of the characters or the narrator, of a moral judgement on the Marchese.'[18] One would imagine that the reception of stories such as *Der Findling* or *Das Erdbeben in Chili* might have led by now to a consensual realization that any number of such 'clear articulations' on the part of the narrator and the other fictional characters does nothing to dissolve the ambiguities of Kleist's narratives. The fallacy lies in the assumption that a successful and straightforward attribution of blame does something for a reader that an ultimately equivocal interplay of perspectives cannot. This bears on the role of seduction in Kleist's narrative technique. For, unlike sexual seduction, Kleist's narrative seduction has no terminal point. It attains its aim by reversing its own convergence and directing the reader back to an awareness of ambiguity. This process is antithetical to the presuppositions of discursive analysis, and so one interpretation of Kleist's stories after another hacks at the web of the text in an effort to clear the way for a speciously unified understanding.

But such a practice surely amounts to misunderstanding the reception of Kleist's stories. If his narratives were such that the presence or absence of one moral judgement, or indeed several, could guide a definitive reading of the text, then the whole edifice of writing on them would never have arisen, since his stories would need to be as simple as the popular genres he mimics, quotes, and ironizes.[19]

The text of *Das Bettelweib von Locarno* contains strong tension between the highly disciplined and cohesive effect conveyed by the mode of narration and the discrepancies that become apparent both in the plot and in the narrative perspective itself. The second to last sen-

---

18 Kevin Hilliard, '"Rittergeschichte mit Gespenst": the Narration of the Subconscious in Kleist's *Das Bettelweib von Locarno*,' in *German Life and Letters*, vol. XLIV (4), 1991, p. 283.

19 Gero von Wilpert, 'Der Ausrutcher des Bettelweibes von Locarno. "Capriccio con fuoco",' in *Seminar*, vol. 26 (4), 1990, pp. 283-93, has taken Kleist's irony a stage further by writing an entertaining parody of Kleist scholarship.

tence of the story produces a curious dissonance in the narrator's attribution of motives: 'Der Marchese, von Entsetzen überreizt, hatte eine Kerze genommen, und dasselbe [the castle], überall mit Holz getäfelt wie es war, an allen vier Ecken, müde seines Lebens, angesteckt' (SW II, 198). Instead of one clear motivation, we are offered two in apposition, which are not immediately consonant. The first, 'von Entsetzen überreizt,' accords with the immediate climax of the ghost story; the second, 'müde seines Lebens,' could be taken to imply that his conviction of the ghost's presence is only the last straw for an aristocrat worn down by an unsatisfactory marriage,[20] his disordered finances,[21] and, of course, the guilt inherent in an unjust social system[22] – or any other thematic combination one prefers.

One aspect of the story's intertextuality with other stories by Kleist that might reasonably give moralistic readings pause is the parallel between the gesture of the Marchese's wife in admitting the beggarwoman to the castle and the action of Piachi at the beginning of *Der Findling*. For both are deeds of compassion that go wrong. Thus, we read in *Das Bettelweib von Locarno*: 'eine alte kranke Frau, die sich bettelnd vor der Tür eingefunden hatte, von der Hausfrau aus Mitleiden gebettet worden war' (SW II, 196), and in *Der Findling*: 'Piachi wollte in der ersten Regung des Entsetzens, den Jungen weit von sich schleudern; doch da dieser, in eben diesem Augenblick, seine Farbe veränderte und ohnmächtig auf dem Boden niedersank, so regte sich des guten Alten Mitleid' (SW II, 199). In both cases, an apparently selfless and humane act begins a chain of events that end in destruction and chaos. But if *Der Findling* has any message to convey to a persevering reader, then it is surely that the attribution of blame is anything other than simple. Just as Piachi's apparently worthy deed may appear quite ambiguous once its context is scrutinized, so critics have asked why the Marchese's wife installs a sick beggar woman in a richly appointed chamber her husband is prone to visit; why it appears to be situated upstairs in the castle when the woman can barely walk; why the ghost refrains from manifesting itself until the visit of the Florentine knight – and so on. Once one begins asking questions of the text that are aimed at producing a unitary reading, such ambiguities tend to multiply, and these have led to analyses such as those of Katherine M. Arens and

---

20 Cf. Gerhard Schulz, 'Kleists *Bettelweib von Locarno* – eine Ehegeschichte?,' in *JbSchG* XVIII, 1974, pp. 436f.

21 Cf. Klaus Müller-Salget, KW III, 858.

22 Cf. Bernd Fischer, *Ironische Metaphysik*, pp. 88f: 'Nicht im übermäßig grausamen oder herrschsüchtigen Charakter des Marchese liegt die Schuld am Tod der Bettlerin, sondern in der bloßen Autorität seines Befehls, . . . letztlich in der feudalen Struktur der Macht . . . Die Schuld liegt außer ihm in der Struktur und historischen Entwicklung der Ständegesellschaft, und eben deshalb kann er seinen Sturz nicht schuldhaft erfahren. . . .'

Kevin Hilliard, which come to opposite conclusions about the psychology of the characters.[23]

The conclusion seems obvious that the text is communicating contrary messages at the same time, much as occurs in *Die heilige Cäcilie*. In order to gain some distance from the bewildering play of thematic ambiguities, we may begin by identifying two strong and contrary movements in the text. As the writing gathers momentum and nears the climax of the ghost story, the text conveys a powerful impression of its own dramatic structure: order perceptibly increases.[24] On a thematic level, by contrast, the lives of the Marchese and his wife pass from orderliness to chaos.

The first sentence of the story cites a 'before' and 'after,' which it ostensibly sets out to explain as an aetiological narrative: in the narrative present the castle may be seen lying 'in Schutt und Trümmern,' whereas it was once intact, 'ein Schloß mit hohen und weitläufigen Zimmern' (SW II, 196). Aetiological narratives are perforce convergent, since they are meant to culminate in a finished explanation, and so this one is introduced by its intention to account for the catastrophe that has devastated the castle. What it explains, however, is not merely a state of disorder, but one that breaks the rules of rationality, and hence of aetiological narratives, in order to come about.

A parallel to the contrary notions of what constitutes order in *Die heilige Cäcilie* may shed some light on this tension. To the civil authorities and the citizens of Aachen, the four brothers are merely insane, an insignificant enclave of chaos within the social order, and are thus incarcerated in the asylum, whence the sound of their 'singing' has long since ceased to disturb the populace. For the Abbess, the miracle that has so transformed the brothers has induced an aspect of divine order into the chaos of the imminent demolition of the convent, and her perspective is shared and confirmed by the Archbishop and Pope. Both notions of order co-exist in the text itself.

One may read *Das Bettelweib von Locarno* in similar terms, if one allows that the story itself is one kind of order, constituting itself as the text progressively unfolds, while, since it is a ghost story that ends cata-

---

23 For Katherine M. Arens, 'Kleist's *Bettelweib von Locarno*: A Propositional Analysis,' in *DVjs* 57 (3), 1983, p. 467, 'they remain schematic figures lacking a psychological consistency with which the reader could identify, either positively or negatively.' I am not sure that this fairly applies to the dog. For Kevin Hilliard, on the other hand, '"Rittergeschichte mit Gespenst",' p. 288: 'The mystery of the story is really psychological: it shows the pressure of an unspoken thought on the false and barren security of a reason which, having sealed itself off prematurely, must allow its defences to be infiltrated by the apparently irrational if it is to achieve the wholeness of true understanding.'

24 This is the main thrust of the reading by Emil Staiger, 'Kleists *Bettelweib von Locarno*. Zum Problem des dramatischen Stils,' in *DVjs* 20 (1), 1942, pp. 10-16.

strophically for the Marchese and his wife, the domestic orderliness of the beginning is, at the same time, brought into chaos on a thematic level.[25]

A typically Kleistian irony rests in the fact that an aetiological narrative culminates in the inexplicable, instead of furnishing the expected rational explanation for the fact that where once there was a castle there is now only a ruin. The rebuff this means to the reader's expectations prompts the asking of questions about the story's thematic coherence, whereupon it becomes apparent that one may make all kinds of conjectures about the Marchese's degree of responsibility, financial difficulties, marital problems, and social prejudices. But the text does not permit any *certainty*, even on the issue of whether he remains in the room to witness the beggar woman's death, after telling her to go behind the stove. The convergence of the narrative can thus return the reader to the initial disorder of a thematic analysis that then yields a choice of answers, which, in turn, contains the temptation to opt for one in particular, so as to restore a sense of expectations fulfilled.

I would argue that this further step is not necessary. When Kleist's stories offer such choices, I feel they are calling attention to their own fictional quality in ways that make fun of judgements made outside the fiction. In a sense, all conjectural verdicts have equal status before the enigma of the text itself, which continues to emerge from the process of judgement unscathed, or, as one of Kleist's most gifted admirers put it: 'Die Schrift ist unveränderlich, und die Meinungen sind oft nur ein Ausdruck der Verzweiflung darüber.'[26]

The reception of Kleist's writings is still haunted by the discrepancy between the mesmeric force of his texts on the page and the efflorescence of divergent meanings in readers' attempts to come to terms with them discursively. I suggest that Kleist produced this effect as one most appropriate to the historical no-man's-land in which he believed his generation to be living. Kleist's genius was for posing questions, as is demonstrated by the forensic panache of every interrogation scene he ever wrote. When it came to answers, he eschewed any certainties that were in vogue, but equally stopped short of risking any innovative position whose complexity came near to that of the enigmas he had formulated. To construct an elaborate filigree around a core of silence may be

---

, 25 Cf. Timothy J. Mehigan, *Text as contract*, pp. 192f: 'Two movements may thus be detected in the narrative: on the one hand, an evolving sense of disorder . . .; on the other hand, an emerging sense of structural order around the figure of the beggar woman, who slowly takes on an apparently irrefutable form . . .. The more the ghost takes on form, the more the existence of the castle is jeopardised, until finally the existence of the former must expunge that of the latter.'

26 Franz Kafka, *Der Prozeß*, p. 185.

aesthetically satisfying, but, in all of Kleist's works, the elusive center is hedged around with so many caveats as to make his readers regret that, in his brief creative life, his conviction never strengthened to the point where this silence could be brought to speak directly and from the heart, rather than veil itself in an unending play of ironies.

This must remain our greatest reservation about Kleist's genius. A few ventures into affirmation of an intellectually sophisticated kind would have done his work no end of good. His somewhat hysterical patriotism of 1808-9 is a sleep of reason, giving birth to monsters, like the ode *Germania an ihre Kinder* (SW I, 25f). Kleist's main strength lies in his ability to tease the wrongness in everything into complex patterns, but his conspicuous weakness is to have no intellectually acceptable answers that carried any commitment, beyond such empty formulae as: "In Staub mit allen Feinden Brandenburgs!" (SW I, 709). Subsequent history has rendered such slogans grotesque, but, even in Kleist's lifetime, they were no answer to even a small proportion of the questions his works ask, and he well knew this.

13

Über das Marionettentheater

Although its title suggests a treatise or essay, *Über das Marionettentheater* is first and foremost a fictional narrative, and thus has its place in a discussion of Kleist's stories. It appeared in December 1810 in four installments in Kleist's venture into journalism, the *Berliner Abendblätter*.[1] The reading I shall offer here is an attempt to restore the fictional quality of the text, which tends to have been buried under a wealth of commentary on statements that may be extracted from it. But it may first be useful to review briefly some of the varied interpretations it has received.

Reconstructions of the original text have seen it as attempting to suggest an ideal relationship between the *Berliner Abendblätter* and its reading public,[2] and have also established entirely credible frames of contemporary references in terms of Kleist's well-documented hostility to Iffland's 'Königliches Nationaltheater,' to official measures against the popular marionette theatre, which flourished in the city's inns, and to the censorship that forbade theatre reviews in Kleist's paper.[3] Significantly, the need to establish how the text might have appeared to its first readers has been more acutely felt in the last decade than in the rest of the 20th century, as it is part of an ongoing reaction to a decontextualized mode of reading *Über das Marionettentheater* as a key to understanding Kleist's whole work that was firmly established by Hanna Hellmann in 1911 and remained dominant well into the 1970s.[4]

Hellmann read the text as consonant with triadic myths of the positive development of human consciousness in the writings of such contemporaries as Novalis, Schlegel, and Schelling, and produced the schema: 'Vom Unbewußten durch Reflexion zum höchsten Bewußtsein:

---

1 For the original division into instalments, see KW III, 1137.

2 Jochen Marquardt, 'Der mündige Zeitungsleser – Anmerkungen zur Kommunikationsstrategie der *Berliner Abendblätter*,' in *Beiträge zur Kleist-Forschung*, Frankfurt/O, 1986, pp. 13f.

3 Alexander Weigel, 'Der Schauspieler als Maschinist. Heinrich von Kleists *Über das Marionettentheater* und das "Königliche Nationaltheater",' *Heinrich von Kleist*, ed. Dirk Grathoff, pp. 264f.

4 Hanna Hellmann, '*Über das Marionettentheater*,' *Kleists Aufsatz über das Marionettentheater*, ed. Helmut Sembdner, Berlin, 1967, pp. 17-31.

Thesis, Antithesis und Synthesis; Marionette, Mensch und Gott.'[5] The next half-century saw the generalization of similar readings of *Über das Marionettentheater*, to the point where they became an accepted means of decoding the intricacies of Kleist's other fictions. These tended to include the implicit, but erroneous, assumption that Kleist's basic mode of thought was as dialectical as that of Hegel or Hölderlin, although a survey of his statements on contemporary history would soon have revealed the contrary. Such wholesale applications of *Über das Marionettentheater* are generally marked by a desire to reduce the multiform ambivalences of Kleist's work to a few propositions that are unambiguous.

As part of a general trend to emphasize the ironic dimension of Kleist's work, the 1970s saw the start of a concerted backlash against taking the more portentous statements in *Über das Marionettentheater* out of context and at face value as descriptions of what Kleist's dramas and stories were essentially about.[6] Wolfgang Binder's essay of 1976 may be seen as beginning a series of readings that are consciously 'deconstructive,' although the label was to be applied only later.[7] Paul de Man's essay of 1984,[8] which deconstructs with a vengeance, has attracted its own hagiography,[9] but my view is that the sustainable parts of his argument were fully anticipated by Wolfgang Binder, Gerhard Kurz, and Beda Allemann.[10] What Binder claims for *Über das Marionettentheater* is essentially no more radical that what other interpretations were claiming at the same time for the other dramatic and prose fictions, namely, that they allow the reader a choice of understandings of the one text.[11] The consensus in today's writing on Kleist that parody plays a significant role in his works rests entirely on such observations.

---

5 Ibid., p. 23.

6 Hilda Brown, 'Kleist's *Über das Marionettentheater*: "Schlüssel zum Werk" or "Feuilleton",' in *Oxford German Studies*, vol. 3, 1968, p. 125, had already made an eloquent plea against the reductionism inherent in treating this text as a key to the whole of Kleist's work.

7 Wolfgang Binder, 'Ironischer Idealismus. Kleists unwillige Zeitgenossenschaft,' *Aufschlüsse. Studien zur deutschen Literatur*, Zurich and Munich, 1976, pp. 311-29.

8 Paul de Man, 'Aesthetic Formalization: Kleist's *Über das Marionettentheater*,' *The Rhetoric of Romanticism*, New York, 1984, pp. 263-90.

9 Cf. Cynthia Chase, 'Models of Narrative: Mechanical Doll, Exploding Machine,' in *The Oxford Literary Review*, vol. 6 (2), 1984, pp. 58f; Harro Müller, 'Kleist, Paul de Man und Deconstruction. Argumentative Nach-Stellungen,' *Diskurstheorien und Literaturwissenschaft*, eds. Jürgen Fohrmann and Harro Müller, Frankfurt/M, 1988, pp. 81-92.

10 Gerhard Kurz, '"Gott befohlen",' pp. 264-77; Beda Allemann, 'Sinn und Unsinn von Kleists Gespräch *Über das Marionettentheater*,' in *KJb* 1981/82, pp. 50-65.

11 Wolfgang Binder, 'Ironischer Idealismus,' p. 311: 'Kleists ironischer Idealismus scheint mir nun so beschaffen, daß er in jeder Setzung zugleich ihre Fragwürdigkeit mitsetzt.'

Awareness of a need to restore ambivalence to Kleist's texts is not unique to recent writing on this one. The problem of *Über das Marionettentheater* is similar to that of interpreting *Die heilige Cäcilie* and *Das Bettelweib von Locarno*. It is the challenge to a reader to see the text as consistently signifying more than one thing at a time. This is easily said, but proves extremely difficult in practice because of the convergent nature of critical argument. The problem also has a clear affinity to the difficulties I have discussed when interpreting *Das Käthchen von Heilbronn*. For it is one thing to say that this drama contains elements of self-parody, creates a tension between its 'fairytale' and experimental aspects, and ironizes its own crassly patriarchal ending, and quite another to keep a duality of perspective constantly open when interpreting individual scenes, incidents, or speeches.[12]

The obstacles in the way of a definitive reading of *Michael Kohlhaas* are another case in point. I have pointed out, when discussing this story, that the intricacy of the text is such that the interactions it establishes between individual and state, and between both of them and the abstract values each purports to espouse, rapidly pass beyond the scope of the formulaic judgements the narrator offers and that readers tend to echo. The choices that the text of *Über das Marionettentheater* progressively allows readers to make may similarly multiply to the point where a reader, perhaps out of self-defence, begins making decisions that close off particular avenues of reference. Such decisions may soon acquire a linear consistency – much as the narrator in one of Kleist's stories may favor one character at the expense of others, while the text as a whole permits a different view to develop, Elvire's 'fidelity' in *Der Findling* being a case in point.[13]

A comparison with *Der zerbrochne Krug* may serve to clarify this point. From the outset, the text of the play incessantly alludes, in its figurative language, to religious myth, especially that of the Fall. Both Eve and Adam, for entirely different reasons, expand this frame of reference to include the Last Judgement.[14] Interpretations, such as that by Oskar Seidlin, have taken this dimension of the text at its word and steered their readings toward a meditation on the Fall of humanity in terms as serious as many readings of *Über das Marionettentheater* – indeed, have cited parts of this as an authority when reading the play.[15]

The point is that the whole text of *Der zerbrochne Krug* does not insist on any one manner of reading such myths. Licht's burlesque and trivializing view of Adam's 'fall' in Scene 1 remains a valid perspec-

---

12 See above, p. 146f. and p. 155f.
13 See above, p. 235.
14 See above, p. 159f. and 62.
15 Oskar Seidlin, 'Was die Stunde schlägt,' pp. 76-79, and see above, p. 67.

tive: 'Der erste Adamsfall,/ Den Ihr aus einem Bett hinaus getan' (SW I, 179) – except that the 'bed' turns out to be the window of Eve's bedroom. This is, in a sense, doubled by Adam's further 'fall' from his seat of office, when his villainy is disclosed, and his replacement by Licht at the end of the play. These quite concrete meanings remain within the comic framework. But just as the world of an internecine feud in *Die Familie Schroffenstein* opens – metaphorically – into a cosmic drama through the way in which the characters cast their perceptions of one another in language, so there is no containing the mythical scope of *Der zerbrochne Krug* once such meanings have been set free in the text. When Eve despairs of ever clarifying the false position in which her own actions, Adam's deceit, and invidious circumstances have placed her, her appeal to a resolution at the Last Judgement is in no way trivialized by the rest of the text, since her suffering is all too real: 'Und ists im Leben nicht, so ist es jenseits,/ Und wenn wir auferstehn ist auch ein Tag' (SW I, 217).

In the same way, certain extremely powerful semantic elements are released into the text of *Über das Marionettentheater*, well before its conclusion, and remain active to the extent that the narrative framework does nothing to discredit them:

> Solche Mißgriffe, setzte er abbrechend hinzu, sind unvermeidlich, seitdem wir von dem Baum der Erkenntnis gegessen haben. Doch das Paradies ist verriegelt und der Cherub hinter uns; wir müssen die Reise um die Welt machen, und sehen, ob es vielleicht von hinten irgendwo wieder offen ist.   (SW II, 342)

> Ich sagte, daß ich gar wohl wüßte, welche Unordnungen, in der natürlichen Grazie des Menschen, das Bewußtsein anrichtet. Ein junger Mann von meiner Bekanntschaft hätte, durch eine bloße Bemerkung, gleichsam vor meinen Augen, seine Unschuld verloren, und das Paradies derselben, trotz aller ersinnlichen Bemühungen, nachher niemals wieder gefunden.   (SW II, 343)

The evocation, from different perspectives, of the motif of the lost paradise by both partners in the dialogue activates its wealth of possible meanings for the whole text in a way similar to that in which Eve opens a perspective from a hearing in a village courtroom onto the Last Judgement – one that is, in turn, enlarged by the other mythical frames of reference in the text. It is not necessary, in *Über das Marionettentheater*, for the two statements about the lost paradise to cohere with each other or their immediate contexts in order to set in motion the same kind of effect that metaphorical language creates in

Kleist's dramas again and again. But it is also open to the reader to ignore these possibilities in favor of the terms of the immediate, fictional situation, and recent writing on *Über das Marionettentheater* shows both options being taken up.

A simple and concrete example of the way in which meanings in Kleist's texts, once set free, may be consolidated at a later point to yield unexpected dimensions of meaning is provided by the dehumanizing effect of Graf Rupert's language in the first scene of *Die Familie Schroffenstein*, which returns to haunt him at the death of his son. Announcing, in the first scene of the play, his campaign of vengeance against Sylvester's branch of the family, he promises: 'Nur eine Jagd wirds werden, wie nach Schlangen' (SW I, 53). In the play's final scene, after he has fatally wounded Ottokar in mistake for Agnes, his henchman, Santing, exclaims: 'Die Schlange hat ein zähes Leben. Doch/ Beschwör ichs fast. Das Schwert steckt ihr im Busen' (SW I, 144). It is as if the dehumanizing connotations of 'Schlange,' once released into the text, have – through all the other transformations of the imagery – been awaiting this moment to reveal, with terrible irony, the full extent of Rupert's blindness to the consequences of his own language. In a similar manner, the final words of *Über das Marionettentheater* – 'das ist das letzte Kapitel von der Geschichte der Welt' (SW II, 345) – return to the motif of the lost paradise, and give it a fresh turning: paradise regained. The obvious difference between the two examples is that the former is convergent, as befits the ending of a tragedy, while the final sentence of *Über das Marionettentheater* has the opposite effect, opening a utopian perspective that the reader may fill out according to a wide range of possible meanings.

So far, I have pursued the option of using intertextuality to explain some of the enigmas of *Über das Marionettentheater* by adducing examples from Kleist's other stories and dramas. It is now most useful to examine briefly its narrative form, before venturing upon those other enigmas with which most of the secondary literature is concerned.

The title suggests a treatise, but the narrative begins, in the first person, as an anecdote. This counterpoint is preserved throughout the text, as many statements, taken in isolation, could form part of various kinds of treatise or essay, while the anecdotal mode is never abandoned – indeed, is strongly reinforced by the two encapsulated narratives of the young man's loss of 'Anmut' and Herr C.'s meeting his master in the guise of a fencing bear. The agonal quality of the discussion is apparent in the narrator's avoidance of any preliminaries and immediate expression of astonishment at Herr C.'s behavior: 'Ich sagte ihm, daß ich erstaunt gewesen wäre, ihn schon mehrere Mal in einem Marionettentheater zu finden. . . .' (SW II, 338). The social setting is marked by Herr C.'s being principal dancer in the ballet of the opera, frequented by the upper and educated classes, while the marionette theater has been hastily put up in the marketplace for the amusement of the common herd: 'und den Pöbel, durch kleine dramatische Burlesken . . . belustigte' (SW II, 339).

Rolf Peter Janz has rightly stressed that the dialogue begins as an interrogation, but turns into something else.[16] The narrator's expressing astonishment at the fact that Herr C. frequents an entertainment below his social station puts the dancer into the position of needing to account for unconventional behavior, and thus the impression is rapidly established that the narrator is in charge of this very mild inquisition. The effect is reinforced by the narrator's sharing with the reader both his astonishment and his intention to pursue an investigation:

> Da diese Äußerung mir, durch die Art, wie er sie vorbrachte, mehr, als ein bloßer Einfall schien, so ließ ich mich bei ihm nieder, um ihn über die Gründe, auf die er eine so sonderbare Behauptung stützen könne, näher zu vernehmen. (SW II, 339)

Immediately before this, Herr C. has begun a different strand of discourse, which presents itself in terms familiar from the Enlightenment's espousal of Horace's maxim that the purpose of art is to edify and delight: *prodesse et delectare*. For, so he declares, visiting the marionette theatre affords him 'viel Vergnügen,' while, at the same time: 'ein Tänzer, der sich ausbilden wolle, mancherlei von ihnen lernen könne.' He has thus countered the narrator's reproach that this entertainment is beneath him socially by presenting its effects as acceptable in terms appropriate to higher forms of art. While the narrator finds this riposte mildly provoking, and is encouraged to pursue the reason for Herr C.'s 'strange assertion,' the latter's gambit is to prove fruitful later in the text, as the narrator relinquishes all pretense of being an inquisitor and becomes, instead, a willing accomplice in the process of his own enigmatic 'edification.' Herr C. is thus allowed to execute the same feat vis-à-vis the narrator as Graf Wetter vom Strahl before the secret court in *Das Käthchen von Heilbronn*. Beginning as the accused, he progressively arrogates the court's authority to himself by his rhetorical strategies. Similarly, from being introduced as someone with incongruous behavior to justify, Herr C., through his own rhetorical skills, becomes

---

16 Rolf Peter Janz, 'Die Marionette als Zeugin der Anklage. Zu Kleists Abhandlung *Über das Marionettentheater*,' *Kleists Dramen*, ed. Walter Hinderer, pp. 31 and 39f.

the authoritative source of statements and narratives that – so the narrator professes – create belief and understanding.

The axis in the text along which this change occurs is the emotional mode of astonishment, where significant modulations occur. The narrator's initial astonishment is a mildly accusing reaction to Herr C.'s seeking entertainment beneath his social station. This is then compounded by a further questioning amazement at the extravagant claims Herr C. makes for the marionettes: 'Ich äußerte meine Verwunderung zu sehen, welcher Aufmerksamkeit er diese, für den Haufen erfundene, Spielart einer schönen Kunst würdige' (SW II, 340). The recurrence of the motif of snobbish disapproval from the beginning of the story may be seen as marking a certain irony on the part of the whole text toward the narrator. For it reveals him as a not very alert inquisitor. Herr C.'s answer to his question as to the role of the 'Maschinist' in the marionette's dance is confusing, to say the least. Instead of pouncing on its apparent incoherence, the narrator reverts to venting his social prejudices about the marionette theatre, thus allowing Herr C. to get away with the first major inconsistency in his argument:

> Inzwischen glaube er, daß auch dieser letzte Bruch von Geist, von dem er gesprochen, aus den Marionetten entfernt werden, daß ihr Tanz gänzlich ins Reich mechanischer Kräfte hinübergespielt, und vermittelst einer Kurbel, so wie ich es mir gedacht, hervorgebracht werden könne. (SW II, 340)

For Herr C. has not been speaking about the need to get rid of any last vestige of spirit from the marionettes at all. Rather, he has mystified the narrator by referring to the line traced by a marionette's center of gravity as 'etwas sehr Geheimnisvolles . . . *der Weg der Seele des Tänzers,*' which he elaborates to mean: 'daß sich der Maschinist in den Schwerpunkt der Marionette versetzt, d. h. mit anderen Worten *tanzt.*' He thus switches from a positive complementarity of marionette and '*Seele des Tänzers*' to evoking an equally – or even more? – graceful dance produced purely mechanically. That the narrator lets this pass is the first sign that his interrogation is becoming dysfunctional.

Herr C. then takes up the motif of astonishment and gives it a new flavor by his preposterous anecdote about the artificial limbs, made in England, that enable their wearers to dance 'mit einer Ruhe, Leichtigkeit und Anmut, die jedes denkende Gemüt in Erstaunen setzen' (SW II, 341). The astonished admiration, which Herr C. signals here, eventually comes to replace the reproving astonishment, with which the narrator began, as the text's dominant emotional tone, but the transition is not immediate. Rather, the narrator rallies and voices his scepticism as amusement: 'Ich äußerte, scherzend, daß er ja, auf diese Weise, seinen Mann gefunden habe.' Herr C. seems momentarily defeated by being taken literally, 'da er seinerseits ein wenig betreten zur Erde sah,' but the narrator, instead of following up his minor victory, asks, instead, a helpful question that allows Herr C. to embark on anecdotes from ballet that have the authority of his own expertise as a successful dancer. These then become the springboard for his first leap into myth, and he evokes humanity's exclusion from paradise 'seitdem wir von dem Baum der Erkenntnis gegessen haben' (SW II, 342).

The narrator's response is initially a sceptical aside to the reader: 'Ich lachte.– Allerdings, dachte ich, kann der Geist nicht irren, da, wo keiner vorhanden ist.' His incredulity is aimed in two directions at once. Herr C. must take his laughter as a lack of conviction, while this is made quite explicit to the reader by confiding the *unspoken* thought Herr C. never gets to hear. This brief aside has a pivotal place in the narrative, for it marks the narrator's beginning to abdicate his initial stance of superiority, as his role now changes, to all intents and purposes, from inquisitor to helper. Herr C. has something he needs to express, and the narrator encourages him: 'Doch ich bemerkte, daß er noch mehr auf dem Herzen hatte, und bat ihn, fortzufahren.' After Herr C.'s account of the marionettes' defying the force of gravity, which simply means that the operator holds them in the air, the narrator makes his last stand as a sceptic:

Ich sagte, daß, so geschickt er auch die Sache seiner Paradoxe führe, er mich doch nimmermehr glauben machen würde, daß in einem mechanischen Gliedermann mehr Anmut enthalten sein könne, als in dem Bau des menschlichen Körpers.

Er versetzte, daß es dem Menschen schlechthin unmöglich wäre, den Gliedermann darin auch nur zu erreichen. Nur ein Gott könne sich, auf diesem Felde, mit der Materie messen; und hier sei der Punkt, wo die beiden Enden der ringförmigen Welt in einander griffen.

Ich erstaunte immer mehr, und wußte nicht, was ich zu so sonderbaren Behauptungen sagen sollte. (SW II, 342f)

It is important to note that the narrator already acts out his own capitulation to Herr C.'s discourse, although neither what has been said nor the manner of delivery has been in the least persuasive in conventional terms. For the astonishment the narrator now manifests is quite different in quality from the superior expression of surprise with which he began the dialogue. He is now simply at a loss for words. Herr C., seizing the chance to take the higher ground, promptly accuses him of ignorance:

Es scheine, versetzte er, indem er eine Prise Tabak nahm, daß ich das dritte Kapitel vom ersten Buch Moses nicht mit Aufmerksamkeit gelesen; und wer diese erste Periode aller menschlichen Bildung nicht kennt, mit dem könne man nicht füglich über die folgenden, um wie viel weniger über die letzte, sprechen.   (SW II, 343)

Thus disarmed, the narrator signifies his defeat by beginning to speak in mythical terms himself. In the remarks that introduce his story about the young man who loses his innocence, he willingly takes up the theme of the lost paradise that, when Herr C. first introduced it, had prompted only a sceptical wink in the reader's direction. In the anecdote that follows, a negative modulation of astonishment occurs in the repetition of the word 'unbegreiflich': 'ging eine unbegreifliche Veränderung mit dem jungen Menschen vor'; 'Eine unsichtbare und unbegreifliche Gewalt schien sich, wie ein eisernes Netz, um das freie Spiel seiner Gebärden zu legen. . . .' (SW II, 344).

From the beginning of this anecdote, the following factors that determine the direction the text henceforth takes become operative: first, the terms of argument are no longer subject to being brought back to everyday experience; second, the imaginative leaps initiated by Herr C. and now imitated by the narrator have established discontinuity, instead of logical succession, as dominant in the discourse; third, Herr C. has won a convert in the narrator, although the manner of conversion has shifted as far as can be imagined from the Enlightenment didacticism suggested by the dancer's opening defense of his preoccupation with the marionette theatre.[17]

The anecdote of the fencing bear, narrated by Herr C., once more contains a dramatization of astonishment, but without the negative overtones of the previous encapsulated story of the young man: 'Ich fiel, da ich mich ein wenig von meinem Erstaunen erholt hatte, mit dem Rapier auf ihn aus; der Bär machte eine ganz kurze Bewegung mit der Tatze und parierte den Stoß' (SW II, 344f). Having gained ascendancy over the narrator by criticizing his acquaintance with the text of Genesis, with all that this is made to imply, Herr C. now stages his own astonished submission to his 'master,' the bear: 'Aug in Auge, als ob er meine Seele darin lesen könnte, stand er, die Tatze schlagfertig erhoben, und wenn meine Stöße nicht ernsthaft gemeint waren, so rührte er sich nicht'

---

17 I thus cannot agree with James A. Rushing Jr., 'The Limitations of the Fencing Bear. Kleist's *Über das Marionettentheater* as Ironic Fiction,' in *The German Quarterly*, vol. 61 (4), 1988, pp. 534f, that the narrator's anecdote about the young man's loss of innocence and the words with which he prefaces it are 'virtually a parody of Herr C.'s manner of speaking,' or that they 'must be seen . . . as an ironic attempt to humour, tease, and/or entertain Herr C.'

(SW II, 345). Thus, the final authority is displaced from the sphere of human language and consciousness altogether. This, in turn, prepares the joyous astonishment of the narrator's final conversion, though, like many a convert, he may not be clear as to the full implications of what he has just bought: 'Glauben Sie diese Geschichte? Vollkommen! rief ich, mit freudigem Beifall. . ..'

The anecdote has not really proven the thesis it is supposed to prove, but what happens within it relegates verbal proofs to an inferior status in the scheme of things. To become Herr C.'s 'master,' the bear need only act, but the capitulation of Herr C. to the bear and of the narrator to Herr C.'s mode of discourse are symmetrical to one another. One may read this doubling as a quite deliberate questioning of the text's own means of operation as it nears its conclusion, since here it opens a perspective onto a non-verbal resolution by combat, before going on to stage an enigmatic conclusion within language itself. The best conversions, it is implied, may be those that do not rely on manipulating the defective machinery of human language.

At the conclusion of the story, the narrator produces a question that assimilates elements from what both Herr C. and he have previously said: 'Mithin, sagte ich ein wenig zerstreut, müßten wir wieder von dem Baum der Erkenntnis essen, um in den Stand der Unschuld zurückzufallen?' But the tone of challenge that marked questions from him earlier in the text is quite absent; he is seeking confirmation and receives it with the statement from Herr C. that concludes the text: 'Allerdings, antwortete er; das ist das letzte Kapitel von der Geschichte der Welt.' The word 'zerstreut' is one of Kleist's favorite dramaturgical gestures, in the stories as well as in the plays, and generally signifies that the course of events, or the implications of the dialogue, have got somewhat beyond a character's control. It is richly ambivalent, and remains so here.

Reading the story along the semantic axis of astonishment thus renders the dynamics of the narrative discourse clearly visible. It also shows it as entirely comparable with others of Kleist's fictions. *Der Zweikampf* is particularly rich in such expressions, and appropriately so, as the plot revolves around events whose understanding requires information the characters – and the reader – simply do not have.[18] In *Über das Marionettentheater*, the narrator has been progressively coaxed out of his depth. Beginning with a certain superciliousness, he has been puzzled, entertained, and baffled by turns. Herr C. has then induced him to adopt a mode of thought and expression from which he preserves a scep-

18 Cf. Klaus Müller-Salget's commentary in KW III, 901: 'Nirgends sonst sind Kleists Personen so oft erstaunt, betroffen, bestürzt, verwirrt, ja "erstarrt wie zu Stein" . . . wie im *Zweikampf*.'

tical distance for as long as he can. His oscillation, at the end, between greeting Herr C.'s story of the bear 'mit freudigem Beifall' and phrasing his own concluding remark as a question, introduced with the phrase 'ein wenig zerstreut,' surely indicates that he is not entirely certain as to where the dialogue has finally brought him. His bemusement is one the reader will doubtless share.

With such a closure, the text opens the way to interpretations of those parts of the dialogue that have led to its being read as an 'Aufsatz' or 'Abhandlung.'[19] The problem with such readings is that Kleist has treated the conventions of discursive argument in as cavalier a manner as his other stories and his dramas are wont to treat the law of causality.[20] The argument has too many gaps to do more than mimic the conventions of reasoned discourse. The dramatization of conviction along the axis of astonishment produces an appearance of convergence in the text, but this is a function of the fictional narrative and not of the fragmentary argument it allows the reader to glimpse along the way.

I suggest that the text opens itself in too many places to diffuse associations to yield any single discursive meaning; readers will always have a wide choice among the plurality of philosophical and mythical discourses of the time to which the text of *Über das Marionettentheater* alludes.[21] Just as the narrative technique of *Der Findling* demands a reader's capacity to view each of the three main characters as alternating between different roles, and not as pursuing the consequential, linear development of the 'Bildungsroman,' so the technique of astonishment, which *Über das Marionettentheater* consistently applies, is aimed at keeping the reader off balance by oscillating between positions that are incompatible within the conventions of reasoned argument.

We have seen how the narrator-as-inquisitor is first outmaneuvred by one such oscillation. Herr C. first proposes a perfect conjunction between the 'soul' of the 'Maschinist' and the inanimate marionette in the formula: 'daß sich der Maschinist in den Schwerpunkt der Marionette versetzt, d. h. mit anderen Worten *tanzt*' (SW II, 340). Taking the cue from the phrase 'etwas ziemlich Geistloses' in the narrator's reply, he then switches to the contrary ideal of eliminating 'Geist'

---

19 The former term is general, the latter is preferred by Rolf Peter Janz, 'Die Marionette als Zeugin der Anklage,' pp. 31f.

20 See above, for example, the discussion of assigning casual motivations to the figure of Graf Wetter vom Strahl, pp. 141-5.

21 For a spectrum of contemporary reference see Gerhard Kurz, '"Gott befohlen",' pp. 265-8; Rolf Peter Janz, 'Die Marionette als Zeugin der Anklage,' pp. 35f; Odo Marquard, 'Felix Culpa? Bemerkungen zum Applikationsschicksal von Genesis 3,' *Text und Applikation: Theologie, Jurisprudenz und Literaturwissenschaft im hermeneutischen Gespräch. Poetik und Hermeneutik 9*, eds. Menfred Fuhrmann, Hans Robert Jauß and Wolfhart Pannenberg, Munich, 1981, pp. 53-77; Bernhard Greiner, 'Die Wende in der Kunst – Kleist mit Kant,' in *DVjs* 64 (1), 1990, pp. 110-15.

altogether with the result: 'daß ihr Tanz gänzlich ins Reich mechanischer Kräfte hinübergespielt, und vermittelst einer Kurbel . . . hervorgebracht werden könne.' The only common denominator between these two positions is the elimination of the human body from ideal forms of movement. It is, in a sense, to the reader's disadvantage that the narrator loses his grasp on the movement of Herr C.'s discourse at this point, and falls back on a repetition of his own opening remarks, since the pattern of oscillating viewpoints, established here with no resistance at all, is to continue for the rest of the dialogue.

Just as the human body has been neatly eliminated from Herr C.'s two ideals of movement, so the text rapidly dispenses with both the 'Maschinist' and the marionette. The human operator disappears for good; the marionette returns at the conclusion, but now in a linking that, ironically, restores the image of the human body, but eliminates human consciousness in a manner that had been anticipated by the superiority of the fencing bear in Herr C.'s anecdote:

so findet sich auch, wenn die Erkenntnis gleichsam durch ein Unendliches gegangen ist, die Grazie wieder ein; so, daß sie, zu gleicher Zeit, in demjenigen menschlichen Körperbau am reinsten erscheint, der entweder gar keins, oder ein unendliches Bewußtsein hat, d. h. in dem Gliedermann, oder in dem Gott.   (SW II, 345)

Once more, it is the middle ground – human consciousness as it expresses itself in language – that is, paradoxically, excluded from the discourse. The strategic value of this is either to suppress positive processes of becoming, or else render them unintelligible, as in the phrase: 'wenn die Erkenntnis gleichsam durch ein Unendliches gegangen ist.' It is significant that the only comprehensible process of change described in any detail in *Über das Marionettentheater* is the wholly negative one of the young man's loss of 'Anmut':

Er fing an, tagelang vor dem Spiegel zu stehen; und immer ein Reiz nach dem anderen verließ ihn. Eine unsichtbare und unbegreifliche Gewalt schien sich, wie ein eisernes Netz, um das freie Spiel seiner Gebärden zu legen, und als ein Jahr verflossen war, war keine Spur mehr von der Lieblichkeit in ihm zu entdecken, die die Augen der Menschen sonst, die ihn umringten, ergötzt hatte.   (SW II, 344)

Where the text most taxes the reader is thus in its elimination of that middle ground, where connections are made and logical orientations occur. Herr C. begins to justify his interests in the marionettes in terms that suggest a middle-of-the-road explanation in the familiar

Enlightenment terms of pleasure and edification. His playing on such terms as 'Grazie,' 'Anmut,' and 'Bildung' then suggests a discourse in the vein of Weimar Classicism, and Bernhard Greiner has rightly drawn attention to the fact that the sculpture alluded to in the story of the young man's loss of innocence was singled out in Goethe's *Über Laokoon* of 1798 as a manifestation, precisely, of 'Anmut.'[22] But the thrust of Kleist's dialogue is to displace 'Anmut' and 'Grazie,' and by extension the human consciousness that apprehends them, from their familiar place as mediators between nature and spirit in contemporary aesthetic discourse. Thus, so concludes *Über das Marionettentheater*, 'Grazie' is simultaneously present in a human frame in which consciousness is either entirely absent or else infinite.

The elimination of consciousness as a mediating function from Kleist's text also serves to prevent the utopian discourse of the development of the individual psyche toward godhead from achieving coherence in terms resembling, for example, Novalis' schema: 'Die individuelle Seele soll mit der Weltseele übereinstimmend werden. Herrschaft der Weltseele und Mitherrschaft der individuellen Seele.'[23] For the movement of the text itself clearly prefers arbitrary leaps to dialectical progressions. When Herr C. alludes to the last 'Periode aller menschlichen Bildung' and 'das letzte Kapitel von der Geschichte der Welt,' the movement of the text itself has been so much the opposite of any orderly sequence that a reader might well ask whether such schematic progressions have any more concrete presence in the text as a whole than the broken promise of an educative discourse for dancers – 'daß ein Tänzer . . . mancherlei von ihnen lernen könne' – or the deceptive centrality of the concept of 'Anmut.'

The point of orientation that the text establishes with its first bold leap away from the world of marionettes and ballet dancers is a mythical time, defined as that 'seitdem wir von dem Baum der Erkenntnis gegessen haben' (SW II, 342). It returns to it in the narrator's concluding question, thus endowing the whole with an illusory, centripetal movement. It is illusory because the myth at the center is, in fact, double – an oscillation between utopian and dystopian variants of the one complex. The myth of the Fall was read positively, as the beginning of the emancipation of the spirit, by Kant, Schiller, Fichte, and other contemporaries, while for Rousseau the manifestation of consciousness in language inaugurated a series of divisions whose sequel is human decadence.[24] The rich allusiveness of Kleist's parody of a Socratic dia-

---

22 Bernhard Greiner, 'Die Wende in der Kunst,' p. 114, note 46: 'Wir gedenken hier nur des anmutigen Knaben, der sich den Dorn aus dem Fuße zieht . . . .'

23 Novalis, *Fragmente, Band II*, ed. Ewald Wasmuth, Heidelberg, 1957, p. 138.

24 See above note 21 and Jean-Jacques Rousseau, *Œuvres complètes*, vol. III, pp. 174f.

logue allows the text to place, in effect, an each-way bet. Whether Rousseau beats Kant by a nose, or Schiller bolts away from the rest down the home straight, a reader will be left with the comforting feeling that there are winnings to collect.

For both readings of the myth were still popular at the time Kleist published *Über das Marionettentheater*, and either option could be taken up by a contemporary reader as the 'message' imparted by its enigmatic whole. Thus, one may see ordinary human consciousness as being displaced from Herr C.'s ideal schema altogether, echoing Rousseau's pessimistic mythicization, or else read 'wenn die Erkenntnis gleichsam durch ein Unendliches gegangen ist' as holding out some distant utopian promise for precisely this human faculty. The affirmative tone of the ending may initially place the utopian option in the foreground, but once a reader begins to question the manner in which the text has arrived at it, then its dystopian alternative is not far to seek in the narration of the young man's irrevocable loss of 'seine Unschuld . . . und das Paradies derselben' – the one coherent, aetiological sequence in the entire text.

It is worth noting that, even here, the loss of innocence need not be taken at face value. The young man has lived as the center of admiring attention, and what he loses is essentially something that lives in others' perceptions of him: 'war keine Spur mehr von der Lieblichkeit in ihm zu entdecken, die die Augen der Menschen sonst, die ihn umringten, ergötzt hatte' (SW II, 344). This seems a clear allusion to the following passage from the end of Rousseau's *Discours*: 'le Sauvage vit en lui-même; l'homme sociable toûjours hors de lui ne sait vivre que dans l'opinion des autres, et c'est, pour ainsi dire, de leur seul jugement qu'il tire le sentiment de sa propre éxistence.'[25] The young man's 'paradise' is thus already marked with all the Rousseauistic attributes of social decadence.

Does 'subversion' of mythical discourse then have the last word? I suggest it cannot, because this would presuppose a firm position from which others *could* be subverted, whereas the oscillating effect within the text seems to me to culminate in an astonishment that leaves several options genuinely open. One may go from a reaction of astonishment to effect a process of re-familiarization by various formulaic reductions of what initially resists rational assimilation, but this is what *Über das Marionettentheater* conspicuously does not do. It leaves the reader at the point where such a process might begin.

If this seems to be taking openness too far, then I repeat, by way of conclusion, that the inability to affirm one clear position as his own is a

25 Ibid., p. 193.

limitation of Kleist's work as a whole. In interpreting the work I regard as his masterpiece, *Penthesilea*, I emphasized the labyrinthine quality of the world that this tragedy creates, and the fact that nothing seems to survive its collapse but a helpless appeal to an Enlightenment humanism whose simplicity stands in no proportion to the complexity of what is destroyed in the heroine's slaughter of Achilles and her own suicide.[26] Similarly, *Über das Marionettentheater* mimics an intellectual quest for a schema to provide an intelligible structure for the relationship of human consciousness to history. By appearing to reach a successful outcome, yet leaving this too in suspension, it also steps back from asserting a positive belief as the author's own; yet it points to the tenuous hope that a quest pursued in terms somewhat *different* from those available to the author and his contemporaries might well be successful.

A precondition of this would be freedom from the compulsion to quote the textual relics of an intellectual and social order, whose fragmentation Kleist had registered and imitated in such wealth of detail, and to incorporate into literary discourse some firm intimations of that 'neue Ordnung der Dinge' (SW II, 761), for which he eventually declined to wait and whose arrival we have yet to witness.

26 See above, p. 122-6.

Abbreviations

AUMLA   Australiation Universities Modern Langauges Association.

DVjs   Deutsche Vierteljahresschrift für Literaturwissenschaft und Geistesgeschichte.

HA   Goethes Werke. Hamburger Ausgabe in 14. Bänden, ed. Erich Trunz, neu bearbeitete Auflage, Munich, 1981.

JbSchG   Jahrbuch der Deutschen Schillergesellschaft.

KJb   Kleist-Jahrbuch.

KN   Heinrich von Kleists Nachruhm. Eine Wirkungsgeschichte in Dokumenten, ed. Helmut Sembdner, Frankfurt/M, 1984.

KW I etc. Heinrich von Kleist. Sämtliche Werke und Briefe in vier Bänden, eds. Ilse-Marie Barth, Klaus Müller-Salget, Walter Müller-Seidel and Hinrich C. Seeba, Frankfurt/M, 1987 etc.

LS   Heinrich von Kleists Lebensspuren. Dokumente und Berichte der Zeitgenossen, ed. Helmut Sembdner, Frankfurt/M and Leipzig, 1992.

PMLA   Publications of the Modern Language Association of America.

SW I, SW II Heinrich von Kleist. Sämtliche Werke und Briefe, ed. Helmut Sembdner, Munich, 1984.

ZfdPh   Zeitschrift für deutsche Philologie.

Bibliography

This bibliography includes only those works cited in the present study. A more comprehensive select bibliography may be found in the notes to the first three volumes of the edition of Kleist's works in the Deutscher Klassiker Verlag.

Allemann, Beda, 'Sinn und Unsinn von Kleists Gespräch *Über das Marionettentheater*,' in *KJb* 1981/82.

Angress, Ruth K., 'Kleist's Treatment of Imperialism: *Die Hermannsschlacht* and *Die Verlobung in St. Domingo*,' in *Monatshefte*, vol. 69 (1), 1977.

Angress, Ruth K., 'Kleists Abkehr von der Aufklärung,' in *KJb* 1987.

Arens, Katherine M., 'Kleist's *Bettelweib von Locarno*: A Propositional Analysis,' in *DVjs* 57 (3), 1983.

Arntzen, Helmut, '*Prinz Friedrich von Homburg* – Drama der Bewußtseinsstufen,' *Kleists Dramen*, ed. Walter Hinderer.

Arntzen, Helmut, *Die ernste Komödie. Das deutsche Lustspiel von Lessing bis Kleist*, Munich, 1968.

Aurnhammer, Achim, *Androgynie. Studien zu einem Motiv in der europäischen Literatur*, Cologne and Vienna, 1986.

Baudelaire, Charles, *Journaux intimes*, *Œuvres complètes*, ed. Claude Pichois, vol. 1, Paris, 1975.

Bentzel, Curtis C., 'Knowledge in Narrative: The Significance of the Swan in Kleist's *Die Marquise von O...*,' in *The German Quarterly*, vol. 64 (3), 1991.

Binder, Wolfgang, 'Ironischer Idealismus. Kleists unwillige Zeitgenossenschaft,' *Aufschlüsse. Studien zur deutschen Literatur*, Zurich and Munich, 1976.

Blumenberg, Hans, *Die Lesbarkeit der Welt*, Frankfurt/M, 1981.

Bogdal, Klaus-Michael, *Heinrich von Kleist: 'Michael Kohlhaas,'* Munich, 1981.

Bohnert, Joachim, 'Kohlhaas der Entsetzliche,' in *KJb* 1988/89.

Boockmann, Hartmut, 'Mittelalterliches Recht bei Kleist. Ein Beitrag zum Verständnis des *Michael Kohlhaas*,' in *KJb* 1985.

Brown, Hilda, 'Kleist's *Über das Marionettentheater*: "Schlüssel zum

Werk" or "Feuilleton,'" in *Oxford German Studies*, vol. 3, 1968.

Brown, Hilda, 'Kleists Theorie der Tragödie – im Lichte neuer Funde,' *Heinrich von Kleist. Studien zu Werk und Wirkung*, ed. Dirk Grathoff, Opladen, 1988.

Brown, Kathryn, and Stephens, Anthony, '"Hinübergehn und unser Haus entsühnen." Die Ökonomie des Mythischen in Goethes *Iphigenie*,' in *JbSchG* XXXII, 1988.

Brunner, Otto, 'Das "Ganze Haus" und die alteuropäische "Ökonomik."' *Neue Wege der Verfassungs- und Sozialgeschichte*, 2. vermehrte Auflage, Göttingen, 1968.

Büchmann, Georg, *Geflügelte Worte. Der Zitatenschatz des deutschen Volkes*, 32. Auflage, Berlin, 1972.

Busst, A. J. L., 'The Image of the Androgyne in the Nineteenth Century,' in *Romantic Mythologies*, ed. Ian Flechter, London, 1967.

Carroll, Lewis, *The Annotated Alice*, ed. Martin Gardner, Harmondsworth, 1970.

Chambers, Ross, *Story and Situation. Narrative Seduction and the Power of Fiction*, Manchester and Minneapolis, 1984.

Chase, Cynthia, 'Models of Narrative: Mechanical Doll, Exploding Machine,' in *The Oxford Literary Review*, vol. 6 (2), 1984.

Cullen, Chris and Mücke, Dorothea von, 'Love in Kleist's *Penthesilea* and *Käthchen von Heilbronn*,' in *DVjs* 63, 1989.

de Man, Paul, 'Aesthetic Formalization: Kleist's *Über das Marionettentheater*,' *The Rhetoric of Romanticism*, New York, 1984.

Denneler, Iris, 'Legitimation und Charisma. Zu *Robert Guiskard*.' *Kleists Dramen*, ed. Walter Hinderer.

Diderot, 'Sacrifices des Hébreux,' *Encyclopédie ou Dictionnaire raisonné des sciences, des arts et des métiers*, reprint, Stuttgart-Bad Cannstadt, 1967, vol. 14.

Dießelhorst, Malte, 'Hans Kohlhase/ Michael Kohlhaas,' in *KJb* 1988/89.

Dyer, Dennis, '"Plus and Minus" in Kleist,' in *Oxford German Studies*, 2, 1967.

Dyer, Denys, *The Stories of Kleist. A critical study*, London, 1977.

Ellis, John M., *Heinrich von Kleist. Studies in the Meaning and Character of his Writings*, Chapel Hill, 1979.

Fichte, Johann Gottlieb, 'Deduktion der Ehe,' *Werke 1797-1798*, ed. Reinhard Lauth and Hans Gliwitzky, Stuttgart-Bad Cannstadt, 1970.

Fink, Gonthier-Louis, 'Das Motiv der Rebellion in Kleists Werk im Spannungsfeld der Französischen Revolution und der Napoleonischen Kriege,' in *KJb* 1988/89.

Fischer, Bernd, 'Der Ernst des Scheins in der Prosa Heinrich von Kleists: Am Beispiel des *Zweikampfs*,' in *ZfdPh*, vol. 105 (2), 1986.

Bibliography

Fischer, Bernd, 'Fatum und Idee. Zu Kleists *Erdbeben in Chili,'* in *DVjs* 58, 1984.

Fischer, Bernd, 'Zur politischen Dimension der Ethik in Kleists *Die Verlobung in St. Domingo,'* *Heinrich von Kleist,* ed. Dirk Grathoff.

Fischer, Bernd, *Ironische Metaphysik. Die Erzählungen Heinrich von Kleists,* Munich, 1988.

Flandrin, Jean-Louis, *Famille. Parenté, maison, sexualité dans l'ancienne société,* Paris, 1976.

Frommel, Monika, 'Die Paradoxie vertraglicher Sicherung bürgerlicher Rechte. Kampf ums Recht und sinnlose Aktion,' in KJb 1988/89.

Gallas, Helga, 'Kleists *Penthesilea* und Lacans vier Diskurse,' *Kontroversen, alte und neue. Akten des VII. Internationalen Germanisten-Kongresses Göttingen 1985,* vol. 6, eds. Inge Stephan und Carl Pietzcker, Tübingen, 1986.

Gallas, Helga, *Das Textbegehren des 'Michael Kohlhaas.' Die Sprache des Unbewußten und der Sinn der Literatur,* Reinbek, 1981.

Genette, Gérard, 'Proust palimpseste,' *Figures I,* Paris, 1966,

Glaser, Horst Albert, *Das bürgerliche Rührstück,* Stuttgart, 1969.

Goethe, Johann Wolfgang von, *Aus meinem Leben. Dichtung und Wahrheit,* HA, vol. X.

Goldmann, Lucien, *The Hidden God. A study of tragic vision in the 'Pensées' of Pascal and the tragedies of Racine,* London, 1964.

Gönner, Gerhard, *Von 'zerspaltenen Herzen' und der 'gebrechlichen Einrichtung der Welt.' Versuch einer Phänomenologie der Gewalt bei Kleist,* Stuttgart, 1989.

Grathoff, Dirk (ed.), *Heinrich von Kleist. Studien zu Werk und Wirkung,* Opladen, 1988.

Grathoff, Dirk, 'Die Zeichen der *Marquise*: Das Schweigen, die Sprache und die Schriften. Drei Annäherungsversuche an eine komplexe Textstruktur,' *Heinrich von Kleist,* ed. Dirk Grathoff.

Grathoff, Dirk, 'Der Fall des *Krug.* Zum geschichtlichen Gehalt von Kleists Lustspiel,' in *KJb* 1981/82.

Grathoff, Dirk, 'Heinrich von Kleist und Napoleon Bonaparte.' *Der Furor Teutonicus und die ferne Revolution, Schreckensmythen – Hoffnungsbilder. Die Französische Revolution in der deutschen Literatur,* ed. Harro Zimmermann, Frankfurt/M, 1990.

Grawe, Christian, 'Zur Deutung von Kleists Novelle *Der Zweikampf,'* in *Germanisch-Romanische Monatsschrift* (NF), vol. 27, 1977.

Greimas, A. J., *Du Sens. Essais sémiotiques,* Paris, 1970.

Greiner, Bernhard, 'Die Wende in der Kunst – Kleist mit Kant,' in *DVjs* 64 (1), 1990.

Grosz, Elizabeth, *Jacques Lacan. A feminist introduction,* London, 1990.

Haase, Donald P., and Freudenburg, Rachel, 'Power, Truth and Interpretation: The Hermeneutic Act and Kleist's *Die heilige Cäcilie*,' in *DVjs*, vol. 60 (1), 1986.

Harms, Ingeborg, '"Wie fliegender Sommer." Eine Untersuchung der "Höhlenszene" in Heinrich von Kleists *Die Familie Schroffenstein*,' in *JbSchG* XXVIII, 1984.

Heller, Erich, 'Goethe and the Avoidance of Tragedy,' *The Disinherited Mind*, Cambridge, 1952.

Hellmann, Hanna, '*Über das Marionettentheater,*' *Kleists Aufsatz über das Marionettentheater*, ed. Helmut Sembdner, Berlin, 1967.

Henkel, Arthur, 'Erwägung zur Szene II, 5 in Kleists *Amphitryon*,' *Festschrift für Friedich Beißner*, eds. Ulrich Gaier and Werner Volke, Bebenhausen, 1974.

Hilliard, Kevin, '"Rittergeschichte mit Gespenst": the Narration of the Subconscious in Kleist's *Das Bettelweib von Locarno*,' in *German Life and Letters*, vol. XLIV (4), 1991.

Hinderer, Walter (ed.), *Kleists Dramen. Neue Interpretationen*, Stuttgart, 1981.

Hoffmann, E. T. A., *Briefwechsel*, ed. Friedrich Schnapp, vol. 1, Munich, 1967.

Hoffmann, Hasso, 'Individuum und allgemeines Gesetz. Zur Dialektik in Kleists *Penthesilea* und *Prinz von Homburg*,' in *KJb* 1987.

Horn, Peter, *Heinrich von Kleists Erzählungen. Eine Einführung*, Königstein/Ts, 1978.

Hoverland, Lilian, *Heinrich von Kleist und das Prinzip der Gestaltung*, Königstein/Ts., 1978.

Hubbs, Valentine C., 'The Plus and Minus of Penthesilea and Käthchen,' in *Seminar*, vol. 6 (3), 1970.

Janz, Rolf Peter, 'Die Marionette als Zeugin der Anklage. Zu Kleists Abhandlung *Über das Marionettentheater*,' *Kleists Dramen*, ed. Walter Hinderer.

Kafka, Franz, *Briefe an Felice*, eds. Erich Heller and Jürgen Born, Frankfurt/M, 1967.

Kafka, Franz, *Der Prozeß*, Frankfurt/M, 1976.

Kafka, Franz, *Sämtliche Erzählungen*, ed. Paul Raabe, Frankfurt/M, 1970.

Kaiser, Gerhard, 'Mythos und Person in Kleists *Penthesilea*,' *Geist und Zeichen. Festschrift für Arthur Henkel zu seinem 60. Geburtstag*, eds. H. Anton, B. Gajek and P. Pfaff, Heidelberg, 1977.

Kaufmann, R. J., 'Tragedy and Its Validating Conditions,' in *Comparative Drama*, vol. I, 1967.

Kayser, Wolfgang, 'Kleist als Erzähler,' *Die Vortragsreise*, Berlin, 1958.

Bibliography

Kittler, Wolf, *Die Geburt des Partisanen aus dem Geist der Poesie. Heinrich von Kleist und die Strategie der Befreiungskriege*, Freiburg i. Br., 1987.

Kleist, Heinrich von, *Das Erdbeben in Chili. Erläuterungen und Dokumente*, eds. Hedwig Appelt and Dirk Grathoff, Stuttgart,1986.

Kleist, Heinrich von, *Die Hermannsschlacht. Ein Drama. Programmbuch Nr. 38*, Bochum, 1982.

Klotz, Volker, 'Tragödie der Jagd. Zu Kleists *Penthesilea*,' *Kurze Kommentare zu Stücken und Gedichten*, Darmstadt, 1962.

Kluge, Gerhard, 'Der Wandel der dramatischen Konzeption von der *Familie Ghonorez* zur *Familie Schroffenstein*,' *Kleists Dramen*, ed. Walter Hinderer.

Koelb, Clayton, 'Incorporating the Text: Kleist's *Michael Kohlhaas*,' in *PMLA*, vol. 105 (5), 1990.

Köller, Wilhelm, *Semiotik und Metapher. Untersuchungen zur grammatischen Struktur und kommunikativen Funktion von Metaphern*, Stuttgart, 1975.

Kreutzer, Hans Joachim, 'Die Utopie vom Vaterland. Kleist's politische Dramen,' in *Oxford German Studies*, vol. 20/21, 1991-1992.

Kreutzer, Hans Joachim, 'Wann lebte Michael Kohlhaas? Über die ästhetische Einheit der Erzählung Kleists,' *Literatur und Geschichte 1788-1988*, eds. Gerhard Schulz and Tim Mehigan, Bern, Frankfurt/M, New York and Paris, 1990.

Kreutzer, Hans Joachim, *Die dichterische Entwicklung Heinrichs von Kleist*, Berlin, 1968.

Kristeva, Julia, 'Women's Time,' *The Kristeva Reader*, ed. Toril Moi, Oxford, 1987.

Krueger, Werner, 'Rolle und Rollenwechsel. Überlegungen zu Kleists *Marquise von O...*,' in *Acta Germanica*, vol. 17, 1984.

Kurz, Gerhard, '"Gott befohlen." Kleists Dialog *Über das Marionettentheater* und der Mythos vom Sündenfall des Bewußtseins,' in *KJb* 1981/82.

Labhardt, Robert, *Metapher und Geschichte. Kleists dramatische Metaphorik bis zur 'Penthesilea' als Widerspiegelung seiner geschichtlichen Position*, Kronberg/Ts. 1976.

Lacan, Jacques, *Écrits*, Paris, 1966.

Lange, Sigrid, 'Kleists *Penthesilea*. Geschlechterparadigmen. Die Frau als Projektionsfigur männlicher Identität – oder doch nicht?,' in *Weimarer Beiträge*, vol 37 (5), 1991.

Laurs, Axel, 'Towards Idylls of Domesticity in Kleist's *Die Marquise von O...*,' in *AUMLA*, vol. 64, 1985.

Ledanff, Susanne, 'Kleist und die "beste aller Welten." *Das Erdbeben in Chili* – gesehen im Spiegel der philosophischen und literarischen

Stellungnahmen zur Theodizee im 18. Jahrhundert,' in *KJb* 1986.

Lessing, Gotthold Ephraim, *Nathan der Weise. Lessings Werke. Mit einer Auswahl aus seinen Briefen und einer Skizze seines Lebens*, ed. Franz Muncker, vol. 4, Stuttgart 1890.

Lessing, Gotthold Ephraim, *Die Erziehung des Menschengeschlechts, Lessings Werke*, vol. 12.

Liewerscheidt, Dieter, "'Ich muß doch sehn, wie weit ers treibt!'" Die Komödie in Kleists *Prinz Friedrich von Homburg*,' in *Wirkendes Wort*, vol. 43 (3), 1990.

Lorenz, Dagmar, 'Väter und Mütter in der Sozialstruktur von Kleists *Erdbeben in Chili*,' in *Etudes Germaniques*, 1978.

Lü, Yixu, *Frauenherrschaft im Drama des frühen 19. Jahrhunderts*, München, 1993.

Lubkoll, Christine, 'Die heilige Musik oder die Gewalt der Zeichen. Zur musikalischen Poetik in Heinrich von Kleists *Cäcilien*-Novelle,' *Heinrich von Kleist*, ed. Gerhard Neumann, Freiburg im Breisgau, 1994.

Lucas, Raymond, 'Die Aporie der Macht. Zum Problem der Amnestie in Kleists *Michael Kohlhaas*,' in *KJb* 1992.

Lüderssen, Klaus, 'Recht als Verständigung unter Gleichen in Kleists *Prinz von Homburg* – ein aristokratisches oder ein demokratisches Prinzip?,' in *KJb* 1985.

Luhmann, Niklas, *Liebe als Passion. Zur Codierung von Intimiät*, Frankfurt/M, 1982.

Lukács, George, 'Die Tragödie Heinrich von Kleists,' *Deutsche Realisten des 19. Jahrunderts*, Bern, 1951.

Lützeler, Paul Michael, *Geschichte in der Literatur*, Munich and Zurich, 1987.

Maas, Joachim, *Kleist. Die Geschichte seines Lebens*, Bern and Munich, 1977.

Marquard, Odo, 'Felix Culpa? Bemerkungen zum Applikationsschicksal von Genesis 3,' *Text und Applikation: Theologie, Jurisprudenz und Literaturwissenschaft im hermeneutischen Gespräch. Poetik und Hermeneutik 9*, eds. Manfred Fuhrmann, Hans Robert Jauß and Wolfhart Pannenberg, Munich, 1981.

Marquardt, Jochen, 'Der mündige Zeitungsleser – Anmerkungen zur Kommunikationsstrategie der *Berliner Abendblätter*,' in *Beiträge zur Kleist-Forschung*, Frankfurt/O, 1986.

Martini, Fritz, '*Das Käthchen von Heilbronn* – Heinrich von Kleists drittes Lustspiel?,' in *JbSchG* XX, 1976.

Mayer, Hans, *Heinrich von Kleist. Der geschichtliche Augenblick*, Pfullingen, 1962.

McGlathery, James M., 'Kleist's *Der Zweikampf* as Comedy,' *Heinrich*

Bibliography

von Kleist-Studien, ed. Alexej Ugrinsky.

McGlathery, James M., *Desire's Sway: The Plays and Stories of Heinrich von Kleist*, Detroit, 1983.

McManners, John, *Death and the Enlightenment. Changing Attitudes to Death among Christians and Unbelievers in Eighteenth-century France*, Oxford, 1981.

Mehigan, Timothy J., *Text as contract. The nature and function of narrative discourse in the Erzählungen of Heinrich von Kleist*, Frankfurt/M, Bern, New York and Paris, 1988.

Michelsen, Peter, 'Die Betrogenen des Rechtgefühls. Zu Kleists *Die Familie Schroffenstein*', in *KJb* 1992.

Michelsen, Peter, '"Wehe, mein Vaterland, dir!" Heinrichs von Kleist *Die Hermannsschlacht*,' in *KJb* 1987.

Milfull, John, 'Oedipus and Adam – Greek tragedy and Christian comedy in Kleist's *Der zerbrochne Krug*,' in *German Life and Letters*, N.S. 27, 1973/74.

Miller, Norbert, 'Verstörende Bilder in Kleists *Hermannsschlacht*,' in *KJb* 1984.

Mitterauer, Michael and Sieder, Reinhard, *The European Family. Patriarchy to Partnership from the Middle Ages to the Present*, trans. Karla Oosterveen and Manfred Hörzinger, Oxford, 1982.

Mommsen, Katharina, *Kleists Kampf mit Goethe*, Frankfurt/M, 1979.

Muecke, D. C., *The Compass of Irony*, London, 1969.

Müller, Harro, 'Kleist, Paul de Man und Deconstruction. Argumentative Nach-Stellungen,' *Diskurstheorien und Literaturwissenschaft*, eds. Jürgen Fohrmann and Harro Müller, Frankfurt/M, 1988.

Müller-Seidel, Walter, 'Kleist. Prinz von Homburg,' *Das deutsche Drama vom Barock bis zur Gegenwart*, ed Benno von Wiese, Düsseldorf, 1964.

Müller-Seidel, Walter, '*Penthesilea* im Kontext der deutschen Klassik,' *Kleists Dramen,* ed. Walter Hinderer.

Müller-Seidel, Walter, *Versehen und Erkennen. Eine Studie über Heinrich von Kleist*, Cologne and Graz, 1961.

Neumann, Gerhard, 'Hexenküche und Abendmahl. Die Sprache der Liebe im Werk Heinrich von Kleists,' in *Freiburger Universitätsblätter*, No. 91, March 1986.

Neumann, Gerhard, '"Ich bin gebildet genug, um zu lieben und zu trauern." Die Erziehung zur Liebe in Goethes *Wilhelm Meister*,' *Liebesroman – Liebe im Roman, Erlanger Forschungen*, Series A, vol. 41.

Neumann, Gerhard (ed.), *Heinrich von Kleist. Kriegsfall – Rechtsfall – Sündenfall*, Freiburg im Breisgau, 1994.

Bibliography

Neumann, Peter Horst, *Der Preis der Mündigkeit. Über Lessings Dramen. Anhang: Über Fanny Hill*, Stuttgart, 1977.

Niejahr, Johannes, 'Heinrich von Kleists *Penthesilea*,' in *Vierteljahresschrift für Litteraturgeschichte* 6 (1893).

Nietzsche, Friedrich, *Jenseits von Gut und Böse*, *Sämtliche Werke*, *Kritische Studienausgabe*, eds. Giorgio Colli and Mazzino Montinari, vol. 5, Berlin and New York, 1980.

Novalis, *Fragmente, Band II*, ed. Ewald Wasmuth, Heidelberg, 1957.

Passage, Charles E., '*Michael Kohlhaas*: Form Analysis,' in *The Germanic Review*, vol. 30, 1955.

Peters, Uwe Henrik, 'Somnambulismus und andere Nachtseiten der menschlichen Natur', in *KJb* 1990.

Peymann, Claus, and Kreutzer, Hans Joachim, 'Streitgespräch über Kleists *Hermannsschlacht*,' in *KJb* 1984.

Propp, Vladimir, *Morphologie du conte*, Paris, 1965.

Puschmann, Rosemarie, *Heinrich von Kleists Cäcilien-Erzählung. Kunst- und literarhistorische Recherchen*, Bielefeld, 1988.

Rastier, F., 'Systématique des isotopies,' *Essais de sémiotique poétique*, ed. A. J. Greimas, Paris, 1972.

Reeve, William C., '*Die Hermannsschlacht*: A Prelude to *Prinz Friedrich von Homburg*,' in *The Germanic Review*, vol. 63 (3), 1988.

Reeve, William C., '"O du – wie nenn ich dich?": Names in Kleist's *Käthchen von Heilbronn*' , in *German Life and Letters*, vol. 41 (2), 1988.

Reimarus, Hermann Samuel, *Handschriftenverzeichnis und Bibliographie*, ed. Wilhelm Schmidt-Biggemann, Göttingen, 1979.

Reinhardt, Hartmut, 'Das Unrecht des Rechtskämpfers. Zum Problem des Widerstandes in Kleists Erzählung *Michael Kohlhaas*,' in *JbSchG* XXXI, 1987.

Rousseau, Jean-Jacques, *Correspondance de J.-J. Rousseau*, vol. 1, Paris, 1839.

Rousseau, Jean-Jacques, *Discours sur l'origine et les fondemens de l'inégalité parmi les hommes, Œuvres complètes*, vol. III, eds. Bernard Gagnebin and Marcel Raymond, Paris, 1964.

Rousseau, Jean-Jacques, *Essai sur l'origine des langues*, Paris, 1969.

Rousseau, Jean-Jacques, *Julie ou La Nouvelle Héloïse*, Paris, 1960.

Rushing, James A. Jr., 'The Limitations of the Fencing Bear. Kleist's *Über das Marionettentheater* as Ironic Fiction,' in *The German Quarterly*, vol. 61 (4), 1988.

Ryan, Lawrence, '*Amphitryon*: doch ein Lustspielstoff!' *Kleist und Frankreich*, ed. Walter Müller-Seidel, Berlin, 1969.

Ryan, Lawrence, 'Die "vaterländische Umkehr" in der *Hermannsschlacht.' Kleists Dramen*, ed. W. Hinderer.

Bibliography

Ryan, Lawrence, 'Kleists "Entdeckung im Gebiete der Kunst": *Robert Guiskard* und die Folgen,' *Gestaltungsgeschichte und Gesellschaftsgeschichte*, ed. Helmut Kreuzer, Stuttgart, 1969.

Ryder, Frank G., 'Kleist's *Findling*: "Oedipus *manqué*?,"' in *Modern Language Notes*, vol. 92, 1977.

Sammons, Jeffrey L., 'Rethinking Kleist's *Hermannsschlacht*,' *Heinrich von Kleist-Studien*, ed. Alex Ugrinsky.

Samuel, Richard H., and Brown, Hilda M., *Kleist's Lost Year and the Quest for 'Robert Guiskard*,' Leamington Spa, 1981.

Samuel, Richard, 'Heinrich von Kleists *Robert Guiskard* und seine Wiederbelebung 1807/1808,' in *KJb* 1981.

Samuel, Richard, 'Kleists *Hermannsschlacht* und der Freiherr vom Stein,' *JbSchG* V, 1961.

Saße, Günter, *Die aufgeklärte Familie. Untersuchungen zur Genese, Funktion und Realitätsbezogenheit des familialen Systems im Drama der Aufklärung*, Tübingen, 1988.

Schings, Hans Jürgen, *Der beste Mensch ist der mitleidigste Mensch. Poetik des Mitleids von Lessing bis Büchner*, Munich, 1980.

Schmidt, Jochen, *Heinrich von Kleist. Studien zu seiner poetischen Verfahrensweise*, Tübingen, 1974.

Schneider, Helmut J., 'Der Zusammensturz des Allgemeinen,' *Positionen der Literaturwissenschaft*, ed. David E. Wellbery.

Schröder, Jürgen, 'Kleists Novelle *Der Findling*. Ein Plädoyer für Nicolo,' in *KJb* 1985.

Schubert, Ernst, 'Der Zweikampf. Ein mittelalterliches Ordal und seine Vergegenwärtigung bei Heinrich von Kleist,' in *KJb* 1988/89.

Schulz, Gerhard, 'Kleists *Bettelweib von Locarno* – eine Ehegeschichte?', in *JbSchG* XVIII, 1974.

Schulz, Gerhard, *Die deutsche Literatur zwischen Französischer Revolution und Restauration. Zweiter Teil. 1806-1830*, Munich, 1989.

Seeba, Hinrich C., 'Der Sündenfall des Verdachts. Identitätskrise und Sprachskepsis in Kleists *Familie Schroffenstein*,' in *DVjs* 44, 1970.

Seidlin, Oskar, 'Was die Stunde schlägt in Kleists *Der zerbrochne Krug*,' *Mythos und Mythologie in der Literatur des 19. Jahrhunderts*, ed. Helmut Koopmann, Frankfurt/M, 1979.

Sieck, Albrecht, *Kleists 'Penthesilea.' Versuch einer Interpretation*, Bonn, 1976.

Staiger, Emil, 'Kleists *Bettelweib von Locarno*. Zum Problem des dramatischen Stils,' in *DVjs* 20 (1), 1942.

Steiner, George, *The Death of Tragedy*, London, 1961.

Stephens, Anthony, 'Zur Funktion der Metapher beim frühen Kleist,' in *Akten des VI. Internationalen Germanisten-Kongresses Basel 1980*,

Bibliography

Bern, Frankfurt/M and New York, 1980.

Stephens, Anthony, 'Kleist's Mythicisation of the Napoleonic Era,' *Romantic Nationalism in Europe*, ed. J. C. Eade, Canberra, 1983.

Stephens, Anthony, 'The Illusion of a Shaped World: Kleist and Tragedy,' in *AUMLA*, vol. 60, 1983.

Stephens, Anthony, '"Eine Träne auf den Brief." Zum Status der Ausdrucksformen in Kleists Erzählungen,' in *JbSchG* XXVIII, 1984.

Stephens, Anthony, 'Name und Identität bei Kleist und Kafka,' in *Jahrbuch des Freien Deutschen Hochstifts*, 1985.

Stephens, Anthony, '"Was hilfts, daß ich jetzt schuldlos mich erzähle?" Zur Bedeutung der Erzählvorgänge in Kleists Dramen,' in *JbSchG* XXIX, 1985.

Stephens, Anthony, '"Wie bei dem Eintritt in/Ein andres Leben." Geburtsmetapher und Individualität bei Kleist,' *Das neuzeitliche Ich in der Literatur des 18. und 20. Jahrhunderts. Zur Dialektik der Moderne. Ein internationales Symposion*, eds. Ulrich Fülleborn and Manfred Engel, Munich, 1988.

Stephens, Anthony, '"Das nenn ich menschlich nicht verfahren." Skizze zu einer Theorie der Grausamkeit im Hinblick auf Kleist,' *Heinrich von Kleist*, ed. Dirk Grathoff, Opladen, 1988.

Stephens, Anthony, 'Kleists Familienmodelle,' in *KJb* 1988/89.

Stephens, Anthony, '"Gegen die Tyrannei des Wahren." Die Sprache in Kleists *Hermannsschlacht*,' '*Die in dem alten Haus der Sprache wohnen.' Beiträge zum Sprachdenken in der Literaturgeschichte*, ed. Eckehard Czucka, Münster, 1991.

Stephens, Anthony, '"Menschen/ Mit Tieren die Natur gewechselt." Zur Funktionsweise der Tierbilder bei Heinrich von Kleist,' in *JbSchG* XXXVI, 1992.

Stephens, Anthony, 'Verzerrungen im Spiegel. Das Narziß-Motiv bei Heinrich von Kleist,' *Heinrich von Kleist*, ed. Gerhard Neumann, Freiburg i. Br., 1994.

Stephens, Anthony, 'Der Opfergedanke bei Heinrich von Kleist,' *Heinrich von Kleist*, ed. Gerhard Neumann, Freiburg i. Br., 1994.

Streller, Siegfried, Heinrich von Kleist und Jean-Jacques Rousseau, in *Weimarer Beiträge*, 8, 1962.

Swales, Erika, 'Configurations of Irony: Kleist's *Prinz Friedrich von Homburg*,' in *DVjs* 56, 1982.

Szondi, Peter, '*Amphitryon*. Kleists "Lustspiel nach Molière,"' *Schriften II*, Frankfurt/M, 1978.

Szondi, Peter, *Versuch über das Tragische*, Frankfurt/M, 1964.

Ueding, Gerd, 'Zweideutige Bilderwelt: *Das Käthchen von Heilbronn*,' *Kleists Dramen*, ed. Walter Hinderer.

Ugrinsky, Alexej (ed.), *Heinrich von Kleist-Studien*, Berlin, 1980.

Weigel, Alexander, 'Der Schauspieler als Maschinist. Heinrich von Kleists *Über das Marionettentheater* und das "Königliche Nationaltheater,"' *Heinrich von Kleist*, ed. Dirk Grathoff.

Weigel, Sigrid, 'Der Körper am Kreuzpunkt von Liebesgeschichte und Rassendiskurs in Heinrich von Kleists Erzählung *Die Verlobung in St. Domingo*,' in *KJb* 1991.

Weiss, Hermann F., *Funde und Studien zu Heinrich von Kleist*, Tübingen, 1984.

Wellbery, David E. (ed.), *Positionen der Literaturwissenschaft. Acht Modellanalysen am Beispiel von Kleists 'Das Erdbeben in Chili,'* ed. David E. Wellberry, Munich, 1985.

Wellbery, David E., 'Semiotische Anmerkungen zu Kleists *Das Erdbeben in Chili,'* *Positionen der Literaturwissenschaft*, ed. David E. Wellberry.

Wilpert, Gero von, 'Der Ausrutcher des Bettelweibes von Locarno. "Capriccio con fuoco,"' in *Seminar*, vol. XXVI (4), 1990.

Wittkowski, Wolfgang, '*Die heilige Cäcilie* und *Der Zweikampf*. Kleists Legenden und die romantische Ironie,' in *Colloquia Germanica*, 1972 (6).

Wittkowski, Wolfgang, 'Skepsis, Noblesse, Ironie. Formen des Als-ob in Kleists *Erdbeben*,' in *Euphorion*, vol. 63, 1969.

Wittkowski, Wolfgang, *Heinrich von Kleists 'Amphitryon.' Materialien zur Rezeption und Interpretation*, Berlin and New York, 1978.

Xylander, Oskar Ritter von, 'Heinrich von Kleist und J.-J. Rousseau,' in *Germanische Studien*, vol. 193, Berlin, 1937.

Zeller, Rosemarie, 'Kleists *Prinz Friedrich von Homburg* auf dem Hintergrund der literarischen Tradition,' in *JbSchG* XXX, 1986.

Zimmermann, Hans Dieter, *Kleist. Die Liebe und der Tod*, Frankfurt/M, 1989.

Ziolkowski, Theodore, 'Kleists Werk im Lichte der zeitgenössischen Rechtskontroverse,' in *KJb* 1987.

Index

This index excludes proper names within Kleist's works and references to secondary literature on Kleist.

Index

violence inherent in , 197, 207
Classical Antiquity, 92, 122, 124
Collin, Heinrich Joseph von, 129–7,
    130–1, 157–3
comedy, 25, 62, 74
    black, 13, 30, 164, 225
    comic hybris, 95
    departure from conventions of, 56, 78–9,
        88, 90
    of manners, 214
    Prinz Friedrich von Homburg read
        as, 177
    Shakespearean, 11
communication
    ideal, 38, 254, 269
    imperfect, 242, 245
    through formal documents, 241, 243–6
community
    leadership, 50
    survival, 46
    voice of, 199
consciouness
    articulated in language, 288
    dislocations of, 4, 119–20, 210, 233
    see also self, divisions in
        contract
    inheritance, 19, 27–8, 75
    metaphor of contract with reader, 256
    social 33–4, 59
crisis of 1801, Kleist's, 3, 12, 25–6
cruelty
    excess of, 4, 196
    motivated by racism, 207
    protests against, 84, 89, 136–7, 155–6
    see also sadism

death
    as entelechy, 211
    virtual, 136
demiurgic
    creation, 14, 205
    text function, 35
demonic, Goethe's concept of, 201
desire
    at odds with moral principles, 256
    consequences of, 197
    enigma of, 114
    expressed in animal imagery, 125
    Lacan's concept of, 112n15
    linked to aggression, 145,159
    linked to death, 31, 114
    unfulfilled, 113, 120
despotism, 182–6, 189
    Enlightened, 190, 213
    see also authority, paternal *and* tyranny

destruction
    pleasurable 15, 163
    universal, 109, 125, 168–9
devil
    Satan, 28, 135, 144,
    self-perception as, 27, 36, 39
devils, 18, 27, 136, 180, 214–15, 224
    Christian, 73
Diderot, Dénis,12n13
dislocations
    in characterization, 107, 144, 149, 155,
        175–76
    in plotting, 132–4
    of perspective, 209
divine
    language, 38
    providence, 12, 41, 205
    vengeance, 12, 27, 198, 208
    benevolence, 105
    inadequacy of, 100, 160
    pedagogue, 79, 87–8
doctrines
    Christian, 12
dreams, 110, 114–15, 140, 145, 147–8,
    152–3, 176–8,

Eichendorff, Joseph von, 263
18 Brumaire 1799, 33
emancipation, 2, 15, 22, 24–7, 51, 117–18
    discourse of, 2, 266–8
    from fathers, 17, 42
    imperfect, 42, 209
    of 18th century sensibility, 223
    from gender roles, 242
    process of, 220
endings
    ambiguous, 13, 128, 210
    choice of, 107, 225, 239–40, 260, 290
    comic, 6, 62, 64, 95
    contrived, 151, 191
    deferred, 56–8, 194, 203–5, 215–17,
        255, 264
    utopian, 6, 260, 281, 290
Enlightenment, 3, 4, 11, 14, 39, 122
    controversies within, 22, 95, 200–1,
        213–14,
    ethical values, 136–8, 156, 159, 193,
        227, 247, 291
    ideals, 26
    myths, 29, 34, 96, 197–8
    philosophy, 3, 12, 91, 201, 213, 236
    popular, 7, 12, 24, 75, 95–7
    religion, 29, 170n28, 186, 226
    view of literature, 282, 285, 289
equality

Index

Index

metaphorical guises, 53
prevented, 48
melodrama, 9, 13, 129
becoming parody, 10
metaphors, 6, 9, 12
cognitive function, 37
creating reality, 39, 118
humans as animals, 35, 53, 103, 116,
138, 142, 154–5, 165, 166, 218–19,
224, 270, 281
impossible to undo, 38
natural, 17
see also Nature
objective correlative, 52
polyphony as structural
metaphor, 270
process of image–making, 35–6
'world of imagery', 132–3, 137–8, 148
Michael Kohlhaas, 159, 244–261
passim, 263, 271, 279
Middle Ages, depicted by Kleist, 15,
44,131, 149, 240–1, 244
mob violence, 31–2, 35, 196, 198–9, 204
mothers
adoptive, 189–90, 229
source of power, 190–1
Molière, Jean Baptiste, 72–95 *passim*
Le Misanthrope, 95
Müller, Adam, 7, 55, 72, 260
mythology
Christian, 23
pagan or Classical, 27, 47, 73–4, 147
myth
conventions of reading, 77
contrast between Goethe and
Kleist, 124–6
myths
Abraham and Isaac, 186, 192
apocalyptic, 5, 163, 289
Diana and Actaeon, 108, 116
Fall of humanity, 7, 17, 21, 28, 33–4, 53,
56, 59, 75, 279, 284, 289–90
Last Judgement, 59–60, 62, 68, 135,
198, 201, 271, 279–80
Narcissus, 124
of feminine, 19
Orpheus and Eurydike, 86
paradise lost, 3, 14, 16, 38, 280–1,
285, 290
paradise regained, 16
utopian, 5
Zeus and Semele, 93

names, 23–24, 118
social determinants, 27, 187–8

Napoleon, 25, 33, 45–7, 50, 54, 121,
153, 157–8, 165, 169, 171
Egyptian campaign, 46
Napoleonic Europe, 5, 25, 48, 169, 213
narcissism, 7n5, 16, 27, 93–4, 178,
181, 187
destructive, 36
structural principle, 122–4
narrative perspective
discrepancies within, 210–11, 263–4,
272–3
shifts within, 234–5, 248, 251–4
narratives, duality of narrative voices, 205,
207, 215, 255–6, 270, 274
encapsulated, 207
in dramas, 23, 57, 70, 79–80, 99–100,
103, 106, 135, 138
plurality of viewpoints, 265, 267
power of, 208–9
self-reflecting, 262
structure, 195
narrator
exerting power on text and
readers, 160, 262
intrusive, 236, 239, 251, 262
ironized by text, 195, 229–30, 235, 238,
283, 286–7
status of in text, 195
unreliable, 194, 210, 228–30, 238, 242
nationalism, German, 159–60, 165, 168–9
Nature
amoral, 17
authority, 121
disunified, 142, 163
fictionalized, 16, 41
idyllic, 16, 24
natural imagery and violence, 17
state of in Rousseau, 226
New Testament, 17, 22–23
gospels, 73
'new beginning', 22–5, 27, 30
'new order of things', 5, 29, 291
Amazon state as spurious, 121
discredited, 43, 212–13
Newton, Sir Isaac 200
Nietzsche, Friedrich, 98, 224
nihilism, 169–70
Novalis (Friedrich von Hardenberg), 4, 29,
120, 126, 277, 289

oaths, 12
as stabilising acts, 209–10
of vengeance, 1, 15–16, 19
Old Testament, 12, 17, 27
Esther, 143

Index

Genesis, 17, 22–3, 67, 285–6
Hosea II–IV, 77
Job, 92
Judges, 168
prophets, 77
Samuel, 211
see also myths

palimpsest, 33, 158
    as structural metaphor, 10–11, 67, 75,
        128–9
parody, 11, 41, 69–70, 136, 143, 146, 173,
        184, 207, 212, 224, 230–1, 278, 289
    by exaggeration, 129, 146, 207, 220–1
    by reversal, 58–9, 97
    Kleist's variant of, 231–4
    of Christian doctrines
        of Rousseau, 222–3, 226–8
        of sentimentalism, 216–17
    parodistic doubling, 249
    reversal, 56–9
    tragic form, 42–3
pastiche, 9, 164
Penthesilea, 9, 33, 45, 51–2, 48, 54, 56,
        95, 97–126 *passim*, 127–30, 132,
        138–9, 159, 174, 212, 291
people
    autonomous voice, 46, 54
    contrasting aspects of 'Volk', 199
    expendable in politics, 49
    swayed by demagogic speech, 48–9, 247
perception
    limited or distorted, 12, 20, 23, 30–1,
        123
pessimism, Kleist's, 5, 25,
playful, (ludic) aspects of texts, 6, 69, 88,
        160–1, 215
Prinz Friedrich von Homburg, 7, 16, 40,
        171–93 *passim*
Prussia, 171–2, 236
    Friedrich Wihlem III, King of, 5, 171
    Prussian burocracy, 244
    Prussian fantasies, 186, 250–2, 254
    Prussian history, 172
    Prussian militarism, 173, 187
    Prussian patriotism, 5, 7, 169, 184, 186,
        190, 251, 260, 276
    Prussian reformers, 157

Racine, Jean, 40
Raphael, 73
readers
    expectations of the text, 39, 205, 210,
        239–40, 275
    manipulation of, 29, 134, 194, 203, 239,

242, 244, 258, 270
reality as text, 29, 31, 53, 188, 194, 200–4,
        206, 242, 244, 268–9
rebellion, thematics of, 47
rebirth, 22
    humanity, 13, 33
    individual, 26, 41, 53, 119–20, 190–3,
Reimarus, Hermann Samuel, 95
religious themes, 11–12, 26–9, 75, 263
Rilke, Rainer Maria, 98
rituals, 2, 11, 22
    centered on truth, 58
    forensic, 57, 70–1, 236
    Kleist's fascination with, 56–7
    of passage, 24
Robert Guiskard, 9–10, 43, 44–54 *passim*,
        191, 194, 199
Romanticism, 122
    absolute love, 141
    concept of individual, 120
    emblems, 151
    experiments with myth, 29
    Kleist at variance with, 126
    Kleist's imitation of, 127–8
    Kleist's work seen as romantic, 129n6
    literature of, 72, 131–2
    motif of sleepwalking, 152, 171, 174,
        178
    religious syncretism, 73, 105
    Romantic Catholicism, 262–3
Rome, sacked by Goths, 163
Rousseau, Jean-Jacques, 3, 16, 18, 28,
        119, 168, 200, 213, 222n17– 20, 224,
        247, 259–60, 289–90
    Discours sur ... l'inégalité, 227–8
    La Nouvelle Héloïse, 222–3

sacraments
    Christian, 12, 19, 23–4, 26, 42, 56
    improvised, 25–26
sacrifice, 7, 30–1
    Abraham and Isaac, 186
    pointless, 31, 50
Sade, Marquis de, 4, 141, 159
    sadism, 90–1, 145, 149,154, 188–9, 215
Schelling, Friedrich Wilhelm Joseph
        von, 277
Schiller, Friedrich von, 209, 289–9
    Don Carlos, 10
    Maria Stuart, 191
Schlegel, Friedrich, 277
scholarship on Kleist, 6–8, 29, 67, 74, 76,
        113, 129–30, 132–4, 139–40,
        158–9,162–3, 172–3, 194–5, 208,
        229–30, 236–9, 258–61, 271–2, 277–9

Index

Index

European tradition, 155
formal problems, 40, 281
Hegelian concept of, 42n48
Kleist's ambitions, 44–5, 157
Kleists place in European tradition, 42
narcissism as tragic theme, 122
of emancipation, 51, 209
potential for, 129
Shakespearean, 11, 76
theory of, 10, 44, 54n17, 127
tragic blindness, 42–3, 186, 206
tragic conversion, 40–1, 209–10
tragic hero or heroine, 41, 122
tragic inevitably, 107
within comic framework, 59, 76, 100, 214–16
within context of fantasy, 171, 191
trust, 1, 10, 23
absence as disease, 34
antidote to suspicion, 41
expectation of absolute, 59–61, 208–9
loss of trust in language, 3
sacrament, 26
truth, 13, 271
ascertaining, 2, 70
at odds with language, 60, 65, 69
disclosure of secret, 65, 80–2, 139–41, 145, 152–3
eluding language, 26, 169
in public discourse, 49
nullified within fictional world, 167
produced in language, 2–3, 38, 57, 270
relation to violence, 61, 64
shown by material tokens, 63–4, 70, 85, 91, 166–8, 286
tyranny, domestic, 220, 231–2
paternal, 183–4, 214
see also authority, paternal and despotism

Über das Marionettentheater, 4, 7, 67, 277–291 *passim*
Über die Aufklärung des Weibes, 25

Die Verlobung in St. Domingo, 22, 24, 59, 206–211 *passim*, 262, 269
violence
done to rationality, 269
excessive, 161, 167, 210, 220–1
see also mob violence
judical, 255
linked to cruelty, 159
reflection of divinity, 125
within the family, 2, 192–3
Voltaire, François Marie Arouet de 200, 226
Dictionnaire philosophique, 77

Wagner, Richard, 98
war
'law of war', 111
affecting civil populations, 50
background to main plot, 99, 118, 269
correlative of inner turmoil, 120
Wedekind, Georg Dr., 44
Weimar Classicism, 39, 95, 122, 159, 167, 193, 289
Kleist's opposition to, 126
Wieland, Christoph Martin, 44–5, 192
Die Prüfung Abrahams, 186, 192
Wilhelmenian Germany, 158

Zenge, Wilhelmine von, 3, 21, 259
Der zerbrochne Krug, 17, 51, 55–71 *passim*, 72, 77–81, 88–90, 100, 130, 142, 194, 279–80
Der Zweikampf, 236–244 *passim*, 263, 286